普通高等教育"十二五"
高职高专规划教材

21世纪高等职业教育财经类规划教材
经济贸易类

国际贸易理论与实务（双语版）

拜文汇 郑美花 ◎ 主编
秦洪武 夏云 姜云臣 ◎ 副主编
高岩 刘娟 丁明华 ◎ 编委成员

International Trade Theory & Practice (English & Chinese)

人民邮电出版社
北京

图书在版编目（CIP）数据

国际贸易理论与实务 ：汉英对照 / 拜文汇，郑美花主编. -- 北京 ：人民邮电出版社，2012.12（2020.8重印）
21世纪高等职业教育财经类规划教材. 经济贸易类
ISBN 978-7-115-30192-5

Ⅰ. ①国… Ⅱ. ①拜… ②郑… Ⅲ. ①国际贸易理论－高等职业教育－教材－汉、英②国际贸易－贸易实务－高等职业教育－教材－汉、英 Ⅳ. ①F740

中国版本图书馆CIP数据核字(2012)第283313号

内 容 提 要

教材内容包括两部分：第一部分为绪论，简单介绍国际贸易原理和国际贸易实务的内容概况；第二部分为国际贸易理论与实务部分，简单介绍国贸理论，重点介绍国贸实务，这部分内容从建立业务关系开始到进行国际贸易综合实习和技能训练为止。

本书的主要内容包括绪论，国际贸易原理与实务，建立业务关系，商品的品名、品质、数量和包装、商品的价格，国际货物运输与保险，国际结算，进出口商品的检验、检疫与报关、索赔、不可抗力与仲裁，进出口业务综合实训。

本教材既可作为高职高专院校国贸专业学生职业能力培养的核心课程用书，也可供英语专业学生作为国际贸易职业方向课程用书，以及外贸从业人员的自学参考用书。

普通高等教育“十二五”高职高专规划教材

21世纪高等职业教育财经类规划教材——经济贸易类

国际贸易理论与实务（双语版）

◆ 主　　编　拜文汇　郑美花
　副 主 编　秦洪武　夏　云　姜云臣
　编委成员　高　岩　刘　娟　丁明华
　责任编辑　刘　琦
　执行编辑　喻文丹

◆ 人民邮电出版社出版发行　　北京市丰台区成寿寺路11号
　邮编　100164　　电子邮件　315@ptpress.com.cn
　网址　http://www.ptpress.com.cn
　北京九州迅驰传媒文化有限公司印刷

◆ 开本：787×1092　1/16
　印张：17.75　　2012年12月第1版
　字数：459千字　　2020年8月北京第10次印刷

ISBN 978-7-115-30192-5

定价：39.00元

读者服务热线：(010)81055256　印装质量热线：(010)81055316
反盗版热线：(010)81055315

前言

随着经济全球化进程的不断深入，我国与世界各国的贸易往来日益频繁，对外贸从业人员的综合素质和业务能力也提出了更高的要求。同时具备专业技能及专业外语知识，并能将专业技能和外语知识融会贯通的复合型人才越来越受用人单位的欢迎和重用。

为适应全球经济一体化对外贸从业人员的要求，培养高职高专学生的外贸业务能力，提高其外贸综合素质，按照中国高等教育学会“普通高等教育‘十二五’高职高专规划教材”的立项要求，本着“理实一体、工学结合”的方针、“实用为主、够用为度、应用为目的”的原则，我们编写了本教材。

本教材的特色及优势体现在以下四个方面。第一，英汉双语。中英文对照介绍进出口业务涉及的各个环节及操作流程。第二，校企合编。从业经验丰富的行业专家、外语专业扎实的资深教授、教学水平高的双师教学团队三方共同研究编写，确保教材内容的前瞻性、科学性、实用性。第三，实战案例丰富。吸收当前外贸企业最前沿的货物进出口案例及外贸单据，实现专业学习与工作岗位的近距离对接。第四，“课证融通、赛考结合”。本教材以当前全国国际贸易职业能力考证和技能竞赛单据的操作实务为标准，保证“课、证、赛、考”的有机融合。

为了支持本课程的教学，方便教师授课，教材编写组还特地配套了教学课件及导入案例和课后复习思考题的双语参考答案等资源。相关资源可参考教材最后一页教学支持证明即可获得。

本教材由山东外国语职业学院的拜文汇、郑美花任主编，并负责全书的策划和统稿；曲阜师范大学秦洪武、夏云教授承担了外语部分的修改、校对工作；山东外国语职业学院姜云臣教授参与了本书的整体内容设计。具体编写分工如下：拜文汇编写了绪论、第十二章；郑美花编写了第一章、第二章、第五章、第六章、第十章；高岩编写了第九章，丁明华编写了第三章、第四章和第十一章，刘娟编写了第七章和第八章。

在本教材编写及出版过程中，山东华信集团提供了大量业务背景素材、相关案例、外贸单证等资源，也得到了中国高等教育学会的支持和指导，另外山东外国语职业学院有关领导、国贸教研室各位同仁也给予大力支持与帮助，在此一并表示感谢。

尽管有资深教授和外贸行业专家的指导和参与，书中难免出现欠缺或疏漏之处，恳请学界专家、同仁及读者不吝指正。反馈邮箱：zmeihua888@163.com。

编　者

2012 年 12 月

目 录

目 录

Contents

Content

Contents

Introduction

绪论

【Learning Objectives】教学目的与要求

After learning this chapter, you will be able to:

1. Grasp both basic concepts of international trade theory and practice;
2. Understand the relationship between theory and practice of international trade;
3. Understand practice learning methods of International Trade Theory.

【Lead-in Case】引导案例

Question: Please explain the reason why we shall study international trade by analyzing the description of Case 1 and Case 2?

问题：请分析案情一和案情二来解释我们为什么要学习国际贸易?

Case 1: German notifies China that China is forbidden to export mutton to German. The reason is that mutton hormone content exceeds the allowed amount, which will affect people's health. After investigation, China finds out that the mutton hormone content is as same amount as that in German, and China also gets the information that German is unceasingly importing the similar quality mutton from India. China believes that German has violated the GATT principles and China's benefits have been violated. German refates, they think they adopt the measures which do not violate the GATT principles, but belong to the general exception that is permitted.

案情一：德国通知中国，禁止从中国进口羊肉，理由是中国羊肉的荷尔蒙含量超标，影响德国国民的身体健康。中国经过调查发现，德国境内销售的羊肉荷尔蒙含量与中国羊肉的荷尔蒙含量是一样的。还发现，德国还不断地从印度进口同样质量的羊肉。中国认为德国违反了 GATT 的原则，中国的利益受到了侵害。德国反驳，他们采取的措施是不违反 GATT 原则的，是属于一般例外所允许的。

Case 2: Elche, a town in Spain became the focus of the global attention on September 14th, 2004. Because the “made in China” shoes which worth nearly $ 10 000 000 had been burned by a local illegal group. This was the first serious violation of the legitimate rights of China in the history of Spain.

案情二：2004 年 9 月 14 日，西班牙小镇埃尔切将近 1000 万美元价值的“中国制造”鞋被当地不法集团烧毁而变成了全球关注的焦点。这是西班牙有史以来第一起严重侵犯华商合法权益、野蛮排斥华人的暴力事件。

Section One International Trade Theory and Practice
第一节 国际贸易理论和实务

1. Study Objective, Main Tasks and Main Contents of International Trade Theory 国际贸易理论的研究对象、主要任务和主要内容

（1）Study Objective 研究对象

International Trade Theory mainly studies the generation and development of international trade as well as trade interests between countries(region)and countries(region). International Trade Theorty summarizes and extracts from the international trade practice, and focuses on the contents of theories and policies of international trade, especially emphasizes on the reasons and results of exchange for goods, services, factors of production and technology among the different countries or regions as well as policies concerned.

国际贸易原理主要研究国际贸易产生、发展的原因或基础以及贸易利益在国家或（地区）之间的分配问题，是对国际贸易实践的总结和提炼。重点关注国际贸易理论与政策内容，尤其是商品、服务、生产要素和技术在各国（或地区）之间交换的原因、结果及相关的政策。

（2）Main Tasks 主要任务

Main tasks of International Trade Principles are to reveal the characteristics of generation and development of international trade, basic theories of international trade, international trade policies and measures, bilateral or regional or multilateral trade relations, distribution of trade interests and the trend of trade development, etc.

国际贸易的主要任务是揭示国际贸易产生、发展的特点，国际贸易的基本理论，国际贸易政策和措施，以及从双边、区域、多边层面上的国家间的贸易关系，贸易利益的协调方式和贸易发展趋势等内容。

（3）Main Contents 主要内容

First, International Trade Principles focus on the description of generation, development and characteristics of international trade theory. International trade theory can be divided into three stages:

首先是关于国际贸易理论的形成、发展和特点的阐述。主要分为三个阶段：

① The early stage is called “the Classical Trade Theory”, represented by the Advantage Trade Theory of Adam Smith and David Ricardo.

早期的国际贸易理论被称为“古典贸易理论”，以亚当·斯密和大卫·李嘉图的优势贸易理论为代表。

② The New-Classical Trade Theory of the early 20th century is represented by Heckscher and Ohlin.

20 世纪初新古典贸易理论，主要代表为赫克歇尔和俄林。

③ The New Trade Theory emerged after World War Ⅱ, with the development of the internalization of multinational corporations and direct foreign investment. The theory mainly includes the New Factor Endowment Theory, the Preference Similarity Theory, the Dynamic Trade Theory, and the Intra-industry Trade Theory, etc.

第二次世界大战后新贸易理论是伴随跨国公司内部化和对外直接投资兴起的，主要理论有新生产要素理论、偏好相似理论、动态贸易理论、产业内贸易理论等。

Second, International Trade Principles focus on international trade policies and measures as well as international trade development trend .【Typical Case Link 2】

其次是国际贸易政策，国际贸易措施和国际贸易的发展趋势。【典例链接 2】

① International Trade Policy 国际贸易政策

International trade policy refers to the principles and policies of administration of the import and export business for all countries and regions in a certain period.【Typical Case Link 1】

国际贸易政策是世界各国和地区在一定时期对进出口贸易进行管理的原则和方针。【典例链接 1】

② International Trade Measures 国际贸易措施

International trade measures are the means to implement policies of international trade, and the measures to protect national trade interests, mainly includes tariff policy, non-tariff policy, export promotion policy, and export control policy.

国际贸易措施是一国实施国际贸易政策的手段，是保护本国贸易利益所采取的一些举措。主要包括关税政策、非关税措施、出口鼓励政策、出口管制政策。

③ Since the 1990s, international trade has undergone many profound changes, illustrating as follows:

进入 20 世纪 90 年代以来，国际贸易领域发生了许多深刻的变化。主要包括以下方面。

- Growing proportion of trade in high-tech products.
  高技术产品贸易比重越来越大。
- Emergence of knowledge-intensive service trade.
  知识密集型服务贸易的崛起。
- Networking of transaction in international trade.
  国际贸易在交易方式上出现网络化趋势。
- Standardization of trade regulation in international trade.
  国际贸易在贸易规则上出现规范化趋势。

Besides, main contents also include the study of the theory of International Division of Labor, Western International Trade Theory, Basic Knowledge on the World Trade Organization, International Trade of Service, International Trade of Technology, etc.

另外，国际贸易的主要内容还包括国际分工理论、西方国际贸易理论、世界贸易组织基础知识、国际贸易服务和国际技术贸易等。

2. Study Objective, Main Tasks and Main Contents of International Trade Practice 国际贸易实务研究对象、主要任务和主要内容

(1) Study Objective 研究对象

It mainly studies the process of concrete operation for exchange of commodities between different countries, including procedures, working methods and skills as well as relative behavioural norms of laws and conventions should be followed.

研究对象是研究国际性商品交换的具体运作过程，包括该过程经历的环节、操作方法和技能，应遵循的法律和惯例等行为规范。

（2）Main Tasks 主要任务

Through studying the international trade practice, students are supposed to master the basic procedures, basic rules and basic skills of international sales of goods; Under the learning to follow the relevant laws, regulations and international trade practices and conventions as well as carrying out the policies of our countries, to fulfill the aim of business operation and make favorable economic efficiency in foreign trade activities.

主要任务是通过国际贸易实务的学习，初步掌握国际货物买卖的基本流程、基本规则和基本技能；学会在遵循有关法律、法规与国际贸易惯例的前提下，正确贯彻我国的方针政策，实现企业的经营意图，在对外贸易活动中实现最佳的经济效益。

（3）Main Contents 主要内容

International Trade Practice is a comprehensive and applied course. Generally, it mainly focuses on sales of contract in international trade, and combining with relevant international practices and laws, giving a detailed description to the clauses of sales contract of international trade, the negotiation of contracts as well as the basic links and relative knowledge execution of contract.

国际贸易实务是一门综合性应用课程。一般来说，主要以国际货物买卖合同为中心，结合有关的国际惯例和法律，详细介绍国际货物买卖合同的条款、合同的磋商和合同的履行的基本环节及有关的知识。

① Relative Law and Convention in International Sale of Goods 国际货物贸易的有关法律和惯例

The Law and convention in international trade are the essential terms and conditions to operate international business effectively. E.g. *United Nations Convention on Contracts for the International Sale of Goods* (*CISG*), *International Rules for the Interpretation of Trade Terms* , *Uniform Rules for Collection, Uniform Customs and Practice for Documentary Credits* (*UCP*) *600* and etc.

国际贸易法律和国际贸易惯例是顺利开展国际贸易的基本条件。如《联合国国际货物销售合同公约》、《国际贸易术语解释通则》、《托收统一规则》、《跟单信用证统一惯例 600》等。

② Clause of Contract for the International Sales of Goods 国际货物买卖合同的条款

a. Commodity Clause: including name of commodity, quality, quantity , packing and commodity inspection.

商品条件：包括商品品名、品质、数量、包装及商品检验。

b. Price Clause: as a rule, it is integrated with Trade Terms.

价格条件：往往与贸易术语联系在一起。

c. Shipment Clause: make sure exporter how to deliver the goods to importer.

装运条件：确定出口方怎样把货物发运给进口方。

d. Insurance Clause: International transportation cargo insurance is achieved through insurance contract, the types of insurance are different to different modes of transportation.

保险条件：是通过订立保险合同来实现的，运输的方式不同，货物运输保险的种类不同。

e. Payment Clause: refers to methods of payment, there are three kinds of payment methods which widely used in the international trade: remittance (including mail, wire T/T, D/D), collection (including

D/P, D/A）and letter of credit.

支付条件：主要指支付方式，国际贸易常用的付款方式是 3 种：汇付（包括信汇、电汇 T/T、票汇）、托收（包括 D/P 付款交单、D/A 承兑交单）和信用证。

f. Disputes and Settlement: include claim, force majeure and arbitration.

争议和违约处理：包括索赔、不可抗力和仲裁。

③ Procedures of Contract Negotiation　合同磋商流程

Business negotiation is an indispensable stage of concluding a transaction, which usually undergoes four steps as: inquiry, offer, counter-offer and acceptance.

交易磋商阶段是谈判成交的不可缺少的过程，通常包括询盘、发盘、还盘、接受 4 个步骤。

④ Implementation of International Trade Contracts　合同的履行

Forwarding all kinds of documents and certificates to the negotiation bank for payment is as follows: 制作各种单证到议付行结汇等，如下：

Bill of Exchange 汇票

Commercial Invoice 商业发票

Bill of Lading 提单

Insurance Policy 保险单据

Certificate of Origin 原产地证

Inspection Certificate 检验证书

Export Cancel Vertification 出口收汇核销单

Customs Invoice 海关发票

Packing List 装箱单

Weight List 重量单

Measurement List 尺码单

Section Two Relationship Between International Trade Theory and Practice
第二节　国际贸易理论与国际贸易实务的关系

1. Summary and Guidance of International Trade Theory to Practice 国际贸易理论对国际贸易实务规律的总结和指导作用

International trade theory comes from practice in international trade, which is the experience generalization and summary of international trade practice.

国际贸易理论源于国际贸易实务，是对国际贸易实务经验的概括和总结。

The function of international trade theory is to guide the realistic practice.It is the summary of the experience of commercial activity since a long time ago.

国际贸易理论是人类长期从事商业活动经验的积淀和结晶，因而它能够作用并指导现实的实践活动。

In the early stage of development of capitalism, international trade policy in Western European countries was mainly based on mercantilist ideas. The only good of international trade is to pursue money, so the Western European countries implemented high tariff and protection policy which restricted the development of capital economy or trade, and implemented trade protection policy of high tariffs, which restricted the economic development of capitalist.

资本主义发展初期，西欧各国在国际贸易政策上主要依据的是重商主义思想，以货币作为国际贸易追求的唯一目标，实行高关税和国内的贸易保护政策，这样制约了资本主义经济的发展。

Bourgeois economists Adam Smith and David Ricardo put forward the Theory of Free Trade. From their perspective, international division of labor will be formed and total production of a country will be creased without any change of labor force by free trade, thereby benefit trade countries respectively. Theoretical barriers to the countries participating in international trade were cleared, and international trade was greatly developed at that time.

资产阶级经济学家亚当·斯密和大卫·李嘉图提出了建立自由贸易秩序的理论。通过自由贸易交换，形成国际分工，在资本劳动力不变的前提下，使国际贸易当事国生产总量增加，从而有利于贸易各国。这样为各国参与国际贸易扫清了理论上的障碍，国际贸易在当时得到了极大的发展。

2. Development, Examination and Revision of International Trade Theory by Practice 国际贸易实务对国际贸易理论的发展、检验和修正

Theory comes from practice, and must accept examination fo practice. When new problems arise from the international trade practice, the original theory could not be suitable for its development, so obstacles will emerge, which will eventually accelerate the development of theory.

理论来源于实践，同时又必须回归实践、接受实践的检验。国际贸易在实际应用中会遇到新的问题，原有的理论不能适应其发展，就会产生阻碍，最终会促进理论的发展。

"International Rules for the Interpretation of Trade Terms" ("INCOTERMS" in the following) formulated by the International Chamber of Commerce is one of the most important and widely used international trade practice in the world. Since the first general rule was drafted in 1936, revisions have been made to adapt to the development of international trade.

国际商会制定的《国际贸易术语解释通则》(以下简称《通则》)是当今世界上最重要、应用最广泛的国际贸易惯例之一。自1936年起草第一部通则以来，就不断定期对其进行修改以适应国际贸易实务的发展趋势。

The "INCOTERMS" was revised to adapt to the demand of the trade terms to cargoes containerization in the containerized traffic, the multi-mode transport and uses the land route vehicles and the railroad flatcar in short distance sea transportation in 1990. In the "INCOTERMS 2000", duties of sellers and buyers were listed in 10 entities instead of the original 13 entities, which facilitate the consultation. Modification of "INCOTERMS 2010" took the increase of world free zones, the widespread use of electronic communications as well as cargo transportation security into account. Terms like DDU, DAF, DES, and DEQ were deleted from the D group in "INCOTERMS 2000". Meanwhile, two new terms were added to group D namely DAT (Delivered At Terminal) and DAP (Delivered At Place), which reflected the practical requirements of international trade, and were compatible with the United Nations Convention on Contracts for the International Sale of Goods (CISG) and the Rotterdam Rules.

1990年《通则》修订的主要原因是适应集装箱运输、多式联运和在短程海运中使用陆路车辆和铁路敞车的滚装运输中的货物集装化发展要求。在《2000年通则》中，将13种术语项下买卖

双方的义务均采用 10 个项目列出，便于查阅。

而通则 2010 的修改考虑了目前世界上免税区的增加，电子通信的普遍使用以及货物运输安全性的提高,删去了通则 2000D 组术语中的 DDU，DAF，DES，DEQ，同时新增加了两种 D 组贸易术语,即 DAT（Delivered at Terminal）与 DAP（Delivered at Place）。这些都在很大程度上反映了国际货物贸易的实践要求，并进一步与《联合国国际货物销售合同公约》及《鹿特丹规则》衔接。

Section Three Learning Methods of International Trade Theory and Practice
第三节 国际贸易理论与国际贸易实务的学习方法

International trade is a practical and foreign-featured course. Most students do not have experience of the particular business of international trade, therefore, during the period of learning the course, they are supposed to combine the theory with the practice of domestic trade or economic life together, and apply more practical skills and techniques to learning this course.

国际贸易是一门实践性、涉外性很强的课程。大多数学生没有接触到国际贸易的具体业务工作，在学习中就应将理论知识的学习尽量地联想到国内贸易或当前的经济生活实际，多运用一些实践性的学习方法。

1. Task-driven Method 任务驱动法

Set up a complete “work tasks” situation for the study of international trade. For example, an export company, on receiving orders from customers, is required to process packaging, transportation, insurance and other operations according to the requirements of the importer and condition of the goods, students can acquire the theoretical knowledge in the process of assignment and accomplishment.

模拟真实场景，制定一套完整的“工作任务”。例如：某出口公司接到客户订单，要根据进口公司的要求及货物的情况，进行货物包装、运输、保险等具体业务操作，学生可以在任务设置和完成的过程中学习到相关的理论知识。

2. Role-play Method 角色扮演法

Set a training environment accessing to the actual scene of real work position , which can help understand the content of the roles and increasing the ability of problem-solving through taking participate in a role-play. For instance, students can be devided into several role-play groups, which act as the role of the exporter, the importer, the bank, and the forwarder respectively and etc. This can help to imitate the procedures of negotiation and payment in international trade contract. Through students' participation and interactive communication, their action-response ability and psychological quality will be enhanced, as the same time students also will recognize their own disadvantages and weaknesses by mutual comments.

设定一个最接近工作岗位的培训环境，指定参加扮演某种角色，借助角色演练来理解角色内容，从而提高解决现实问题的能力。例如，学生可以分成若干小组，小组成员分别扮演出口商、进口商、银行、货代企业等，模拟真实的国际贸易磋商与合同结算，通过学生的参与和互动交流，使学生的反应能力和心理素质得到强化；同时通过互相点评，学生认清了自身的缺点和不足。

3. Case-analysis Method 案例分析法

The teacher can design a specific given knowledge point Case-Problem, supply with massive background materials and demonstrate the real scene of international business. The participants can analyze the question and propose solved methods with the professional knowledge.

针对某个重要知识点，由教师设置一个特定案例，提供大量背景材料，展示真实背景，让学生依据专业知识来分析问题，提出解决问题的方法。

In the process of learning, a variety of specific case analysis can enable students to understand what is a contract, contract-signed, the performance of the contract, the duties and obligations between the importers and exporters, and so on. This can guide students to generalize the regularity through discussions, develop the ability of analyzing and solving problems independently and flexibly, and form cultivate good study habits.

在学习过程中，通过各类具体案例分析，使学生更加深刻的理解什么是合同、合同签订的方式、合同的履行、进出口商的责任义务等内容，从而引导学生通过思考讨论得出规律，培养独立、灵活分析问题和独立处理问题的能力，养成良好的学习习惯。

4. Bilingual Teaching Method 双语教学法

The foreign-featured in international trade field determines the importance of foreign language acquisition for students. Therefore, on one hand, the students should acquire the professional knowledge of foreign trade; on the other hand, they should also develop the ability of English of foreign trade during the study of this book. A gradual and graded immersion teaching method can be adopted on the basis of students' foreign language levels respectively. The whole semester will be roughly divided into three stages with different proportion of Chinese and English used in professional curriculum teaching. The proportion of English will gradually increase.

国际贸易专业的涉外性决定了学生的外贸外语学习很重要。因此，在本书的学习中，一方面要学好专业知识，另一方面也要培养外贸英语的能力。可以根据学生各自的外语基础，采用循序渐进，分级渗透式的方法，将整个学期的学习大致分成 3 个阶段，不同的阶段，中英文语言讲授专业课程的比例不同，英语所占的比重逐渐加大。

In the first stage, for important knowledge, using Chinese to teach first and then using English to repeat, to emphasize, to explain and to memorize the important theory and trade terms; in the second stage, gradually increased English proportion will be, attaching Chinese explanation to complex and difficult professional knowledge, to encourage students to learn how to use English to express professional content; in the third stage, applying English language for teaching basically, students ability to express professional knowledge in English will be improved.

在第一个阶段使用中英文结合，对于重要的知识，使用中文讲授一遍后，再使用英文讲授一遍，重要的定理和关键词，使用英文强调重复讲解、记忆；第二阶段逐步加大英文的比例，复杂难解的专业知识附以中文解释，在教学互动环节，鼓励学生学会如何使用英文表达专业内容；第三阶段，基本使用英语进行讲解，提高学生用英语思考表述专业问题的能力。

5. Select Competitive Course and Obtain Related Qualification Certificate 选取优势课程，考取专业相关的证书

Students of international trade majors can obtain many professional certificates. It is impossible for students to obtain all certificates in school, but they can select appropriate certificates according to their learning strength. There are lots of certificates related to international trade such as Foreign Trade Documentary Clerk, Export Sales Staff, Export Trader, Customs Declaration, Foreign Trade Merchandiser, Inspection Staff. See Fig. introduction-1.

国际贸易专业的学生可以考取的专业证书有很多，学生不可能在学校期间考完所有的证书，可以根据自己在学习中的优势，选取合适的证书考取，国际贸易相关证书主要有：单证员、外销员、高级国际贸易业务员、报关员、跟单员、报检员，如图绪-1 所示。

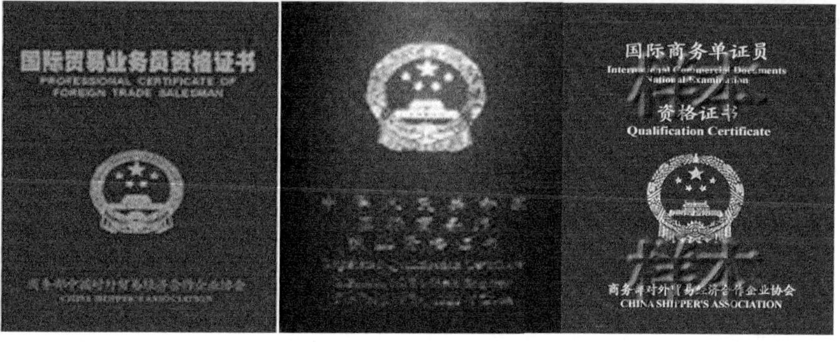

图绪-1 相关证书样例

【Review Questions】复习思考题

【Typical Case Link 1—典例链接 1】

Question: Analyze development prospects of China's foreign trade based on the data of Shanghai foreign trade development.

问题：从上海外贸发展数据试分析我国对外贸易发展的前景。

According to statistics, foreign capital enterprises in Shanghai have occupied a considerable proportion of the economy. In 2010, export and import of foreign capital enterprises accounts for 67.8% of the total share of international trade in Shanghai, foreign capital enterprises accounts for 62.9% of all industrial enterprises; 30.3% of the labor force concentrated in these enterprises, by the end of 2010, the foreign capital enterprises in Shanghai amounted to 34 400, the highest among the provinces in China. Foreign trade enterprises play a very important role in Shanghai's economic development.

根据资料统计，外资企业在上海经济中占有相当大的比重。2010 年，上海外资企业进出口额占全市总比重的 67.8%，外资企业占全市工业企业的比重为 62.9%；全市劳动力的 30.3%集中在外资企业，截至 2010 年年底，上海的外资企业达 3.44 万家，在全国各省区市中最高，外贸企业在上海市的经济发展中起到举足轻重的作用。

【Typical Case Link 2—典例链接 2】

Question: What are the problems of foreign capital enterprises to be concerned in foreign trade development?

外贸企业在国际贸易发展中应该注意哪些问题?

Some company in Wenzhou is a business group including various industries such as shoemaking, real estate. In the year of 2010, shoe exports of the company exceed $100 million, paying more than $50 million tax. The products have been exported to Germany, France, the United States, Spain, Eastern Europe and many other countries and regions. Trade prospects are very good, but from 2011, the Group's international trade orders were relatively reduced. The economy became sluggish, and through investigation, we know that though the shoes export is very good during these years, there is a problem of low price at the expense of quality. Therefore, with more and more strictly quality standards, shoes export is facing severe challenges, and thus also affects the export growth in profits.

温州某家企业集团是一家集制鞋、房地产等各类行业于一体的外贸企业集团，公司 2010 年鞋类出口突破 1 亿美元，纳税超 5000 万美元。产品远销德国、法国、美国、西班牙、东欧等国家或地区，贸易前景非常好，但是从 2011 年开始，集团的国际贸易订单量相对减少，经济出现了疲软，根据调查得知，多年来该集团的外贸鞋虽然出口销量很好，但是很多产品存在价格低，品质要求不高的现象，因此在品质标准越来越严格的情况下，鞋的出口面临着严峻的挑战，进而也影响了企业的出口利润增长。

Chapter One International Trade Theory

第一章　国际贸易理论

【Learning Objectives】教学目的与要求

After studying this chapter, you should be able to:

1. Have a good understanding of the relative contents of international trade;

2. Know the early ideas of regarding the basis for international trade and the distribution of the benefits to be gained from the trade;

3. Understand main trade policies and measures in international trade.

【Lead-in Case】引导案例

Question: Try to use international trade theory to explain the trade phenomena.

问题：请运用国际贸易原理来解释这一贸易现象。

In 2009, the European Union started to impose heavy tariffs on China's iron and steel fasteners. On July 31, 2009, China brought an accusation against EU in WTO. There was no result in the consultation, which are the first necessary procedure. On October 12, China asked for the establishment of a panel of experts. Some countries such as Brazil, Canada, Chile, Colombia, India, Japan, Norway, Thailand, Turkey, the United States and Taiwan of China took part in the proceedings as a third party.

On December 3, 2010, the WTO Panel made an adjudication regarding to EU's antidumping measure to China's iron and steel fasteners, which supported China's 8 appeals.

2009 年，欧盟开始对进口中国的钢铁扣件课以重税。2009 年 7 月 31 日，中国在 WTO 起诉欧盟。首先进行的是必经的磋商程序，但磋商无果。同年 10 月 12 日，中国要求成立专家组进行审理。巴西、加拿大、智利、哥伦比亚、印度、日本、挪威、泰国、土耳其、美国以及中国台湾地区以第三方身份参加诉讼。

2010 年 12 月 3 日，WTO 专家组就中国诉欧盟对中国钢铁扣件反倾销案做出一审裁决，对其中双方争议的 8 项诉求做出裁决，支持了中国的 8 项诉求。

Section One Overall of International Trade 第一节 国际贸易概述

1. Definition of International Trade 国际贸易的定义

Trading is one of the most basic activities of mankind. It has existed in every society, every part of the world, and in fact every day since the caveman came into trading.

贸易是人类最为基本的活动之一。每个社会都有贸易活动，并存在于世界各地，事实上，从洞穴人开始就有了贸易交往活动。

International trade, in essence, is the fair and deliberate exchange of commodity, technology and services between countries and regions. As this exchange takes place worldwide, it is also called World Trade or Global Trade. When viewed from those between a country and the other countries or their externals, international trade may also be called Foreign Trade. A nation's foreign trade can sometimes be called Overseas Trade, because of the nation's geographical characteristics or historical traditions. International trade may also be called Import and Export Trade because of concerning trade operations of both import and export.

国际贸易，从本质上说，是指不同国家（或地区）之间在平等的基础上，有意识地进行商品、技术和服务的交换活动。由于这一交换活动是世界范围内的，所以亦称世界贸易或全球贸易。从一个国家或地区和其他国家或地区的对外关系的角度看国际贸易又叫对外贸易。一个国家的对外贸易由于地理位置或历史传统的原因，有时又叫海外贸易。国际贸易由进口贸易和出口贸易两部分组成，故有时也称为进出口贸易。

International trade is a commercial activity across counties, which includes not only international trade and oversea production, but also emerging service industries, such as transportation, tourism, banking, advertising and so on. The main motivation of international trade is not only to acquire benefits, seek resources and develop diversification to expand sales, scatter business risks, in many cases, but also an extension of a country's foreign policy.

国际贸易是人们跨越国界所进行的商务活动，不仅包括国际贸易及国外生产，同时还包括新兴的服务行业，诸如交通运输业、旅游业、银行业、广告业等。一国或地区进行国际贸易的主要动机不仅在于追求利润，寻求资源和开展多元化经营，扩大销售，分散企业风险，很多情况下还是一国对外政策的延伸。

2. Characteristics of International Trade 国际贸易的特点

International trade is a business activity with foreign features, which has its characteristics different from domestic trade, which is far more complicated procedures involved in its transaction process, trading terms and conditions, international trade practices than domestic trade in the following aspects.

国际贸易是一项具有涉外性质的商务活动，具有不同于国内贸易的特点，其交易过程、交易条件、贸易做法及所涉及的问题，都远比国内贸易复杂。具体表现在如下几个方面。

（1）Complication 复杂性

It is more complicated than we can imagine. A minor mistake may affect the smooth implementation of economic interests because of both sides of transaction between different countries and regions involves the problems of adaptation of related different trade laws and regulations of different countries which give rise to the discrepancies and conflicts between two culture backgrounds, conventions and customary habits during the course of business negotiation and executing contracts.

国际贸易比我们想象的要复杂得多。稍有疏忽，就可能影响经济利益的顺利实现。因为交易双方处在不同国家或地区，在洽商交易和履约的过程中，涉及各自不同的法律制度和规则，会因为文化背景、惯例和习惯做法互有差异而引起争议和矛盾。

（2）Risk 风险性

Both the quantities and revenues of international trade in goods are larger than those of domestic trade. There is always a long time span between the signing of a contract and fulfillment of it, because it takes quite a long time to transport goods from one country to another. The consignments in transit may meet with all kinds of natural disasters, accidents, other extraneous risks when traveling a long distance. Under such circumstances, there exists an inevitably greater risk in the international trade.

在国际货物贸易中，成交的数量和金额相对较大，履约时间往往很长，而且交易的商品需要长途运输。在远距离的运输过程中，可能会遇到各种自然灾害、意外事件和各种其他外来风险，从而更加大了国际贸易的风险程度。

（3）Instability 不稳定性

International trade is instable and susceptible to the turbulence of international situation and changes of market. Especially under the situation of current instable international situation, increasingly intensified international market competition and trade friction as well as frequently floating market exchange rates, international commodity price, the instability of international trade is more obvious and it is more difficult to engage in international trade.

国际贸易易受国际局势和市场变化的影响，具有不稳定性。尤其在当前国际局势动荡不定、国际市场竞争和贸易摩擦愈演愈烈以及国际市场汇率经常浮动和货价瞬息万变的情况下，国际贸易的不稳定性更为明显，从事国际贸易的难度也更大。

（4）Multi-Intermediate Links 多环节性

International Trade has an extensive coverage and a large scope, involves many intermediate links. Apart from both parties of two sides, international trade also involves various intermediaries, agents and departments provide services as commodity inspection, transportation, insurance, finance, railway stations, ports, customs and soon. One problem in any part will affect the normal conduct of the whole transaction, and finally may lead to legal disputes.

国际贸易覆盖面广、范围大。国际贸易中除交易双方当事人外，还涉及各种中间商、代理商以及为国际贸易服务的商检、运输、保险、金融、车站、港口和海关等部门。任何一个环节出了问题，就会影响整笔交易的正常进行，并有可能引起法律上的纠纷。

3. Importance of International Trade 国际贸易的重要性

First, for the customers, international trade bring news living styles, updated concepts, great variety of demand. For example, Mobile phones, computers, cameras are cheaper than before. What is more, since the early 90's China has become a net importer of oil. In 1993, the oil imports of China was about 9.2 million ton. In 45 main mineral products which was necessary in development of China's economy, there were 5 of which relied on imports solution, and 15 kinds of which required long-term import by 2010. International trade can solve the contradictions between the limited domestic resources and the variation demand of people, which can promote better economic development.

首先，发展国际贸易，对个体来说，能带给人们新的生活方式、新的理念、满足生活的多样化需求。如手机、电脑、相机越来越价廉物美；再如，中国自 20 世纪 90 年代初已成为石油净进口国，1993 年石油进口达 920 万吨；到 2010 年中国经济发展所必需的 45 种主要矿产品，有 5 种主要依靠进口解决，15 种需要长期进口。通过国际贸易可以解决国内资源有限与人民生活需求多样化的矛盾，更好地发展经济。

Second, developing international trade and participation in the international division of labor may saving social labor, and increase economic efficiency for companies. By direct investment in other countries, such as setting up joint venture and wholly-owned subsidiaries or multi-national companies, it can enjoy the advantage of economies of scale, which create the effect of reducing the cost when the size of production reaches a certain scale.

其次，发展国际贸易，对于公司来说，可以参与国际社会分工、节约社会劳动、提高经济效益。通过直接投资，如建立合资企业和独资企业或跨国公司，其可以享有规模经济优势，这种优势在生产达到一定时会产生降低成本的效益。

Third, development of international trade may promote economic development and makes contribution to the increase of economic growth rate, and enhance competitiveness in the world trade for countries. WTO data showed that international trade of China got a rapid development in the ten years after joining the WTO, China became the largest exporter of goods and the second largest merchandise importer in the world. Development advantages of industries such as textiles, home appliances, and electronics are obvious. Sectors such as automobiles, ships, railway locomotives also developed rapidly as a new growth point of foreign trade. In the past ten years China has become an important member of the international trade system. The economic strength and competitiveness of China has also been significantly improved.

再次，发展国际贸易，能够促进国家经济发展、提高经济增长率、增强竞争力。世贸组织的数据表明，入世十年是中国国际贸易飞速发展的十年，中国成为世界上最大的商品出口国、第二大商品进口国。尤其是纺织、家电、电子等产业发展优势明显，汽车、船舶、铁路机车等行业也迅速发展为新的外贸增长点。十年的时间中国已成为世界国际贸易体系重要的一员，国家的经济实力和竞争力也得到了大幅度提高。

Besides, with the development of international trade, the government introduced foreign capitals and brought in investment in local area, which would provide more job opportunities.

此外，随着国际贸易的发展，政府吸引外资，给当地的居民提供更多的就业机会。

Section Two Protectionist Theories and Free Trade Theories
第二节 保护贸易理论和自由贸易理论

1. Overview 概述

Why is trade conducted between countries? How can trade generate wealth for various trading partners? Why do some nations want free trade while some others want to restrict trade? In different historical periods and international market environment, economists have tried to answer the questions by putting forward different theories, which have already formed two major types of theories systems, that is, Protectionist Theories and Free Trade Theories.

国家之间为什么要进行贸易？如何从事生产和进行贸易才能使各国利益最大化？为什么一些国家想自由贸易而另一些国家想限制贸易？在不同的历史发展阶段和国际市场环境，经济学家们提出了不同的理论观点，也逐渐形成了保护贸易和自由贸易两大理论体系来解释这些问题。

Free Trade Theories are to deal with the natural order of trade, that is, it examines and explains trade patterns under certain conditions. Theories of this type pose questions of how much, which products, and with whom a country will trade in the absence of restrictions among countries; Protectionist Theories prescribes governmental interference with the free movement of goods and services among countries in order to alter the amount, composition, and direction of trade.

自由贸易理论解释的是自然状况下进行的贸易，即解释了在一般条件下的贸易模式。这种理论解释了用多少钱、针对某种产品，和不受贸易限制的国家做交易的问题；而保护贸易理论则是指国家间为了调节贸易份额、贸易结构和贸易方向而由政府出面干预货物和服务贸易自由流动的模式。

Both the descriptive and prescriptive theories have considerable impacts on international business. They provide insights with favorable markets as well as potentially successful products. The theories also help to wnderstand the governmental trade policies that might be enacted, and predict how those policies might affect competitiveness.

以上这两种理论对国际贸易产生很大的影响。他们为畅销市场和潜在产品的成功交易提供视角，这些理论也有助于了解各国政府实施的贸易政策，并且预示着这些政策可能引起的竞争。

2. Protectionist Theories 保护贸易理论

Trade protectionism holds that governments should intervene with trade to prevent the free interflow of foreign products into their domestic markets, and in order to protect domestic industry from foreign competition. Tariff, import quota, foreign exchange control, convoluted formalities of imports and exports, discriminatory government procurement policy are the important means of international trade protection.

贸易保护主义认为政府应该干预贸易，去阻止外国产品自由流入他们的本国市场，以保护国内产业免受外国商品的竞争。关税、进口配额、外汇管制、烦琐的进出口手续、歧视性的政府采购政策等都是国际贸易保护的重要手段。

2.1 Mercantilism 重商主义

Trade protectionism was first voiced by mercantilism, which formed the foundation of economic thought from 16th to 17th centuries, and dominated the policies of the main industrial nations in 17th and 18th centuries.

贸易保护主义第一次被重商主义来表述，该贸易理论产生于 16～17 世纪，盛行于 17～18 世纪中叶的主要工业国家。

This theory held that a country wealth was measured by its ownership of treasure, which was usually in the form of gold. According to this theory, countries should export more than import, if succeed, would receive their trade surpluses in the form of gold from the country that ran deficits. In this case, the governments should establish monopolies over their countries' trade and impose restrictions were imposed on most imports and subsidies on exports.

重商主义者认为一个国家的财富凭其拥有的贵重物品来衡量，如黄金。基于此，国家应该出口大于进口，这样的话，这个国家会由于贸易顺差拥有更多的黄金。为了达到此目的，政府应该垄断国家贸易，限制进口，奖励出口。

Trade surplus—*the amount by which the value of exports exceeds the value of imports in a given time period.*

贸易顺差是指在特定年度一国出口贸易总额大于进口贸易总额，又称“出超”。

Trade deficit —*the amount by which the value of imports exceeds the value of exports in a given time period*。

所谓贸易逆差是指一国在一定时期内进口贸易总值大于出口总值，俗称“入超”，或叫“贸易赤字”。

Mercantilism can also be grouped into early and late stage of mercantilism. 重商主义又可分为早期重商主义和晚期重商主义。

(1)Early mercantilism(16th century~in the middle of 17th century): Early mercantilist also was known as monetary balance theory, emphasized on the absolute trade surplus, control of commodity imports, currency output ban to accumulate money wealth. In order to accumulate money as much as possible, mercantilists required their governments to control currency activities. See Fig. 1-1.

早期重商主义（16 世纪～17 世纪中叶）又称为货币差额论。强调绝对的贸易顺差，控制商品进口，禁止货币输出以积累货币财富。为保证贮藏尽量多的货币，力求政府使用行政手段控制货币运动，如图 1-1 所示。

图 1-1　货币财富

(2) Late mercantilism(in the middle of 16th century-17th century): The late mercantilism is also called the trade balance theory. The theory does not against monetary output, and holds that currency output can bring in more currencies, which advocates currency output to purchase raw material or conduct transshipment trade and promotes production to gain more currencies from overseas. In order to guarantee the surpluses of foreign trade, mercantilists required their governments to take some measures to protect tariff.

晚期重商主义（17 世纪中叶～18 世纪）又称为贸易差额论。该理论不反对货币输出，在货币输出能带来更多货币的前提下，主张输出货币购买原材料或进行转口贸易，发展生产以便从国外获取更多货币。为保证对外贸易顺差，力求政府采取保护关税的措施。

2.2　Protecting Manufacturing Industry Theory of A. Hamilton 汉密尔顿的制造业保护论/关税保护学说

Protecting Manufacturing Industry Theory is the oldest economic argument for government intervention, dating to the year of 1792 and Alexander Hamilton(1757～1804)，American. See Fig. 1-2.

制造业保护论是最古老的政府干预经济的论据，对它的研究可以追溯到 1792 年美国的亚历山大·汉密尔顿（1757～1804），如图 1-2 所示。

图 1-2　亚历山大·汉密尔顿

This theory held that it is necessary to develop manufacturing industry in order to have American economic independance on one hand; On the other hand, the new infant manufacturing industries established by developing country have to be protected by taking customs tariff measures so as to avoid the competition from England that was well developed.

他主张为使美国经济自立。一方面，要发展制造产业，另一方面，新的已建立的幼稚产业难以与发达的英国竞争，必须采用关税保护措施。

2.3　Protecting Infant Industry Theory of F. List 李斯特的幼稚产业保护论

Friedrich List，1789～1846
《政治经济学的国民体系》
（The National System of Political Economy）

图 1-3　李斯特

Friedrich List, a German economist, was a representative protectionist in the early 19th century when Adam Smith had initiated free trade theory. His masterpiece is *The National System of Political Economy.* See Fig. 1-3.

弗里德里希·李斯特(Friedrich List，1789～1846)，德国经济学家，当亚当·斯密开创他的自由贸易理论的时候，李斯特就成了19世纪早期贸易保护主义者的代表，如图1-3所示。他的代表作是《政治经济学的国民体系》。

He is affected deeply by the thought of Alexander Hamilton and proposed the Protecting Infant Industry Theory. The core idea of the theory is productivity theory, he held that the productivity was the competence of creating treasure, the governments had to execute the protecting trade policies on the growth of its new infant and potential industry so as to ensure productivity development, even loss may be caused at the early date.

李斯特深受汉密尔顿的影响,提出了保护幼稚工业理论。他的核心理论是生产力理论，他认为生产力就是创造财富的能力，为使生产力发展，国家必须对其新兴而有发展前途的工业实行暂时的保护政策，即使开始时可能受到损失。

Like this, in order to protect the interest of Germany, which is a less developed nation than Britain at that time, he held that if the less developed nations were only concerned with the trade interest in the short time and adopted free trade in practice, then they would forever be dominated by the more developed nations. He held that Germany at that time should sacrifice its interest in the short time and restrict import and levy a higher customs tariff so as to help the growth of its new infant and potential industry and to achieve its interest in the long run.

同样的道理，作为一个不太发达的国家——德国相对落后于发达的英国，不能因为短期的利益而采用自由贸易政策，否则这样就会永远被发达国家所控制。因此，他认为德国应该牺牲短期利益，要以限制进口并征收高关税的办法对其新兴而有发展前途的工业进行暂时的保护，以免被当时先进的英国工业挤垮。

2.4 Super-protectionism Theory 超保护贸易理论

凯恩斯（John Maynard Keynes）1936 年发表《就业、利息和货币通论》The General Theory of Employment, Interest and Money

图1-4　凯恩斯

J. M. Keynes, a British economist, renovated and consolidated Super-protectionism Theory or Mercantilism in the 30's of the 20th century. His masterpiece is *The General Theory of Employment, Interest and Money* published in 1936. See Fig. 1-4.

凯恩斯（John Maynard Keynes，1883～1946）是英国资产阶级经济学家，是超保护贸易理论或者是说 20 世纪 30 年代的重商主义的创始人，如图 1-4 所示。他的代表作是《就业、利息和货币通论》，于 1936 年出版。

From 1929 to 1933, a serious economic crisis took place in the field of capitalism, which had a further exerted great influence in the market. He maintained that only the policies of protection trade can make sure brisk economy, enlarge employment and ease crisis. To protect their own industries from the competition of foreign entry, the government should take some measures like as prohibition tariff, dump policy, foreign exchange war and quantity restriction to work as ways of scrambling foreign markets.

从 1929 年到 1933 年，资本主义世界爆发严重经济危机，市场问题进一步尖锐化。他认为只有采取保护贸易的政策才能够保证经济繁荣，扩大就业，缓和危机。为保护本国产业免受国外商品的竞争，政府应该采取禁止性关税、倾销政策、外汇战争、数量限制等措施作为争夺国外市场的手段。

All these means proposed by him, of which are highlight different from traditional protectionism on the purposes of protection, the objectives of protection, the methods of protection, and the characteristics of protection, the theory is called Super-protectionism Theory. In detailed as Table 1-1.

他提出的这些保护手段，无论在保护目的、保护对象、保护手段及保护特点上都与传统的保护主义政策有很大的不同，所以被称为超保护贸易理论，如表 1-1 所示。

Table 1-1　Differences between J. M. Keynes' Super-protectionism and Traditional Protectionism.

	Traditional Protectionism	**J. M. Keynes' Super-protectionism**
Purpose of protection	Developing own state productivity	Enhance the control to foreign market, pursuing Trade surplus
Objective of protection	The infant industries of less developed nations	Backward industries of developed nations
Methods of protection	Tariff measure	Tariff and non- Tariff measures
Characteristics of protection	Prohibit and restrict import of goods	Export Promotion Measures by export subsidies and dumping

表 1-1　　凯恩斯的贸易保护观点与传统贸易保护的区别

	传统保护贸易政策	超保护贸易政策
保护目的	发展本国生产力	加强对国外市场的控制，争取贸易顺差
保护对象	落后国的幼稚工业	发达国家的夕阳工业
保护手段	关税措施	关税与非关税措施
保护特点	防御性限制进口为主	以政府补贴和商品倾销主动向别国进攻

3. Free Trade Theories 自由贸易理论

The free trade theory means there if no intervention of government over import and export trade and free competition in foreign market.

自由贸易理论是指国家对进出口贸易不加干预，任其自由竞争。

3.1 Absolute Advantage Theory 绝对优势理论

英国的经济学家亚当·斯密(Adam smith)在其 1776 年出版的《国民财富的性质和原因的研究》一书中，提出了绝对优势理论

图 1-5 亚当·斯密

Adam Smith, classical economist of Britain, proposes the Absolute Advantage Theory, the core idea of which is that if the production costs of a country of a certain product are lower than the same product in another country, it is called the absolute advantage, in that way, this country ought to produce and export this kind of product exclusively; On the contrary, if the production costs of a country of a certain product are higher than the same product in another country, it is called the absolute inferior position, then this country should not produce this kind of product, and may import from another country. In this way, each country produces their products with absolute advantage respectively and exchanges each other so that they can gain benefits. See Table. 1-2.

英国古典经济学家亚当·斯密提出绝对优势理论，如图 1-5 所示。其核心思想认为，若一国生产某产品的成本小于另一国同类产品的生产成本，即处于绝对优势，那么，该国就应该专门生产并出口这种产品；若一国生产某产品的成本大于另一国，即处于绝对劣势，则该国就不应该生产这种产品，而是从另一国进口这种产品。这样，各自生产自己具有绝对优势的产品并进行交换，从中获得利益，如表 1-2 所示。

表 1-2　　绝对优势比较

		英国	法国	合计
分工前	毛呢/wool	100 人·年/单位	110 人·年/单位	2 单位
	葡萄酒/wine	120 人·年/单位	80 人·年/单位	2 单位
分工后	毛呢/wool	220 人·年 2.2 单位		2.2 单位
	葡萄酒/wine		190 人·年 2.375 单位	2.375 单位

See from Table.1-2, for example, if the woolen and vintage all be produced both in Britain and France, in order to produce a certain number of woolen, Britain needs 100 labor a year, while france needs 110 labor a year; for a certain quantity of vintage, Britain needs 120 labor a year, while france only need 80 labor a year. Therefore, input vintage from France and output woolen. France is just the opposite, output vintage to the British in exchange for the woolen. The two countries can both gain benefits from the international trade.

例如英国和法国都生产毛呢和葡萄酒。生产一定数量毛呢，英国一年需要 100 人的劳动，法国则一年需要 110 人的劳动；而如果要配制一定数量的葡萄酒，英国一年需要 120 人劳动，法国则一年只需要 80 人劳动。因此，英国从法国输入葡萄酒而输出毛呢。法国则刚好相反，向英国输出葡萄酒以交换毛呢。两国都能从中获得贸易所带来的利益。

3.2 Theory of Comparative Advantage 比较优势理论

英国经济学家大卫·李嘉图（David Richard B）在其 1817 年出版的《政治经济学及赋税原理》详细地阐述了比较优势理论。《Principles of Political Economy》

图 1-6 大卫 · 李嘉图

Based on the research of Adam Smith, David Ricardo puts forward with a different point of view against Adam Smith, which believes that a country can produce and export absolute advantage product and import absolute inferior commodities from other countries even if a country does not have any absolute advantage in production. Compared with other countries, the relative cost of comidites is different, the country can still produce and export products of low relative cost in exchange for products of high relative cost to gain benefits. See Table 1-3.

大卫 · 李嘉图基于亚当 · 斯密研究的基础上，提出了与亚当 · 斯密不同的观点，如图 1-6 所示。他认为一国不仅在本国商品相对于别国同种商品处于绝对优势时可以生产和出口该种商品，在本国商品相对于别国同种商品处于绝对劣势时可以进口该种商品，而且即使一个国家在生产上没有任何绝对优势，只要它与其他国家相比，生产各种商品的相对成本不同，仍可以通过生产相对成本较低的产品并出口，来换取自己生产中相对成本较高的产品，从而获得利益，如表 1-3 所示。

表 1-3 比较优势

		英国	葡萄牙	合计
分工前	毛呢	100 人 · 年/单位	90 人 · 年/单位	2 单位
	葡萄酒	120 人 · 年/单位	80 人 · 年/单位	2 单位
分工后	毛呢	220 人 · 年 2.2 单位		2.2 单位
	葡萄酒		170 人 · 年 2.125 单位	2.125 单位

3.3 Factor-Endowment Theory 要素禀赋理论

图 1-7 赫克歇尔

图 1-8 詹姆斯 · 米德

赫克歇尔在 1919 年的论文《对外贸易对国民收入的影响》中首先使用了要素禀赋这一概念来解释贸易原因

1933 年俄林在著作《域际贸易与国际贸易》中继承了他老师赫克歇尔的思想，更详尽的阐述了此理论，并因此在 1977 年与另一名英国经济学家詹姆斯 · 米德分享了当年的诺贝尔经济学奖

The Factor Endowment Theory is also known as H-O theory, proposed by the Swedish economists Heckscher and Ohlin. The main content of the Factor-Endowment Theory is comparative advantage in one country is determined by the factor endowments, factor endowment difference is the root cause of international trade. See Fig. 1-9.

要素禀赋理论又被称为 H-O 理论，是由瑞典经济学家赫克歇尔（Heckscher）和俄林（Bertil Ohlin）师徒俩提出的，如图 1-7 和图 1-8 所示。要素禀赋理论的主要内容是一国的比较优势由要素禀赋决定，要素禀赋不同是国际贸易产生的根本原因如图 1-9 所示。

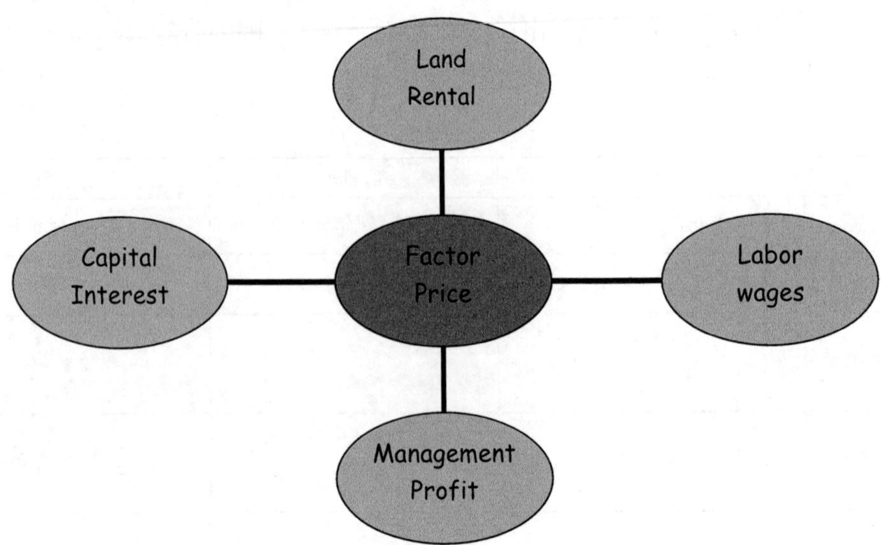

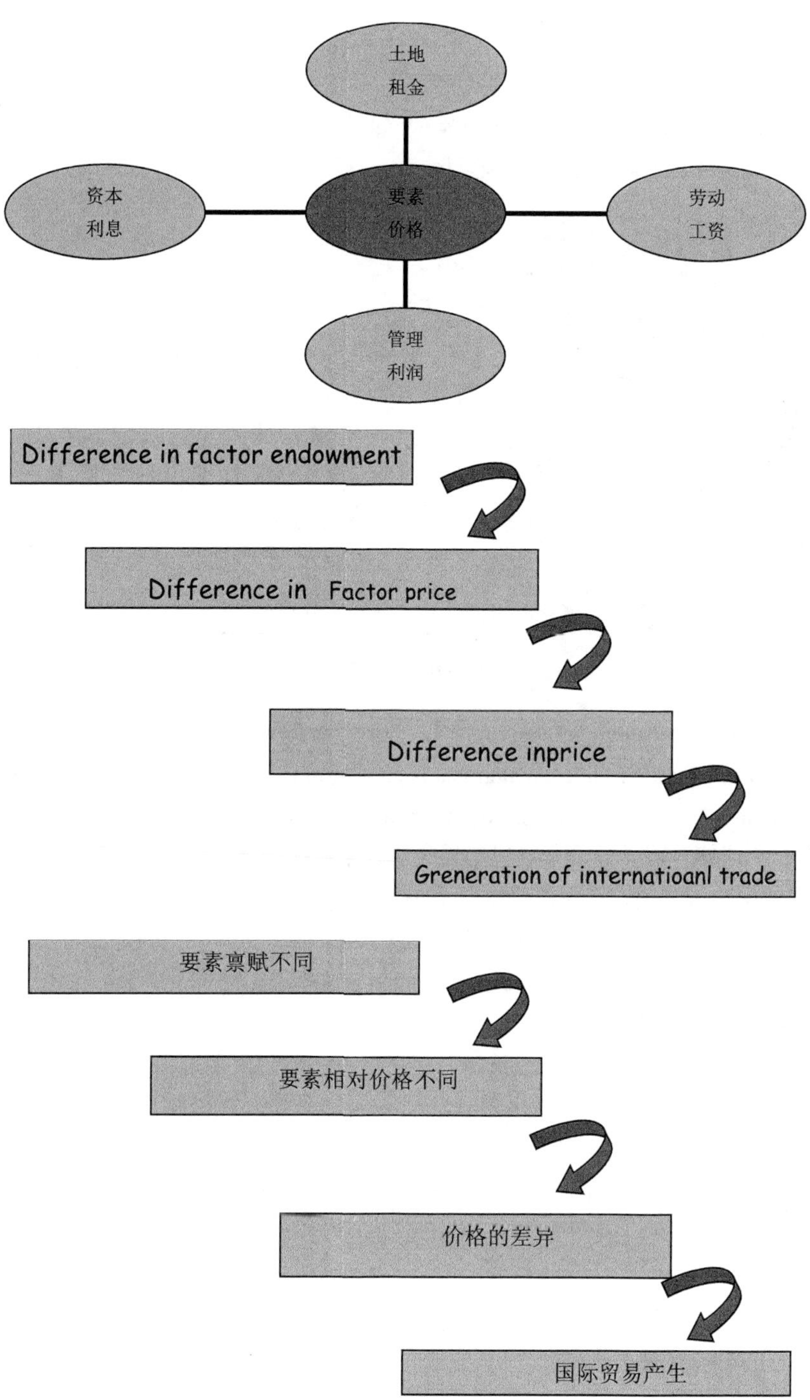

图 1-9　比较优势

With certain production factor stock of each country, the country will produce and export products with extensive use of its opulent factors and import products with extensive use of its rare factors. In short, countries with a plentiful supply of labor force export labor-intensive products, import capital-extensive products. On the contrary, countries with abundant capital export capital-intensive products and import labor-intensive products.

在各国生产要素存量一定的条件下，一国将生产和出口较密集使用其丰裕要素的产品，进口较密集使用其稀缺要素的产品。简而言之，劳动力丰富的国家出口劳动密集型产品，进口资本密集型产品；相反资本丰富的国家出口资本密集型产品，进口劳动密集型产品。

3.4 The Leontief Paradox 里昂惕夫之谜

Wassily Leontief：美国著名当代经济学家（俄裔）

21 岁获得柏林大学的博士学位，1931 年加入美国国籍，长期担任哈佛大学教授、美国经济学会会长

因在投入产出学中的开创性贡献，于 1973 年获得诺贝尔经济学奖

图 1-10 里昂惕夫

In the early 1950s, the American economist Leontief put forward the factor endowment theory that is known as the "Leontief Paradox" later, which has been a turning point of new contemporary development of western traditional microeconomic theory of international trade.

20 世纪 50 年代初，美国经济学家里昂惕夫对要素禀赋的理论提出了质疑，被后人称为"里昂惕夫之谜"，它的提出成为西方传统微观国际贸易理论在当代新发展的转折点，如图 1-10 所示。

Leontief selected 10 types of commodities' data with maximum net imports and exports from 167 industries in the data of the year 1947 to see the factor proportion of which in total exports and imports of per million dollars. See Table.1-4.

在 1947 年的数据中，里昂惕夫从 167 个行业的商品中选出净进出口额最大的 10 类商品，分别看看它们每 100 万美元的出口总额和进口总额中的要素比例，如表 1-4 所示。

表 1-4 数据分析

净出口	K/L	净进口
批发贸易	7638	农业和渔业
机动车辆	10447	纸和纸箱厂
谷物制品	21022	橡胶
纺织产品：纺纱、编织、印染	10738	榨汁机
铁路运输	21022	食品：罐头、保鲜、冷冻
海洋运输	15945	其他非铁矿（不包括铜、铅、锌和铝）
钢制品和轧钢机	15273	原油及天然气
采煤	8491	狩猎器具
特殊的工业机械	10439	原生铜
石油产品	27139	其他原生金属（不包括铅、铜、铝）
平均值	14788.4	平均值

Table 1-4 Data Analysis

Net Export	K/L	Net import
Wholesale Trade	7638	Agriculture and Fisheries
Motor Vehicle	10447	Paper and Carton Factory
Cereal Products	20752	Rubber
Textile Products: Spinning, Weave	10738	Juicer
Prinling and dyeing	21022	Food: Can, Fresh, Freezing
Maritime Transport	15945	Other than iron (not including copper, lead, zinc and aluminum)
Steel products and Rolling Machine	15273	Crude Oil and Natural Gas
Coal Mining	8491	Hunting Tools
Special Industrial Machinery	10439	Native Copper
Petroleum Products	27139	Other Primary Metal (not including lead, copper, aluminum)
Average	14788.4	Average

	1951 年	
	出口	进口
资本（美元）	2256800	2303400
劳动（人/年）	173.91	167.81
资本/劳动	12977	13726
美国出口劳动密集型产品，进口资本密集型产品。		

	1951 年	
	Export	Import
Capital (US. $)	2256800	2303400
Labor (per / year)	173.91	167.81
Capital / Labor	12977	13726
Ameria export Labor-intensive products, import capital-intensive products.		

In 1951, the United States imported capital-intensive commodities, while labor-intensive goods are exported. Thus, Leontief pointed out that the United Stated participated in the international division of labor on the basis of specialization in labor-intensive production. In other words, the country uses foreign trade to save capital and organize surplus labor, not on the contrary.

1951 年，美国进口的是资本密集型商品，而出口的则是劳动密集型商品。由此，里昂惕夫指出，美国参加国际分工是建立在劳动密集生产专业化基础之上的。换言之，这个国家是利用对外贸易来节约资本和安排剩余劳动力，而不是相反。

According to Heckscher-Ohlin model, the United States should export capital-intensive products and import labor-intensive products, while the actual verification result shows the opposite. This is known as the “Leontief Paradox”.

按赫克歇尔—俄林模型推断，美国应出口资本密集型产品，进口劳动密集型产品，而实际验证结果却与此相反。这被称为“里昂惕夫之谜”。

3.5 New Theory of Free Trade 自由贸易新理论

Since the 1950s, many new phenomena appeared in the international trade.

20 世纪 50 年代以来，国际贸易出现了许多新的现象。

（1）Trade between similar products significantly increased.

同类产品之间的贸易量大大增加。

（2）The volume of trade between developed countries significantly increased.

发达国家之间的贸易量大大增加。

（3）Position of industry shifted constantly.

产业领先地位不断转移。

After the establishment of the European Community, intra-industry development in dept and breadth among western European countries shows that the smaller the difference in factor endowments between countries, the greater possibility of intra-industry trade is, and so does the trade flow. This phenomenon can not be well explained by the factor endowment theory, since factor endowments, technology and factor intensive level of products are in same industrial sector that make little difference among European countries, so new trade theory comes into being.

尤其是欧洲（经济）共同体成立后，西欧国家之间产业内贸易向纵深发展显示出：国家之间要素禀赋差别越小，发生产业内贸易的可能性越大，贸易流量也越大。这种现象使用要素禀赋理论无法做出满意的解释，因为西欧国家的要素禀赋状况差别不大，技术水平差别不大，同一产业部门产品的要素密集程度差别也不大，由此产生了新的贸易理论。

3.5.1 Intra-industry Trade Theory 产业内贸易理论

Intra-industry international trade refers to the phenomenon that a country or region not only proceed exporting but also importing products of the same industrial sector for a certain period.

产业内国际贸易是指一个国家或地区，在一段时间内，同一产业部门产品出现既进口又出口的现象。

As in the case, trade activities such as cases that Japan exports cars to the United States, while imports the same products from the United States; China exports shirts of a certain brand to South Korea, while at the same time imports T-shirts from South Korea. Intra-industry trade also includes intermediate products trade, namely the trade of semi-finished products, parts of a certain products in trade between two countries. Intra-industry trade theory holds that:

如日本向美国出口轿车，同时又从美国进口轿车的现象；中国向韩国出口某种品牌的衬衣，同时又从韩国进口某种 T 恤衫的这种贸易活动。产业内贸易还包括中间产品的贸易，即某项产品的半制成品、零部件在两国间的贸易。产业内贸易理论认为：

（1）Product heterogeneity is the basis for international trade within the industry;产品的异质性是产业内国际贸易的基础；

（2）Demand preference similarity and diversity are the guarantee of intra-industry trade;需求偏好的相似性和多样性是产业内贸易的保证；

（3）The intra-firm increasing return to scale is the main interest resource of trade within a industry. 企业内部规模收益递增是产业内贸易的主要利益来源。

3.5.2 Economies of Scale Theory 规模经济理论

Main representative of economies of scale theory is Paul R. krugman, whose theory pointed out that product price superiority or the cost superiority may not be caused by technical level differences, or factor endowment differences, but the production scale of the product. Therefore, the new trade theory believed that the economies of scale is the key factor leading to the appearance of modern international trade.

规模经济理论的主要代表是克鲁格曼，规模经济理论指出，一国某种产品的价格优势或成本优势可以既不是因技术水平差异所引起的，也不是因要素禀赋的不同所引起的，而是由生产该产品的生产规模所造成的。因此，新贸易理论认为，规模经济是现今国际贸易产生的一个重要因素。

3.5.3　Theory of Preference Similarity 需求偏好相似理论

The main representative is Linde, who held that the decisive factor of production are demand and market rather than cost. Further more, since a country's potential export products are based on its consumption structure which is decided by the country's level of per capita income. The basis of the export is established because of similarity to domestic market. See Fig. 1-2.【Typical Case Link 1】

需求偏好理论的主要代表是林德，他认为企业生产的决定因素不是成本而是需求和市场，进一步说，本国的潜在出口产品由本国的消费结构决定，本国的消费结构又由本国的人均收入水平决定。出口市场的形成是因为与国内市场相似，如图 1-11 所示。【典例链接 1】

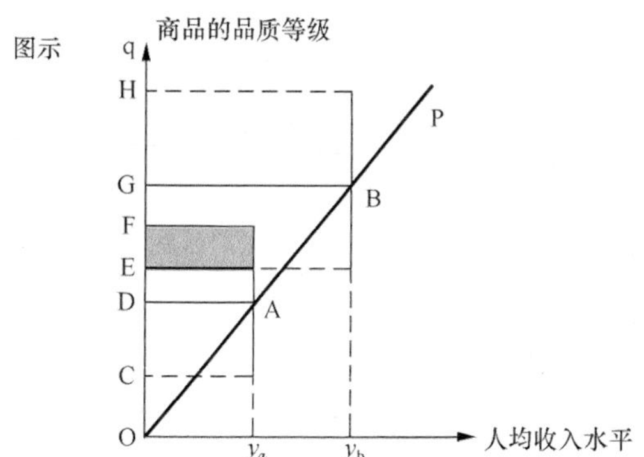

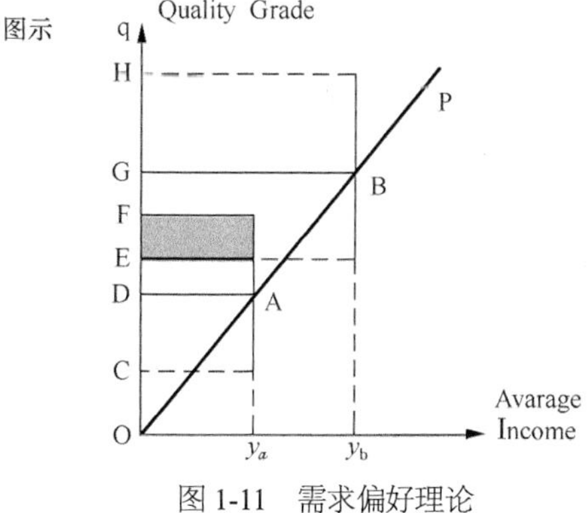

图 1-11　需求偏好理论

3.5.4　Product Life Cycle Theory 产品生命周期理论

Product life cycle theory, of which the main representatives are Welsh and Vernon, who mainly employ the marketing theory to analyze the possibility of international trade. The first stage is new product stage, which is talent-United States-knowledge-intensive. The second stage is maturity stage of products, which is capital-other developed countries-technology-intensive and capital-intensive. The third stage: standardization stage, that is price-developing countries-labor-intensive. See Fig. 1-12.

产品生命周期理论的主要代表人物有威尔士和弗农，其理论内容主要是运用市场营销理论来分析国际贸易上的可能。第一阶段：产品的创新阶段：人才——美国——知识密集型。第二阶段：产品的成长、成熟阶段,资本——其他发达国家——技术密集型和资本密集型。第三阶段：标准化阶段，价格——发展中国家——劳动密集型，如图 1-7 所示。

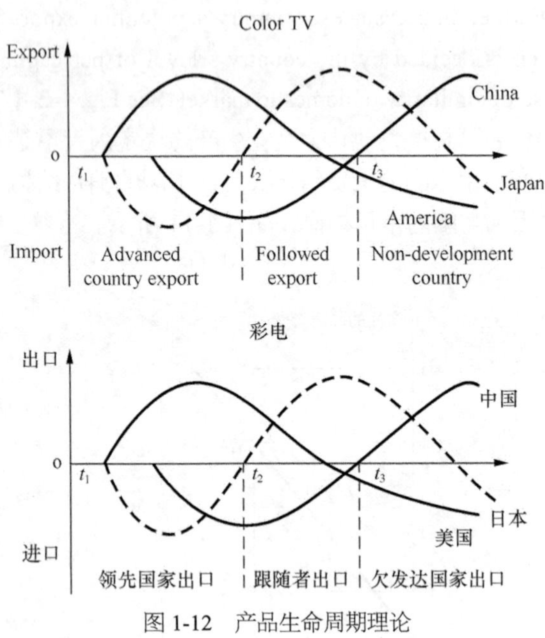

图 1-12　产品生命周期理论

3.5.5　Competitive Advantage Theory 竞争优势理论

Main representative of the competitive advantage theory is Michael E. Porter, an American economist. The main element of the theory is that a country's advantage in the international market mainly comes from competitive advantage rather than comparative advantage. A country's competitive advantage refers to the competitive advantage of enterprise and industry, including production factors (demands for basic factors and advanced factors), size and structure in demand, related and supporting industries (upper industries efficient favorable to downstream), enterprise organization, strategy and competition, policy of the government , the opportunity. See Fig. 1-13.

竞争优势理论的代表人物主要是美国经济学家麦克尔·波特，理论的主要内容是指，一国在国际市场中的优势主要来自于竞争优势而不是比较优势，一国的竞争优势是指企业和行业的竞争优势。包括：生产要素状况（基本要素和高等要素需求状况）、市场需求的规模和结构、相关与辅助行业（上游企业有效率对下游企业有利）、企业组织结构、战略和竞争状况，政府的策略和机遇，如图 1-13 所示。

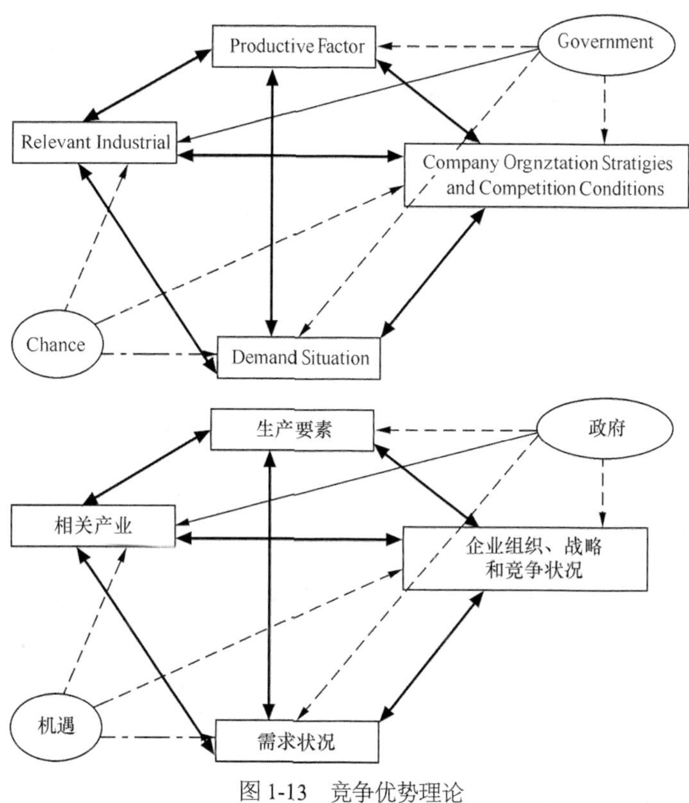

图 1-13　竞争优势理论

Section Three International Trade Policy and Measure 第三节 国际贸易政策与措施

1. International Trade Policy 国际贸易政策

International trade policy refers to the government of a country made and executed some policies to the national import and export trade in order to fulfill the goal of policies during a certain period.

国际贸易政策是一国政府在一定时期内为实现一定的政策目标对本国的进出口贸易制定并实施的政策。

As a tool of state intervention on foreign economic relations, international trade policy is not only an important content of economic policy, but also an important component of foreign policy. In different historical periods, on one hand, the government of a state always adopt its trade policy to fit in with the needs of changes of economic situations abroad. On the other hand, the government adjusted foreign policies according to economic demand on one own nation.

国际贸易政策，作为国家干预对外经济关系的工具，不仅是经济政策的重要内容之一，也是对外政策的重要组成部分。在不同历史时期，一方面，一国政府往往根据国外经济形势的变化调整其贸易政策；另一方面，根据自己国内的经济需求来调整对外政策。

As concluded in previous section, international trade benefits its practicing nations generally and helps them to develop their economies. Therefore, all the governments in the world will make relative trade policies to adjust the interest of some nation among international trade and achieve its economic purpose accordingly. So far, international trade policy can categories into two types, which are Free Trade Policy and Protectionist Policy.

像上面的章节中所讲过，一般说来国际贸易受益于进行贸易的国家并且帮助这些国家发展经济。因此，世界各国的政府都要制定有关的贸易政策来调整一国在国际贸易中的利益，实现本国的经济目的。迄今为止，国际贸易政策主要有两种基本类型：自由贸易政策和保护贸易政策。

1.1 Free Trade Policy 自由贸易政策

Free Trade Policy refers to no intervention on import and export trade and free competition. The implementation of free trade policy is characterized by lower tariffs, reduction of taxable products as well as reduction cancel of non-tariff barriers.

自由贸易政策是指国家对进出口贸易不加干预，任其自由竞争。自由贸易政策实施表现为关税的降低和应税商品的减少、非关税壁垒等的减少与取消。

Free Trade Policy is adopted by countries with strong economic strength, driven by domestic grown industrial group that are the main beneficiaries. For countries with weak economic power and infant industries, it means that the market is occupied by a foreign country, they were the main victims. Thus free trade was considered to be policy of "the strong".

自由贸易政策为经济实力强的国家所采用，为其国内成熟产业集团所推动，它们是主要受益者。对经济实力薄弱的国家及幼稚产业，却意味着市场被外国占领，它们是主要受害者。因而自由贸易被认为是“强者”的政策。

1.2 Trade Protection Policy 贸易保护政策

Trade Protection policy refers to the international trade theory or policy that limits imports through tariff and various non-tariff trade barriers, in order to protect domestic industry from foreign competition. Tariff, import quota, exchange control, convoluted imports and exports procedure, discriminatory government procurement policy are important means of international trade protection. See Fig. 1-14.

贸易保护政策是指通过关税和各种非关税壁垒限制进口，以保护国内产业免受外国商品竞争的国际贸易理论或政策。关税、进口配额、外汇管制、烦琐的进出口手续、歧视性的政府采购政策等都是国际贸易保护的重要手段，如图 1-14 所示。

图 1-14　贸易保护主义

"Super-protectionism" or "new mercantilism", emerging in the early 1980s, is mainly characterized by green barriers, technology barriers and non-tariff barriers such as anti-dumping and intellectual property protection. Characteristics are as folluows:

超贸易保护主义是20世纪80年代初才兴起的，是以绿色壁垒、技术壁垒、反倾销和知识产权保护等非关税壁垒措施为主要表现形式，又被称为"超贸易保护主义"。它具有以下特点：

（1）Use WTO rules, implement the trade protection. 利用WTO规则，实行贸易保护。

（2）Through regional trade organizations to protect the interests of members. 通过区域贸易组织保护成员方利益。

（3）More diversified means of protection.保护手段更趋多样化。

（4）Make strategic trade policy.制定实施战略性贸易政策。

1.3 GATT & WTO 关贸总协定与世界贸易组织

GATT, *the General Agreement on Tariffs and Trade,* the major trade-liberalization organization, which began in 1947 with 23 members and had 117 members by 1993, signifies the main efforts that international society had made to coordinate with the policies of various members. GATT changed its name into WTO (*The World Trade Organization*)on January 1st 1995, according to Uruguay Round Negotiations (1986～1994).

GATT，即关税与贸易总协定，在1947年由23个成员组成，到1993年止发展成117个成员，主要的努力意在协调各成员的贸易政策。GATT于1995年1月1日根据乌拉圭回合谈判（1986～1994）更换名字为WTO（世界贸易组织）。

WTO is the only global international organization dealing with the rules of trade between nations so far. With its headquarters located in Geneva, Switzerland, its core are the WTO agreements, negotiated and signed by the bulk of the world trading nations and ratified in their parliaments. See Fig. 1-15.

WTO是目前唯一处理国际贸易规则的国际贸易组织。它的总部设在瑞士日内瓦，其核心是WTO协议，由世界贸易组织全体成员磋商和签署，并在议会中通过，如图1-15所示。

图1-15 世界贸易组织总部

By the end of 2010, WTO has had 153 members including China which entered into WTO on December 11th, 2001. The present WTO Director-General Mike Moore has well performed his duties in helping China to enter into WTO. The goal of WTO is to help to make a deal for producers of goods and services, exporters, and importers conduct their business.

截至2010年年底，WTO发展到包括中国在内的153个成员，中国于2001年12月11日加入。现任WTO总干事麦克·穆尔在中国加入WTO进程中很好地履行了他的职责。WTO的目标意在帮助产品和服务的生产者、出口方、进口方达成交易。

1.3.1 The Function fo WTO 世界贸易组织的作用

WTO is an international organization, mainly responsible for administering the multilateral and plurilateral trade agreements which make up the WTO together. As a forum for multilateral trade negotiations, it is dedicated to settling trade disputes and monitoring its members' trade policies, providing technical assistance and training to developing countries, and cooperating with other international institutions who formulate policies for global economy.

WTO是一个国际性的组织，主要是管理和执行共同构成世贸组织的多边及诸边贸易协定。作为一个多边贸易谈判的论坛，WTO致力于解决贸易争端，监督各成员贸易政策，为发展中国家提供技术援助和培训，并与其他制订全球经济政策的国际机构进行合作。

1.3.2 Purposes of WTO 世界贸易组织的宗旨

（1）Improving the living standard, guaranteeing full employment and raising real income and effective demand dramatically and steadily.

提高生活水平，保证充分就业和大幅度、稳步提高实际收入和有效需求。

（2）Expanding production and trade in goods and services.

扩大货物和服务的生产与贸易。

（3）Persisting taking the road of sustainable development, each member shall promote the optimal use of resources in the world, and protect the environment in a way that meets the needs of all members whose economic development vary from one to another.

坚持走可持续发展之路，各成员方应促进对世界资源的最优利用、保护和维护环境，并以符合不同经济发展水平下各成员需要的方式，加强采取各种相应的措施。

（4）Making efforts to ensure that developing countries, especially the least developed among whom, secure a share in the growth of international trade commensurate with their level of economic development and share of interests.

积极努力确保发展中国家，尤其是最不发达国家在国际贸易增长中获得与其经济发展水平相适应的份额和利益。

（5）Establishing an integrated multilateral trading system.

建立一体化的多边贸易体制。

1.3.3 Principles WTO 世界贸易组织的基本原则

（1）Reciprocity principle;互惠原则

（2）Transparency principle;透明度原则

（3）Market access principle;市场准入原则

（4）Principle of fair competition;促进公平竞争原则

（5）Economic development principle;经济发展原则

（6）Non-discrimination principle;非歧视性原则

2. International Trade Measure 国际贸易措施

International trade measures are specific means of implementation of the international trade policy. Therefore, all the governments in the world have to take some measures to encourage export for accumulation of more foreign currencies and restrict import in order to protect infant industry, and to prevent domestic markets from being occupied too much by foreign entries. To encourage export and restrict import, establishment of free trade zones, export subsidies, return of product tax, and some other methods like tariff and non-tariff trade barriers are often used. Specific measures of international trade are the following.

国际贸易措施是国际贸易政策的具体执行手段。因此，世界各国的政府都要采取各类国际贸易措施，鼓励出口以积累更多外汇，限制进口以保护本国幼稚产业以及阻止本国市场被外资过多占领。为了鼓励出口和限制进口经常采取的措施有：建立自由贸易保护区、出口补贴、出口退税以及其他关税及非关税壁垒。具体措施如下。

2.1 Tariff 关税

Tariff is the duties levied by the customs that is established by the representative nation from importers and exporters when products pass by the customs frontier of one country.

关税是指进出口商品经过一国关境时，由海关代表国家向进出口商征收的一种赋税。

2.1.1 Classifications According to Expropriation 按照征收的对象分类

（1）Import Duty 进口税

The import duty is a tariff levied by the customs of importing country from native imports based on customs tariff when input oversea commodities. Import duties are divided into General taxes and MFN taxes.

进口税是进口国家的海关在外国商品输入时，根据海关税则对本国进口商所征收的关税。进口税分为普通税和最惠国税两种。

The general tax rate is usually the highest rate of a country's tax regulations, usually 1 ~ 5 times higher than the preferential tariff rate. For example, general tax rate on imported toys in the US is 70%, while MFN is only 6.8%.

普通税率通常为一国税则中的最高税率，一般比优惠税率高 1～5 倍。例如，美国对进口玩具征税的普通税率为 70%，而最惠国待遇仅为 6.8%。

（2）Export Duty 出口税

An export duty is a tariff levied by customs on the export goods when domestic goods leave the country. Since the imposition of export tariffs will increase the cost of exported goods, with no good to the competition of domestic goods in the international market, many countries have cut or abolished export tariffs.

出口税是指当本国货物出境时，海关对出口货物征收的一种关税。由于征收出口关税会增加出口货物的成本，不利于本国货物在国际市场的竞争，许多国家纷纷削减或废除出口关税。

（3）Transit Duty 过境税

Transit duty is levied on goods during border transportation. Now most countries impose only a small number of permit fees, stamp duty, registration and statistic taxes when foreign goods pass by the territory.

过境税是指对通过本国关境运输的货物所征收的一种关税。目前大多数国家在外国商品通过其领土时，仅征收少量的准许费、印花税、登记税和统计税等。

2.1.2 Classifications According to Discrimination Treatment and Specific Implementation Situation 按差别待遇和特定的实施情况划分

（1）Import Surtax 进口附加税

Importing customs imposes additional import tax according to a certain purpose temporarily other than a general import tax, which is called Import Surtax. Mainly have the following two kinds as follows.

进口国海关对进口商品，除了征收一般进口税外，临时根据某种目的再加征进口税，就叫做进口附加税，主要有以下两种。

① Countervailing Duty: A countervailing duty is a kind of import surtax on oversea commodities received bonus or subsidies directly or indirectly when being imported.

反补贴税：反补贴税是对于直接或间接地接受奖励或补贴的外国商品进口所征收的一种进口附加税。

② Anti-dumping Duty: An anti-dumping duty is a kind of import surtax imposed on dumping imported goods.

反倾销税：反倾销税是对于实行商品倾销的进口商品所征收的一种进口附加税。

（2）Variable Levy 差价税

① Variable Levy: In order to protect domestic production and market, weaken competitiveness of import goods, duties imposed on according to the difference between domestic and imported prices is called Variable Levy.

差价税：为了保护国内生产和国内市场，削弱进口商品的竞争能力，按国内价格与进口价格之间的差额征收关税，就叫差价税。

② Preferential Duty 特惠税

A preferential duty refers to special low tariffs or duty-free preferential treatment given to all or some goods imported from a certain country or region. Some of them are reciprocal, while some are not. Rates are generally lower than the MFN rate and agreement rate.

特惠税是指对从某个国家或地区进口的全部商品或部分商品，给予特别优惠的低关税或免税待遇。特惠税有的是互惠的，有的是非互惠的。税率一般低于最惠国税率和协定税率。

③ Generalized System of Preferences 普遍优惠制

Generalized system of preferences, also called GSP for short, refers to general, non-discriminatory and non-reciprocal tariff preferences given to import commodities (especially manufactured goods and semi-manufactured goods) from developing countries or regions by developed countries.

普遍优惠制简称普惠制，是发达国家承诺对从发展中国家或地区输入的商品，特别是制成品和半制成品，给予普遍的、非歧视的和非互惠的关税优惠待遇。

2.1.3 Classifications According to the General Method to Levy Duties 按照征税的一般方法分类

（1）Specific Duty 从量税

A specific duty is a tariff levied on the basis of measurement units such as product weight, quantity, capacity, length and area. Calculation method of specific duty is very simple. Formula is as follows:

从量税是以商品的重量、数量、容量、长度和面积等计量单位为标准计征的关税。从量税额的计算非常简单，公式如下：

Specific Duty Amount = quantity of commodities × unit specific duty

从量税额=商品数量 × 单位从量税

（2）Advalorem Duty 从价税

Advalorem duty is a tariff levied based on the prices of imported goods, of which tax rate is the percentage of the price of goods. Advalorem tax is calculated as follows:

从价税是以进口商品的价格为标准计征的关税，其税率表现为货物价格的百分率。从价税额的计算公式如下：

Advalorem Duty Amount= total value of commodities × advalorem duty rate

从价税额=商品总值 × 从价税率

（3）Mixed Duty 混合税

Mixed duty, also known as compound duty, refers to the method of taxation levying both specific duty and advalorem duty on certain imported commodities. It has two situations during application. One is imposing specific duty as dominated and advalorem duty as added, the other is imposing advalorem duty primarily and levying additional specific duty.

混合税又称复合税，是指对某些进口商品，既采用从量税，又采用从价税的一种征税方法。在应用时有两种情况：一是以从量税为主，加征从价税；二是以从价税为主，加征从量税。

（4）Alternative Duty 选择税

The alternative duty is a tariff with choice of a relatively high taxation between two kinds of tax rates of advalorem duty and specific duty on import goods at the same time. But sometimes in order to encourage certain goods to be imported, the lower one may also be chosen.

选择税是对于一种进口商品同时有从价税和从量税两种税率，在征税时选择其税额较高的一种征税。但有时为了鼓励某种商品进口，也会选择其中税额低者征收。

2.2 Non-tariff Measures 非关税措施

Non-tariff measures, also known as non-tariff barriers, are all other measures to restrict imports except tariff measures that is compared to tariff barriers.

非关税措施，又称非关税壁垒，是与关税壁垒相对而言，是指除关税措施以外的一切限制进口的各种措施。

（1）Import Quotas 进口配额制

An import quota is that the government sets a direct limit on the quantity or the amount of goods that can be imported into a country in a given period of time. In the limit prescribed time, goods within that quota can be imported while goods exceeds the amount are prohibited to be imported , or can be imported under high tariffs. There are mainly two kinds of import quotas, absolute quota and tariff quota.

进口配额制是一国政府在一定时期内，对进口的某些商品的数量或金额加以直接限制。在规定的期限内，配额以内的货物可以进口，超过配额的不准进口，或者征收较高关税后才能进口。进口配额制主要有绝对配额和关税配额两种形式。

（2）Voluntary Export Restriction “自动”出口限制

A voluntary export restraint is an exporting country or region stipulated export quota to some goods that can be exported out of a country during a specified period of time voluntarily under the pressure of the import country. This limit is self-controlled, the export are prohibited in excess of the quota . Voluntary export restraint mainly includes two forms, which are non-agreement voluntary export and agreement voluntary export restraint.

“自动”出口限制是指出口国家或地区在进口国的要求和压力下，“自动”规定在某一时期内某些商品对该国的出口限额，在该限额内自行控制出口，超过限额即禁止出口。“自动”出口限制主要有两种形式：非协定的“自动”出口限制和协定的“自动”出口限制。

（3）Import License System 进口许可证制

An import license system refers to the measure that regulated import of certain goods only for approved and obtained license. No goods without a license could be imported. The license is often used together with exchange quota management. Import license can be divided into fixed import permit and quota-free import licenses according to its relationship with import quota.

进口许可证制度是指国家规定某些商品进口，必须得到批准，领取许可证后方能进口的措施。没有许可证的商品一律不准进口。许可证常与配额外汇管理等结合使用。进口许可证按照其与进口配额的关系，可分为有定额的进口许可证和无定额的进口许可证。

（4）Foreign Exchange Control 外汇管制

Foreign exchange controls are measures imposed on a country on the purchase/sale of foreign currencies and international settlement in order to balance international payments and maintain the exchange rate of domestic currency. Foreign exchange controls include quantity control and exchange rate control.

外汇管制是一国为平衡国际收支和维持本国货币汇价而对外汇买卖和国际结算实行的限制。外汇管制的方式包括数量管制和汇率管制。

（5）Discriminatory Government Procurement Policy 歧视性政府采购政策

A discriminatory government procurement policy is that a country made laws and decrees to provide a preference with local goods in government purchases. Due to the large number of government procurement, this made imported goods suffer discrimination. For example, the “Buy American Act” of the US required that any goods purchased by the United States Federal Government must be manufactured in the United States, or made of American-sourced raw materials. Only when products produced or manufactured in the United States are in shortage of quantity or prices of which are too high, or under the circumstances that the interests of the United States will be harmed without buying foreign goods, are purchases of foreign goods allowed.

歧视性政府采购政策是指国家制定法令，规定政府机构在采购时要优先购买本国产品的做法。由于政府采购数量较大，政府采购本国货使得进口商品受到歧视。如美国“购买美国货法案”规定：凡是美国联邦政府采购的货物，应该是美国制造的，或者是用美国原料制造的。只有在美国自己生产的商品数量不够时，或者国内价格过高，或者不买外国货就会伤害美国利益的情况下，才能购买外国货。

（6）Technical Barriers to Trade 技术性贸易壁垒

Technical barriers to trade takes the forms of national or regional technical regulations, protocols, standards and certification systems (conformity assessment procedures). It involves a wide range of fields, covering science and technology, health, quarantine, safety, environmental protection, product quality and certification, and many other technical indicator systems, and applied in international trade.It takes flexible methods, numerous provisions. The methods to set technical barriers to trade include technical regulations, technical standards, conformity assessment procedures, and so on.【Typical Case Link 2】

技术性贸易壁垒是以国家或地区的技术法规、协议、标准和认证体系（合格评定程序）等形式出现，涉及的内容广泛，涵盖科学技术、卫生、检疫、安全、环保、产品质量和认证等诸多技术性指标体系，运用于国际贸易当中，呈现出灵活多变、名目繁多的规定。技术性贸易壁垒的方法有技术法规、技术标准、合格评定程序等。【典例链接 2】

2.3 Export Promotion Measures 鼓励出口措施

Measures of encourage exports refers to the measures taken by governments of the exporting countries through economic, administrative and organizational methods to promote export and expand foreign markets. Different from import restrictions, it is of high concealment. It can be divided into several kinds the following.

鼓励出口的措施是指出口国政府通过经济、行政和组织等方面的措施，促进本国商品的出口，开拓和扩大国外市场。在形式上与进口限制有所不同，隐蔽性较强，其中主要有以下几种。

（1）Export Subsidies 出口补贴

Export subsidy is a cash subsidy or financially preferential treatment given by governments to export companies in order to reduce the price of export goods and strengthen their competitiveness in foreign markets.

出口补贴是一国政府为降低出口商品的价格，加强其在国外市场上的竞争能力，在出口某种商品时给予出口厂商的现金补贴或财政上的优惠待遇。

（2）Export Credit 出口信贷

In order to support export of their products, and enhance their international competitiveness, export countries with the support of their governments, would allow its own specialized banks or commercial banks to loan to their exporters or foreign importers (or banks) in a rate slightly below the current market rate, in order to address the needs of the buyers to pay for the import commodities. Export credits can be divided into seller's credit and buyer's credit.

出口国为了支持本国产品的出口，增强国际竞争力，在政府的支持下，由本国专业银行或商业银行向本国出口商或外国进口商（或银行）提供较市场利率略低的贷款，以解决买方支付进口商品资金的需要。出口信贷有卖方信贷和买方信贷。

（3）National Guarantee of Export Credit System 出口信贷国家担保制

The National Guarantee of Export Credit System means that export country establish a specialized agency to guarantee foreign importers or banks to get credit from exporters or commercial banks so as to enlarge exports.

出口信贷国家担保制是国家为了扩大出口，对于本国出口商或商业银行向国外进口商或银行提供的信贷，由国家设立的专门机构出面担保。

（4）Commodity Dumping 商品倾销

Commodity dumping refers that below a price of raw material obviously in foreign markets than the international price so as to attack competitors, occupy or consolidate foreign markets.

商品倾销是指商品以明显低于正常价格的价格，在国外市场上大量抛售，以打击竞争对手，占领或巩固国外市场。

2.4 Export Control Measures 出口管制措施

Due to some political, economic and military reasons, different countries might effect administrations on certain commodities.

由于某些政治、经济和军事的目的，各国也都可能对某些商品实行出口管制。

（1）Export License 出口许可证

Export license is the legal certificate which is for regulation on cargo export. All import or export enterprises should apply for a license from the specified issuing agency according to related regulations for their cargos before imports or exports. Customs will accept declaration by presentation of the export license.

出口许可证是国家管理货物出境的法律凭证。凡实行出口许可证管理的商品，各类进出口企业应在出口前按规定向指定的发证机关申领出口许可证，海关凭出口许可证接受申报。

（2）Export Quotas 出口配额

Export quota is a government policy to restrict exports, that is, a control on the quantity of export commodities. Some quota are actively set by the national government, while others are set on the requirements of the import country.

实行出口配额是政府限制出口的一种政策，即控制出口商品的数量。有些出口配额是本国政府主动设立的，也有的配额是适应进口国政府的要求而设立的。

（3）Export Ban and Trade Embargo 禁止出口与贸易禁运

Export Ban is a way to strictly control one country's strategic materials or imperative commodities of shortage at home, while trade embargo is a trade measure taken by some country to impose sanctions on their hostile states.

禁止出口一般是一国对其战略物资或急需的国内短缺物资进行严格控制的手段。而贸易禁运则是一些国家为了制裁其敌对国家而实行的贸易控制措施。

Section Four New Trends in International Trade 第四节 国际贸易新趋势

1. Coexistence of Visible Trade and Invisible Trade 有形贸易与无形贸易并存

The coexistence of visible and invisible trade means the three fields of merchandise trade, technology trade and service trade exist at the same. Generally speaking, developed countries need merchandise and developing countries need technology. The proportion of service industry in one country's GDP marks its economic development level with developed ones being 65% and developing ones 15%～30%. Service trade occupies around 20% of the total volume of global imports and exports.

有形贸易与无形贸易并存，主要是指商品贸易，技术贸易，服务贸易三大领域同时存在。一般来讲发达国家需要商品，发展中国家需要技术。服务业在一个国家 GDP 的比重标志着这个国家的经济发展水平，发达国家达到 65%，发展中国家只有 15%～30%。全球进出口总额中，服务贸易占 20%左右。

2. Coexistence of Free Trade and Trade Protection 自由贸易与保护贸易并存

WTO rules advocate free trade, which are supported by developed countries and expected by developing countries. Uruguay Round appeals for the opening of agricultural products market and developing countries ask for the most-favored-nation treatment, reducing tariffs and canceling quantitative restrictions so as to realize free trade. However, developed countries impose trade protection on anti-dumping and countervailing actions.

WTO 规则提倡贸易自由，这是发达国家主张的，也是发展中国家希望的。乌拉圭谈判呼吁开放农产品市场，发展中国家要求得到最惠国待遇，削减关税，取消数量限制，实现自由贸易，而发达国家又以反倾销，反补贴等实行贸易保护。

3. Coexistence of Global Trade and Regional Trade 全球贸易与区域贸易并存

Global trade intends to establish a single market without trade barriers according to WTO rules. Regional trade means geographical neighbors cancel quantitative restrictions and trade barriers among them and take steps to phase out tariffs according to multi-lateral agreements so as to realize regional free trade step by step, while the member states apply foreign trade and tariff policies to the non-members. Typical examples include East Asia, Central Asia, ASEAN, EU.

全球贸易是通过 WTO 规则，建立全球统一的无贸易壁垒的区域；区域贸易是地理上比邻的国家，通过多边协定，在成员方之间取消数量限制和贸易壁垒，分阶段降低关税，逐步实现区域自由贸易，成员方对外实行对外贸易政策和关税政策，如东亚、中亚、东盟、欧盟。

4. Coexistence of External Trade and Internal Trade 外部贸易与内部贸易并存

International trade is generally understood as the exchange of goods, technology, and service among different countries. The exchange of goods, technology, and services are apparently done through relevant departments and enterprises in the countries.

国际贸易一般理解为不同国家之间的商品、技术、服务的交换，如果具体分析，不难看出国家间商品、技术、服务贸易又是通过所在国的相关部门、企业来完成交换。

When one country's industry exchanges part of its products with another country, such as the exchange between China's home appliances and American aerospace manufacturing industry, it is inter-industry trade. When one company in a country, such as TCL, Changhong, Konka, and Haier, exchanges its own products with another foreign company, it is called inter-company trade. Inter-industry trade and inter-company trade are all external trade, which hold a leading post in trade.

一个国家的产业与另一个国家的产业部分产品交换，例如中国家电业与美国航空制造业之间的贸易称为产业间交换；一个国家某个企业，如 TCL，长虹，康佳，海尔，用自己的产品与另外一国某企业产品相交换，称为企业间贸易。产业间与企业间的贸易称外部贸易，在贸易中占主导地位。

Intra-country trade includes intra-industry trade and intra-company trade. Intra-country trade means two countries exchange similar products between their same or similar industries. Intra-company trade is the exchange of goods, technology and service within TNCs.

内部国家贸易包括：产业内部与企业内部贸易。所谓产业内部贸易，是参与贸易的两个国家，相同或相类似产业部分之间相互进出口同类产品。企业内部贸易是跨国公司内部进行的商品、技术和服务交换。

【Review Questions】复习思考题

【Typical Case Link 1—典例链接 1】

Question: Try to analyze this Case from the perspective of the international trade theory .

问题：试用国际贸易理论来分析该案例。

Procter & Gamble is the biggest producer of baby diapers in the United States. In the 1980s, it penetrated the most popular diapers in the American market to Hong Kong of China and Germany markets. But to its surprise, sales were completely different. Hong Kong of China Mothers think much of their baby's comfort so that they change immediately after baby's urine. Hong Kong of China consumers thought that the diaper was too thick, while German mothers change diapers once a day when taking care of their babies, German consumers came to the opposite conclusion that the diaper was too thin and of lower hygroscopicity.

宝洁公司是美国最大的婴儿尿布生产商，在 20 世纪 80 年代把美国市场上最受欢迎的婴儿尿布同时打入相类似的中国香港和德国市场。但是销量却完全不一样，大大出乎宝洁公司的预料。中国香港母亲重视婴儿的舒适，尿后即换,故中国香港的消费者认为，宝洁公司的尿布做得太厚；而德国母亲看顾婴儿注重一天换一次规则，故德国的消费者却得出相反的结论，宝洁公司的尿布太薄，吸水性不足。

【Typical Case Link 2—典例链接 2】

Question: Try to explain this Case from the view of foreign trade policies.

问题：试用对外贸易政策解释这一贸易现象。

China is a leading producing and export country for agricultural products. However, with various inspection and quarantine measure came in, we are facing severe challenges to export agricultural products and foodstuff. For example, there are as much as 56 inspection items required by Japan on China's rice, of which more than 90% are sanitary and quarantine measures (usually only 9 items will be inspected). Another example is our poultry exported to Japan. Its sanitation standard is 500 times higher than international one. There was more than 30,000 ton honey exported to Germany withdraw from European market just because it cannot meet the special sanitary requirements of the importer.

我国是农产品生产和出口的大国，但是随着各种名目的检疫检测措施的出现，我国农产品和食品的出口正面临着严峻的考验，如我国出口日本的大米，日方规定的检验项目多达 56 个，其中有 90%以上是卫生和检疫措施项目（一般仅检 9 个项目）；又如我输日的家禽，其卫生标准要求竟高出国际卫生标准 500 倍；出口至德国的蜂蜜曾经因为不能满足进口方的特殊卫生要求使输往德国 3 万多吨蜂蜜不得不停止出运而一度退出欧洲市场。

Chapter Two Establishing Business Relations and Signing Contract

第二章 建立贸易联系和合同的签订

【Learning Objectives】教学目的与要求

After studying this chapter, you should be able to:

1. Master the procedures of international business negotiations;
2. Know about some information channels of supply and demand;
3. Learn some skills and techniques in international transaction;
4. Be familiar with main clauses of international trade contract.

【Lead-in Case】引导案例

Question: Is the contract effective?

问题：合同是否生效？

A makes B an offer: "OFFER 50 SETS COMPUTERS USD 1500 PER SET CIF HONGKONG LOADING WITHIN 2 MONTHS AFTER CONTRACT IRREVOCABLE L/C, PLS REPLY", B replies to A : "ACCEPTED, LOADING UPON CONTRACT".

A 向 B 发盘，发盘中说"供应 50 台计算机、每台 1500 美元 CIF 中国香港订立合同后 2 个月内装船，以不可撤销 L/C 付款、请复电"。B 收到发盘后，立即复电："我接受你的发盘，在订立合同后立即装船"。

Section One General Procedures of Import & Export Business

第一节 进出口贸易的一般程序

Any person who takes part in foreign trade has to be familiar with the whole procedures of import and export business. It mainly includes two parts, which are Export Procedures and Import Procedures.

任何想从事对外贸易的人都必须事先了解外贸进出口的程序。它主要包括出口程序和进口程序。

1. Procedures of Export Business 出口贸易流程

Merchandise exports are sent goods out of a country, it is the process of selling goods and services from China to customers living in another country. Any exporter who wants to sell his products to a foreign country must know about the procedures of export. See Fig. 2-1.

商品出口是指货物输往国外，是从中国销售货物和服务到另一个国家的一种形式。任何想做出口贸易的人都必须事先了解出口贸易的程序，如图 2-1 所示。

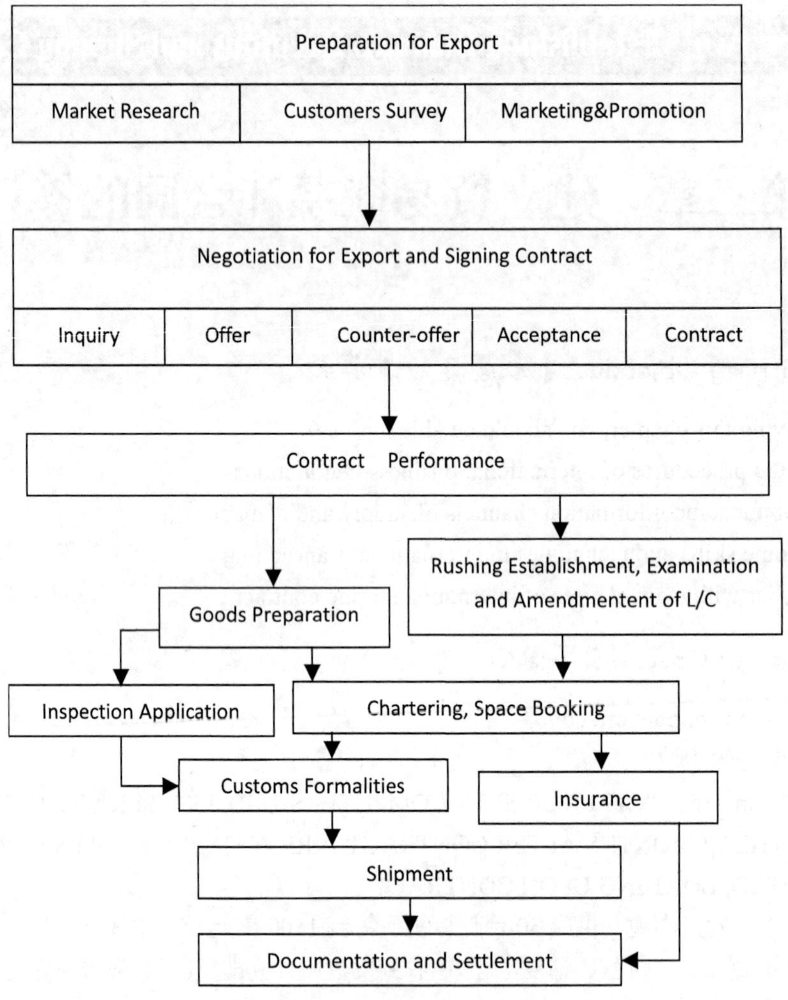

Fig.2-1 Procedures of Export Business

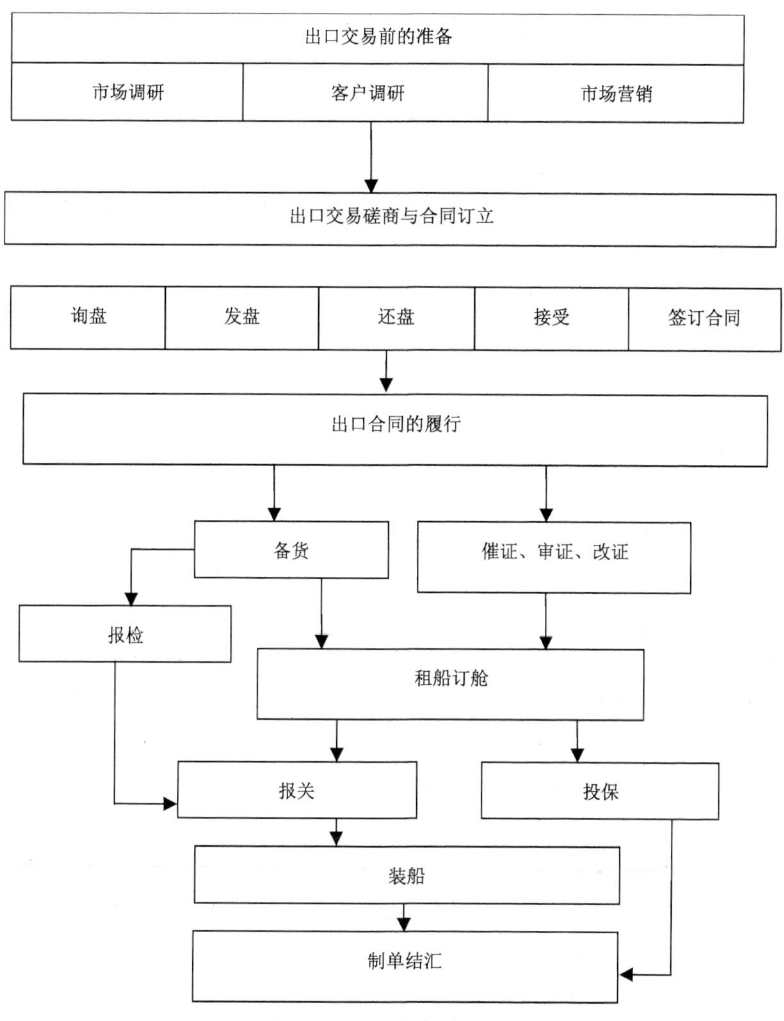

图 2-1　出口交易流程图

From figure the above, general procedures of export business generally include three stages is preparations for export, business negotiations, signing contract and contract performance.

由上可以看出，出口交易的一般程序主要包括交易前准备工作、进行交易磋商并签订合同和履行合同三个阶段。

1.1　Preparation for Export 出口交易前的准备工作

Exporters must prepare carefully before business negotiations. The more sufficient and careful the preparation is, the more smooth negotiation and contract signing will be.

在出口交易磋商开始前，出口商必须认真做好交易前的各项准备工作。准备工作做得越充分和细致，进行业务洽谈和签订合同的过程也会越主动和顺利。

（1）Market Research 市场调研

① Survey the product quality requirements of the target market.

调查目标市场对产品的质量要求。

② Survey the supply-demand relationship of the target market.

调查目标市场的供求关系。

③ Survey the target market sales price.

调查目标市场的销售价格。

④ Survey the law provisions and trade barriers of the target market.

调查目标市场的法律规定及贸易壁垒。

⑤ Survey the target market cultural background, local customs, including consumer preferences, and customary business practices.

调查目标市场的文化背景、风俗习惯：包括消费者个人偏好、贸易习惯等。

⑥ Survey the foreign exchange control of target market.

调查目标市场的外汇管制。

（2）Customers Survey 客户调研

Namely, 4C, that is Credit, Character, Capital, Capacity.

即“四个 C”：信誉，性格，资信，能力

① Understanding Customers' payment capacity.

了解客户的支付能力。

② Understanding customers' management ability.

了解客户的经营能力。

③ Understanding customers' business scope.

了解客户的经营范围。

④ Understanding customers' operating style.

了解客户的经营作风。

（3）Marketing &Promotion 市场营销

Export commodities marketing project may vary from one to another because of the commodity difference. It generally includes the following aspects:

出口商品营销方案内容因商品不同而不一，大致包括以下几个方面：

① Supply market;　货源情况；

② Foreign market;　国外市场情况；

③ Exportation operation;　出口经营情况；

④ Marketing plans and measures.　推销计划和措施。

In a word, we can do this by offering the right "The Market Concept ", which is the 4Ps:

为此，我们提供正确的营销综合结构——“四个 P”：

① the right Product;　正确的商品；

② the right Price;　正确的价格；

③ the right channels of distribution: Place;　通过恰当的分销渠道，地点；

④ presented the right way: Promotion.　用正确的方式展示促销。

1.2 Negotiation of Contract 合同的磋商

1.2.1 Form and Content 磋商的形式和内容

Business negotiation has both oral and written forms.

交易磋商在形式上有口头和书面两种。

Oral business negotiation mainly refers to the face-to-face talks on the negotiation table, such as participation in various exhibitions, fairs and trade visits, and invitations of foreign customers to China, and so on. In addition, it also includes the business negotiations of both parties by international long-distance call and other forms. See Fig. 2-2.

口头交易磋商主要是指在谈判桌上面对面的商谈，如参加各种交易会、洽谈会以及贸易小组出访，邀请客户来华洽谈等。此外，还包括双方通过国际长途电话等形式进行的交易磋商，如图 2-2 所示。

The written form mainly refers to doing transactions through mail, fax, e-mail, online trading, etc.

书面交易磋商主要是指通过信件、传真、电邮、网上交易等通信来洽谈交易。

图 2-2　书面交易磋商

Contents of business negotiations includes all items in the contract, which name, quality, quantity, packaging, price, shipment and payment are the 6 main conditions of trade. Other conditions, such as inspection, claims, arbitration and force majeure, are regarded as general ones.

交易磋商的内容，涉及签订的买卖合同的各项要款，其中品名品质、数量、包装、价格、装运和支付这 6 项交易条件，被认为是交易的主要条件。而其他条件，如商检、索赔、仲裁和不可抗力等，作为一般交易条件。

1.2.2　General Procedures of the Business Negotiation 磋商的一般程序

Business negotiation generally consists of four steps, namely, inquiry, offer, counter-offer and acceptance. Among them, offer and acceptance are the essential two steps for a transaction.

交易磋商的程序一般包括 4 个环节，即询盘、发盘、还盘和接受。其中，发盘和接受是达成一笔交易所不可缺少的两个基本环节。

1.2.2.1　Inquiry 询盘

Inquiry is the enquiry for trading terms by one party to the other in order to purchase or sell goods. Inquiry can be sent out either by the buyer or the seller. The content can be enquiry for prices, or other trading terms and requirement of offer. Inquiry is just general commercial relations between both parties, only playing a role of inviting the other party to send offer, with no legal bindings to both parties. Inquiry is usually the starting point of a trade so that great importance would be attached by the inquired party and reply be given time.

询盘是指交易的一方为了购买或销售货物，向对方提出有关交易条件的询问。询问可以由买方发出，也可以由卖方发出。询盘的内容可以只询问价格，也可以询问多项的交易条件，要求对方发盘。询盘只是询盘人与被询盘人之间的一般性的商务联系，只起到邀请对方发盘的作用，对双方都没有法律上的约束力。但询盘通常是交易的起点，因此，被询盘人必须十分重视并及时地作出回应。

Sample of Inquiry（询盘实例）

Dear sirs,

We need your quotation for 100 M/T soybean. Items include packaging, delivery time, and price term is CIF. Port of destination: Singapore.

Looking forward to your reply.

Best regards

Tracy

Manager of MINC

尊敬的先生:

我需要您的 100 吨的大豆报价，包括包装、交货时间、报价、价格是到岸价格、目的港新加坡。

期待您的回复。

特雷西

MINC 公司经理

1.2.2.2 Offer 发盘

An offer is a positive approval of signing a contract with the other party following the terms sent by the offerer to the offeree. offers are mostly sent by the seller. If it is sent by buyer, it is called the "Bid".

发盘是指买卖双方中的一方（发盘人）向对方（受盘人）提出各项交易条件，并愿按照这些条件与对方达成交易的一种肯定的表示。发盘大多是卖方提出的。若买方提出，则叫“递盘”。

An offer is a business practice and also a legal action, which is called “offer” in the contract law. It is legal bindings on the offerer upon an offer sent. Offerer could not cancel or change the quotation within the validity. In practice, offer is usually sent by the other party upon inquiry but it can also be sent directly without inquiry.

发盘既是商业行为，也是法律行为，在合同法中称之为“要约”。一项发盘一经发出，对发盘人就立即产生法律上的约束力，在发盘的有效期内，发盘人不得任意撤销或修改内容。实际业务中，发盘通常是一方收到对方的询盘之后做出的，但也可不经询盘直接向对方发盘。

（1）Condition for Validity of an Offer 构成一项发盘的有效条件

① Submitting to one or more specific persons.

向一个或一个以上特定的人提出。

② The offer must be confirmed with correct contents and complete terms.

内容必须十分确定，要求发盘的全部内容是明确的，发盘的各项条件要完整。

③ Indicating offerer is binding. 表明发盘人受约束。

Offer shall be final with no restrictive conditions. Once accepted by offeree, offerer should establish contract relations with offeree according to the terms and conditions in the offer.

发盘应是终局的，没有限制性条件。发盘一经受盘人接受，发盘人必须按发盘条件与受盘人建立合同关系。

The offer should be sent to offeree. 发盘应送达受盘人。

In international trade, offer validity refers to the validity of the offer that allows the offeree to make decisions on accepting the offer.

国际货物买卖中，发盘一般应有有效期，发盘的有效期是指可供受盘人对发盘做出接受的期限。

（2）Enter into Force and Withdrawl of Offer 发盘的生效和撤回

An offer usually has a period of validity (a deadline or a period before acceptance). It comes into effect upon arriving at the offeree. Therefore, offerer could withdraw the offer before it arrives at offeree when it has no binding force. It can be concluded that offer withdrawal is actually a method to prevent the offer being effective.【Typical Case Link 1】

发盘中通常有明确的有效期（或是一个最迟接受的期限，或是一段接受的时间），并在送达受盘人时生效，因此，发盘在到达受盘人之前对发盘人没有约束力，发盘人也可以将其撤回。可见，撤回发盘实质上是阻止发盘生效。【典例链接 1】

（3）Revocation 发盘的撤销

Revocation of the offer refers to the act taken by the offerer to cancel the offer and terminate the validity after the offeree received the offer.

发盘的撤销是发盘送达受盘人后，发盘人取消发盘，解除效力的行为。

An offer could not be withdrawn under the following circumstances: ① the offer is irrevocable as indicated by the period of validity or other terms. ② Offeree has taken measures on the offer relying on the belief that the offer is irrevocable.下列情况不能撤销：① 发盘规定有效期或以其他方式表明是不可撤销的；② 受盘人有理由信赖这项发盘是不可撤销的，并已本着这种信赖采取了行动。

（4）Invalidity 发盘的失效

The offer would be invalid in following circumstances: ①counter offer; ②offer revocation; ③offer invalidation; ④force majeure; ⑤either party become incapacitated or dead or go bankruptcy before the offer is accepted.

在下列情况下发盘失效：①受盘人还盘；②发盘人撤销发盘；③发盘过了有效期；④不可抗力事件发生；⑤在发盘被接受前，当事人丧失行为能力或死亡或法人破产等。

Sample of Offer（发盘实例）

Dear Joni,

We well received your inquiry. We quote below as you required:

Name of commodity: Soybean

Quality: Grade A

Packaging: In bulk

Quantity: 100/MT

Price: CIF Singapore 1.80

Payment terms: Irrevocable LC

Delivery date: No later than 30/12/2011

Any further questions, please feel free to let me know.

Best regards!

琼妮，您好：

我们收到了您的询盘，按您的要求，我方报价如下：

品名：大豆

品质：A 级

包装：散装

数量：100 吨

价格：每公吨大豆 USD 1.80 CIF 新加坡

付款条件：不可撤销信用证

交货日期：不迟于 30/12/2011

如有任何疑问，请随时让我知道。

此致！

1.2.2.3 Counter-Offer 还盘

Counter-offer is also known as bargaining. It happens when the offeree does not agree with or totally agree with terms and conditions the offerer put in the offer. It is an indication of the offeree to change and amend the original offer.【Typical Case Link 2】

还盘又叫还价，它是指受盘人不同意或不完全同意发盘人在发盘中提出的条件，为与发盘人协商而提出修改或变更的表示。【典例链接 2】

Counter-offer is the offeree's refusal to the original offer, as well as a new offer made by offeree to the previous offerer. Once counter offer, the previous offer will be invalid, with no bindings on the previous offerer, and the offeree becomes the new offerer.

还盘是受盘人对原发盘的拒绝，也是受盘人向原发盘人做出的新的发盘。还盘后，原发盘即失去效力，原发盘人亦不再受其约束，还盘人便变成了新发盘人。

Sample of Counter-Offer（还盘实例）

Dear Mr. Black,

Thanks for your offer. After our carefully study, we found your price is on the high side. We know your goods are of high quality, but we do hope you kindly reduce the price approximately by 5% for our long term cooperation.

We look forward to your reply.

Best regards!

布莱克先生，您好：

谢谢您提供的发盘，经过我们仔细研究，我们认为你方价格太高，我们知道您的商品质量高，但为了我们的长期合作，我们希望您能降低价格约 5%。

期待您的回复。

此致！

1.2.2.4 Acceptance 接受

Acceptance is one party's approval of a contract to close a deal with the other party in line with his conditions when offeree receives the offer or offerer receives the counter-offer from offeree. Acceptance , the same with offer, is both a business practice and legal action, which is called "promise" in the contract law. When acceptance happens, it is resulting in signing a contract and concluding a deal.

接受是指受盘人接到发盘人的发盘或发盘人接到受盘人的还盘，同意对方提出的条件，愿意与对方达成交易，订立合同的一种表示。接受和发盘一样，既属于商业行为，又属于法律行为，合同法中称为“承诺”。接受产生的法律后果是“达成交易，成立合同”。

（1）Acceptance Conditions 构成接受的条件

There are 4 conditions for acceptance: ①It has to make by the offeree; ②It must be indicated in some way; ③It shall be completely consistent with the offer; ④It must be delivered to the offerer within validity.

构成接受的条件也是 4 个：①必须由受盘人做出；②必须用某种方式表示出来；③接受的内容须与发盘相符；④必须在发盘的有效期内送达发盘人。

（2）Methods of Acceptable 接受的方式

Acceptance must be indicated to offerer in a certain way by offeree, usually by email or verbally. It can also be indicated by "action" in international practice, but it is not applicable in our country.

接受必须由受盘人以某种方式向发盘人表示出来。接受的形式一般用函电和口头的方式来表达。在国际上"接受"也可以"用行为表示出来"，但我国不适用以"行为"表示接受这一规定。

（3）Entry into Force and Withdrawl of Acceptance 接受的生效和撤回

Since the legal consequence of the acceptance is to set up a contract, acceptance can only be withdrawn, and not be revoked. Revocation of acceptance means canceling a contract, whereas contract revocation shall be approved by both parties, not just one party.

因为接受的法律后果是成立合同，所以接受只能撤回，不能撤销。撤销接受就是撤销合同，而撤销合同须买卖双方都同意，不能只一方同意。

（4）Late Acceptance 逾期接受

Acceptance must be delivered within the validity period specified in the offer. If the offer validity period is not provided, it shall be delivered within a reasonable period. If acceptance is delivered to the offerer later than the period of validity or the reasonable period, the acceptance will be become a late acceptance or delayed acceptance, usually of no legal bindings. However, it could be effective if the offerer considers acceptable.

接受必须在发盘规定的有效期内送达，如果发盘未规定有效期，须在合理的时间内送达发盘人。如果接受晚于有效期或合理的时间才送达发盘人，该项接受便成为一项逾期接受或称迟到的接受。逾期接受一般无效，但只要发盘人认为该接受依然有效，逾期接受还是有效的。

Sample of Counter Acceptance（接受实例）

Dear Mr. Brown,

We have received your offer of soybean, and we are pleased to confirm buying soybean from you on the terms and conditions in your offer.

We enclose our Sales Confirmation in duplicate, a copy of which please sign and return to us for our file.

Best regards!

布朗先生，您好：

我们已经收到您关于大豆的发盘，我们非常愿意按照发盘的条件从你方购买大豆。

兹随函附寄我方销售确认书一式两份，其中一份请签退我方，以便存档。

此致！

1.3 Signing the Contract for International Sale of Goods 国际货物买卖合同的签订

Once offer are accepted, purchase and sale contract for international business will be able to be signed.

发盘一经接受便可以签订国际货物买卖合同。

"United Nations Convention on Contracts of International Sales of Goods" is currently the most important international convention on international sales of goods which is passed in March 1980 by congress of Vienna participated by representatives from 62 countries or regions. From January 1, 1988, the Convention took effect among 11 members, including our country. It has 65 members until June of 2005.

《联合国国际货物买卖合同公约》为当前在国际货物买卖方面最重要的国际公约。1980 年 3 月在由 62 个国家或地区代表参加的维也纳外交会议上通过。自 1988 年 1 月 1 日起，公约对包括我国在内的 11 个成员方生效。截至 2005 年 6 月，加入该公约的国家或地区已有 65 个。

1.3.1 Contract Form 合同的形式

Contracts are formed according to the United Nations Convention on Contracts of International Sales of Goods and the Contract Law of The People's Republic Of China. The contract forms include written, oral and other forms.

根据《联合国国际货物销售合同公约》和《中华人民共和国合同法》的有关规定，当事人订立合同，有书面形式、口头形式和其他形式。

In the international trade, the common used written contracts are sales contract, purchase contract, letter of confirmation, agreement, memorandum, letter of intent, order and so on. In China's trade business, we usually employ Sales Contract and Sales Confirmation as written contract.

在国际贸易中，一般常用的书面合同有销售合同、购货合同、成交确认书、协议、备忘录、意向书、订单等。我国外贸业务中，主要采用的书面合同是销售合同、销售确认书等。

Oral form of transactions is to conclude a contract by dialog between two parties, including face-to-face negotiations and phone calls.

口头形式是交易双方当事人之间通过对话方式，包括当面谈判和通过电话方式而订立的合同。

Other forms mean those forms to conclude a contract apart from written and oral form. An example is to confirm the contract by shipment of goods, advance payments or other behaviors.

其他形式指可能存在的除书面形式、口头形式之外的合同形式。如通过发运货物或者预付货款等行为形式表示对合同内容的确认。

1.3.2 Clauses in the Contracts of the International Sale of Goods 国际货物买卖合同的主要条款

（1）Quality Terms 品质条款

Quality terms including product name, stipulating methods of product quality and so on.

国际货物买卖合同中品质条款包括品名、商品品质的表示方法等。

（2）Quantity Terms 数量条款

Quantity terms consist of figures and measurement unit.

数量条款主要由数字和计量单位构成。

（3）Package Terms 包装条款

Package terms mainly include: packaging, specifications, packaging materials, cost and shipping mark. Packaging material, style and specifications need to be confirmed before the setting of the package terms.包装条款的主要内容有：包装方式、规格，包装材料、费用和唛头。制定包装条款要明确包装的材料、造型和规格。

（4）Price Terms 价格条款

The price refers to the value of each unit of goods. Price terms include price of each unit of goods, valuation currency, designated place of delivery, trade terms and methods to set price.

价格是指每一计量单位的货值。价格条款的主要内容有：每一计量单位的价格金额，记价货币，指定交货地点，贸易术语与商品的作价方法等。

（5）Shipping Terms 装运条款

Shipping terms, are also known as terms of delivery, should specify delivery time, place of shipment, destination, whether partial shipment and transshipment are allowed, and so on.

国际货物买卖合同的装运条款，又称交货条款。合同中的装运条款，应具体规定交货时间、装运地、目的地、能否分批装运和转运等内容。

（6）Insurance Terms 保险条款

In general, insurance terms include insurance amount, insurance conditions, insurance premium, insurance policy and terms that insurance applied.

一般来说，保险条款所涉及的内容有保险金额、投保险别、保险费、保险单证和保险适用条款等。

（7）Payment Terms 支付条款

Payment terms generally include currency, premium, method of payment and payment time.

国际货物买卖合同中的支付条款一般包括支付货币、支付金额、支付方式和时间。

（8）Inspection Terms 检验条款

Inspection terms include time and place of inspection, inspection authority, certification, inspection bases and inspection methods re-inspection and so on.

国际货物买卖合同中的检验条款，主要包括检验的时间与地点、检验机构、检验证书、检验依据与检验方法以及商品的复验等。

（9）Arbitration Terms 仲裁条款

It is a written document agreed by both parties to present their differences that are going to happen or have happened to arbitration committee on the basis of voluntariness and unanimity through negotiations, as well as equality and mutual benefit. Arbitration is the most commonly used method in the settlement of disputes in international trade on the premise of signing arbitration agreement by both parties.

仲裁条款是指双方当事人在自愿、协商、平等互利的基础之上将他们之间已经发生或者可能发生的争议提交仲裁解决的书面文件。仲裁是国际贸易中解决争议时最常用的方法,并以双方订有仲裁协议为前提。

Sample of Sales Contract 合同格式示例

CHINA SHANDONG CHEMICAL PURCHASING AGENT 中国山东化工产品采购代理

FAX: 86-533-2106787 TEL: 86-533-2106771

传真：86-533-2106787 电话：86-533-2106771

SALES CONTRACT 销售合同

NO.: CC0704-M19 合同号码：CC0704-M19

Date: APR. 12, 2008 日期：2008-04-12

This Contract is made by and between CHINA SHANDONG CHEMICAL PURCHASING AGENT

Jinjing Road, High-New Tech Development District, Zibo City, Shandong Province, China(herein-after called the Sellers)and PROGRESSIVE TRADRS (PVT)LTD, (Herein-after called the buyer), whereby the Sellers agree to sell and the Buyers agree to buy the under-mentioned commodity according to the terms and conditions stipulated below:

本合同由中国山东省淄博市天津路高新技术开发区中国山东化工产品采购代理（以下称卖方）和PVT 贸易公司（以下称买方）签署，双方同意按下列条款，由卖方出口，买方购买如下货物：

Name of Commodity, Specification and Packing 货物名称、规格及包装	Quantity 数 量	Unit Price 单 价	Total value 总 值
SAY TOTAL：大写总值：			

1. Shipping Mark: 运输标志：
2. Shipping Date: 装运期限：
3. Port of Loading: 装运港：

   Port of Destination: 目的港：
4. Transshipment: 转运：

   Partial Shipment: 分批装运：
5. Insurance: 保险：
6. Terms of payment: 付款方式：
7. Other requirements: 其他要求：
8. Discrepant documents: When the issuing bank refuses to take payment, due to the documents not to be in compliance with the terms and conditions of the credit, the Sellers and Buyers should confirm the new terms of payment by negotiation within 3 days as of the date of refuse. If not, the terms of payment hereunder will be altered to be D/P at sight.

单证不符条款：若开证行因卖方提交的单据不符信用证要求而拒绝付款，买卖双方应在拒付之日起三天内商定新的付款方式，否则付款方式自动转为即期 D/P 付款。

9. Examination period and organization : The buyers should examine the goods within 15 days as of the date of the arrival of the goods at the discharge port. The buyers should entrust the examination organization which is approved by the sellers, and if there is no agreement on examination organization by the both parties, the buyers may entrust the SGS of Switzerland or its branches, to examine the goods and take the examination certificate as the preliminary evidence of the claim to the sellers.

检验期限和机构：买方应在货物到达卸货港 15 天内对货物进行检验，并必须确保选择的检验机构是卖方认可的，如果双方没有商定检验机构，买方可以委托 SGS 或其分支机构检验货物，检验证书可作为向卖方索赔的原始证据。

10. Special declaration: 特别声明：

① The ownership shall belong to the seller if the buyers fail to pay the price;

若买方不履行付款义务，则货物所有权归卖方所有；

② The risk of damage or missing of the goods shall be borne by the buyers after the delivery of goods by the seller.

卖方发货后，若货物丢失，则损失由买方承担。

11. Force Majeure: In case of Force Majeure, the Sellers shall not be held responsible for late delivery or non-delivery of the goods, but shall notify the Buyers by cable. The Sellers shall deliver to the Buyers by registered mail, if requested by the Buyers, a certificate issued by the China Council for the Promotion of International Trade or/and competent authorities.

不可抗力：由于不可抗力事故，使卖方不能在本合同规定期限内交货或不能按期交货，卖方不负责任。但卖方必须立即以电报通知买方。如买方提出要求，卖方应以挂号函向买方提供由中国国际贸易促进委员会或有关机构出具的发生事故的证明文件。

12. Dispute settlement and applicable law:

纠纷解决及适用法律：

① Any dispute arising from this contract or in connection with this contract shall be submitted to China International Economic and Trade Arbitration Commission or its Peking branch for arbitration in accordance with Rules of Arbitration. The arbitral award is of legal binding upon both parties.

任何本合同产生的纠纷应交由中国国际经济与贸易仲裁委员会或其在北京的分支机构依据其仲裁条款裁决。仲裁裁决书对双方均有约束力。

② This contract is governed by the Contract Law of the People's Republic of China. The terms such as FOB terms in the contract are based on INCOTERMS 2000, and the terms of letter of credit are based on UCP 600.

该合同受中华人民共和国合同法约束。其他如 FOB 条款依据 INCOTERMS 2000，信用证条款依据 UCP 600。

13. Effectiveness of contract: This contract comes into effect after being signed by representatives of each party.

合同生效：该合同自买卖双方代表签字盖章后生效。

The seller(signature and seal)	The buyer(signature)
卖方（签字盖章）	买方（签字盖章）

1.4 Performance of Export Contract 出口合同的履行

Performance of export contract is complex. For example , payment by letter of credit generally includes stocking, pressing for L/C, L/C verification, vessel booking, customs declaration, inspection declaration, insurance, loading, documents making and exchange settlement with inseparable relation between each other.

出口合同的履行手续繁杂、环节众多，以信用证支付方式为例，一般包括备货、催证、审证、改证、租船订舱、报关、报验、保险、装船、制单结汇等环节，各环节之间存在密不可分的关系。

2. Procedures of Import Business 进口贸易流程

We have studied the general procedures of export transactions and dealt with different stages and steps in the view of exporter. Having been familiar with the process of the export business, we find it much easier to understand how an importer handles with his import business. After all, the export and import trades are two sides of one coin.

我们已经学习了出口贸易的一般程序，并从出口商的角度简要地了解了其各个阶段和步骤。因此，我们也就很容易理解进口商是如何进口交易的。毕竟，出口贸易和进口贸易是同一件事物的两个方面。

Importing is referred to the purchase activities of foreign products produced in the world market or those services provided by foreign companies. See Fig. 2-3.

进口贸易是将外国所生产或加工的商品购买后输入本国市场的贸易活动，如图 2-3 所示。

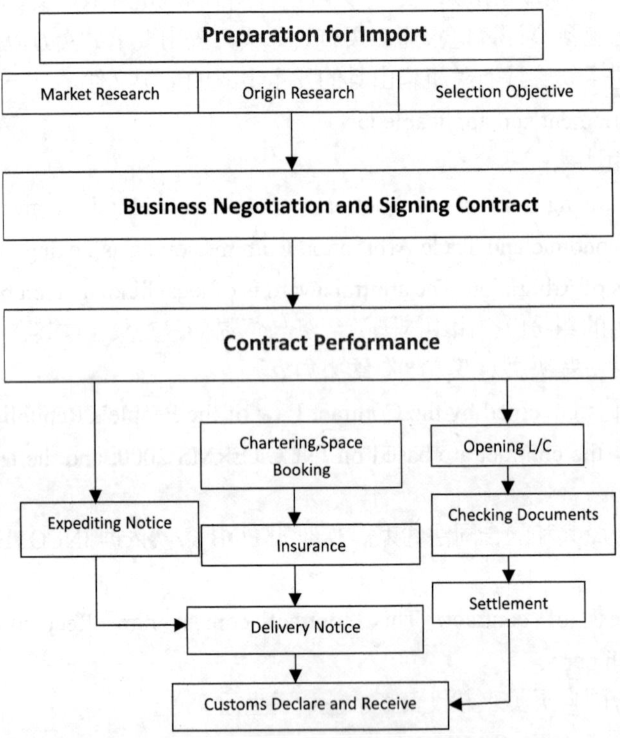

Fig.2-3　Procedures of Import Business

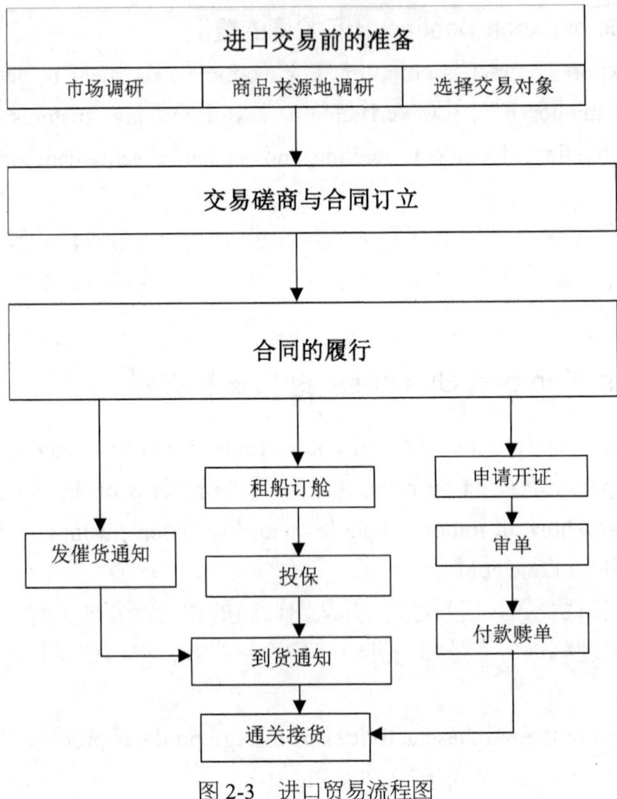

图 2-3　进口贸易流程图

From the above, the general procedures of import business also include three stages, which are preparations for export, business negotiations, signing contract and contract performance that is the same as procedures of export business .

由上可以看出，进口交易的一般程序和出口贸易程序相同也包括交易前准备工作、进行交易磋商并签订合同和履行合同三个阶段。

2.1　Preparation for Import 进口交易前准备工作

The knowledge we have acquired from the previous preparations for export is also applicable to import business. With the fundamental knowledge of export transaction, we can grasp the essential points of preparations for import easily and manage import trade well and smoothly.

我们前面学过的出口贸易的知识同样适用于进口贸易。具备了出口贸易交易前的准备知识后，我们很容易掌握进口交易准备前的要点，从而顺利地进行进口贸易。

（1）Market Research 市场调研

The technical and economic benefits of the import commodity as well as price trends and supply position of the supplying country and leading manufacturers should be analyzed. On the basis of cost accounting, it is also necessary to learn about the operating status, credit status of traders, and commodity quality, price and payment terms of different suppliers.

正确分析进口商品的技术经济效益，以及主要供应国和主要生产厂商供应情况和价格趋势，了解商品经营情况，不同厂商的商品品质、价格、成交条件、交易者的资信状况等，并进行进口成本核算。

（2）Origin Research 货源地调研

In order to ensure the quality and quantity of import goods, it is an prerequisite to conduct foreign market on the production, supply and selling of the products, customer information, price trend as well as supplier's credit status.

为了保质、保量地得到进口采购的商品，在进行进口交易前必须对国外市场进行调查，包括有关商品的产供销和客户情况，商品的价格趋势及供应商的资信情况等，做到货比三家。

（3）Objective Selection　交易对象的选择

When you select a transaction object, you should first pay attention to their credit status, business ability and management style. It also must get hang of your customer's situation by establishing customer cards so as to record their credit status, business scope and ability, managerial style, details about dealing and contract performance, and attitudes towards compensation. In addition, regular research is also needed in order to provide reference when selecting a business trader.

选择交易对象时，首先要注意他们的资信情况、经营能力和经营作风。必须经常了解和掌握客户情况。通常的做法是建立客户卡片，详细记录其资信情况、经营范围、经营能力和作风、成交情况、履约情况、对索赔的态度等，并定期分析研究做出鉴定，供选择交易对象时参考。

2.2　Negotiation, Signing and Performance of Contract 进口合同的磋商、签订和履行

The procedures of negotiation of signature of import contract is almost the same as export contract(see the section 1.2 and 1.3).There is only a little difference in the part of implementation. Take payment by letter of credit as an example, it generally includes opening L/C, vessel booking, pressing loading, insurance, examine documents and payment, customs and inspection declaration for imports, acceptance and goods distribution.

进口合同的磋商和签订的程序几乎和出口合同是一样的（参见上述1.2和1.3），只是在履行的部分稍微有些差异。以信用证支付方式为例，一般包括开立信用证、租船订舱和催装、办理货运保险、审单付款、进口报验与检验、验收与拨交货物等环节。

Section Two Ways to Establish Business Relations
第二节 建立业务关系的途径

1. Ways on the Internet 网络途径

1.1 E-business 电子商务

Among various business activities all over the world, e-business is a new business operating model under Internet environment base on use of browser and server, in which buyers and seller close a variety of deals without facing each other so as to realize shopping on the Internet of consumers, business transactions among traders, online electronic payment and other transaction activities and financial operations.

电子商务通常是指是在全球各地广泛的商业贸易活动中，在因特网开放的网络环境下，基于浏览器/服务器应用方式，买卖双方不谋面地进行各种商贸活动，实现消费者的网上购物、商户之间的网上交易和在线电子支付以及各种商务活动、交易活动、金融活动和相关的综合服务活动的一种新型的商业运营模式。

1.2 Main Commercial Websites 主要商务网站

（1）主要B2B商务网站 http://www.alibaba.com
http://www.made-in-china.com
http://www.cycbiz.com.cn
http://www.tradekey.com
http://www.globalsources.com
http://www.tradeeasy.com
http://www.ec21.com

（2）主要搜索引擎 http://www.google.com
http://www.altavista.com
http://www.lycos.com
http://search.msn.com
http://www.europages.com

（3）部分网络资源（国内）中国国际贸易网 http://www.guomaoren.com
中华人民共和国商务部 http://www.mofcom.gov.cn
中国外经贸 http://www.chinamarket.com.cn
中国贸促网 http://www.ccpit.org
阿里巴巴 http://www.alibaba.com
中国国际贸易发展网 http://www.itdn.com.cn
国际商务桥 http://www.ibb.cn

2. Commodity Trade Fair 商品交易展览会

As an import or export enterprise, participating in commodity trade fairs is another main channel to search for customers and supply of goods in addition to e-commerce. At present, the trade fairs can mainly be divided into the domestic fairs and the overseas fairs.

作为进出口企业，参加商品交易会是除电子商务外，寻找客户和货源的另一大主要渠道。目前商品交易会主要分为国内展览会和国外展览会。

2.1 Domestic Fair 国内展览会

The main domestic fair is China Import and Export Fairs, it's also called Canton fair, which was founded in the spring of 1957. It is held in Guangzhou during spring and autumn every year. At present in China, it has the longest history of 50 years. With the highest level, largest scale and most commodity species, Canton Fair is a comprehensive international trade event wining largest number of visitors and best effects.

国内主要的展览会是中国进出口商品交易会，又称广交会，创办于 1957 年春季，每年春秋两季在广州举办，迄今已有 50 多年历史，是中国目前历史最长、层次最高、规模最大、商品种类最全、到会客商最多、成交效果最好的综合性国际贸易盛会。

Other domestic fairs include International Textile Exhibition, Arts and Crafts International Gift Fair, International Building Materials Exhibition, China Electronics Fair, Hospitality Equipment, Supplies Fair, printing and packaging Industry Exhibition, International Food and Beverage Exhibition, International Machinery and Electronic Products Exhibition, Shoe Leather Exhibition, Textile and Apparel Sourcing Fair, Medical Equipment Import and Export Trade Fair, International Logistics Exhibition, International Chemical Industry Exhibition, International Packaging Materials Exhibition, International Toy Fair, etc..

其他国内展览会有国际纺织品展览会、国际礼品工艺品展览会、国际建筑材料展览会、中国电子展、酒店设备用品展览会、印刷包装工业展览会、国际食品饮料展览会、国际机电产品展览会、鞋业皮具展览会、纺织品服装跨国采购交易会、医疗器械进出口交易会、国际物流展览会、国际化工展览会、国际包装材料展览会、国际玩具用品展等。

2.2 Foreign Exhibition 国外展览会

At present, there are some popular oversea fairs that China's enterprises tend to participate in , such as the Spring and Autumn Goods Fair in Frankfurt, Cologne Hardware Exhibition, Milan maqifu Exhibition, Chicago International Fair in the Autumn, of which machinery and electronics products were displayed most and achieved the most obvious trade effects. Germany has the most exhibit items among the 60 countries and regions where China's enterprises take part in. Europe, North America, Japan are the traditional markets for China's enterprises. It is the golden era to develop the markets of Asia, Africa, Latin America, Eastern Europe and CIS.

目前，我国企业出国展览已形成了一些热点，如法兰克福春秋季消费品博览会、科隆五金制品展览会、米兰马契夫展览会、芝加哥五金展览会等，其中机械、电子类展览参展比例最高，取得的贸易效果也最明显。在我国企业出国展览的 60 个国家和地区中，德国是参展项目最多的国家，欧洲、北美、日本是我国出国经贸展览的传统市场，目前正是开拓亚洲、非洲、拉美、东欧和前独联体市场的黄金时期。

3. Other Channels 其他途径

Banks at home and abroad;（国内外银行）
Chambers of Commerce;（商会）
Trade Directories; （贸易指南）
Business Associates; （生意伙伴）
Commercial Counselors' Office; （商务参赞处）
Commercial Office of Embassies; （大使馆商务处）
Advertisements;（广告）
Recommendations by Business Partners or Clients;（贸易伙伴的推荐）

Section Three Cultural Differences and Taboos in International Trade 第三节 国际业务交往中的文化差异及禁忌

In international trade, we should attach great importance to cultural differences when doing international trade, since merchants and consumers of different countries differ in their national character, religious belief and custom, and they might even have a taboo or preference on color, number and pattern. These differences could be found in languages, values, gestures, laws, religion, politics, education and technology, etc..

在国际贸易中，由于各国贸易商和消费者的民族特性、宗教信仰、风俗习惯可能有较大的差别，甚至对颜色、数字、图案都有不同的忌讳和偏好，这就需要外贸工作人员在国际业务交往时，考虑到各国的文化差异。这些差异具体表现在语言、价值观念、姿势手势、法律、宗教、政治、教育程度、技术水平等方面。

1. Cultural Differences in International Business 国际业务交往中的文化差异

1.1 Language Differences 语言差异

There are more than 3,000 different kinds of languages in the world. It will be at least 10,000 different languages and dialects around the world if count various dialects in. Difficulties would come to us when doing business when we lack the knowledge of customers language habit. American Automotive Companies come across many difficulties due to the lack of other nations' language knowledge.

For example, the reason why "Nova", a kind of car under Chevrolet, is unpopular in Spanish-speaking countries is that the name"Nova" spells like "nova" in Spanish, meaning "don't go".

世界上有三千多种不同的语言，加上各种各样的方言，全世界至少有一万种不同的语言和方言。如果没有了解对方语言习惯，就可能遇到许多业务上的困难。美国的汽车公司，由于缺乏其他国家的语言知识而遇到不少困难。

如雪佛莱的“Nova”牌汽车，在讲西班牙语的国家不受欢迎的原因，据说就是其名字“Nova”类似西班牙语中的“nova”，意思是“不走”。

1.2 Non-linguistic Differences 非语言方面的差异

It is known that non-linguistic sign of one side, such as facial expressions, body movements, gestures, directly affect the other side's understanding and acceptance. In international trade, the intentions of non-linguistic sign, the same as language, vary wildly. As can be seen from the table, these non-linguistic greetings can be nod, bow, handshake, hug or eyebrow's movement. And its intention needs to be understood according to the different culture and habits of different countries. See Table 2-1.

众所周知，贸易一方的非语言示意，如面部表情、身体动作、姿势手势等都直接影响到贸易另一方对内容的理解和接受。在国际贸易中，非语言示意的含义就如同各国语言一样，差异很大。从表中可以看出，这些国家非语言表示的问候可以是点头、鞠躬、握手、拥抱或眉毛的动作，具体情况则要根据各国不同的文化习俗决定，如表 2-1 所示。

Table 2-1　　Cultural Differences

Country	Non-verbal greetings
USA	Handshake with enthusiasm and strength
Japan	Bow, bend at the same time and to the same position with customer
Australia	Warm handshake between men (handshake is also ok between men and women when women give their hands first)
France	Handshake (but American-style handshake is regarded as offensive)
Argentina	Slight nod and handshake at the same time (For long separation, ladies can kiss each other's cheeks, and men may hug each other)
Belgium	Handshake for everybody, just shaking gently
Chile	Shake hands and kiss on the right cheek
Pei Ji	Smile, eyebrow move (Handshake is also ok)
Greece	Hug and kiss on the cheeks or shake hands
India	Closed palm under mouth with thumb near chest and nod slightly at the same time
Portugal	Warm and tight handshake for everybody

表 2-1　　各国不同的文化习俗

国家	非语言表示的问候方式
美国	热情、紧紧、使劲地握手
日本	鞠躬，弯腰程度和时间与对方相同
澳大利亚	男士之间热情握手（男女之间也可握手，但必须是女方先伸出手来）
法国	握手（但美国式的使劲握手被视作无礼）
阿根廷	轻微点头，同时进行握手（如分别较长，女士可互相亲吻脸颊，而男士则可互相拥抱）
比利时	人人都握手，只是轻轻一握
智利	握手，并在右脸颊上吻一下
斐济	微笑，并把眉毛一竖（握手也可以）
希腊	拥抱，并在双颊上吻一下或握手
印度	双手手掌在嘴巴下合拢，拇指贴胸，并轻微点头
葡萄牙	人人都热情紧紧握手

2. Measures to Deal with Cultural Differences in International Trade 应对国际贸易中文化差异的措施

（1）Cultivate Cross-cultural Awareness 培养跨文化意识

Cross-cultural awareness is the consciousness of business people to understand cultural differences and respond appropriately to them. Higher Cross-cultural awareness is required in many steps of international business operations, such as international marketing, human resource management and incentive mechanism. Therefore, the personnel engaged in international trade must have a basic cross-cultural awareness.

跨文化意识是指商务人员对文化差异的理解并做出适当反应的一种商务意识。国际化的企业运作的各个环节，例如国际营销、人力资源管理、激励机制等都需要较高的跨文化意识。因此,从事国际贸易的人员必须拥有基本的跨文化意识。

（2）Master the Skills of Cross-cultural Business 掌握跨文化商务技巧

Cross-cultural business contacts require the understanding ability to the culture and organization, adaptability, ability to establish relations, systemic and multi-angled views, attitudes, sensitivity, language ability, decision-making ability under culture influence, skilled diplomacy and cross-cultural ability. Therefore, in-service staff should strengthen the training on related abilities. For those business talents who are accepting the higher education, they should cultivate the awareness of cross-cultural business. In addition, related courses and practice should be provided by colleges.【Typical Case Link 3】

跨文化商务交往中应当具备的能力有对文化和组织的理解力，适应能力，建立关系能力，系统和多视角的思维能力，态度、敏感性，语言能力，文化影响下的决策能力，外交能力和跨文化能力。因此对于在职人员来说,应该加强相关能力的培训，对于接受高等教育的商务人才来说,应加强跨文化商务交往意识的培养，同时学校应提供相关的课程以及实践机会。【典例链接 3】

（3）Focusing on Cultural Integration 注重文化的融合。

When a multinational company invests in other countries, it needs to integrate with three kinds of culture, which are culture of his native country, culture of the target country, and its corporate culture. Only by focusing on cultural integration, can a company adapt fully to the market, and thereby expand the market. For example, KFC launched the Mexico chicken rolls "into the market earlier. It is followed by the launch of "Lao Beijing Chicken Rolls" which is integration with Chinese culture and won the Chinese market by adding China's traditional sweet soybean taste and shredded green onion.

一个跨国公司跨国投资经营时，往往需要融合三种文化：自己国家的文化、目标市场国家的文化、企业的文化。只有注重文化的融合，才能深入地适应市场，进而拓展市场。例如肯德基早期推出了“墨西哥鸡肉卷”，在该产品投入市场后不久，肯德基又推出了一款融合了中国文化的“老北京鸡肉卷”，该产品添加了中国传统的甜面酱、葱丝等原料，因此在中国市场上获得成功。

（4）Enhance Cultural Exchange and Display 加强文化交流与展示

It is an effective way to understand cultural difference by multilevel and multiform cultural exchanges and displays. Not only does it contribute to the cultural exchange among countries and regions, but also forcefully promotes the economic and trade cooperation. China-France Culture Year is a good platform to show culture and promote culture communication.

进行多层次、多形式的文化交流与展示，是一个了解文化差异的有效途径。它不仅有利于国家或地区之间的文化交流，还有力地推动了经贸合作，已成功举办的中法文化年就是一个展示文化、交流文化的平台。

With the changing international situation, the influence of cultural differences on international trade will keep on changing. New influencing factors will come into being. Only active concern were shown on the change of situation could you have the initiative in international trade and move further.

随着国际形势的不断变化，文化差异对国际贸易的影响会不断变化，会有新的影响因素出现，要在国际贸易中掌握主动必须积极关注形势的变化，同时做出对自己最好的解决方法，只有如此才能越走越远。

【Review Questions】复习思考题

【Typical Case Link 1—典例链接 1】

Question: Is the contract effective?

问题：合同是否成立?

In the morning of February 17, A sends an offer to B by the air mail. The offer requires that it will be effective if B replies before February 25. But A sends a notice to revoke the offer in the afternoon of February 17(by cable). The notice reached B in the morning of February 18 while B received the offer sent by the air mail on February 25. Since B thinks the price is in his favor, he accepts immediately and sends a acceptance note by cable. Is this contract effective? And what is the reason?

A 在 2 月 17 日上午用航空信件形式邮出一份发盘给 B。发盘中规定 B 在 2 月 25 日前答复有效。但 A 又于 2 月 17 日下午发出撤回发盘的通知（用电报）。该通知于 2 月 18 日上午到达 B；而 2 月 25 日 B 才收到那封发盘的航空信。由于 B 考虑到该商品价格对其有利，所以立即做出接受，并用电报发出接受通知。问：合同能否成立？为什么?

【Typical Case Link 2—典例链接 2】

Question: Is this counter-offer or acceptance?

问题：这是还盘还是接受?

On 18th of some month, we sent the following offer to A. “We could offer 100 metric ton soybean of A grade with the price being USD 1,500 per MT, CIF Hamburg. Packing would be suitable for sea voyage. We would arrange shipment after contract. Payment method is an irrevocable letter of credit at sight. Looking forward to your earlier reply”.

某月 18 日，我方向 A 公司发盘“可供一级大豆 100 公吨，每公吨 1500 美元 CIF 汉堡，适合海运包装。订约后即装船，不可撤销即期信用证付款，请速回电。”

A answers immediately by telegram. “We accept your email on 18th. Pls pack with double gunny bags and an inner plastic bag.” We begin to prepare goods after receiving the reply. Several days later, the market price of soybean falls, and A company informed by cable that the contract is not formed. However, we hold the contract is effective. Is this contract effective?

A 立即电复“你方 18 日电我方接受，用双层麻袋装，内加一层塑料袋。”我方收到复电后着手准备，数日后，大豆的市场价格下跌，A 商来电称“合同未成立”，我方坚持合同已经成立。该合同是否成立?

【Typical Case Link 3—典例链接 3】

Question: What attention should we pay to when communicating with foreign merchants?

问题：与国外商人交往应注意什么问题？

Several merchants are attending an international trade conference on a ship. Suddenly the ship begins to sink. "Ask them to wear the life vest and jump off the ship at once." The captain ordered the chief mate. Several minutes later, the chief mate came back. "But those guys didn't want to jump." The chief mate reported to the captain. So the captain had to go himself. Sooner, the captain came back, saying "they all had jumped overboard." "How could you make it?" The chief mate asked curiously. "I told the English that diving is good for his health, so he did jump. I told the French that it is quite fashionable. I told the German that it is an order to jump and I told the Russian that it is quite revolutionary." "But how did you persuade the American?" "That was quite easy; I told them that they have already been insured." The captain said.

几个商人在一条船上开国际贸易大会。突然船开始下沉。“快去叫那些人穿上救生衣，跳下船去。”船长命令大副。几分钟后，大副回来了。“那些家伙不肯跳！”大副报告说。于是，船长亲自出马。不一会儿，船长回来说：“他们都跳下去啦。”“那你用了什么方法啊？”大副忍不住问。“我告诉英国人跳水是有益的运动，他就跳啦。我告诉法国人那样做很时髦，告诉德国人说那是命令，告诉苏联人说那样很革命。”“你是怎么说服美国人的呢？”“这很容易。”船长说：“我就说已经帮他们上了保险啦。”

Chapter Three　Quality of Commodity

第三章　商品品质

【Learning Objectives】教学目的与要求

After learning this chapter, you will be able to:

1. Understand clearly the name of commodity;
2. Master various methods of quality stipulated;
3. Master quality clause of in a sales contract.

【Lead-in Case】引导案例

Question: in this situation, does the buyer hold the repudiation rights? Why?
问题：在上述情况下，买方有无拒付的权利？为什么？

One Chinese company exported a contract of grade B peanuts to a foreign country importer. When the seller was working on the delivery of the goods, he found that the grade B peanuts were out of stock. Without prior consent of the buyer, the seller delivered the grade A peanuts instead of grade B peanuts and stated on the invoice Grade A peanuts. Price is the same, while the buyer refused the consignment.

我国某公司向某国出口花生一批，合同规定为 B 级花生。卖方交货时发现 B 级花生无货，中国公司在未征得买方同意的情况下，用 A 级花生代替了 B 级花生并在发票上注明"A 级花生、价格照旧"，货运抵买方后，遭买方拒绝。

Section One　Name of Commodity
第一节　商品的品名

1. Name of Commodity 商品的品名

Name of Commodity is an address or concept of some commodity, which is different from other commodities. The name of commodity, to a certain extent, reflects the natural attribute of commodity, as well as the main performance characteristics. The name also represents the goods that usually should have the quality, is the essential main trading conditions in the contract.

商品品名，它是某种商品区别于其他商品的一种称呼或概念。商品的名称在一定程度上体现了商品的自然属性、用途以及主要的性能特征。品名也代表了商品通常应具有的品质，是合同中不可缺少的主要交易条件。

As the following naming ways:

（1）With its main usage to name: travel shoes, insecticide, bicycle.

（2）With main raw materials to name: sweater, glass.

（3）With its main components to name: American ginseng royal jelly, aloe cream.

（4）With the appearance to name: red bean, tapered roller bearing.

（5）The commendatory term to name: Youth treasure, robust fruit milk.

（6）The character to name: wine of Home Kong Fu, Kong Yiji fennel.

（7）Process for the production to name: Erguotou, refined oil.

例如以下命名方式。

（1）以其主要用途命名：旅游鞋、杀虫剂、自行车。

（2）以其所使用的主要原材料命名：羊毛衫、玻璃杯。

（3）以其主要成分命名：西洋参蜂王浆、芦荟乳霜。

（4）以其外观造型命名：赤豆、圆锥滚子轴承。

（5）以其褒义词命名：青春宝、乐百氏果奶。

（6）以人物名字命名：孔府家酒、孔乙己茴香。

（7）以制作工艺命名：二锅头、精制油。

2. Significance of the Name of Commodity 列明品名的意义

（1）From the perspective of the law, stipulate in the contract that the subject matter of the specific name, relationship to both the transfer of goods with respect to the rights and obligations of a contract for the sale, is the main trading conditions.

从法律的角度来看，在合同中规定标的物的具体名称，关系到买卖双方交接货物方面的权利和义务，是买卖合同的主要交易条件。

（2）From business point of view, the name or description of the rules are both the substance of the transaction, which is the foundation and precondition.

从业务的角度看，品名或说明的规定是双方交易的物质内容，是交易赖以进行的物质基础和前提条件。

（3）Good names of commodities can generalize the characteristics of goods, with the purchase of consumer psychology, but also can meet the consumer's purchase desire.

好的商品名称既能概括商品的特性，符合购买者的消费心理，又能增进消费者的购买欲望。

3. Commodity Name Clause in a Sales Contract 合同中的品名条款

（1）Make a realistic stipulation based on the goods, avoiding exaggeration about the commodity.

针对实际做出实事求是的规定，对商品的品名不要做夸大的宣传。

（2）In the description of commodity clause of the sales contract, the stipulation of the commodity must be precise and specific.

在签订买卖合同的品名条款时，对品名必须明确、具体。

（3）In the contract, it should be possible to use the international common name. Internationaly in order to have the statistic of commodity taxation, the common classification criteria is available. The Customs Cooperation Council chaired made "harmonized commodity description and coding system" (The Harmonized Commodity Description and Coding System, H.S coding system). The system was formally implemented in January 1, 1988. China using the system in January 1, 1992. The preparation of Customs statistics, the GSP treatment are according to H.S. Therefore, the commodity name we use should be consistent with H.S..

If the seller delivers the goods do not conform with the contract name or description, the buy side has right to reject the goods, and asked to put in a claim for damages.

在合同中，应尽可能使用国际上通用的名称。国际上为了便于对商品的统计征税时有共同的分类标准，海关合作理事会主持制定了《协调商品名称及编码制度》（The Harmonized Commodity Description and Coding System,简称 H.S.编码制度）。该制度于 1988 年 1 月 1 日起正式实施，我国于 1992 年 1 月 1 日起采用该制度。目前各国的海关统计、普惠制待遇等都按 H.S.进行。所以，我国在采用商品名称时,应与 H.S.规定的品名相适应。

如果卖方交付的货物不符合合同规定的品名或说明，则买方有权拒收货物，并要求提出损害赔偿。

Section Two Stipulating Methods of Commodity Quality
第二节　商品品质的表示方法

The quality of goods is the integration of intrinsic and the outer forms or shapes of goods. Intrinsic attributes includes chemical, physical, mechanical properties and biological structure. The outer forms or shapes of goods includes shape, color, transparency, or style of the goods.

商品品质指的是商品的内在质量和外观形态的综合。内在质量包括商品的化学成分，物理和机械性能以及生物结构等；外观形态包括商品的外形、色泽、透明度或款式。

Quality of goods is indispensable to international trade. The goods sold have their own qualities, and the quality determined commodity market share and market price. Therefore, the quality of the goods is among the main terms upon which a sales contract is based and constructed.

商品的品质是国际贸易不可缺少的部分。国际贸易中所销售的商品都有其自身的品质，而且该品质决定商品的市场占有率和市场价格。因此，品质是销售合同中的最主要的条款，也是签订合同的基础。

Commodity provides the material basis for international trade. All of commodities present certain qualities, which should be agreed upon by the exporter and the importer while the business is being negotiated.

商品是进行国际贸易的基础，所有的商品都表现出一定的品质，是进出口商品进行交易磋商时首先取得一致意见的事项。

1. Methods of Stipulating Quality of Commodity 商品品质的表示方法

Commodities traded in international trade have various types and characteristics, so are the methods of stipulating quality of goods. Generally, there are two ways to indicate quality of goods either by description or by physical commodity. See Fig. 3-1.

在国际贸易中所交易的商品，种类繁多，特点各异，所以表示品质的方法也多种多样。但归纳起来可分为两大类：用实物表示和用文字表示，如图 3-1 所示。

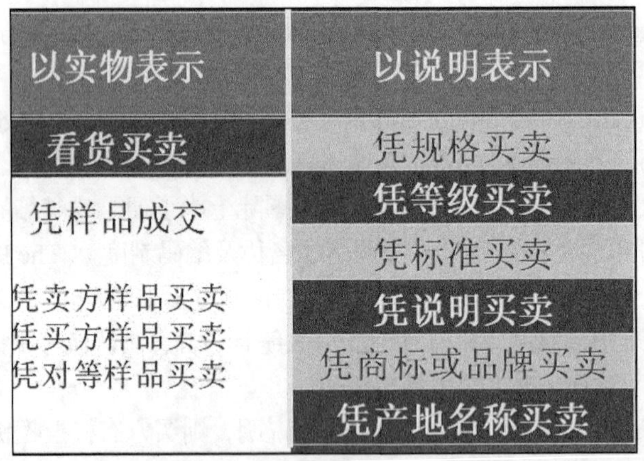

图 3-1　国际贸易商品品质分类

1.1　Sale by Physical Commodity 以实物表示

1.1.1　Sale by Sample 凭样品买卖

The sample refers to the article which can be used to represent the quality of the whole lot. In merchandising, a sample is a small quantity of a product, often taken out from a whole lot or specially designed and processed, which is given to encourage customers to buy the product.

Sale by sample refers to the sale of the two sides agreed that consultations and open a contract based on samples as the basis for quality. This method is used when the transaction is hard to conclude by standard, grade or words, such as some arts and crafts, clothing, native products, light industrial products, etc.

凭样品买卖是指买卖双方同意根据样品进行磋商和开立合同，并以样品作为交货品质的依据。凭样品买卖的方法一般适用于难于标准化、规格化，难于用文字说明其品质的商品，如部分工艺品、服装、土特产品、轻工产品等。

Sale by sample includes 3 cases, which are sale by the seller's sample, sale by the buyer's sample, and the counter sample. See Fig. 3-2.

样品就是指能够代表一整批货物的质量的实物，通常是指从一批货物中抽取出来或由生产和使用部门特别设计加工出来的能够代表出售货物品质的少量实物，用于向客户推广自己的产品，如图 3-2 所示。

图 3-2　样品

凭样品买卖主要有凭卖方样品、凭买方样品和凭对等样品三种成交方式。

① Sale by the seller's sample 凭卖方样品买卖

Seller's samples are the samples which are usually sent by the seller to the buyer, which are also called original samples. The seller provide a little objecs that can represent the whole batch of delivery quality, namely "a representative sample". At the same time keep a copy or copies of the same sample, the sample is called "duplicate". The sample dispached and the duplicate sample/file sample kept shall have the same article number so as to make it convenient for delivery, verification when handling quality dispute or future transactions.

凭卖方样品是指由卖方向买方提供货物的样品，即原样。卖方所提供的能代表整批交货品质的少量实物，即为“代表性样品”。同时，卖方应留存一份或数份同样的样品，该样品称为“复样”。一般来说，发出的样品和复样具有相同的编号，以备交货或处理品质纠纷时作核对之用。

② Sale by the buyer's sample 凭买方样品买卖

Sale by the buyer's sample is defined by Buyer's sample through consulting transaction and contract, and by Buyer's sample delivery quality as basis, which is also known as "sample contract".

凭买方样品买卖是指凭买方提供的样品磋商交易和订立的合同，并以买方样品作为交货品质的依据，也称“来样成交”。

③ Sale by the counter sample 凭对等样品买卖

A counter sample is a duplicate made by the seller according to the sample provided by the buyer. After the confirmation of the buyer, the sample will serve as the basis of the transaction and delivery. A counter sample is also called a return sample. Actually, counter sample is a transfer from sale by buyer's sample to sale by seller's sample. When a transaction is made based on the sample, the seller should keep one or more equivalent samples for file, which are called duplicate samples.

卖方根据买方提供的样品，加工一个类似的样品交买方确认，在买方确认后，这一样品就作为成交和交货的依据，称之为对等样品，也叫回样。实际上是把凭买方样品买卖，转化为凭卖方样品的买卖。根据样品成交的交易，卖方应留存一个或一个以上的样品备案，即复样。

1.1.2 Sale by physical goods 看货买卖

Trading under this term, the buyer inspects the goods on the spot. For instance, various trade fairs, transaction and consignment of bulk agricultural products and heavy machinery, auction, exhibition, etc.

现场实际看货成交。如各种展销会以及大宗农副产品、大型机器设备的交易和寄售、拍卖、展卖等贸易方式都属于看货成交。

2. Sales by Description 以文字说明表示商品的品质

2.1 Sales by Specification 凭规格买卖

Sales by Specification, which reflect the quality of some main indicators, such as composition, content, purity, performance, thickness, length. Sale by specification is more convenient, accurate, which can also be adjusted according to different applications, so this method is widely used in the international trade.【Typical Case Link 1】

凭商品规格，即反映商品品质的一些主要指标，如成分、含量、纯度、性能、长短、粗细。凭规格买卖比较方便、准确，还可以根据不同用途予以调整，故这种方法在国际贸易中广为运用。【典型链接 1】

2.2 Sales by Grade 凭等级买卖

Sale by grade means that devide quality into grade which are in terms of the provisions of each grade specifications. For example, fresh hen eggs, shell light brown and clean, ever in size.

凭等级买卖，最好在品质条款中规定每一等级的具体规格。如，新鲜的鸡蛋，成色好、个头大、颜色干净的会更贵，如图 3-3 所示。

图 3-3 鸡蛋的等级

Grade AA:60—65gm per egg

Grade A:55—60gm per egg

Grade B:50—55gm per egg

Grade C:45—50gm per egg

Grade D:40—45gm per egg

Grade F:35—40gm per egg

2.3 Sales by Standard 凭标准买卖

The standard is the government agency or the business community to unify specifications or grades of some goods, being published to the public. There are specific corporate standards, , national standards, regional standards or international standards.

标准是政府机构或商业团体对某一些商品统一其规格或等级，并予以公布，具体有企业标准，团体标准、国家标准、区域标准或国际标准。

In addition, in international trade, for some commodities that quality changes greatly, which are hard to define with scientific method and to establish uniform standards, such as agricultural and sideline products have the following two kinds of standards:

另外，在国际贸易中，对一些品质变化较大，不能因科学方法定义，难确定统一标准的商品，如农副产品，有以下两种标准：

A. Fair average quality (Fair average quality, FAQ)is the standard in international market of agricultural and sideline products. The agricultural product of each production year intermediate goods, or a quarter or a shipment in place of a single commodity “average quality”.

For example:

Chinese Groundnut, 1994’s crop, FAQ

Moisture (max.)13%

Admixture (max.)5%

Oil Content (min.)44%

A. 良好平均品质俗称大路货，是国际农副产品市场上通用标准。即农产品的每个生产年度的中等货，或某一季度或某装船月份在发运地的同一种商品的“平均品质”。

如：

中国花生仁，1994 年产，大路货

水分：最高 13%

杂质：最高 5%

含油量：最低 44%

B. Good merchantable quality (G.M.Q)

For the trading of wood and aquatic products, GMQ is used to indicate the quality. GMQ means the goods are free from defects and good enough for use or consumption. GMQ is usually not supplement with specification and when disputes arise because of the quality of the goods, exporters will have to be invited to make the arbitration.

B. 上等可销品质也称“精选货”。在买卖木材和水产品时，可以采用“凭上等可销品质”方式。“凭上等可销品质”是指卖方必须保证其交付的货物品质良好，合乎商销，而无需以其他方式证明商品的品质。但如果出现纠纷时，卖方卷入纠纷的仲裁。

2.4　Sales by Description and Illustration 凭说明书和图表买卖

Consider the commodity with complex structure, strict requirement on the material and design, such as machinery, electrical, instrumentation, sales by description and illustration generally require the vendor quality assurance technical terms of service.

针对结构复杂、材料和设计的要求非常严格的一些商品，如机器、电器、仪表等，凭说明书和图表买卖时，一般需订立卖方品质保证条款和技术服务条款，如图 3-4 所示。

图 3-4　说明书

2.5　Sales by Trade Mark or Brand 凭商标或牌号买卖

Brand name refers to commodity brands that the manufacturer or seller produce or sale, which is also known as brand. Trademark is a brand of patterned, which is a specific commodity sign. Trademarks and brand are protected by the trademark law. See Fig. 3-5.

商标的牌名是指厂商或销售商所生产或销售的商品的牌号，又称品牌。商标则是牌号的图案化，是特定商品的标志。商标与牌号受商标法保护，如图 3-5 所示。

图 3-5　商品品牌

2.6　Sales by Origin 凭产地名称买卖

Oue to some special factors like natural conditions and traditional production techniques in origin, the native products are renowned for their unique specialty in quality. So we can take the origin of the goods as characteristic of the commodity when stipulating the quality of goods such as France Perfume,

German Beer, China Northeast Rice. See Fig. 3-6.

某些商品由于产地的自然条件等特殊因素和产地的传统工艺，使该产品具有与众不同的特殊品质。我们在规定产品的品质时，可以以商品的产地作为商品品质的特点。如法国香水、德国啤酒、中国东北大米，如图 3-6 所示。

图 3-6　特殊品质商品

Section Three　Quality Clauses in Sales Contract
第三节　合同中的品质条款

Because quality clause is one of the essential terms and conditions in a contract, a breach of contract by the seller will lead to a very serious consequence. In order to facilitate the seller's performance of the contract, certain tolerance is allowed in commodity quality. In the quality clause concerning byproducts, quality latitude is stipulated, As to manufacture goods, the concept of quality tolerance is applied.

因为品质条款是合同的要件条款，如果卖方违约将产生十分严重的后果。为了便于卖方履约要给予卖方在品质掌握上一定的宽容度。对于农副产品在品质条款中规定品质机动幅度，对于工业制成品采用品质公差的概念。

1. Quality Range 品质机动幅度

For some primary products with unstable quality like bulk agricultural byproduct , metal and mineral, which is allowed some flexibility in the quality indicators within a certain range.

对一些质量不甚稳定的某些初级产品：大宗农副产品、五金矿产品，允许卖方所交货物的品质指标在一定幅度内有灵活性。

There are several order methods.　有以下几种制定方法。

（1）To stipulate a certain scope, such as S: 0.5% ~ 0.6% 0.5% / 0.6%;

规定范围，如 S：0.5%～0.6% 0.5%/0.6%

（2）To stipulate “max” or “min” such as　the highest, largest (Max: 0.5%); the lowest, minimum (Min: 0.6%);

规定极限：最高、最大（0.5%）；最低、最小（0.6%）；

（3）To stipulate more or less allowance , e.g. down content of down garment 16% ± 1%.

规定上、下差异：羽绒含绒量 16% ± 1%。

Commodity price can be adjusted within the range of quality latitude. Fix the price according to the quality and stipulate "Price Adjustment Clause Relating to Quality". Some commodities` price can be adjusted base on the actual delivery performance. Adopt discount price when the quality is below the stipulation of the contract.

在品质机动幅度范围内价格可以调整。体现按质议价，有些商品可根据实际交货品质情况调整价格，规定"品质增减价条款"。对低于合同规定采用折扣价。

2. Quality Tolerance 品质公差

Quality tolerance is recognized internationally, which is the process error of industrial manufactured goods. The existence of error is absolute, some are due to the limit of technological level and production level. These errors are allowed by the same industry. This is a quality tolerance given to the seller delivery. Within the range of tolerance, goods seller delivered are qualified, the buyer can neither reject the goods nor require adjustment to the price and require returning goods and compensation. 【Typical Case Link 2】

品质公差是国际上公认的产品品质的允许误差。品质公差是工业制成品在加工过程中所产生的误差，这种误差的存在是绝对的，其大小是由科技水平、生产力水平决定的，是同行业公认允许的误差。这是给卖方交货的宽容度。只要在品质公差范围内，卖方的交货都是合法的，买方不得拒绝接受，不得要求调整价格，也不得要求退货和赔偿。【典型链接 2】

【Review Questions】复习思考题

【Typical Case Link 1—典例链接 1】

Question: What mistakes did the company A make?

Can Company A just turn a blind eye and ignore it by saying that the deal is not by the sample?

问题：A 公司的失误在哪里？是否可以以该商品并非凭样成交为由而不予理赔？

One Chinese foreign trade company A exported to German company B a batch of marijuana. In the contract, it was stipulated that the water should not exceed 15%, impurity not more than 3%. Before the deal, company A sent the sample to the customer and after the contract Company A advised "the sample is similar to the goods". After the arrival of the goods in Germany, the buyer B showed the inspection certification, reading the goods quality was 7% inferior to the quality of the sample, therefore the buyer claimed for 600 pounds of compensation. Company A refused the compensation and stated its reason by saying that the merchandisc on delivery was selected, because of the agricultural products, it was not possible to be made exactly like the sample. But it was also not so far as below the sample's quality by 7%.

中国 A 外贸公司向德国 B 公司出口大麻一批，合同规定水分最高 15%，杂质不超过 3%，但在成交前，中国公司曾向对方寄过样品，合同订立后又电告对方"成交货物与样品相似"。货到德国后，买方出具了货物品质比样品低 7%的检验证明，并要求赔偿 600 英镑的损失。中国公司拒绝赔偿，并陈述理由说：该方商品在交货时是经过挑选的，因为是农产品，不可能做到与样品完全相符。但也不至于比样品低 7%。

【Typical Case Link 2—典例链接 2】

Question: What can be learned from the case?

问题：我们应从中吸取什么教训？

In October, 2007, a company of Hong Kong of China placed an order of 5 000 metric tons of iron manhole cover with a business enterprise in mainland on FOB basis. The total amount of the contract was USD 3.05 million (approximately RMB 22.9 million). Goods production was subject to the drawings supplied by the buyer. This contract provision stipulated that the quality of casting surface should be smooth, no casting cracks, porosity, and should not have blisters, shrinkage, slag and other defects. (1) Within 10 days after the contracting, the seller shall give the buyer about RMB 250 000 as the "anti-deposit", which will be returned within five days after the first shipment. (2)Before shipment, the seller should notify the buyer to come to the production site to do sample inspection and sign the quality confirmation. If the quality was not in conformity with what was required, the buyer should have the right to refuse the contract goods. Without agreement upon the terms and conditions of transaction between the seller and the buyer, noone could terminate the contract, otherwise that party that initated contract termination should bear all economic losses.

2007 年 10 月，中国香港某商行向中国内地一企业按 FOB 条件订购 5000 公吨铸铁井盖，合同总额为 305 万美元（约人民币 2290 万元）。货物由买方提供图样进行生产。该合同品质条款规定：铸件表面应光洁；铸件不得有裂纹、气孔、砂眼、缩孔、夹渣和其他铸造缺陷。（1）订约后 10 天内卖方须向买方预付约人民币 25 万元的“反保证金”，在交第一批货物后 5 天内退还。（2）货物装运前，卖方应通知买方前往产地抽样检验，并签署质量合格确认书。若质量不符合合同要求，买方有权拒收货物。不经双方一致同意，任何一方不得单方面终止合同，否则由终止合同的一方承担全部经济损失。

Chapter Four　Quantity of Commodity

第四章　商品数量

【Learning Objectives】教学目的与要求

After learning this chapter, you will be able to:

1. Understand the various calculation units

2. Have a good cornmand of calculating methods.

【Lead-in Case】引导案例

Question: Please explain the reasons.

问题：请说明原因。

A foreign trade company exported 1 000 sets of typewriters. The L/C stipulated that partial shipment was prohibited. But when the consignments were gathering at the port for shipment, the seller found that 45 sets of goods got problem in packing and quality. Since it was an emergency and in order to assure of the quality, the exporter believed that according to *the Uniform Customs and Practice for Documentary Credits* 600, even if it doesn't allow the partial shipment, there is a more-or-less clause by 5%. Eventually, the seller loaded 955 sets virtually whereas the goods were rejected by the negotiating bank.

某外贸公司出口打字机 1000 台。信用证付款规定不许分批装运。但是货物集港准备装船时才发现有 45 台包装及质量有一定的问题。临时更换已经来不及，为了保证质量，出口商认为，根据《跟单信用证统一惯例 600》的规定，即使不准分批，在数量上也允许有 5%的伸缩。少装 45 台，也未超过 5%。于是实际装船 955 台，当去银行议付时，遭到银行的拒绝。

Section One Calculating Units of the Commodity Quantity 第一节 商品数量的计量单位

Quantity clause in contract of sale is an important clause. "*The United Nations Convention on the international sale of goods*" mentioned that to deliver base on the agreed quantity is a basic obligation of the seller. Representation methods of the quantity units is different due to the different nature of the goods and the different measurement system of countries, The systems in common use in the world are the Metric System, the British System and the US System. The units of measurement generally used in international trade are listed in the table as follows. See Table 4-1.

数量条款是买卖合同中的一项重要条款。《联合国国际货物销售合同公约》规定：按约定数量交货是卖方的一项基本义务。由于商品的性质不同和各国采用的度量衡制度不同，表示数量的单位方法也不同。目前国际上通常使用的度量衡制度有米制、英制和美制。国际贸易中经常使用的计量单位，如表4-1所示。

Table 4-1 Units of Measurement

Weight	gram(g),kilogram(kg), ounce(oz), pound(lb), metric ton(M/T), long ton(L/M), short ton, etc.
Number	Piece(pc), package(pkg), pair, set, dozen(doz), gross(gr), ream(rm),etc.
Length	meter(m), centimeter(cm), foot(ft), yard(yd）,etc.
Area	square meter(sq m), square foot(sq ft), square yard(sq ya）,etc.
Volume	cubicmeter(cu m), cubiccentimeter(cu cm), cubic foot(cu ft), cubic yard(cu yd）,etc.
Capacity	Liter(L), gallon(gal), pint(pt), bushel(bu）,etc.

表4-1 度量衡单位

重量	克、千克、盎司、磅、公吨、长吨、短吨等
数量	只、件、双、套、打、罗、令等
长度	米、厘米、英尺、码等
面积	平方米、平方英尺、平方码等
体积	立方米、立方厘米、立方英尺、立方码等
容积	升、加仑、品脱、蒲式耳等

The following measuring units are usually adopted in China.

我国通常采用下列计量单位。

1. Weight 重量单位

If trade in weight,the units in common use are gram(g),kilogram(kg), ounce(oz),pound(lb),metric ton(M/T),long ton(L/M), short ton, etc. This measurement method is used for agricultural and sideline products, mineral products and some industrial products, such as soybean, iron ore, steel.

按重量交易时，其常用的单位有克、千克、盎司、磅、公吨、长吨、短吨等。这种计量方法多用于农副产品、矿产品和某些工业产品，如大豆、铁矿、钢材。

2. Number 数量单位

If trade in quantity, the units in common use are piece(pc), pair , set, dozen(doz), roll, ream(rm), gross(gr), bag , bale, etc., For products, light industrial and mechanical products industrial manufactured goods such as consumed and some native products, such as clothing, sports goods, vehicles, livestock etc..

按数量计量的单位有：件、双、套、打、卷、令、罗、袋、包等。多用于消费品、轻工业品和机械产品等工业制成品及部分土特产品，如服装、文体用品、车辆、活牲畜等。

3. Length 长度单位

It is mostly used for textile products, metal cords, electric wires, such as meter(m), foot(ft), yard(yd),etc.

有些商品如布匹、绳索、电线电缆等常采用长度计算单位如米、英尺、码等。

4. Area 面积单位

It is often used in trade of leather, wooden board glass, carpets, such as, square meter(sq m), square foot(sq ft), square yard(sq ya),etc..

面积多用于皮革、木板、玻璃、地毯等商品交易，其表示单位有平方米、平方英尺、平方码等。

5. Volume 体积单位

It is mostly used for wood, sand, etc.. It includes cubicmeter(cu m),cubic foot(cu ft), cubic yard(cu yd), etc..

按体积表示多用于木材、砂石等商品交易，计量单位如立方米、立方英尺、立方码等。

6. Capacity 容积单位

It is mostly used for grain, oil, etc., such as Liter(L), gallon(gal), bushel(bu),etc..

常用于粮食、石油等，如升、加仑、蒲式耳等。

Section Two Calculating Methods of the Commodity Weight
第二节 商品重量的计量方法

1. Gross Weight 毛重

Gross weight is the total weight of the commodity itself and the package(the tare).

毛重是指商品本身的重量加包装（皮重）的重量。

2. Net Weigh 净重

Net weight is the actual weight of commodity without the weight of the package.

净重是指商品本身的实际重量，不包括包装的重量。

3. Conditioned Weight 公量

Conditioned weight refers to the sum weight of the commodity that extracted moisture with scientific methods,and added the weight of standard moisture. This method is mainly used for larger economic value and water content volatile commodities, such as wool, silk, cotton yarn.

公量是指用科学的方法抽出商品所含水分，再另加标准水分求得的重量。这种方法主要用于经济价值较大而水分含量不稳定的商品，如羊毛、生丝、棉纱等。

Conditioned Weight = Dried Weight + Standard Moisture

$$= \frac{\text{Actual weight} \times (1+ \text{standard regaining rate of water})}{1 + \text{actual regaining rate of water}}$$

$$\text{公量} = \text{干量} + \text{标准水分量}$$

$$= \frac{\text{实际重量} \times (1+\text{标准回潮率})}{1 + \text{实际回潮率}}$$

Internationally recognized wool, silk moisture regains 11% GB standards. Serrated cotton impurity rate was 2.5%, cotton moisture regains of 8.5%.

国际上公认的羊毛、生丝的公定回潮率为 11%；国标规定锯齿棉标准含杂率为 2.5%，棉花公定回潮率为 8.5%。

4. Theoretical Weight 理论重量

Theoretical weight applied to the fixed size of goods. The piece weight of the fixed size of goods is almost same. It is easy to get the sum weight by piece weight adding up the pieces, such as steel board.

理论重量适用于有固定尺寸的商品。只要尺寸符合，规格一致，其重量大体相等，根据件数就可以推算出重量，如规格钢板等。

5. Legal Weight 法定重量

Legal weight is pure commodity weight plus the weight of inner packaging materials.

法定重量是纯商品的重量加上直接接触商品的包装物料（如内包装等）的重量。

Section Three Quantity Clause in the Contract 第三节 合同中的数量条款

1. More or Less Clause 溢短装条款

The buyer and seller stipulate in a sales contract that the seller is allowed to deliver the goods within a certain percentage of more or less than the contracted quantity. For example，10 000 square metre 5% more or less at seller`s option.

溢短装条款是指买卖双方在合同中规定卖方的实际交货数量可以比合同规定的数量多交或少交百分之几，但不超一定的范围。如：10 000 平方米，卖方可溢短装 5%。

The quantity difference is usually expressed by percentage such as range from 3% to 5%. Different commodities decide how much the range of quantity difference should be. For some commodities with low value such as sandstone or coal, it is allowed to stipulate a wider range, usually 10% more or less. For some products like metals and minerals, quantity difference should be set within a smaller margin. Who should determine how much more or less would be allowed? Generally, the seller is to decide the quantity difference in practice. As stipulated in a contract, it is also practical to allow the shipper or the party in charge of shipment to decide the quantity according to the capacity of cabin. Under the more or less clause, the payment for the over-load or under-load portion will be made either according to contract price or at the international market price at the time of shipment arrival so that when international market price fluctuates, the seller cannot take advantage of the more or less clause to load more or less on purpose and harm the interests of the buyer. 【Typical Case Link 1】

数量机动幅度的大小通常都以百分比表示，如3%到5%不等。溢短装幅度的大小，根据具体商品的不同来决定。对某些价值较低的商品，如沙石、煤炭等可以规定较大的幅度10%。对某些价值较高的五金矿产品，溢短装幅度规定的要小些。溢短装多装少由谁来选择，按照惯例一般由卖方来决定，也可按合同的规定，根据舱容的大小由船方或负责安排运输的一方来决定。溢短装部分的价格既可按照合同的价格来规定，也可不按合同的价格，根据装船时或到达时国际市场的价格另定。以免卖方利用溢短装条款在国际市场价格波动时有意多装或少装，给买方带来不便。【典例链接 1】

2. About or Approximate 约量

In quantity clause,sometime “about”, “approximately”, “percentage of more or less” delivery will be used. But internationaly that is not a standard for such “about”or “approximate” sometime it’s 2.5%, sometime it's 5%. International Chamber of Commerce “UCP” (600th Publications)stipulate it’s within 10%. In order to facilitate the performance of the contract and to avoid controversy, import and export quantity clause in the contract should be clear and specific, for example, in terms of trade turnover number, should be provided the unit of measurement. For weight-measured goods, shall be prescribed in the weight calculation method. 【Typical Case Link 2】

在交货数量前加上“约”、“大约”、“左右”、“近似”等规定数量机动幅度，可以少交或多交约定数量的百分比。但国际上对约量的含义解释不一，有的解释为2.5%，有的解释为5%。国际商会《跟单信用证统一惯例》（第 600 号出版物）则认为，凡“约”，“大约”视为不超过10%的增减幅度。不同的解释和理解容易引起纠纷，为了便于履行合同和避免引起争议，进出口合同中的数量条款应当明确具体，比如，在规定成交商品数量时，应一并规定该商品的计量单位。对按重量计算的商品，还应规定计算重量具体方法。【典例链接 2】

【Review Questions】复习思考题

【Typical Case Link 1—典例链接 1】

Question：(1) How much are you going to deliver as seller? Why?

(2) Standing in the position of the buyer, what should pay attention to during the negotiation of the terms of the contract?

问题：（1）作为卖方你准备交付多少？为什么？

（2）如果站在买方的立场上，磋商合同条款时，应注意什么？

An ore report exntract specified as follows: “25 000M/T, 3% more or less at seller′s option.” When the seller prepared to take delivery, the international market price of ore went upward.

一笔出口矿砂的合同规定：“25 000M/T，3%卖方溢短装条款。”卖方准备交货时，矿砂的国际市场价格上涨。

【Typical Case Link 2—典例链接 2】

Question：What can be illustrated from this case?

问题：本案例说明了什么问题?

A Chinese export company exported a batch of donkey meat to Japan. The provision of the contract was: net weight 16.6 kilograms per carton, a total of 1500 boxes with total amount of 24.9 metric tons. When inspected by the Japanese customs, they found that the net weight was 20 kilograms per carton, a total of 1500 boxes with total amount of 30 metric tons. That is to say each carton has overloaded 3.4 kilograms. But in the document the weight was 24.9 metric tons. When negotiating, the bank only made the settlement according to the documents, paid only for 24.9 metric tons. The export company gave away 5.1 metric tons donkey meat to the customer. In addition, the Japanese customs considered that the weight delivered did not match with the voucher, the Chinese exporter was suspected to help the importer take tax evasion by doing so. Therefore, the Japanese customs sent the Chinese company their complaints. After negotiations with them, the Japanese customs forgave the Chinese exporter. But the over-delivery of 5.1 metric tons of donkey meat was not returned to the Chinese exporter and no more payment for it.

中国某出口公司出口一批驴肉到日本，合同规定，该批货物共 25 公吨，装 1500 箱，每箱净重 16.6 千克。如按规定装货，则总重量应为 24.9 公吨，余下 100 千克可以不再补交。当货物运抵日本港后，日本海关人员在抽查该批货物时，发现每箱净重不是 16.6 千克而是 20 千克，即每箱多装了 3.4 千克。因此，该批货物实际装了 30 公吨。但在所有单据上都注明了 24.9 公吨，议付货款时也按 24.9 公吨计算，白送 5.1 公吨驴肉给客户。此外，由于货物单据上的净重与实际重量不符，日本海关还认为我方少报重量有帮助客户逃税之嫌，向中方提出意见。经中方解释，才未予深究。但多装的 5.1 吨驴肉，不再退还，也不补付货款。

Chapter Five Packing and Marks of Commodity

第五章 商品的包装和标志

【Learning Objectives】教学目的与要求

After learning this chapter, you will be able to:

1. Acknowledge the definition and function of packing;
2. Understand and grasp the kinds and marks of packing;
3. Familiar with the stipulations of packing clause in a contract.

【Lead-in Case】引导案例

Question: How does this situation occur?

问题：其故何在？

In a supermarket in the Netherlands, there is a set of yellow bamboo canned tea with characters of "Chinese tea" on one side and ancient costumed maids on the other side, engraved with delicate looks and considerable ethnic characteristics, but few foreign consumers are interested in.

在荷兰某一超级市场上有黄色竹制罐装的茶叶一批，罐的下面刻有中文"中国茶叶"四字，另一面刻有我国古装仕女图，看上去精致美观，颇有民族特点，但国外消费者少有问津。

Section One Overall of Packing 第一节 包装概述

1. Definition 定义

Packing is used for the general operation of putting goods into containers for shipment and storage. From the view of the law, packaging is a part of the commodity instructions. In international business, packing clause is an essential term of a sales contract. By law of some countries, the buyer is entitled to reject the goods if the seller delivered goods failing to be packaged in accordance with the agreed terms.

包装是把货物放到容器中用来运输和储存的一般过程。从法律角度讲，包装还是说明货物的重要组成部分；在国际货物买卖中，包装条件是买卖合同中的一项主要条件。按照某些国家的法律规定，如果卖方交付的货物未按约定的条件包装，或者货物的包装与行业习惯不符，买方有权拒收货物。

2. Purpose and Significance of Packaging 包装的目的和重要性

2.1 Three Main Purposes of Packaging 包装的三大目的

One of the basic purposes of packing is to protect the product. This is important because the product may have to withstand a lot of handling during transportation between the factory and the consumer.

The second purpose of packaging is to make the product appealing to the buyer. Products with an eye-catching package are better to sell.

The other common purposes of packing are to provide information about the product inside, make it easy to carry the product, and provide convenience in using the product. See Fig. 5-1.

包装的基本目的是用来保护货物。这是因为产品从出厂到流通领域的客户手中需要经受很多次搬运。

包装的第二个功能是美化商品，吸引消费者。包装美观的商品有利于吸引顾客，扩大销售。

包装的最普遍的目的是给内部的商品提供信息，方便存储、保管或使用，如图 5-1 所示。

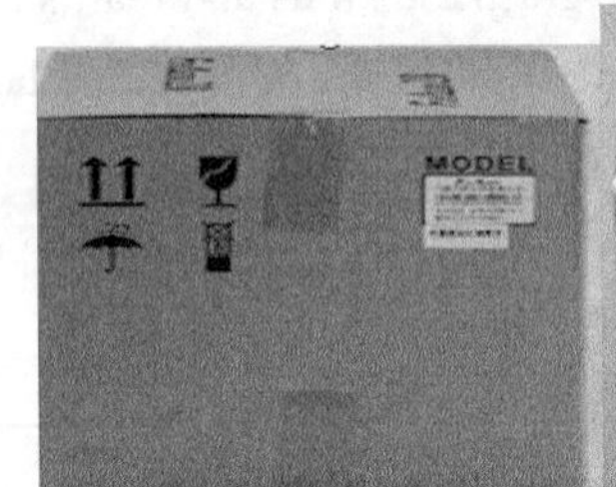

图 5-1　各种包装图示

2.2 Significance of Packaging 包装的重要性

Packaging is a continuation of the commodity production. The vast majority of goods can only go into circulation to realize its use value and value after package. In the export trade, packaging is of great importance to protect, glorify, promote commodities and plays a significant role in storage, transportation, sale and the use of the goods. Apart from a few products which do not need to be packaged and adopt under pack or conveyance in bulk, it has been estimated that as much as 70% of cargo loss could be prevented by proper packaging and marking. Therefore, packing is truly a major competitive force in the struggle for markets. Packing is one of the most important problems that confront the merchants engaged in foreign trade. Hence, in this respect, suitable packing is of great necessity and importance.

包装是商品生产的继续，绝大多数商品只有进行了包装，才能进入流通领域，从而实现其使用价值与价值。在出口贸易中，包装对保护商品、美化商品、宣传商品以及对商品的贮藏、运输、销售和使用，都起着重要作用，除少数商品不需要包装而采用裸装或散装。据统计如果有合适的包装和标识，70%的货物损失都是可以避免的。因此，包装已经成为对外竞销的强有力手段之一，是对外贸易必须面对的最重要的问题之一。从这个意义上讲，合适的包装有着非常重要的意义。

Section Two Kinds of Packing
第二节　商品包装的种类

1. Kinds of Cargoes 货物的分类

The kinds of cargoes are various in international trade. From the view point of whether they need packing, they fall into three kinds, which are Nude Cargo, Cargo in Bulk/Bulk Cargo and Packed Cargo.

贸易中的货物是多种多样的，根据包装的不同可以分为以下 3 种：裸装货、散装货和包装货。

1.1 Nude Cargo 裸装货

Nude cargoes or nude packed commodities refer to those kinds of cargoes whose qualities are more stable and to be shipped without any packages or in simple bundles.

For example, rubber, steel plates, timber, automobiles, etc. See Fig. 5-2.

所谓裸装货是指有些商品的品质比较稳定，只要将商品无包装运输或以其自身进行捆扎的货物，如钢材、铅锭、木材、橡胶、车辆等，如图 5-2 所示。

图 5-2　各种裸装货图示

Characteristics: 特征

- Without any packages; 形态上自然成件；
- Not easy to be influenced by outside circumstances; 能抵抗外界影响；
- In simple bundles; 略加捆扎；
- Difficult to be packed. 难以包装。

1.2 Bulk Cargo 散装货

Cargo in bulk refers to goods which are shipped or even sold without packages on the conveyance in bulk, such as oil, ore, grain, coal, etc. Cargo in bulk can be transported, loaded and unloaded by conveyance and loading and unloading equipment designed particularly. Bulk shipment is usually applicable for large quantity of commodities that are to be shipped by means of transport with special purposed shipping equipment. Bulk shipment has the advantages of space saving, quick handling and lower freight. See Fig. 5-3.

所谓散装货是指未加任何包装、直接付运至销售的货物，通常适用于不需要包装即可直接进入流通区域，或不容易包装或不值得包装的货物，例如石油、煤炭、矿砂、粮食等。散装货物运输可以借助于传输带，装卸设备通常是特殊设计的，它使用的是大宗货物运输工具，相应地运输过程也是较特殊的。散装货的优势是节省船位、操作迅速、运费低廉，如图 5-3 所示。

图 5-3　各种散装货图示

Characteristics: 特征：

- Without packages on the conveyance; 不需要包装；
- Applicable for large quantity of commodities; 大宗商品的运输和装卸；
- Space saving, quick handling and lower freight. 节约舱位，装运快捷，运费低廉。

1.3　Packed Cargo 包装货

Packed Cargo refers to those which need shipping packing, sales packing or both. Most of commodities in international trade need certain degree of packing during the shipping, storing and sales process. See Fig. 5-4.

所谓包装货是指需要运输包装、销售包装或两者都需要的货物。大多数国际贸易货物都需要某种程度的包装以便运输、仓储和销售，如图 5-4 所示。

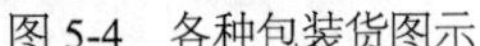

图 5-4　各种包装货图示

2. Kinds of Packing 包装的分类

In international trade, according to the function of the goods in the process of circulating and the packing materials and methods, packing can be divided into transport packing (also called outer packing), sales packing (also called inner packing), and neutral packing.

在国际贸易中，根据商品包装在流通过程中的作用的不同，包装材料和包装方法的不同，包装可分为运输包装（又称外包装），销售包装（又称内包装）和中性包装。

2.1　Shipping packing(Outer Packing) 运输包装（外包装）

Transport/shipping packing is also called outer packing or giant packing. It is used mainly to keep the goods safe during transportation. Not only must it be solid enough to prevent the packed goods from any damage, but also be easy to store, discharge, convenient to load and unload. The methods of shipping packing usually fall into two kinds which are single piece packing and collective packing.

运输包装又称外包装或大包装，它的作用主要在于保护运输途中的商品，同时便于防盗、运输、卸载、储存和分配。运输包装通常分为两类：单件运输包装和集合运输包装。

2.1.1　Classifications 分类

2.1.1.1　Single Piece Packing 单件运输包装

The cargoes are packed as a single unit in the transportation.

单件运输包装是指货物在运输过程中作为一个计件单位的包装。

It can be sub-divided into the following two kinds：常细分如下：

According to the style （按包装造型分有）：箱（Case）、桶（Drum）、袋（Bag）、包（Bale）、捆（Bundle）、罐（Can）等，如图 5-5 所示。See Fig. 5-5.

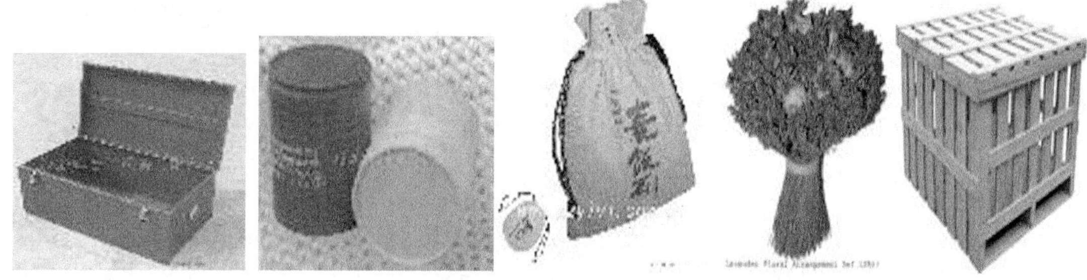

图 5-5　各种单件包装图示

According to the material（按使用材料分有）：纸箱（Carton）、木箱（Wooden Case）。

图 5-6　各种不同材料单件包装图示

铁桶（Iron drum）、塑料桶（Plastic drum）、纸袋（Paper Bag）、麻袋（Gunny bag）、塑料袋（Plastic bag），如图 5-6 所示。See Fig. 5-6.

2.1.1.2　Collective Packing 集合运输包装

Collective Packing is also called Group Shipping Packing.

A certain number of single pieces are grouped together with a big packaging or are packed in a big container. It can be sub-divided into the following three kinds:

集合运输包装也称作集团运输包装，是指在单件运输包装的基础上，为了适应运输、装卸作业的要求，将若干单件包装组合成一件大包装。又可细分如下：

- Container 集装箱
- Pallet 托盘
- Flexible Container 集装包和集装袋

（1）Container 集装箱

The container is a kind of tool used for transportation which can be thought as a particular shipping packing of the cargo, usually provided by the shipping company in cycle use.

集装箱是指一种运输工具，被认为是一种特殊的运输包装，它一般由运输公司提供周转使用。

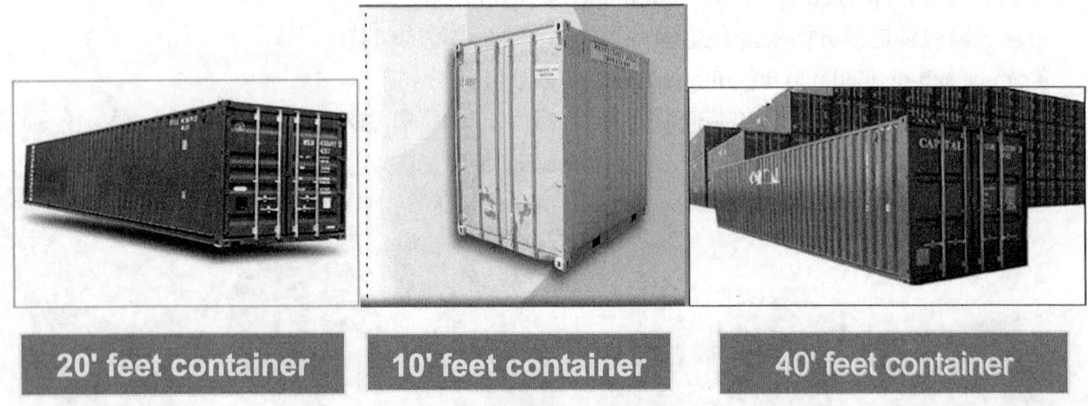

图 5-7 三种普遍采用的集装箱规格

Nowadays, the specifications of the container in common use in the world are the first series in ISO, including 1A, 1AA, 1B, 1C, 1D, 1E and 1F.The most common specification is 1C, i.e. 8 × 8 × 20 feet, and the actual largest load weight is 17.5 Metric Ton and volume is 24~26 Cubic Metre. When calculating the circulating quantity of the container, we often take the 20 foot container as a measurement unit, i.e. TEU (Twenty-foot Equivalent Unit)to indicate it, meaning “being equal to a 20-foot unit”. See Fig. 5-7.

目前国际上普遍采用的集装箱是 ISO 的第一系列规格，包括：1A、1AA、1B、1C、1D、1E 和 1F 型号的集装箱。最常用的规格为 8 英尺 × 8 英尺 × 20 英尺的集装箱，其实际最大载重为 17.5 吨，体积为 24～26 立方米。一般计算集装箱流量时，都以这种规格为一个标准单位，称为“TEU”意为“20 英尺相当单位”，如图 5-7 所示。

（2）Pallet 托盘

It is a kind of single-layer or double-layer flat carrier which is made according to a certain specification. Certain quantities of single pieces are packaged collectively on the flat carrier and tied up in the light of the requirements to form a shipping unit, which makes it convenient to load, unload, lift and pile the goods by using machinery in the shipping process.

托盘指用木材、金属或塑料制成的托板，将货物堆放在托板上方，并用箱板纸、塑料薄膜或金属绳索加以固定，组合成一件包装，这样更方便货物的装卸、堆码，以及叉车操作。

This is a typical pallet and has a capacity of two tones. In appearance, it looks like a platform on which the cargo is placed. An aperture is provided at each side to enable the fork lift truck to handle the pallet. See Fig. 5-8.

这是一个典型的托盘，载重量为 2 吨。从外表看，它像一个平台可以堆放货物，下面有插口，供铲车装卸使用，如图 5-8 所示。

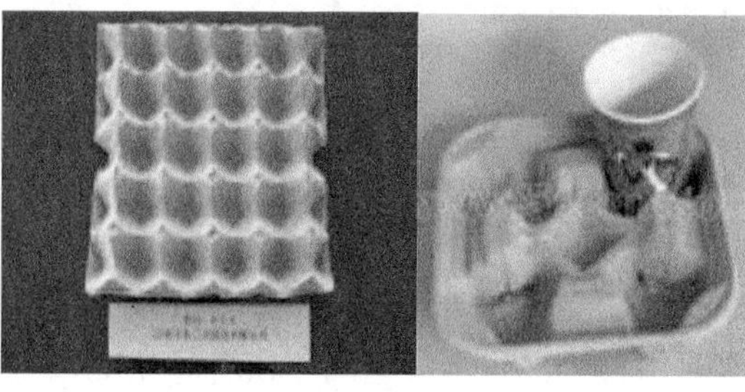

图 5-8　几种托盘图示

（3）Flexible Container 集装袋和集装包

- Kinds of round-shaped or square-shaped bag which weaved by synthetic fiber or composite material.
- The capacity varies usually from 1~4 metric tons. The maximum capacity can reach about 13 metric tons.
- Be suitable for powder or cargoes such as fertilizer, flour, sugar, cement, etc.

集装包或集装袋（Flexible Container）是指用合成纤维或复合材料编织成的圆形大口袋或方形大包。这种集装包容量不一，一般为 1～4 吨，最高达十几吨。可广泛用于肥料、粮谷、糖、水泥等粉状、块状物品的包装，如图 5-9 所示。

图 5-9　集装包

2.1.2　Requirements for Shipping Packaging　对运输包装的要求

（1）Be suitable for the features of commodities. 必须适应商品的特性；

（2）Be suitable for the requirements of transportation methods. 必须适应运输方式的要求；

（3）Think about relevant legal stipulations of some countries and request of customers, e.g. applying straw materials to be packed is prohibited in some countries.

必须考虑有关国家的法律规定和客户的要求，如有的国家禁止使用稻草之类的材料做包装用料；

（4）Easy to operate for all kinds of intermediate links.

要便于各种流转环节人员进行操作；

（5）To save expenses before premising the packag on strong basis.要在保证包装牢固的前提下节省费用。

2.2 Sales Packing 销售包装

It's also called inner packing, small packing or immediate packing.

Its functions:

- A form of protection to reduce the risks of goods being damaged in transit and prevent pilferage;
- A form of promoting sales;
- A decisive aid in selling household consuming goods.

销售包装又称内包装或小包装，是直接接触商品并随商品进入零售网点和消费者或用户直接见面的包装。这类包装除了必须具有保护商品的作用外，更应具有促销的功能。

2.2.1 Classifications 分类

Sales packing can be designed with various packaging materials, different structures and styles, with results in the diversity of the sales packaging. See Fig. 5-10.

销售包装可采用不同的包装材料和不同的造型结构与样式，因而产生了销售包装的多样性，如图 5-10 所示。

Sales package can be divided into:

- Piling-up pattern; 堆叠式包装；
- Hanging-up pattern; 挂式包装；
- Pattern for carrying about; 便携包装；
- Pattern for easily opening; 易开包装；
- Pattern for spraying out; 喷雾包装；
- Pattern for showing off a gift. 礼品包装。

See Fig. 5-10.

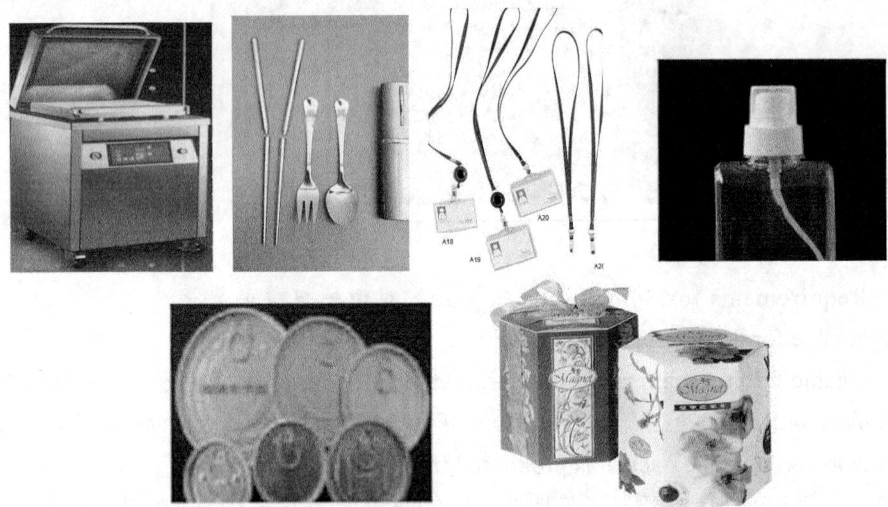

图 5-10 销售包装的分类图示

2.2.2 Requirements for Sales Packaging 对销售包装的要求

（1）Easy to display; 便于陈列；

（2）Easy to identify; 便于识别；

（3）Easy to carry and use; 便于携带和使用；

（4）Artistically attractive; 有艺术的吸引力；

（5）Verbal Instructions; 文字说明。

There should be necessary verbal instructions on the sales packaging, such as trademark, brand name, commodity name, name of origin, quantity, specification, composition, purpose, and usage. The verbal instructions and decorative pictures should be closely coordinated.The words must be concise and understandable to the consumers in the sales market, using a foreign language at the same time if it is necessary. See Table. 5-1.

销售包装上应有必要的文字说明，如商标、品牌、品名、产地、数量、规格、成分、用途和使用方法等。文字说明应同装潢画面紧密结合、互相衬托、彼此补充，以达到宣传和促销的目的，使用的文字还须简明扼要，并能让销售市场的顾客看懂，必要时也可以同时使用出口目的国语言。

（6）Note the toboos of package as follows: 注意包装禁忌，如表 5-1 所示。

Table 5-1 Taboos of Sales Package

Country or Region	Favorite Patternrs	Aversion Pattern	Favorite Color	Aversion Color
Britain		Elcphant, goat		Red
France		Spade		Darkgreen
Italy		Chrysanthemum	Green	
Iran	Lion			
Southeast Asian countries	Elephant		Green	Yellow
Singapore	Double happiness			
Japan		Lotus	Black	Green
Turkey	Duck			
America		Bear		
Some South American Countries	Owl			Purple, yellow
Islamic Countries		Pig and similar pattern	Green	Blue
Some North African Countries		Dog		

表 5-1 销售包装的禁忌

国家或地区	喜爱的图案	厌恶的图案	喜爱的色彩	厌恶的色彩
英国		象、山羊		红色
法国		黑桃		墨绿色
意大利		菊花	绿色	
伊朗	狮子			
东南亚国家	象		绿色	黄色
新加坡	双喜			
日本		荷花	黑色	绿色
土尔其	鸭子			
美国		熊		
南美一些国家	猫头鹰			紫、黄色
伊斯兰教的国家		猪及类似图案	绿色	蓝色
北非一些国家		狗		

2.3 Neutral Packing 中性包装

Neutral packing is a kind of packing which does not show:

- Origin of country;
- Name and address of the manufacturer;
- Trade mark and brand on both shipping and sales packing.

In short, there is no information of manufacturer.

中性包装是一种在运输和销售包装均不显示原产国制造商名称、地址、商标及品牌的包装。简言之，没有生产者的任何资料。

The purpose of using neutral packing is to break down the discriminatory tariffs and restrictions of some importing countries. It is also a flexible method adopted by some exporting countries to expand export.

中性包装的出现是为了打破某些进口国关税歧视和限制，也是某些出口商为了扩大出口采取的一些灵活的做法。

2.3.1 Classifications 分类

There are two cases for neutral packing which are neutral packing with designated brand name and neutral packing without designated brand name. See Fig. 5-11.

中性包装又分为无牌中性包装和定牌中性包装两种，如图 5-11 所示。

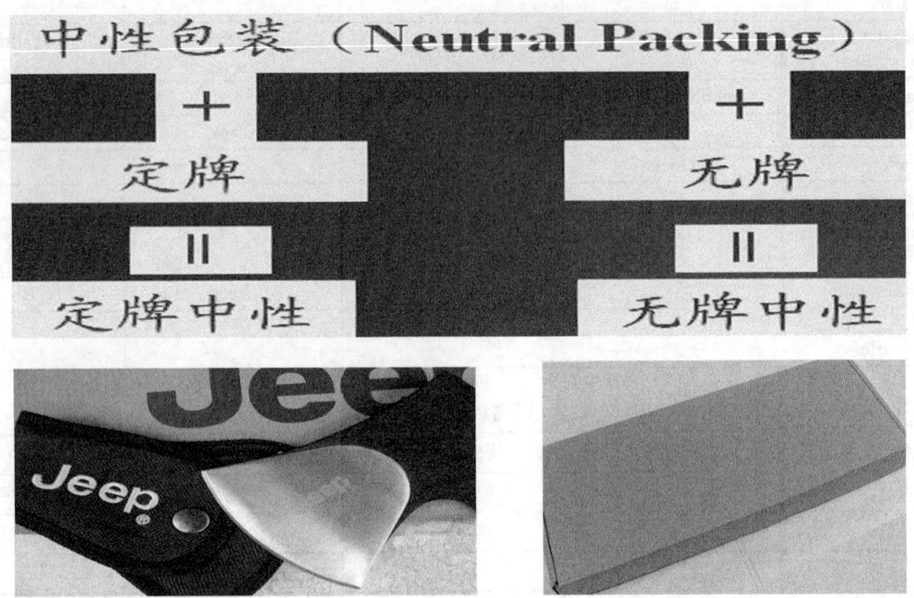

图 5-11 中性包装的分类图示

- Unlicensed Packing

Unlicensed Packing means that there are no mark or brand name designated by the buyer on the package of commodities or commodity, according to the requirement of the buyer.

无牌中性包装是指在商品和包装上均不使用任何商标/牌名。

- Brand Designated Packing 定牌中性包装

Designated Brand Packing means that the seller marked the trade mark or brand name designated by the buyer on the package of commodities or commodity itself according to the requirement of the buyer.

所谓定牌中性包装是指卖方按照买方要求在其出售的商品或包装上标明买方指定的商标或牌号的包装。

At present, in many countries in the world, commodities sold by supermarkets, large department stores, specialized stores, chain stores are usually marked with their own trademarks or brand names on the package, in order to raise their name recognition and promote the worth of goods. Exporters in many countries would like to accept brand designated by the buyer with the purpose of taking advantage of the operation abilities and the business and brand reputation of the buyer, so as to raise price and expand production. For example, manufacturers of sports shoes' production who have the world famous trademarks like NIKE and REEBOK have their main production in China.

当前，世界许多国家的超市、大百货公司和专业商店、连锁店出售的商品都要在商品或包装上标有本商店使用的商标或品牌，以扩大本店的知名度和显示该商品的身价。许多国家的出口商为了利用买主的经营能力及其商业信誉和品牌信誉，提高售价和销路，也愿意接受定牌生产。如运动鞋生产的世界著名商标 NIKE、REEBOK，它们的主要生产地就是中国。

2.3.2 Stipulation of Designated Brand in China 中国定牌生产的规定

In the exportation of China, the exporter must mark "Made in China" on the commodities itself and its packing, unless there are some otherwise stipulations, when designated brand production is adopted.【Typical Case Link 1】

我国出口贸易中，采用定牌生产时，除非另有规定，出口商品或包装上均需标明“中国制造”字样。【典例链接 1】

2.3.3 Requirements for Neutral Packing 对中性包装的要求

(1) To checkup the pattern, letter and content provided by the importer if there is any inappropriate.

(2) Stipulate in the contract "in case the buyer's sample results in any disputes of infringement of industrial property, the seller will have nothing to do with it."【Typical Case Link 2】

应审查外商提供的图样、文字、内容有无不妥之处；

应在合同中规定“如发生工业产权争议，或侵权行为卖方概不负责”。【典例链接 2】

Section Three Marks of Packing
第三节 商品包装的标志

1. Concept and Significance of Packing Marks 包装标志的概念和意义

Packing mark refers to different, words diagrams and figures which are written, printed, or brushed on the outside of the commodity packing in order that it is easy and convenient for goods loading, unloading, store, inspection, customs clearance and discharge. Package should not be marked with crayons, tags or card.

包装标志是指在商品包装上书写、压印、刷制各种有关的标志，如文字、图形和数字，为了便于货物交接、防止错发错运，便于识别，便于运输、仓储、商检和海关等有关部门进行查验等工作，也便于收货人提取货物。包装不能用粉笔、标签或卡片来做包装标志。

2. Classifications 分类

According to the uses of the packing marks as follows：shipping mark, indicative mark, warning mark and bar code mark as follows. See Fig. 5-12.

根据用途可分为运输标志、指示性标志、警告性标志和条形码标志，如图 5-12 所示。

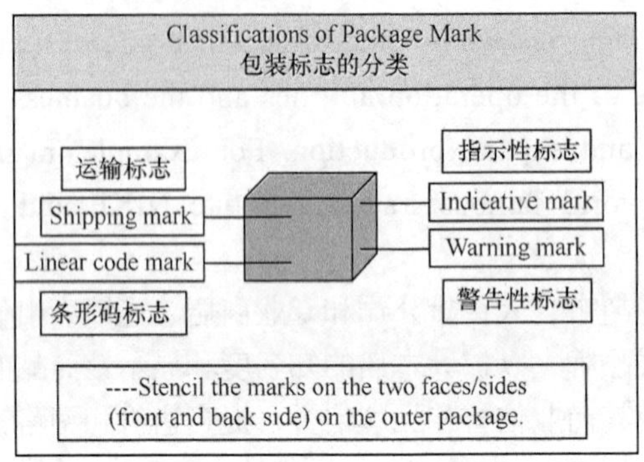

图 5-12　包装标志分类

2.1　Shipping Mark 运输标志

It is an identical symbol, which is composed of a specific geometric figure, abbreviations or initials of consignee. 【Typical Case Link 3】

运输标志，即唛头（Shipping Mark），是一种识别标志，通常由一个简单的几何图形和一些字母、数字及简单的文字组成。【典例链接 3】

The contents of shipping mark and sample as follows. See Fig. 5-13.

其主要内容和样例如下，如图 5-13 所示。

- Name of destination; 目的港；
- Code of consignee; 收货人名称或代码；
- Reference No.; 参考号,如订单、发票号码；
- Number of package; 包装物件号，顺序号和总件数。

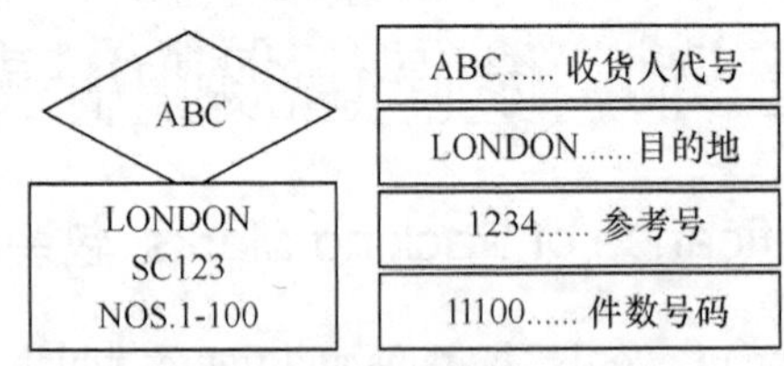

图 5-13　“普通唛头”样例

ISO Shipping Mark：ISO has developed new standard shipping marks, which are widely adopted by all countries in international trade.标准化运输标志：国际标准化组织发展了新的标准运输标志，这一运输标志在对外贸易中被世界各国广泛采用。

ISO Shipping Mark consists of 4 lines, not more than 17 letters including numbers and signs,not applying to geometrical diagrams.

标准运输标志由 4 行组成，每行不超过 17 个字母（包括数字和符号），不采用几何图形。

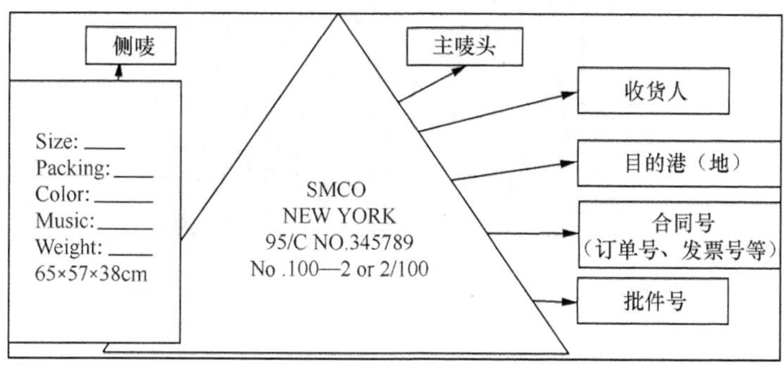

图 5-14　标准化运输标志

In practice, the shipping mark may further devide into “front mark” and “side mark”. The front mark usually stencils on the two bigger sides of the outer packing while side mark prints on the two smaller areas of the one, (side mark often refers to size, color,net weight, gross weight, the origin country, etc. See Fig. 5-14.

有时实际业务中，把“唛头”分为“正唛”和“侧唛”。正唛一般刷在外包装较大的两个侧面上，而侧唛则多印刷在面积较小的两个侧面上，如图 5-14 所示（侧唛：货号、颜色、净重、毛重、包装尺寸、生产国别等）。

2.2　Indicative Mark 指示性标志

We usually make use of the simple, noticeable design, remarkable diagrams and simple words on the packages to remind the relative workers of the items for attention when they load, unload, carry and store the goods, such as: Handle With Care, This Side Up, etc.Printed in black color generally. See Fig. 5-15. and Fig.5-16.

指示性标志又称安全标志、保护性标志，是指在包装上用简单醒目的图形和文字提醒各个环节的操作者在运输、装卸、存储时需要注意的事项。如“小心轻放”、“此端朝上”指示标志一般应印成黑色，如图 5-15、图 5-16 所示。

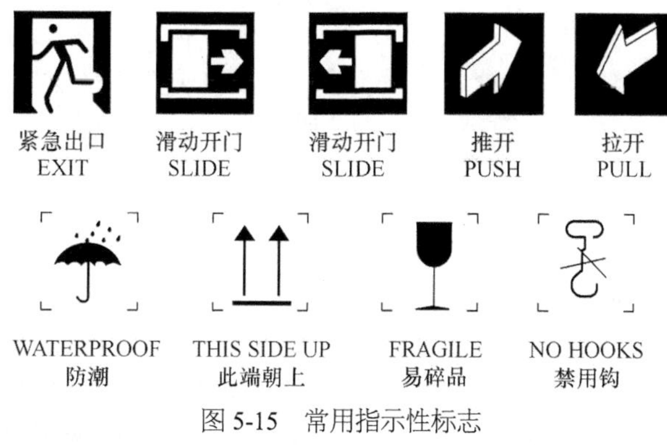

图 5-15　常用指示性标志

Do Not Drop	切勿乱摔
Keep Dry	保持干燥
Handle with Care	小心轻放
Fragile	易碎物品
Guard against Damp	防潮
Keep in Dark Place	暗处存放
This Side Up	此端向上
No Turning Over	切勿倒置

Common Markings & Phrases 常用指示标志标语

易碎物品

运输包装件内装易碎品，因此搬运时应小心轻放。

禁用手钩

搬运运输包装时禁用手钩。

向上

表明运输包装件的正确位置是竖直向上。

怕晒

表明运输包装件不能直接照射。

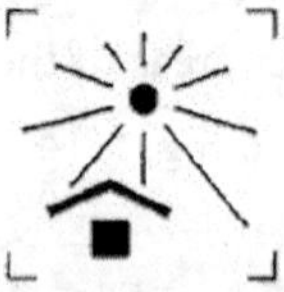

怕辐射

包装物品一旦受辐射便会完全变质或损坏。

怕雨

包装件怕雨淋。

重心

表明一个单元货物的重心。

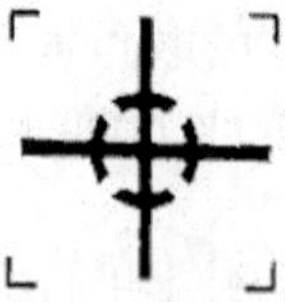

禁止翻滚

不能翻滚运输包装。

此面禁用手推车

搬运货物时此面禁放手推车。

堆码层数极限

相同包装的最大堆码层数，n 表示层数极限。

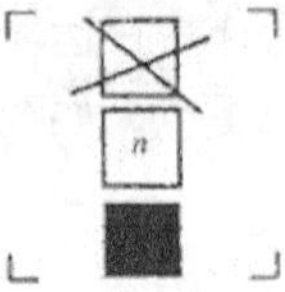

堆码重量极限

表明该运输包装件所能承受的最大重量极限。

禁止堆码

该包装件不能堆码并且其上也不能放置其他负载。

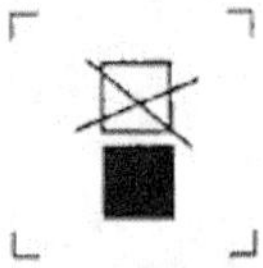

图 5-16　常用指示性标志

2.3　Warning Marks 警告性标志

The warning mark is also called dangerous cargo mark or shipping mark for dangerous commodities, which is printed clearly and definitely on the shipping packaging of the inflammable, explosive, poisonous, corrosive or radioactive goods, so as to give warnings to the workers/dockers/crew. See Fig. 5-17.

警告性标志又被称为危险品标志，是清晰地印刷在外包装上的警告性短语，警告性标志是由卖方参照一些危险的特征如燃烧、爆炸、有毒、腐蚀性、放射性等而在外包装上印刷的图片与短语的结合，以示警告，使装卸、运输和保管人员按货物特性采取相应的防护措施，以保护物资和人身安全，如图 5-17 所示。

图 5-17 常用警告性标志

2.4 Bar Code Mark 条形码标志

Universal Product Code (short for UPC) is also called Bar Code which refers to the electronic identification code attached on the commodities. The product code on the packing is a group of parallel stripes with numbers, which are black and white and of different intervals. The standard bar code is a special code language read by the optical scanning device in order to input data on the computer.

通用产品码，也被称为条形码，是指附在产品上用以进行电子识别的代码。即，条形码是一组带有数字的黑白及粗细间隔不等的平行条纹所组成，是利用光电扫描阅读设备为计算机输入数据的特殊的代码语言。

UPC-Universal Product Code compiled by Universal Code Council of America and Canada and EAN-European Article Number compiled by European Article Number Association, which is later called as Article Number Association (IANA)are the two most commonly adopted universal product codes. There are now five versions of UPC and two versions of EAN. See Fig. 5-18.

国际通用的条形码有两种：UPC 码和 EAN 码。（1）美国、加拿大组织的统一编码委员会的 UPC 码（Universal Product Code）;（2）欧盟国际物品编码协会的 EAN 码(European Article Number) 如图 5-18 所示。

EAN symbols have 12 digits and one check digit, and an EAN symbol uses the first three characters to designate the country of the EAN. International organization issuing the number, 4 digits centered indicates a manufacturer code, 5 digits suffix stands for product code. See Fig. 5-19.

EAN 共 13 位：由 12 位数字的产品代码和 1 位校验码（最后一位）组成。前三位为国别码，中间四位为厂商码, 后五位为产品代码，如图 5-19 所示。

图 5-18　条形码标志

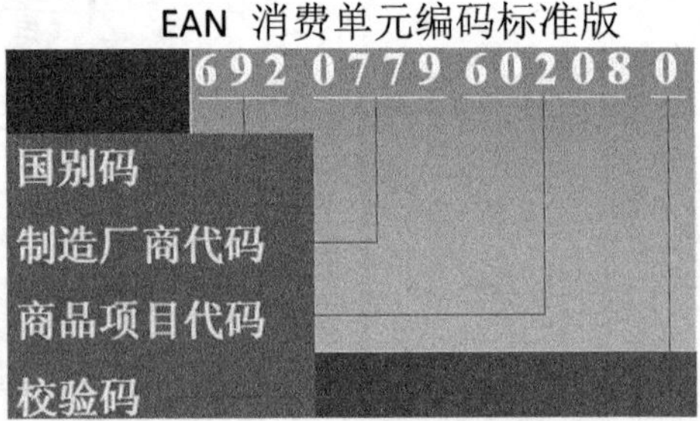

图 5-19　消费单元编码标准版

At present, the bar code used for all of sales packaging in the world. Commodity without bar code, even if famous commodity, cannot enter into supermarket; it can only be classified as low-grade goods to enter into discount stores. Some countries prohibit importing products without bar code mark. The application of bar codes mark improves efficiency and accuracy of settlement and convenience for customers.

目前，许多国家超级市场的商品包装均有条形码，如果商品包装上没有条形码，即使是名优商品，也不能进入超级市场，只能以低级产品进入折扣店；有些国家则规定，如果包装上没有条形码就不予进口。条形码的使用，大大提高了结算的效率和准确性，也方便了顾客。

China formally joined the International Article Number Association in April, 1991, and is assigned to the number of “690~699”(not including HangKong 489, Maco 958, Taiwan 471). Commodity with this kinds of numbers in bar codes which means they are made in China.

我国于 1991 年 4 月正式加入国际物品编码协会，成为正式会员。该会分配给我国的国别号为“690～699”（不包括中国香港 489、中国澳门 958、中国台湾 471），凡适用于使用此条形码的商品，即表示为中国产品。

Section Four　Packing Clause in a Sales Contract
第四节　合同中的包装条款

1. Clause of Packing in a Sales Contract 合同中的包装条款

Clauses of packing usually include packing material, packing manner, packing expenses and shipping marks. The following points need good attention.

合同中的包装条款一般包括：包装材料、包装方式、包装费用和运输标志等内容。注意如下几点。

（1）Stating the Stipulations of Packing Clearly 对包装的规定要明确具体

Detailed requirement for packaging materials and techniques should be clearly stated. Such ambiguous expression as “seaworthy packing” or “customary packing” should be avoided.

商品包装材料、包装方式、包装规格应当根据商品的特点和运输方式而定，在合同中明确规定。不要采用笼统含糊的语言规定包装条款。比如：习惯包装、适合海运包装等。

（2）Paying Attention to Commodity Characteristics and Law Requirement 考虑商品特性及有关法律

The seller should adopt appropriate package according to different characteristics of goods and transportation. For instance, for ceramic, glass and other commodities, packaging that is anti-collision and shatter-resistant should be used.

卖方应根据商品的特点以及不同的运输方式，采用合适的包装。如针对陶瓷、玻璃等商品，应采取防碰撞、防碎的包装。

（3）Specifying the Bearer of Packing Charges 明确包装费用由谁负担

The packaging expenses are usually included in the price, and shall be afforded by the seller. Who delivers the goods as well as the packing to the buyer. However, it should be stipulated in the contract that who bears the cost if the buyer requests the special packing.

包装费用一般包括在货价之内，不另计收，由卖方负责。如果买方要求特殊包装，双方应在合同中具体规定负担的费用和支付的办法。

（4）Which Party Provide Shipping Mark 何方提供运输标志

Which party provid shipping mark should be stated out. According to the practice, shipping mark is always given by the seller. However, it should be stipulated in the contract that who bears the cost if the buyer requests the special requirement.

何方提供运输标志应明确订立。按照国际贸易习惯，唛头一般由卖方决定；但如果买方有特殊要求，则应在合同中具体规定。

2. Samples of Packing Clause 买卖合同的包装条款样例

（1）"In cartons of 10 kilos net each." 纸箱装，每箱净重 10 千克。

（2）"In cloth bales each containing 10 pcs. of 42 yd." 布包，每包 10 匹，每匹 42 码。

（3）"10 pieces to a box, 20 boxes to an export carton." 每 10 件装一盒子，20 盒装一出口纸箱。

（4）"Shipping mark is to be determined by the seller." "唛头" 由卖方决定。

（5）"All the packing charges have been included in the Unit Price."

全部包装费用都已经包括在单价里面了。

（6）"Suitable for the long-distance sea transportation exports wooden box packaging, and have good moisture-proof, moisture resistance and anti-corrosion properties."

适合长途海运出口的新木箱包装，并具有良好的防潮、防湿、防震和防锈性能。

3. Attentions in Packaging Clause 包装条款应注意的问题

We should pay attention to these questions:

（1）Packing must be suitable for ocean shipment and sufficiently strong to withstand rough handling. Bales must be press-packed and hoped; with adequate inside waterproof protection and the outer wrapping must comprise good quality canvas.

（2）Cases or other outside containers must be externally of the smallest cubic dimension consistent with adequate protection of the goods.

（3）Packages must bear full marks and shipping numbers stenciled in good quality stencil ink in large plain characters on two sides and one end of each package.

（4）All bales must be marked "use no hooks".

在订立包装条款时应注意下列问题：

（1）包装必须适合海运，并能经受住粗暴的操作。包装必须经过紧压，内部用适当的防水保护层，外部由上好品质的帆布包裹。

（2）包装箱或其他外部的集装箱在外形上必须体积最小并能对货物起到充分的保护作用。

（3）包装上必须有运输标志，包装物的两面及每一件包装的底部都要用良好的印刷墨水印刷大而清晰的运输数目。

（4）所有的包装上都要标明"勿使用吊钩"。

【Review Questions】复习思考题

【Typical Case Link 1—典例链接 1】

Question: Try to analyze the case.

问题：试对此案例作出评析。

One Chinese export company exported some goods to Canada, valued at USD 900 000. The contract stated that it should be packed in plastic bags marks with English and French on each item. But the Chinese company used other packaging instead in the actual delivery, and still used only English marks. The foreign merchant, in order to adapt to the requirements of the local market and sales, hired people to change the packing and shipping marks, then they filing claim to China. The Chinese company recognized they were wrong and compensated the customer.

中国某出口公司出口到加拿大一批货物，价值 90 万美元。合同规定用塑料袋包装，每件要使用英、法两种文字的唛头。但中国公司实际交货改用其他包装代替，并仍使用只有英文的唛头，国外商人为了适应当地市场的销售要求，不得不雇人重新更换包装和唛头，后向中方提出索赔，中方理亏只好认赔。

【Typical Case Link 2—典例链接 2】

Question: Why is this?

回答：买方为何提出这种要求？

A Singapore client with Shanghai Bicycle Factory to import "Forever" brand bicycle of 12 000 sets, but the Singapore client requested the Shanghai Factory to use "sword" brand trademark, and shall not indicate in the packaging of "Made in China".

新加坡某客户与中国上海某自行车厂洽谈进口"永久牌"自行车 12 000 辆，但要求中方改用"剑"牌商标，并在包装上不得注明"中国制造"字样。

【Typical Case Link 3—典例链接 3】

Question: Please analyse whether the customs' act is right or not.

回答：请分析海关的处理是否正确。

During the 2002 World Cup, a Japanese importer placed an order with a Chinese exporter of T-shirts for promotion sports drinks, requesting the red grounding color printing " Japan Korea World Cup", no other printing is needed. All the shirts should be given with beverage sales to the fans during the World Cup as promotion method. Being stipulated in the contract, the deadline of shipment was May 20th, 2002. The Chinese exporter organized the production and on May 25th, sent the goods and prepared all the documents to the negotiating bank. However, because the Japanese team went no further to top 16, to avoid the possible backlog, the Japanese side, with an excuse of documents presented with discrepancies refused to pay. After several times of null negotiation, the exporter could only ship the goods back to China to reduce losses, but the customs thought the "Japan Korea World Cup" and the English intellectual property are held by FIFA, and the Chinese exporter cannot issue a real effective use of commercial documents, thus infringing an intellectual property right so the customs destroyed the impounded T-shirts.

2002 年世界杯期间，日本一进口商为了促销运动饮料，向中国出口商订购 T 恤衫，要求以红色为底色，并印制"韩日世界杯"字样，此外不需印制任何标识，以在世界杯期间作为促销手段随饮料销售赠送现场球迷。合同规定 2002 年 5 月 20 日为最后装运期，中方组织生产后于 5 月 25 日将货物按质量装运出港，并备齐所有单据向银行议付货款。然而货到时由于日本队止步于 16 强，日方估计到可能的积压损失，以单据不符为由拒绝赎单。在多次协商无效的情况下，我方只能将货物运回以在国内销售减少损失，但是在货物途经海关时，海关认为由于"韩日世界杯"字样及英文标识的知识产权为国际足联所持有，而中方外贸公司不能出具真实有效的商业使用权证明文件，因此海关以侵犯知识产权为由，扣留并销毁了这一批 T 恤衫。

Chapter Six　Trade Terms and Price of Goods

第六章　国际贸易术语与价格条款

【Learning Objectives】教学目的与要求

After learning this chapter, you will be able to:

1. Acknowledge the importance and function of various kinds of Trade Terms;
2. Understand the calculation of commission and discount;
3. Familiar with the calculation & quotation of goods Price.

【Lead-in Case】引导案例

Question: Do you think the contract signed like this is correct?

问题：如此签约是否正确?

A company exported a batch of strong seasonal goods to a British customer on CIF terms. The two parties agreed to stipulate in the contract：The buyer should send the relative L/C before the end of September, while the seller should guarantee that the vessel arrived at the port of destination by 2nd December. Once the vessel arrived at the destination later than 2nd December, the buyer has the right to cancel the contract. If payment has been made, the seller should return it to the buyer.

某公司按 CIF 伦敦向英国出口一批季节性较强的货物，双方在合同中规定：买方须于 9 月底前将信用证开到，卖方保证运货船只不得迟于 12 月 2 日驶抵目的港。如货轮迟于 12 月 2 日驶抵目的港，买方有权取消合同。如货款已收，卖方须将货款退还买方。

Section One Trade Terms
第一节 贸易术语概述

1. Trade Terms 贸易术语

1.1 Concept 概念

Trade terms, also reference to as Price Terms or Price Conditions, are abbreviations of letters or words specifying specific price composition and liabilities, cost and risk in the delivery of goods between the seller and buyer.

贸易术语也称为价格术语或价格条件，它是指利用短语或英文缩写说明商品的价格构成及买卖双方在货物交接的过程中有关风险、责任和费用的划分的专门用语。

It covers two basic meanings. Firstly trade terms indicate commodity price composition, e.g. FOB excludes freight and insurance premium which are paid by the buyer, while CIF is the opposite. Second, trade terms are specified terms concerning place of delivery, risks, obligations and costs during delivery of goods between the seller and the buyer.

这一定义包含两层意思。第一层含义：贸易术语说明了商品价格的构成，例如，用 FOB 不包含运费、保费，称离岸价，运保费要由买方出；CIF 则相反，运费、保费都已在包含的货价中，由卖方承担。第二层含义：贸易术语是买卖双方在货物交接过程中，关于交货地点、风险、责任、费用如何划分的专门用语。

1.2 Function 作用

Price term lies at the core of the terms and conditions of a contract. In international trade, the pricing problem is far more complicated than that in domestic trade. Because quotation should also indicate which party is to bear the expenses of freightage insurance and other relevant charges except cost of goods, and which party is to bear the risks in case of the goods being damaged. In order to complete their deals successfully, make clear to each other their respective obligations, at the very beginning of the deal, and find the full expression of these in the trade terms. Therefore, trade terms, which are used unified and specific language for worldwide merchants, they take shape gradually in international practice greatly simplify dealing procedures, improve efficiency, promote the development of international trade and play significant roles in international trade.

价格条款是合同中所有条款的核心。在国际贸易中，进口商和出口商所要解决的价格问题比国内贸易中的价格问题复杂得多，因为出口报价除了要包括成本以外，还要指明由哪一方承担运费，保险费和其他相关费用，由哪一方承担货物受损的风险。只有通过贸易术语（又称价格术语），才能明确双方的责任，从而顺利地完成交易。因此，作为全世界国际贸易商人的统一专门用语，贸易术语的出现大大简化了交易程序，提高了交易效率，有力地促进了国际贸易的发展，在国际贸易中具有重要的作用。

2. International Trade Practice 有关国际贸易术语的国际贸易惯例

2.1 Definition 国际贸易惯例的定义

International trade customs are universally recognized customary ways of doing business and explanation evolving in the long process of trade development and has been compiled by relative international organizations into rules and regulations which are acquainted, recognized and adopted by many trading organization in most countries.

国际贸易惯例是在国际贸易的长期实践中逐步发展形成的具有普遍意义的一些习惯做法和解释，经过有关国际组织的编纂与解释成为规则、条文，并为较多的国家或贸易团体所熟悉、承认和采用。

2.2 Feature 国际贸易惯例的性质

（1）International trade customs are neither legislations or laws for all countries, nor laws of a certain country.

它不是各国的共同立法，也不是某一国的法律，不具有法律的强制性。

（2）When both parties cite one international custom, it becomes legally valid and both parties are subject to it. If the contract clause conflict with customs, the contract to be followed is as a basic principle. Even if the contract does not indicate which custom the contract is subject to, the custom still has binding force.

当买卖双方在合同中援引某项惯例时，则该惯例即具有法律效力，对双方均有约束力，有法律强制性。如果合同的条款与惯例有冲突，将遵循合同优先惯例的原则。合同中未引入某项惯例，惯例仍有约束力。

（3）Both parties could make out some clause different from customs when signing a contract on the principle of contract first.

遵循契约至上原则，合同双方当事人在签订合同时也可以作出与惯例不同的规定。

Nowadays, some international conventions and laws endow the customs legality. E.g. CISG (UNIITED NATIONS CONVENTION ON CONTRACTS FOR THE INTERNATIONAL SALE OF GOODS (1980)[CISG] stipulates that the commonly used and universally know customs which are not excluded from the contract are binding to both parties. China's laws indicate what the law fails to cover is subject to international trade customs.

目前新的趋势是，某些国际公约或某些国家以立法的形式直接赋予惯例法律效力。如《联合国国际货物销售合同公约》规定：合同没有排除的惯例，已经知道或应当知道的惯例和经常反复遵守的惯例对双方当事人均有约束力；再如，我国的法律规定：凡是中国法律没有规定的适用国际贸易惯例。

2.3 International Practice of Trade Terms 贸易术语的国际惯例

2.3.1 Characteristics 特征

In order to avoid, or at least reduce to a considerable degree, the uncertainties of different interpretations of such terms in different countries, the international Chamber of Commerce (ICC) first published a set of international rules for the interpretation of the most commonly used trade terms in foreign trade in 1936. These rules were known as "INCOTERMS 1936". Amendments and additions were later made in 1953, 1967, 1976, 1980, 1990, 2000 and presently 2010 in order to bring the rules in line with current international trade practices. The latest version, INCOTERMS 2010 came into force on 1st January 2011.

为了避免在不同的国家对这类术语可能产生的歧义，或者至少把产生歧义的可能性降到最低程度，国际商会于 1936 年首次出版了一套国际通则，解释对外贸易中最常用的贸易术语，即《1936 年国际贸易术语解释通则》（简称《1936 年通则》）。为了使这些通则符合现实的国际惯例，后来曾于 1953 年、1967 年、1976 年、1980 年、1990 年、2000 年和最近的 2010 年对其进行了修改和补充。最近的一次修订是 2011 年 1 月 1 日起生效的《2010 通则》。

Therefore, International Convention of Trade Terms are not a common legislation and without legally binding force upon both parties to a contract. This implies that if the stipulations in a contract are in conformity with that of the law but not with trade terms, parties thereto should follow the relevant legislation rather than trade convention. If a contract stipulates that a certain convention should be applicable, this convention will be binding upon both parties. In case of a dispute, courts or arbitrators will judge the case according to the convention cited in the contract.

因此，国际贸易术语惯例是在国际贸易业务中反复实践的习惯做法，经国际贸易组织加以编纂而成的，其本身不是法律，不具有强制性，这隐含着合同中的规定必须合法而不是符合贸易术语。合同中贸易双方当事人必须合法贸易。如果合同都同意采用某种惯例来约束该项贸易，并在合同中作出明确规定时，这项约定的惯例就有了强制性。

It should be stressed that the scope of INCOTERMS is limited to matters relating to the rights and obligations of the parties to the contract of sale with respect to the delivery of goods sold (in the sense of "tangible").

需要强调指出的是这些《通则》涵盖的范围主要指销售合同当事人的权利和义务中与已售货物（仅指"有形货物"）交货的有关事项。

2.3.2 Three Most Influential Trade Terms Conventions 三个有影响力的贸易术语惯例

（1）"WARSAW-OXFORD RULES 1932" 《1932 年华沙—牛津规则》

It is mainly used to indicate the nature and characteristic of the CIF contract and drafted at a conference of the international law association in Warsaw. In the mid 19th century, CIF is widely applied in international trade, however, there are no unified explanations or rules on each party's obligation drafted and adopted rules for CIF contracts in the capital of Poland, Warsaw in 1928. After that, this rule is combined into 21 provisions in Oxford conference in 1932 and renamed as Warsaw-Oxford rules 1932 used till now.

这是国际法协会制定的，专门解释了 CIF 这一贸易术语的本质特性。19 世纪中叶起，CIF 贸易术语在国际贸易术语中得到了广泛的应用，由于这一贸易术语对买卖双方各自承担的义务没有统一的规定和解释，在交易中经常发生争议和纠纷。国际法协会于 1928 年在波兰首都华沙起草并制定 CIF 统一规则。其后，于 1932 年牛津会议上，将此规则定为 21 条，更名为《1932 年华沙—牛津规则》，沿用至今。

（2）Revised American Foreign Trade Definitions 1941 《1941 年美国对外贸易定义修订本》

It is drafted by the constitutors are chamber of Commerce of the United States of America, American importers association (AIA) and National foreign trade council, etc. It includes 6 Terms namely, EX (Point of Origin), FOB (Free on Board), FAS, C&F,CIF and EX dock and is used in some North American and Latin American countries.

它是由美国商会、美国进口商会和美国对外贸易协会等联合制定。主要适用于北美及拉丁美洲国家。内容包括 6 六种术语，即：

① Ex Point of Origin（原产地交货）

② Free on Board（运输工具上交货）

该术语有以下 6 种解释：

- FOB (named inland carrier at named inland point of departure) 即在指定的发货地点于指定的内陆运输工具上交货；
- FOB (named inland carrier at named inland point of departure) freight prepaid to (named point of exportation)即在指定的内陆发货地点的指定的内陆运输工具上交货，运费预付到指定的出口地点；
- FOB (named inland carrier at named inland point of departure) freight allowed to (named point)即在指定的内陆发货地点的指定的内陆运输工具上交货，减除至指定地点的运费；
- FOB (named inland carrier at named of exportation) 即在指定的出口地点的指定的内陆运输工具上交货；
- FOB Vessel (named port of shipment) 即指定装运港船上交货；
- FOB (named inland point in country of importation) 即在指定进口国内陆地点交货。

③ Free Along Side（运输工具旁边交货）

④ Cost and Freight（成本加运费）

⑤ Cost，Insurance and Freight（成本加保险费、运费）

⑥ Ex Dock（目的港码头交货）

（3）INCOTERMS 2000 《2000 年国际贸易术语解释通则》

INCOTERMS 1990 consists of 13 trade rules. INCOTERMS 2000 groups the 13 rules into 4 categories. See Fig. 6-1.

1990 年修订是主要内容包含 13 个贸易术语。《2000 通则》保留了这 13 个贸易术语，并把贸易术语分成 4 组，如图 6-1 所示。

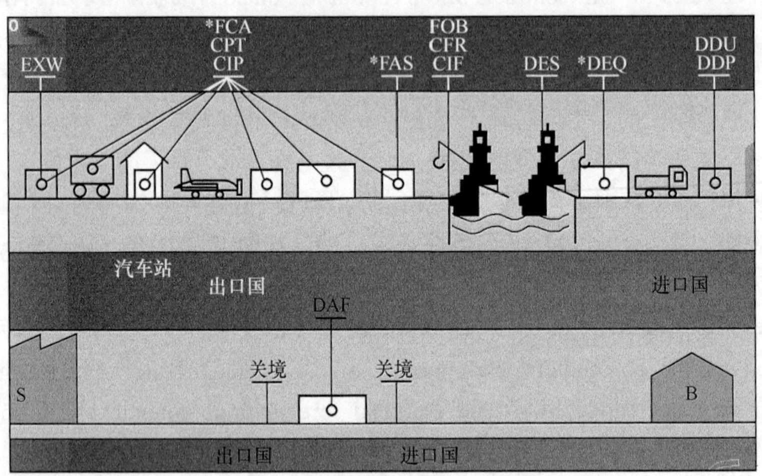

图 6-1　2000 年国际贸易术语解释通则

Compared with INCOTERMS 2000, the key changes of INCOTERMS 2010 consolidates the “delivered” rules, reducing the total number of rules from 13 to 11. The INCOTERMS 2010 rules, DAF, DES, DEQ and DDU are replaced by two new INCOTERMS Crules DAT and DAP. Consolidation of “D” Terms as follows:

与《2000 通则》相比，《2010 通则》改为 11 个贸易术语，删去了原来 D 组的 DAF、DES、DEQ、和 DDU，新增加了 DAT 和 DAP 如下：

- DAF-Delivered At Frontier 边境交货；
- DES-Delivered Ex Ship 目的港船上交货；
- DEQ-Delivered Ex Quay 目的港码头交货；
- DDU-Delivered Duty Unpaid 未完税交货。
- The DDP (Delivered Duty Paid) is unchanged and is joined by the following new “D” rules. 只有“完税后交货术语”不变，并且再加入如下两个新的术语。
- DAT-Delivered at Terminal 运输终端交货

DAP-Delivered at Place 目的地交货，如图 6-2 所示。See Fig. 6-2.

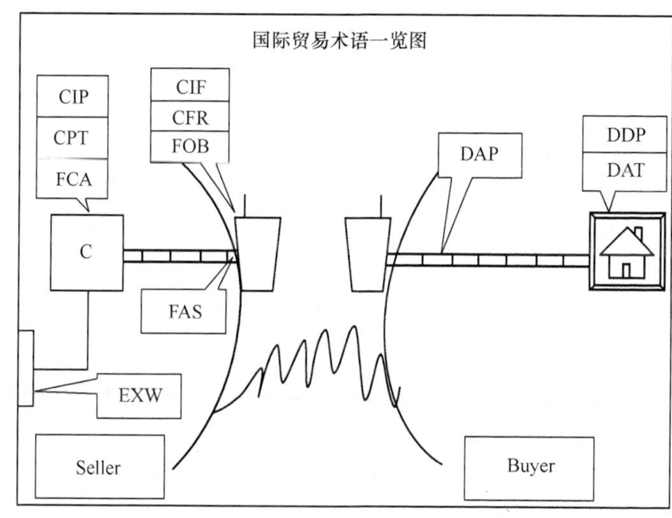

图 6-2 2010 国际贸易术语解释通则

As in 2000, INCOTERMS 2010 was very prevailing and grouped into four basically different categories, namely starting with the term whereby the seller only makes the goods available to the buyer at the seller’s own premises (the “E”-terms Ex Works), followed by the second group whereby the seller is called upon to deliver the goods to a carrier appointed by the buyer (the “F”-term FCA, FAS and FOB), which continuing with the “C”-terms wcrc the seller has to contract for carriage but without assuming the risk of loss of or damage to the goods or additional costs due to events occurring after shipment and dispatch (CFR,CIF,CPT and CIP); and finally the “D”-terms whereby the seller has to bear all costs and risks needed to bring the goods to the pace of destination (DAT,DAP and DDP). The following chart sets out the classification of the trade terms. See Fig. 6-3.

与 2000 年版本一样，《2010 年通则》中的贸易术语被广泛地使用并划分为四组不同的基本类型：第一组“E 组”只有一个术语（EX Works），即卖方在自己的地点为买方备妥货物；第二组“F 组”（FCA、FAS 和 FOB），要求卖方将货物交给买方指定的承运人；第三组为“C 组”（CFR、CIF、CPT 和 CIP），卖方须订立运输合同，但对货物灭失或损坏的风险以及装船和启运后发生意外事故所产生的额外费用，不予承担责任；最后一组为“D 组”（DAT、DAP 和 DDP），卖方必须承担把货物交至目的地国所需要的全部费用和风险。下面是列明贸易术语这种分类的图表，如表 6-1 所示。

表 6-1　　2010 INCOTERMS 2010 国际贸易术语解释通则

组别	术语	合同性质	含义
E 组（启运） Group E Departure	EXW	出口地交货贸易术语，合同为装运合同 Shipment Contract	工厂交货 EX works
F 组（主运费未付） Group F Main Carriage unpaid	FCA FAS FOB		货交承运人 Free carrier 船边交货 Free alongside ship 船上交货 Free on board
C 组（主运费已付） Group C Main Carriage Paid	CFR CIF CPT CIP		成本加运费 Cost and Freight 成本、保险费加运费 Cost, Insurance and Freight 运费付至 Carriage Paid to 运费、保险费付至 Carriage and Insurance Paid To
D 组（到达） Group D Arrival	DAT DAP DDP	到达合同 Arrival Contract	运输终端交货 Delivered at terminal 目的地交货 Delivered at place 完税后交货 Delivered duty paid

In details, the terms have been grouped in four basically different categories.

具体地讲，贸易术语可分为四组。

（1）Namely starting with the only terms where-by the seller makes the goods available to the buyer at the seller's own premises (the "E" terms Ex-works).

（2）Then the second group where-by the seller is called upon to deliver the goods to a carrier appointed by the buyer (the "F" terms FCA, FAS and FOB).

（3）Then the "C" terms where-by the seller has to contract for carriage, but without assuming the risk of, loss of, or damage to the goods or additional costs due to events occurring after shipment and dispatch (CFR, CIF, CPT and CIP), but the seller doesn't need shoulder the risk or extra payment caused by goods loss after shipment. By CIF and CIP terms, the seller have to cover insurance for the goods shipped and pay the premium as well. The contract based on the "C" terms is a shipment contract, in which the delivery term is the shipment time or delivery time, but not the arrival destination port or destination time.

（4）Finally, the "D" terms which the seller has to bear all costs and risks mean to carry the goods to the country of destination (DAT, DAP and DDP). So we say the contract based on these terms can be called arrival contract, in which, both the place and the time of destination should be stipulated clearly in the contract. The "D" terms can be divided into two groups which are DAT and DAP, which the seller is not responsible for customs clearance; DDP, the seller is responsible for customs clearance.

E 组为发货（启运，Departure）术语，只有 EXW 一种。就此术语，卖方在他自己的处所将货物提供给买方，即履行了交货义务。

F 组为主运费未付（Main Carriage Unpaid）术语，共有 FCA、FAS、FOB 三种。按 F 组术语，卖方必须将货物交给由买方指定的承运人或运输工具，即完成交货义务。由买方自负费用订立运输合同并指定承运人。

C 组为主运费已付（Main Carriage Paid）术语，包括 CFR、CIF、CPT、CIP 四种。按这些术语，卖方必须负责按通常条件订立运输合同，并支付到合同规定的目的港或目的地的正常费用，但不负担由于装运和发运后发生的事故所引起的货物灭失的风险或额外费用。其中 CIF 和 CIP 术语的卖方尚需负责投保货物运输险和支付保险费。按 C 组术语达成的合同属装运合同（Shipment Contract），在合同中规定交货期条款时，只能规定装运期或发货期，而不能规定到达目的港或目的地的日期。

D 组为到达（Arrival）术语，共有 DAT、DAP 和 DDP 三种。按这类术语达成的交易，卖方必须负担将货物运至目的地国家所需的一切费用和风险。因此，用 D 组术语达成的合同术语到达合同（Arrival Contract），在合同中规定交货期条款时，要规定货物到达目的港或目的地的期限。D 组分为两类：DAT 和 DAP，即卖方不负责货物进口清关和卖方负责进口清关。

In a word, one of the main features of the INCOTERMS 2010 is that they are available for international and domestic sale contracts. The forming of various trade blocs, like the European Union, has been made as a must for the rules to be application for both international and domestic trade. Hence, "International rules for the interpretation of trade terms，2010", are the most widely used, influential and important international practices published by ICC and all trade terms in this textbook are subject to it .

总之，《2010 通则》的一个很重要的特点是其中所涉及的国际贸易术语对国际和国内货物买卖合同均可适用。由于像欧盟这样的贸易同盟的出现使国际贸易术语必须在适用于国际贸易的同时也能适用于国内贸易。因此，《国际贸易术语解释通则 2010》（简称"INCOTERMS 2010"）是目前使用最广泛、影响最大、最重要的一个国际贸易惯例，本课程所提到的贸易术语的解释都以该通则为准。

Section Two Six Symbolic Delivery Trade Terms
第二节 六种象征性交货贸易术语

1. Symbolic Delivery 象征性交货

In international trade, FOB, CFB, CIF, FCA, CPT and CIP are the most widely used terms of 11 trade terms. nowadays, they are used as trade terms for symbolic delivery. FOB, CFR and CIF are suitable for sea and inland waterway transport. FCA, CPT and CIP are used irrespective of modes of transportation.

在 11 种国际贸易术语中 FOB、CFR、CIF、FCA、CPT 和 CIP 是六个最常用的贸易术语，在现代的国际贸易中，它们已经升华为象征性交货的贸易术语。其中的 FOB、CFR 和 CIF 适合海上和河内运输，而 FCA、CPT 和 CIP 适合任何运输方式。

Symbolic Delivery is compared with physical delivery.

所谓象征性交货是针对实际交货（Physical Delivery）而言。

Symbolic Delivery refers to that the seller fulfills obligation on condition that the seller ships the goods on board as the contract stipulates at port of shipment within due time and delivers related entitled documents as stipulated on the contract. The risks are transferred when the goods are on board. The seller is liable for loading the goods in due time and has no guarantee for the arrival of goods.

象征性交货是指卖方只要按照合同规定的时间在装运港把货物装上船并向买方提交了合同规定的代表货物所有权凭证的有关单据，就算完成了交货义务。风险在货物装上船时由卖方转移给买方，卖方只负责按时装运，无需负责保证到货。

The core of Symbolic delivery is the buying and selling of related documents instead of physical goods, in other words, delivering the documents is delivering goods by the seller to the buyer.

象征性交货的核心是单据的买卖，双方交易的是单据而不是货物，也就是说卖方只要向买方交货。

The seller delivers the goods against documents and the buyer pay for the goods against the documents. As long as the seller provides all sets of qualified documents in due time and even if the goods are damaged or lost during shipment.

卖方是凭单交货，买方是凭单付款，只要卖方如期向买方提交了全套合格单据，即使货物在运输途中损坏或灭失，买方也必须履行付款义务。

The buyer shall pay, reversely, if the seller provides wrong documents and even if the goods are in goods shape, the buyer may refuse to pay.

相反地，如果卖方提交的单据不符合要求，即使货物完好无损地到达目的地，买方仍有权拒绝付款。

Symbolic delivery creates a new epoch of international trade. And symbolic delivery is the basic of understanding modern international settlement and credit dealings.

象征性交货开创了国际贸易的新纪元。理解什么是象征性交货才能理解现代的国际结算、信用证交易。

2. FOB、CFR、CIF 装运港交货的三种常用贸易术语

2.1 FOB: Free on Board (named port of shipment) 装运港船上交货（指定装运港），又称“离岸价”

It shall be followed by the name of port of shipment, like FOB London.

采用这术语后加注装运港名称：如 FOB London。

（1）Definition 定义

The seller is responsible for shipping the contracted goods on board. The ship nominated by the buyer at the port of shipment within specific period and beared all costs and risks before the goods are on board the vessel.

卖方在合同规定的装运港和期限内将合同规定的货物装到买方指定的船上，并负担货物装上船为止的一切费用和风险。

（2）Obligations 买卖双方的义务

“Free on Board” means that the seller fulfills his obligation to deliver when the goods have passed over the ship’s rail at the named port of shipment. This means that the buyer has to bear all costs and risks of loss or damage to the goods from that point. The FOB term requires the seller to clear the goods for export. When the ship’s rail serves no practical purpose, such as in the case of roll-on/roll-off or container traffic, the FCA term is more appropriate.

“装运港船上交货”是指当货物在指定装运港越过船舷时，卖方即履行了义务，这是指买方必须自该交货点起，负担一切费用和货物灭失或损失的风险。FOB 术语要求卖方办理货物出口清关。如果船舷不适合实际需要，比如在滚装运输或集装箱运输的情况下，则 FCA

术语更为适用。

（3）The Cancellation of the Concept “Cross the Rail” “船舷为界”概念的取消

It is a historic practice before INCOTERMS 2010 to regard the rail as the boundary. However, some defects were found in practical application. Moreover, the meaning of it is obscure. “Revised American Foreign Trade Definition 1941” has stipulated that the risk of transfers when the goods are on board the ship. INCOTERMS 2010 specified that the risk of loss and damage to the goods passes when the goods are on board the vessel, and the buyer bears all costs from that moment onwards. It could be an engagement that both parties agree to regard boarding on ship as the boundary. The concept of “cross the rail” was cancelled thereafter.

以船舷作为划分风险的界限是《2010 通则》以前长期沿用的一种惯例，但是在实际应用中有很多缺陷，不是很确切。《1941 年美国对外贸定义》是以货物装上船作为风险划分的界限，有它的科学性。《2010 通则》在关于 FOB 风险划分时就作了重新规定：货物的灭失和损坏的风险在货物装上船时起即由卖方转移至由买方承担，取消了以船舷为界划分风险的概念，明确规定以货物装上船作为风险划分的界限。

（4）Methods of Transport 运输方式

This term can only be used for sea and inland waterway transport.

该术语只能适合于海运和内河运输。

（5）Variations of FOB FOB 术语变形

In order to make it clearly who is responsible for loading the goods, the buyer and the seller may add some additional conditions, which become the variations under FOB. These variations concern only problems relating to different kinds of charges. They do not affect the separation of risk and the property transfer in the goods.

为了明确由谁来负担装船费用，买卖双方往往在 FOB 术语后加列附加条件，这就形成了 FOB 术语变形。这些变形主要解释买卖双方所负费用问题，而不影响风险转移和货物的交接。FOB 术语变形主要有：

We may adopt, if necessary, the variations of FOB to indicate who shall bear the loading expense. The most commonly used variations of FOB are:

a. FOB Liner Terms

On FOB liner terms, the seller is responsible only for delivering the goods to the Liner Company’s warehouse, CY or to the place within the reach of the tackle of the ship. This means that the loading expense is borne by the party who pays the freight, i.e., the buyer, just as the goods are transported by the liner. So the seller is not responsible for the loading expenses.

a. FOB 班轮条件：指卖方负责将货物交到班轮公司仓库、CY 或吊钩所及之处，有关装船费用按班轮条件办理，即卖方不负担有关装船的费用。

b. FOB Under Tackle

The seller is responsible for delivering the goods under the tackle of the buyer’s named ship, and shall not bear the expenses for loading the goods into the ship’s hold and other expenses.

b. FOB 吊钩下交货：指卖方仅负责将货物交到买方指定船只的吊钩所及之处，有关装船的各项费用如衬垫费、驳船费、保护加固费等一概由买方负担。

c. FOB Stowed(FOBS)

The seller shall be responsible for loading the goods into the hold, and bear the loading expense, including the stowing expense.

c. 船上交货并理舱：指卖方负责将货物装入船舱并支付包括理舱费在内的装船费用。

d. FOB Trimmed(FOBT)

The seller shall be responsible for loading the goods into the hold and bear the loading expense, including the trimming expense. i.e., the seller has to bear the cost of leveling the goods, especially the bulky cargoes so that the ship will sail smoothly and steadily.

d. 船上交货并平舱：指卖方负责将货物装入船舱并支付包括平舱费在内的装船费用，如衬垫费、驳船费、保护加固费等。

e. FOB Stowed and Trimmed(FOBST)

Loading, stowing and trimming charges are to be borne by the seller.

e. 船上交货并理舱和平舱：指卖方负责将货物装入船舱并支付包括理舱费和平舱费在内的装船费用。

（6）Some points to FOB 关于 FOB 的几个问题

When adopting the FOB terms, we shall pay attention to the following points:

① Delivery of the goods on board the vessel;

② Link-up of vessel and goods;

③ Expense for loading the goods on board the vessel.

Under the FOB terms, in case the buyer charters a liner to carry the goods, since liner charges contain loading and unloading expenses, therefore the loading expense is actually borne by the buyer. In case the goods are carried by a chartered vessel, the two parties shall negotiate who shall bear the loading expense and stipulate it clearly in the contract.

使用该术语时要注意以下三点：

① 船上交货的要求；

② 船货衔接问题；

③ 货物装船的费用问题。

在 FOB 术语下，如果是买方负责派船到装运港区接货，由于租船费用包括装货和卸货费用，那么，实际上装货费用是由买方负责。如果是班轮条件办理，那么买卖双方可以协商由买方还是卖方承担装货费用，并在合同中明确规定。

2.2 CFR: Cost and Freight(named port of destination) 成本加运费（指定目的港）

It shall be followed by the name of port of destination, like CFR London.

采用这术语后加注目的港名称：如 CFR 伦敦。

（1）Definition 定义

The seller is responsible for shipping the contracted goods on board. The ship nominated by the buyer at the port of shipment within specific period and beared all costs and freight necessary to bring the goods to the named port of destination.

卖方在合同规定的装运港和期限内把合同规定的货物装到买方指定的船上，并负担将货物运至指定目的港所必需的费用和运费。

（2）Obligations 买卖双方的义务

"Cost and Freight" means that the seller is responsible for chartering a liner and loading the goods on the liner at the stipulated time in the contract. The buyer must undertake the costs and freight necessary to bring the goods to the named port of destination but the risk of loss of or damage to the goods, as well as any additional costs due to events occurring after the time the goods have been delivered on board the vessel, is transferred from the seller to the buyer when the goods pass the ship's rail at the port of shipment. The CFR term requires the seller to clear the goods for export. When the ship's rail serves no practical purpose, such as in the case of roll-on/roll-off or container traffic, the CPT term is more appropriate to use.

"成本加运费"是指卖方负责租船或订船，在合同规定的期限内将货物装到运往指定目的港的船上，卖方必须支付将货物运至指定目的港所必须的费用和运费。但当货物在装运港越过船舷时，货物灭失或损坏的风险，以及由于货物已装上船后发生的事件而引起的任何额外费用，自卖方转移到买方。该术语要求卖方办理货物出口清关，并只能适合于海运和内河运输。如果船舷不适合实际需要，比如在滚装运输或集装箱运输的情况下，则 CPT 术语更为适用。

（3）Methods of Transport 运输方式

This term can only be used for sea and inland waterway transport.

该术语只能适合于海运和内河运输。

（4）Some Points to CFR 关于 CFR 的几个问题

When adopting the CFR term, we shall pay attention to the following points:

① Bearing unloading expenses;

② Responsibilities of chartering;

③ Shipping advice.

使用该术语时要注意以下几点：

① 卸货费用的负担；

② 租船或订舱的责任；

③ 关于装船通知。

In case the goods are delivered by a chartered vessel, the two parties shall stipulate who shall pay the unloading/discharging expenses at the port of destination in the contract. In order to make it clearly who is responsible for the loading of the goods, the buyer and the seller may add some additional conditions, which become the variations under CFR. These variations concern only problems relating to different kinds of charges. They do not affect the separation of risk and the property transfer in the goods. We may adopt, if necessary, the variations of CFR to indicate who shall bear the unloading expense. The most commonly used variations of CFR are:

a. CFR Liner Terms

The unloading expenses are borne by the party who pays freight, i.e., the seller or the shipping company.

b. CFR Ex ship's hold

The buyer shall bear the expenses for slinging up the goods from the hold to the dock. The discharging charges shall be borne by the buyer.

c. CFR Landed

The seller shall bear the expenses for unloading/landing the goods from the ship onto the dock or wharf or land at the port of destination, including the expenses of lighterage and dockage.

如果货物是有班轮条件办理，那么买卖双方必须在合同中明确规定货物在目的港的卸货费用由哪方承担。为了明确由谁来负担装船费用，买卖双方往往在 CFR 术语后加列附加条件，这就形成了 CFR 术语变形。这些变形主要解释买卖双方所负费用问题，而不影响风险转移和货物的交接。CFR 术语变形主要有：

a. CFR 班轮条件：指卸货费用由支付运费的一方负担，即卖方或承运人负担。

b. CFR 舱底交货：指货物运抵目的港后，自船舱起吊直到卸到码头的卸货费用由买方负担。

c. CFR 卸到岸上：指由卖方负担卸货费，包括驳船费和码头费。

2.3　CIF: Cost, Insurance and Freight (named port of destination) 成本、保险费加运费（指定目的港）又称“到岸价”

It shall be followed by the name of port of destination, like CIF London.

采用这术语后加注目的港名称：如 CIF 伦敦。

（1）Definition 定义

The seller is responsible for shipping the contracted goods on board, the ship nominated by the buyer at the port of shipment within specific period and bearing all costs, insurance and freight necessary to bring the goods to the named port of destination.

卖方在合同规定的装运港和期限内把合同规定的货物装到买方指定的船上，并负担支付将货物运至指定目的港所必需的费用、运费和保险。

（2）Obligations 买卖双方的义务

CIF means that the seller has the obligations to procure marine insurance against the risks of losses of or damage to the goods during the carriage. In other words, CIF means that the seller has the same obligations as under CFR but with the addition that he has to procure marine insurance against the buyer’s risk of loss of or damage to the goods during the carriage. The seller contracts for insurance and pays the insurance premium.

“成本、保险费加运费”是指卖方负责为货物在运输途中可能遭受的风险、灭失或损失投保。换句话说，其含义与 CFR 基本一致，只是在 CIF 价格条件下，卖方还要办理保险手续并交付保险费，在签订合同时卖方就应规定保险险别。

If CIF terms are adopted, the seller shall contract for insurance and pay the premium. But the buyer should note that under the CIF terms the seller is only required to obtain insurance for minimum coverage customary for a particular trade and clear the goods for export If the buyer needs particular coverage for the goods, it should be clearly stipulated in the contract, or the buyer should insure the goods themselves. When the ship’s rail serves no practical purpose such as in the case of roll-on/roll-off or container traffic, CIP is more appropriate.

如采用 CIF 术语，卖方必须办理保险手续并交付保险费。因此，卖方应订立保险合同并支付保险费。买方应注意到，“成本、保险费加运费”术语只要求卖方投保最低限度的保险险别。如买方需要更高的保险险别，则需与卖方明确达成协议，或者自行做出额外的保险安排。如果船舷不适合实际需要，比如在滚装或集装箱运输的情况下，则 CIP 术语更为适用。

（3）Methods of Transport 运输方式

CIF can only be used for sea and inland waterway transport.

CIF 术语只适用于海运和内河运输。

（4）Some Points to CIF 关于 CIF 的几个问题

① Duty of Insurance 保险责任

In different rules there are different stipulations. INCOTERMS 2010 stipulates "failing express agreement in the contract, be in accordance with minimum cover of the Institute Cargo Clause or any similar set of clauses when required by the buyer. The seller shall provide, at the buyer's expense, war, strikes, riots and civil commotion risk insurance if procurable. The minimum insurance shall cover the price provided in the contract plus 10% (i.e. 110%) and shall be provided in the currency of the contract". In international business practice, in case under the CIF terms, the two parties shall usually stipulate the specific cover and amount of insurance.

应保何种险别，不同惯例所做规定不一。《2010 通则》规定："若在合同中没有规定，投保范围应为协会（伦敦保险协会）货物条款或者其他类似保险条款中规定的最小范围。但在买方要求，并由买方承担费用的情况下，可加保战争、罢工、暴乱和民变险，保险金额则最少应为合同金额的 110%，并应采用合同中的货币"。在实际业务中，CIF 术语下买卖双方通常在合同中明确规定具体的保险险别和保险金额。

② Variations of CIF　CIF 术语的变形

It means the charges of unloading. It should be clearly stipulated in the contract or by using CIF variations. On CIF terms there are the same variations as those on CFR terms. They are as follows.

卸货费用的划分，可以在合同中用文字作出具体规定，也可以采用 CIF 术语的变形来表示。CIF 术语的变形与 CFR 术语的变形相同。他们主要有以下这些。

a. CIF Liner Terms

The unloading expenses are borne by the party who pays freight, i.e., the seller or the shipping company.

b. CIF Ex ship's hold

The buyer shall bear the expenses for slinging up the goods from the hold to the dock. The discharging charges shall be borne by the Buyer.

c. CIF Landed

The seller shall bear the expenses for unloading/landing the goods from the ship onto the dock or wharf or land at the port of destination, including the expenses of lighterage and dockage.

a. CIF 班轮条件：指卸货费用由支付运费的一方负担，即卖方或承运人。

b. CIF 舱底交货：指货物运抵目的港后，自船舱起吊直到码头的卸货费用由买方负担。

c. CIF 卸到岸上：指由卖方负担卸货费，包括驳船费和码头费。

2.4　Similarities FOB、CFR、CIF 三种术语的共同点

FOB, CFR and CIF are classified into one group as they are alike in characters from the below 6 aspects:

（1）They are used for port-to-port waterway transportation.

（2）Place of delivery of the seller is on board a ship in the export country.

（3）Risks are borne by the seller until the goods are on board the vessel.

（4）Symbolic trade terms, documents instead of goods selling and buying.

（5）The risks are transferred to the buyer once the seller delivery the goods on board the vessel.

（6）Contracts signed under the above three are referred to shipment contracts, in other words, the seller is only responsible for punctual shipment and disregard when it arrives.

我们把 FOB、CFR、CIF 放在一起来论述，是因为这三个贸易术语在性质上是一样的，有着它们共同的规律，可以从以下六个方面来看：

（1）这三个贸易术语都是适用于港到港的海洋运输。

（2）卖方的交货地点都是在出口国的装运港船上。

（3）风险的划分都是在出口国装运港以货物装上船为界。

（4）都是象征性交货的贸易术语，以交单代替了交货。

（5）卖方只要在装运港把货物装上船就完成了交货义务，风险就转移给了买方。

（6）这三个术语签订的合同术语装运合同，也就是说买方只管按时装运，不管何时到达。

3. FCA、CPT、CIP 货交承运人三种常用贸易术语

3.1 FCA: Free Carrier at(named place) 货交承运人（指定地点）

It shall be followed by the named place, like FCA London.

采用这术语后加注指定地点：如 FCA 伦敦。

（1）Definition 定义

The seller delivers the goods to the carrier nominated by the buyer at the place and time stipulate in the contract.

卖方在合同规定的时间和地点把合同规定的货物交给买方指定的承运人。

（2）Obligations 买卖双方的义务

“Free Carrier” means that the seller deliver the goods, cleared for export, to the carrier nominated by the buyer at the stipulated place. It should be noted that the chosen place of delivery has an impact on the obligations of loading and unloading the goods at that place. If delivery occurs at the seller’s premises, the seller is responsible for loading. If delivery occurs at any other place, the seller is not responsible for unloading.

“货交承运人”是指卖方只要在指定的地点将货物交给买方指定的承运人，并办理了出口清关手续，即完成了交货责任。需要注意的是，交货地点的选择对于在该地点装货或卸货的义务会产生影响。若卖方在其所在地交货，卖方应负责装货，若卖方在任何其他地点交货，卖方则不负责卸货。

“Carrier” means any person who, in a contract of carriage, undertakes to perform or to procure the performance of transport by rail, road, air, sea, inland waterway or by a combined of such modes.

“承运人”是指在运输合同中承诺通过铁路、公路、空运、海运、内陆水运或这些运输的联合方式履行运输或由其他人履行运输的人。

If the buyer nominates a person other than a carrier to receive the goods, the seller is deemed to fulfill his obligation to deliver the goods when they are delivered to that person.

若买方指定的提货人并非是承运人，则当卖方在货物交给此人时，便被认定为已经履行了交货责任。

（3）Methods of Transport 运输方式

This term may be used irrespective of the mode of transport, including multi-modal transport.

这一术语可用于各种运输方式，包括多式联运。

3.2 CPT: Carriage Paid to (named place of destination) 运输付至（指定目的地）

It shall be followed by the destination, like CPT London.

采用这术语后加注目的地：如 CPT 伦敦。

（1）Definition 定义

The seller delivers the goods to the carrier nominated by the buyer at the place and time stipulate in the contract and pay the freight necessary to the destination of import country.

卖方在合同规定的时间和地点把合同规定的货物交给买方指定的承运人,并支付将货物运至目的地的运费。

（2）Obligations 买卖双方的义务

"Carriage Paid To…"means that the seller delivers the goods to the carrier nominated by him but the seller in addition pay the cost of carriage necessary to bring the goods to the named destination. This means that the buyer bears all risks and any other costs occurring after the goods have been delivered.

"运费付至"是指卖方向其指定的承运人交货，但买方还必须支付将货物运至目的地的运费，即买方承担交货后发生的一切风险和其他费用。

"Carrier" means any person, who in a contract of carriage, undertakes to perform or to procure the performance of transport, by rail, road, air, sea, inland waterway or by a combination of such modes. If subsequent carriers are used for the carriage to the agreed destination, the risk passes when the goods have been delivered to the first carrier.

The CPT term requires the seller to clear the goods for export.

"承运人"指的是在运输合同中通过铁路、公路、海运、内陆水运或这些运输的联合方式承担或让他人承担运输的人。如果还使用接运的承运人将货物运至目的地，则风险在货物交给第一承运人时转移。

"运费付至"术语要求卖方办理货物的出口清关手续。

（3）Methods of Transport 运输方式

This term may be used irrespective of the mode of transport including multi-modal transport.

这一术语课适用于各种运输方式，包括多式联运。

（4）Some Points for Attention 使用 CPT 应当注意的问题

Risks Transfer 风险划分界限

As INCOTERMS 2010 explained, the buyer bears all risks and any other costs occurring after the goods have been so delivered. In multi-modal transport, risks transfer to the buyer when the seller delivers the goods to the first carrier.

按照《2010 通则》的解释，货物自交货地点至目的地的运输途中的风险由买方承担，而不是卖方，卖方只承担货物交给承运人控制之前的风险，在多式联运的情况下，卖方承担的风险自货物转嫁给第一承运人控制时即转给买方。

3.3 CIP: Carriage and Insurance Paid to (named place of destination) 运费和保险费付至（指定目的地）

It shall be followed by the destination of import country, like CIP London.

采用这术语后加注进口国目的地：如 CIP 伦敦。

（1）Definition 定义

The seller delivers the goods to the carrier nominated by the buyer at the place and time stipulated in the contract, and pays the freight and insurance necessary to destination of import country.

卖方在合同规定的时间和地点把合同规定的货物交给买方指定的承运人，并支付将货物运至目的地的运费和保险费。

（2）Obligations 买卖双方的义务

Carriage and lnsurance to means that the seller delivers the goods to the carrier nominated by him but the seller must in addition pay the cost of carriage necessary to bring the goods to the named destination. This means that the buyer bears all risks and any additional costs occurring after the goods have been so delivered. However, in CIP the seller also has to procure insurance against the buyer's risk of loss of or damage to the goods during the carriage. Consequently, the seller contracts for insurance and pays the premium.

"运费和保险费付至"指卖方向其指定的承运人交货，但卖方还必须支付将货物运至目的地的运费，即买方承担卖方交货之后的一切风险和额外费用。但是，按照"运费和保险费付至"术语，卖方还必须办理买方货物在运输途中灭失或损坏的风险的保险。因此，由卖方订立保险合同并支付保险费。

The buyer should note that under the CIP term the seller is required to obtain insurance only on minimum cover. Should the buyer wish to have protection of greater cover, he would either need to agree as such expressly with the seller or to make his own extra insurance arrangements.

买方注意到，"运费和保险费付至"术语要求卖方投保最低限度的保险险别。如买方需要更高的保险险别，则需要与卖方明确地表达协议，或者自行作出额外的保险安排。

"Carrier" means that any person, who in a contract of carriage, undertakes to perform or to procure the performance of transport, by rail, road, air, sea, inland waterway or by a combination of such modes. If subsequent carriers are used for the carriage to the stated destination, the risk passed when the goods have been delivered to the first carrier. The CIP term requires the seller to clear the goods for export.

"承运人"指的是在运输合同中通过铁路、公路、空运、海运、内陆水运或这些运输的联合方式承担或让他人承担运输的人。如果使用接运的承运人将货物运至约定的目的地，则风险在将货物交给第一承运人时转移。"运费和保险费付至"术语要求卖方办理货物出口清关手续。

（3）Methods of Transport 运输方式

This term may be used irrespective of the mode of transport including multi-modal transport.

这一术语可适用于各种运输方式，包括多式联运。

Section Three Five Physical Delivery Trade Terms
第三节 五种实质性交货贸易术语

1. Physical Delivery 实质性交货

Physical delivery refers to that the seller deliver the goods to the buyer in due time and at due place as agreed in the contract and does not effect documents replacing of delivering goods. The seller fulfills obligation on condition that the seller ships the goods on board the vessel as the contract stipulates at port of shipment within due time and has no guarantee for the arrival of goods.

实质性交货是指卖方要在规定的时间和地点将合同要求的货物提交给买方或其指定人，而不能以交单代替交货。卖方在约定装运地点装运，并向买方提交合同规定的包括物权凭证在内的有关单据就算完成了交货义务。

2. EXW and FAS 出口国交货的两个术语

2.1 EXW: Ex Works (named place) 工厂交货（指定地点）

It shall be followed by the named place, like EXW Warehouse.

采用这术语后加注指定地点：如 EXW 仓库交货。

（1）Definition 定义

The seller delivers when it places the goods at the disposal of the buyer at the seller's premises or at another named place (i.e. works, factory, warehouse, etc).

卖方在其所在地或其指定的地点（如工场、工厂或仓库等）将货物交给买方处置时即完成交货。

（2）Obligations 买卖双方的义务

EXW means that the seller's only responsibility is to make the goods available at his premises during the contracted time and bear the charges and risks before the goods are delivered to the buyer. He is not responsible for loading the goods onto the vehicle provided by the buyer and clear the goods for export, unless otherwise agreed. The buyer bears the full cost and risks involved in carrying the goods from there to the desired destination.

这一术语是指卖方只需在合同规定的日期或期限内在指定的工厂（或仓库）将货物交给买方支配，并承担货物交给买方支配之前的费用和风险。除非另有规定，否则，卖方不用负责将货物装上买方备妥的运输车辆和办理出口清关手续。

（3）Methods of Transport 运输方式

EXW is widely used in any means of transport including multi-modal transport in both domestic trade and international trade.

EXW 事实上是按国内贸易的方法进行交货，但也可用于国际贸易。适用范围很广，适合任何一种运输方式，包括多式联运。

（4）Advantages 好处

But the buyer can get the cargoes at a lowest price. Freight and insurance charges can be paid with native currency, so the foreign exchange can be saved, gaining better service from the shipping or insurance agent in the export country.

根据此术语，买方可以获得最低价；运费与保费可以用本国货币支付，因而可以节省外汇；可以从出口国的船公司或保险公司获得较好的服务。

EXW thus represents the minimum obligations, costs and risks among 11 terms undertaken by the seller. It is frequently used in coastal areas in mainland, Hong Kong and Macao.

因此，EXW 术语是 11 种术语中卖方承担义务、费用和风险最小的术语。在我国沿海开放地区和靠近港澳的地区经常使用这一术语。

2.2 FAS: Free Alongside Ship(named port of shipment) 启运港船边交货（指定的装运港）

It shall be followed by the nominated place of shipment, like FAS London.

采用这术语后加注指定装运港：如 FAS 伦敦。

（1）Definition 定义

The seller places the goods alongside the vessel nominated by the buyer at the named port of shipment to fulfill his delivery obligation under this term.

卖方将货物运到指定的装运港码头船边，即船舶吊钩所及之处，即履行交货。

（2）Obligations 买卖双方的义务

Under FAS terms the seller's obligations are fulfilled when the goods have been placed alongside the vessel on the quay or in lighters. This means that the buyer has to bear all cost and risks , losses of, or damage to the goods from that moment. FAS term requires the seller to clear the goods for export. Pay attention here, in the previous INCOTERMS, under this term, the buyer is responsible for clearing the goods for export, INCOTERMS 2010 has been reversed.

这一术语是指卖方在装运港将货物放置在码头买方所指派的船只的船边，即完成了交货。买方必须自该时刻起，负担一切费用和货物灭失或损坏的一切风险。FAS 术语要求卖方办理货物出口清关。应注意，《通则》先前的版本都规定，在 FAS 术语下的货物出口清关需由买方负责办理。《2010 年通则》对此作了与上述相反的规定。

（3）Methods of Transport 运输方式

This term is used for waterway transport.

它仅适用于水上运输方式。

（4）Different Definition Under American Trade Terms 与美国对外贸易定义的区别

In American, FAS is free along side,while in INCOTERMS 2010, FAS is free alongside ship.

In American, FAS is used in any means of transportation.

In INCOTERMS 2010, FAS is used in ocean marine transportation to be equivalent, word "vessel" must be added after FAS in American Trade Definition.

美国定义的 FAS 中为 along side,而 INCOTERMS 2010 中的 FAS 为 alongside ship。

美国定义的 FAS 可在任何运输工具旁，不一定在港口。

INCOTERNS 2010 中的 FAS 与美国定义的 FAS + Vessel 具有相同的意义，可用于海运。

3. DAT, DAP and DDP 进口国目的地交货的三种贸易术语

3.1 DAT=(INCO2000 DEQ): Delivered At Terminal(Named Terminal at Port or Place of Destination)

运输终端交货（指定港口或目的地的运输终端）

It shall be followed by the terminal place of destination, like DAT London.

采用这术语后加注目的地运输终端：如 DAT 伦敦。

（1）Definition 定义

"Definition at Terminal" means that the seller delivers when the goods, once unloaded from the arriving means of transport, are placed at the disposal of the buyer at a named terminal at the named port or place of destination. "Terminal" includes any place, whether covered or not, such as a quay, warehouse, container yard or road, rail or air cargo terminal. The seller bears all risks involved in bringing the goods to the unloading them at the terminal at the named port or place of destination. DAT requires the seller to clear the goods for export，which are applicable. However, the seller has no obligation to clear the goods for import duty or carry out any import customs formalities.

"运输终端交货" 是指当卖方在指定港口或目的地的指定运输终端将货物从抵达的载货运输工

具上卸下，交给买方处置时，即为交货。“运输终端”意味着任何地点，而不论该地点是否有遮盖，例如码头、仓库、集装箱堆积场或公路、铁路、空运货站。卖方承担将货物送至指定港口或目的地运输终端并将其卸下期间的一切风险。如适用时，DAT 要求卖方办理出口清关手续。但卖方无义务办理进口清关、支付任何进口税或办理任何进口海关手续。

（2）Obligations 买卖双方的义务

The Seller's Obligations 卖方义务

① Provide the Goods and the Documentaries 提供合同约定的货物和单据

The seller must invoice in conformity with the contract of sale and any other evidence of conformity that required by the contract.

卖方必须提供符合买卖合同约定的货物和商业发票，以及合同可能要求的其他与合同相符的证据，亦可以是同等作用的电子记录或程序。

② Security Clearance 负责通关

The seller must obtain，at its own risk and expense，any export license and other official authorization and carry out all customs formalities necessary for the export of the goods and for their transport through any country prior to delivery.

卖方必须自担风险和费用，取得所需的出口许可证和其他官方授权，办理货物出口和交货前从他国过境运输所需的一切海关手续。

③ Contract of Carriage 签订运输合同

The seller must contract at its own expense for the carriage of the goods to the named terminal at the agreed port or place of destination. If a specific terminal is not agreed or is not determined by practice，the seller may select the terminal at the agreed port or place of destination that best suits its purpose.

卖方必须自付费用签订运输合同，将货物运至约定港口或目的地的指定运输终端。如未约定特定的运输终端或不能由惯例确定，卖方则可选择最适合其目的在约定港口或目的地的运输终端。

④ Contract of Insurance 关于保险合同

The seller has no obligation to the buyer to make a contract of insurance. However, the seller must provide the buyer, at the buyer's request, risk, and expense (if any), with information that the buyer needs for obtaining insurance.

卖方对买方无订立保险合同的义务。但应买方要求并由其承担风险和费用（如有的话），卖方必须向买方提供后者取得保险所需的信息。

⑤ Redelivery 交货

The seller must unload the goods from the arriving means of transport and must then deliver them by placing them at the disposal of the buyer at the named terminal at the agreed port or place of destination on the agreed date or within the agreed period.

卖方必须在约定日期或期限内，在买方指定的港口或目的地运输终端将已从抵达的运输工具上卸下的货物交给买方处置的方式交货。

⑥ Transfer of Risks 风险转移

The seller bears all risks of loss of or damage to the goods until they have been delivered by placing the goods at the disposal of the buyer at the named terminal at the agreed port or place of destination.

卖方承担完成交货前货物灭失或损坏的一切风险。

⑦ Allocation of Costs 费用划分

The seller must pay all costs resulting from transportation and all costs relating to the goods until they have been delivered, other than those payable by the buyer from the time the goods have been delivered.

卖方必须支付因运输发生的费用，以及交货前与货物相关的一切费用，但自交货日起应由买方支付的费用除外。

The costs of customs formalities which are necessary for export as well as well duties, taxes and other charges payable upon export and the costs for their transport through any country, prior to delivery shall be paid by the seller.

货物出口所需海关手续费用，出口应交纳的一切关税、税款和其他费用，以及货物从他国过境运输的费用亦由卖方支付。

⑧ Notice to the Buyer 通知买方

The seller must give the buyer any notice needed in order to allow the buyer to take measures that are normally necessary to take delivery of the goods.

卖方必须向买方发出所需通知，以便买方采取收取货物通常所需要的措施。

（3）The Buyer's Obligations 买方义务

① Payment 支付价款

The buyer must pay the price of the goods as provided in the contract of sale. Any document referred to in the following items may be an equivalent electronic record or procedure if agreed between the parties or customary.

买方必须按照买卖合同约定支付价款，同时可以是同等作用的电子记录或程序。

② Clearance for Import 进口通关

The buyer must obtain, at its own risk and expense, any import license or other official authorization and carry out all customs formalities for the import of the goods.

买方必须自负风险和费用，取得所有进口许可或其他官方授权，办理货物进口的一切海关手续。

③ Taking Delivery and Proof of Delivery 收取货物和交货凭证

The buyer must take delivery of the goods when they have been delivered as agreed. The buyer must accept the delivery document provided by the seller.

当货物按照约定交付时，买方必须收取货物，并接受卖方提供的交货凭证。

④ Transfer of Risks 风险转移

The buyer bears all risks of loss of or damage to the goods from the time they have been delivered.

买方承担卖方交货时起货物灭失或损坏的一切风险。

The buyer must, whenever it is entitled to determine the time within an agreed period and/or the point of taking delivery at the named terminal, give the seller sufficient notice thereof. In the event that the buyer fails to give notice, then it bears all risks of loss of or damage to the goods from the agreed date or the expiry date of the agreed period for delivery.

当买方有权决定在约定期间的具体时间和/或指定运输终端内收取货物的地点时，应向卖方发出充分通知。如买方未能发出充分通知，由此造成货物灭失或损坏的一切风险由买方承担。

⑤ Allocation of Costs 费用划分

The buyer must pay all costs relating to the goods from the time they have been delivered.

买方必须支付完成交货之时起与货物相关的一切费用。

Any additional cost incurred by the seller if the buyer fails to fulfill its obligations in obtaining import license or other official authorization or fails to inform the seller in time.

如因买方未能办好进口报关或进口许可或未及时向卖方发出通知，由此导致卖方发生的额外费用由买方支付。

The costs of customs formalities as well as duties, taxes and other charges payable upon the goods imported.

买方必须支付办理进口海关手续的费用以及进口需缴纳的所有关税、税款和其他费用。

⑥ Notice to the Seller 通知卖方

The buyer must, whenever it is entitled to determine the time within an agreed period and/or the point of taking delivery at the named terminal, give the seller sufficient notice thereof.

当有权决定在约定期间内的具体时间和/或指定运输终端内的收取货物的地点时，买方必须向卖方发出充分通知。

⑦ Inspection of Goods 货物检验

The buyer must pay the costs of any mandatory pre-shipment inspection.

买方必须支付货物强制性装运前的检验费用。

⑧ Assistance with Information and Related Costs 协助提供信息及相关费用

The buyer must provide to or render assistance in obtaining for the seller, at the seller's request, risk and expense, any document and information, including security-related information, that the seller needs for the transport and export of the goods and for their transport through any country.

买方应卖方要求由其承担风险和费用，买方必须及时向卖方提供或协助其取得货物运输和出口及从他国过境运输所需要的任何单证和信息，包括安全相关信息。

（4）Methods of Transport 运输方式

Delivered rule may be used any mode of transport and may also be used where more than one mode of transport is employed.

该术语可适用于任何运输方式，也可适用于多种运输方式。

（5）Some Points to DAT 关于 DAT 的几个问题

The parties are well advised to specify as possible the terminal and, if possible, a specific point within the terminal at the agreed port or place of destination, as the risks to that point are for the account of the seller. The seller is advised to procure a contract of carriage that matches this choice precisely.

由于卖方承担在特定地点交货前的风险，特别建议双方尽可能确切地约定运输终端，或如果可能的话，在约定港口或目的地的运输终端内的特定的地点。建议卖方取得的运输合同应能与所作选择确切吻合。

Moreover，if the parties intend the seller to bear the risks and costs involved in transporting and handing the goods from the terminal to another place，then the DAP or DDP rules should be used.

此外，如果双方希望由卖方承担将货物由运输终端运输和搬运至另一地点的风险和费用，则应当使用 DAP 或 DDP 术语。

Under both new rules，delivery occurs at a named destination. In DAT，at the buyer's disposal unloaded from the arriving vehicle (as under the former DEQ rule). In DAP, likewise at the buyer's disposal, but ready for unloading (as under the former DAF, DES and DDU rules). The new rules make the INCOTERMS 2000 rules DES and DEQ superfluous. The named terminal in DAT may well be in a port, and DAT can therefore safely be used in cases where the INCOTERMS 2000 rule DEQ once was.

使用 DAT 时卖方要负责把货物从运输工具上卸下，由买方处置，而 DAP 则不同，在目的地由买方自行卸货。因此，DAT 可以适用原来 DEQ 的场合。DAP 可以适用原来 DES 的场合。

3.2 DAP: Delivered at Place (Named Place of Destination) 目的地交货（指定目的地）

It shall be followed by the place of destination, like DAP London.

采用这术语后加注目的地：如 DAP 伦敦。

（1）Definition 定义

"Delivered at Place" means that the seller delivers when the goods are placed at the disposal of the buyer on the arriving means of transport ready for unloading at the named place of destination. The seller bears all risks involved in bringing the goods to the named place.

"目的地交货"是指当卖方在指定目的地将还在运抵运输工具上可供卸载的货物交由买方处置时，即为交货。卖方承担将货物运送到指定地点的一切风险。

（2）Obligations 双方义务

The Seller's Obligations 卖方义务

① Provide the Goods and the Documentaries 提供合同约定的货物和单据

The seller must provide the goods and the commercial invoice in conformity with the contract of sale and any other evidence if conformity that may be required by the contract.

卖方必须提供符合买卖合同约定的货物和商业发票，以及合同可能要求的其他与合同相符的证据，也可以是同等作用的电子记录或程序。

② Security Clearance 负责通关

The seller must obtain, at its own risk and expense, any export license and other official authorization and carryout all customs formalities necessary for the export of the goods and for their transport through any country prior to delivery.

卖方必须自负风险和费用，取得所需的出口许可和其他官方授权，办理货物出口和交货前从他国过境运输所需的一切海关手续。

③ Contract of Carriage 签订运输合同

The seller must contract at its own expense for the carriage of the goods to the named terminal at the agreed port or place of destination. If a specific terminal is not agreed or is not determined by practice, the seller may select the terminal at the agreed port or place of destination that best suits its purpose.

卖方必须自付费用签订运输合同，将货物运至约定港口或目的地的指定运输终端，如未约定特定的运输终端或不能由实务确定，卖方则可选择最适合其目的在约定港口或目的地的运输终端。

④ Contract of Insurance 关于保险合同

The seller has no obligation to the buyer to make a contract of insurance. However, the seller must provide the buyer, at the buyer's request, risk, expense (if any), and information that the buyer needs for obtaining insurance.

卖方对买方无订立保险合同的义务。但应买方要求并由其承担风险和费用（如有的话），卖方必须向买方提供后者取得保险所需的信息。

⑤ Delivery Goods and Documentaries 交货和交货凭证

The seller must deliver the goods by placing them at the disposal of the buyer on the arriving. This means of transport ready for unloading at the agreed point, if any, at the named place of destination on the agreed date or within the agreed period.

卖方必须在约定日期或期限内，将货物放在已抵达的运输工具上，准备好在指定的目的地（如有的话）的约定点卸载，听由买方处理。

The seller must provide the buyer, at the seller's expense, with a document enabling the buyer to take delivery of the goods.

卖方必须自付费用，向买方提供凭证，以确保买方能够收取货物。

⑥ Transfer of Risks 风险转移

The seller bears all risks of the loss or the damage to the goods until they have been delivered by placing the goods at the disposal of the buyer at the named terminal at the agreed port or place of destination.

卖方承担完成交货前货物灭失或损坏的一切风险。

⑦ Allocation of Costs 费用划分

The seller must pay all costs resulting from transportation and a relating to the goods until they have been delivered, other than those payable by the buyer from the time goods have been delivered.

卖方必须支付因运输发生的费用，以及交货前与货物相关的一切费用，但自交货日起应由买方支付的费用除外。

Any charges for unloading at the place of destination that were for the seller's account under the contract of carriage; and the costs of customs formalities necessary for export as well as duties, taxes and other charges payable upon export and the costs for their transport through any country prior to delivery shall be paid by the seller.

运输合同中规定的应由卖方支付的在目的地卸货的任何费用及交货前发生的货物出口所需海关手续费用，出口应交纳的一切关税、税款和其他费用，以及货物从他国过境运输的费用亦由卖方支付。

⑧ Notice to the Buyer 通知买方

The seller must give the buyer any notice needed in order to allow the buyer to take measures that are normally necessary to enable the buyer to take delivery of the goods.

卖方必须向买方发出所需通知，以便买方采取收取货物通常所需要的措施。

⑨ Checking-Packaging-Marking 查对—包装—标记

The seller must pay the costs of those checking operations (such as checking quality, measuring, weighing, counting) that are necessary for the purpose of delivering the goods, as well as the costs of any pre-shipment inspection mandated by the authority of the country of export. The seller must, at its own expense, package the goods, unless it is usual for the particular trade to transport the type of goods sold unpackaged. The seller may package the goods in a appropriate manner for their transport, unless the buyer has notified the seller of specific packaging requirements before the contract of sale is concluded. Packaging is to be marked appropriately.

卖方必须支付为了进行交货所需要进行的查对费用。如查对质量、丈量、过磅、点数的费用，以及出口国有关机构强制进行的装运前检验所发生的费用。除非买方在特定贸易中，某类货物的销售通常不需要包装，卖方必须自付费用包装货物。除非买方在签订合同前已通知卖方特殊包装要求，卖方可以选择适合该货物运输的方式对货物进行包装。包装应作适当标记。

The Buyer's Obligation 买方义务

① Payment 支付价款

The buyer must pay the price of the goods as provided in the contract of sale. Any document referred to in the following items may be an equivalent electronic record or procedure if agreed between the parties or customary.

买方必须按照买卖合同约定支付价款，同时可以是同等作用的电子记录或程序。

② Clearance for Import 进口通关

The buyer must obtain, at its own risk and expense, any import license or other official authorization and carry out all customs formalities for the import of the goods.

买方必须自负风险和费用，取得所有进口许可或其他官方授权，办理货物进口的一切海关手续。

③ Taking Delivery and Proof of Delivery 收取货物和交货凭证

The buyer must take delivery of the goods when they have been delivered as agreed. The buyer must accept the delivery document provided by the seller.

当货物按照约定交付时，买方必须收取货物，并接受卖方提供的交货凭证。

④ Transfer of Risks 风险转移

The buyer bears all risks of loss or damage to the goods from the time they have been delivered.

The buyer must, whenever it is entitled to determine the time within an agreed period and/or the point of taking delivery at the named terminal, give the seller sufficient notice thereof. In the event that the buyer fails to give notice, then it bears all risks of loss or damage to the goods from the agreed date or the expiry date of the agreed period for delivery.

买方承担卖方交货时起货物灭失或损坏的一切风险。

当买方有权决定在约定期间内的具体时间和/或指定运输终端内收取货物的地点时，应向卖方发出充分通知。如买方未能发出充分通知，由此造成货物灭失或损坏的一切风险由买方承担。

⑤ Allocation of Costs 费用划分

The buyer must pay:

买方必须支付：

- All costs relating to the goods from the time they have been delivered as agreed;
- All costs of unloading necessary to take delivery of the goods from the arriving means of transport at the named place of destination, unless such costs were for the seller's account under the contract of carriage;
- Any additional costs incurred by the seller if the buyer fails to fulfil its obligations in obtaining import license or other official authorization or fails to inform the seller in time;
- The costs of customs formalities as well as all duties, taxes and other charges payable upon import of the goods.
- 按约定完成交货时起与货物相关的一切费用；
- 在指定目的地从到达的运输工具上卸载货物必须收取的一切费用，但运输合同规定该费用由卖方承担者除外；

- 因买方未能办好进口报关或进口许可或其他正式（官方）授权未及时向卖方发出通知，由此导致卖方发生额外费用；
- 办理进口海关手续的费用以及进口需缴纳的所有关税、税款和其他费用。

⑥ Notice to the Seller 通知卖方

The buyer must, whenever it is entitled to determine the time within an agreed period and/or the point of taking delivery at the named place of destination, giving the seller sufficient notice thereof.

当有权决定在约定期间内的具体时间和/或指定目的地内的收取货物的地点时，买方必须向卖方发出通知。

⑦ Inspection of Goods 货物检验

The buyer must pay the costs of any mandatory pre-shipment inspection.

买方必须支付货物强制性装运前的检验费用。

（3）Methods of Transport 运输方式

This rule may be used irrespective of the mode of transport selected and may also be used where more than once mode of transport is employed.

该术语可适用于任何运输方式，也可以适用于多种运输方式。

（4）Some Points to DAP 关于 DAP 的几个问题

The parties are well advised to specify as clearly as possible the point within the agreed place of destination, as the risks to that point are for the account of the seller. The seller is advised to procure contracts of carriage that match this choice precisely. If the seller incurs costs under its contract of carriage related to unloading at the place of destination, the seller is not entitled to recover such costs from the buyer unless otherwise agreed between the parties.

由于卖方承担在特定地点交货前的风险，特别建议双方尽可能清楚地订明指定的目的地内的交货地点。建议卖方订立的运输合同应能与所作选择确切吻合。如果卖方按照运输合同在目的地发生了卸货费用，除非双方另有约定，卖方无权向买方要求偿付。

DAP requires the seller to clear the goods for export, where applicable. However, the seller has no obligation to clear the goods for import, pay any import duty or carry out any import customs formalities. If the parties wish the seller to clear the goods for import, pay any import duty and carry out any import customs formalities, the DDP term should be used.

如适用时，DAP 要求卖方办理出口清关手续。但是卖方无义务办理进口清关、支付任何进口税或办理任何进口海关手续。如果双方希望卖方办理进口清关、支付所有进口关税，并办理所有进口海关手续，则应当使用 DDP 术语。

3.3　DDP: Delivered Duty Paid (Named Place of Destination) 完税后交货（指定目的地）

It shall be followed by the named place of destination, like DDP London.

采用这术语后加注指定目的地：如 DDP 伦敦。

（1）Definition 定义

"Delivered Duty Paid" means that the seller delivers the goods when the goods are placed at the disposal of the buyer, clear for import on the arriving means of transport ready for unloading at the named place of destination.

"完税后交货"是指当卖方在指定目的地将仍处于抵达的运输工具上，但已完成进口清关，且可供卸载的货物交由买方处置时，即为交货。

DDP represents the maximum obligation for the seller.

DDP 代表卖方的最大责任。

（2）Obligations 买卖双方义务

The Seller's Obligations 卖方义务

① Provide the Goods and the Documentaries 提供合同约定的货物和单据

The seller must provide the goods and the commercial invoice in conformity with the contract of sale and any other evidence if conformity that may be required by the contract.

卖方必须提供符合买卖合同约定的货物和商业发票，以及合同可能要求的其他与合同相符的证据，亦可以是同等作用的电子记录或程序。

② Security Clearance 负责通关

The seller bears all the cost and risks involved in bringing the goods to the place of destination and has an obligation to clear the goods not only for export but also for import, to pay any duty for both export and import and to carry out all customs formalities.

卖方承担将货物运至目的地的一切风险和费用，并且有义务完成货物出口和进口清关，支付所有出口和进口的关税和办理所有海关手续。

③ Contract of Carriage 签订运输合同

The seller must contract at its own expense for the carriage of the goods to the named place of destination or to the agreed point, of any, at the named place of destination. If a specific point is not agreed or is not determined by practice, the seller may select the point at the named place of destination that best suits its purpose.

卖方必须自负费用签订运输合同，将货物运至指定目的地或指定目的地内的约定的地点（如有约定）。如未约定特定的支付点或该交付点不能由惯例确定，卖方则可在指定目的地内选择最合适其目的地的交货点。

④ Contract of Insurance 关于保险合同

The seller has no obligation to buyer to make a contract of insurance. However, the seller must provide the buyer, at the buyer's request, risk, and expense (if any), with information that the buyer needs for obtaining insurance.

卖方对买方无订立保险合同的义务。但应买方要求并由其承担风险和费用（如有的话），卖方必须向买方提供后者取得保险所需的信息。

⑤ Delivery Goods and Documentaries 交货和交货凭证

The seller must deliver the goods by placing them at the disposal of the buyer on the arriving means of transport, cleared for import ready for unloading at the agreed point, if any, at the named place of destination on the agreed date or within the agreed period.

卖方必须在约定日期或期限内，在指定的目的地或目的地约定地点（如有的话）将可卸载的货物交由买方处置完成交货。

The seller must provide the buyer, at the seller's expense, with a document enabling the buyer to take delivery of the goods.

卖方必须自付费用，向买方提供凭证，以确保买方能够收取货物。

⑥ Transfer of Risks 风险转移

The seller bears all risks of loss or damage to the goods until they have been delivered by placing the goods at the disposal of the buyer at the named terminal at the agreed port or place of destination.

卖方承担完成交货前货物灭失或损坏的一切风险。

⑦ Allocation of Costs 费用划分

The seller must pay all costs resulting from transportation and all costs relating to the goods until they have been delivered, other than those payable by the buyer from the time the goods have been delivered.

卖方必须支付因运输发生的费用，以及交货前与货物相关的一切费用，但自交货日起应由买方支付的费用除外。

Any charges for unloading at the place of destination that were for the seller's account under the contract of carriage and the costs of customs formalities necessary for export and the cost for their transport through any country are prior to delivery shall be paid by the seller.

运输合同中规定的应由卖方支付的在目的地卸货的任何费用及交货前发生的货物出口所需海关手续费用，出口应缴纳的一切关税、税款和其他费用，以及货物从他国过境运输的费用亦由卖方支付。

⑧ Notice to the Buyer 通知买方

The seller must give the buyer any notice needed in order to allow the buyer to take measures that are normally necessary to enable the buyer to take delivery of the goods.

卖方必须向买方发出所需通知，以便买方采取收取货物通常所需要的措施。

The Buyer's Obligations 买方义务

① Payment 支付价款

The buyer must pay the price of the goods as provided in the contract of sale. Any document referred to in the following items may be an equivalent electronic record or procedure if agreed between the parties or customary.

买方必须按照买卖合同约定支付价款，同时可以是同等作用的电子记录或程序。

② Customs Formalities 通关

The seller must provide assistance to the seller, at the seller's request, risk and expense, in obtaining any import license or other official authorization for the import of the goods.

应卖方要求并由其承担风险和费用，买方必须协助卖方取得货物进口所需的任何进口许可或其他官方授权。

③ Taking Delivery 收取货物

The buyer must take delivery of the goods when they have been delivered as agreed.

当货物按照约定交付时，买方必须收取货物。

④ Transfer of Risks 风险转移

The buyer bears all risks of loss or damage to the goods from the time they have been delivered.

买方承担卖方交货时起货物灭失或损坏的一切风险。

The buyer must, whenever it is entitled to determine the time within an agreed period and/or the point of taking delivery at the named terminal, giving the seller sufficient notice thereof. In the event that the buyer fails to give notice, then it bears all risks of loss or damage to the goods from the agreed date or the expiry date of the agreed period for delivery.

买方有权决定在约定期间内的具体时间和/或指定运输终端内收取货物的地点时应向卖方发

出充分通知，如买方未能发出通知，由此造成的货物灭失或损坏的一切风险由买方承担。

⑤ Allocation of Costs 费用划分

The buyer must pay:

买方必须支付：

- All costs relating to the goods from the time they have been delivered as agreed;
- All costs of unloading necessary to take delivery of the goods from the arriving means of transport at the named place of destination, unless such costs were for the seller's account under the contract of carriage;
- Any additional costs incurred by the seller if the buyer fails to fulfill its obligations in obtaining import license or other official authorization or fails to inform the seller in time.
- 按约定完成交货时起与货物相关的一切费用；
- 在指定目的地从到达的运输工具上卸载必须收取的一切费用，但运输合同规定该费用有卖方承担者除外；
- 因买方未能办好进口报关或进口许可或未及时向卖方发出通知，由此导致卖方发生额外费用。

⑥ Notice to the Seller 通知卖方

The buyer must, whenever it is entitled to determine the time within an agreed period and/or the point of taking delivery at the named place of destination, give the seller sufficient notice thereof.

当有权决定在约定期间内的具体时间和/或指定目的地内的收取货物的地点时，买方必须向卖方发出通知。

⑦ Inspection of Goods 货物检验

The buyer has no obligation to the seller to pay the costs of any mandatory pre-shipment inspection mandated by the authority of the country of export or import.

买方对卖方不承担义务支付任何进出口国有关机构装运前强制进行的检验费用。

（3）Methods of Transport 运输方式

This rule may be used irrespective of the transport selected and may also be used where more than one mode of transport is employed.

该术语可适用于任何运输方式，也可适用于多种运输方式。

（4）Some points to DDP 关于 DDP 的几个问题

The parties are well advised to specify as possible the point within the agreed place of destination, as the costs and risks to that point are for the account of the seller. The seller is advised to procure contracts of carriage that match this choice precisely. If the seller incurs costs under its contract of carriage related to unloading at the place of destination, the seller does not entitle to recover such costs from the buyer unless otherwise agreed between the parties.

由于卖方承担在特定地点交货前的风险和费用，特别建议双方尽可能清楚地订明在指定目的地内的交货点。建议卖方订立的运输合同应能与所做选择确切吻合。如果按照运输合同卖方在目的地发生了卸货费用，除非双方另有约定，卖方无权向买方要求偿付。

The parties are well advised not to use DDP if unable directly or indirectly to obtain import clearance. If the parties wish the buyer to bear all risks and costs of import clearance, the DAP rule should be used. Any VAT or other taxes payable upon import are for the seller's account unless express agreed otherwise in the sale contract. See Table 6-2.

如卖方不能直接或间接地完成进口清关，则特别建议双方不使用 DDP。如双方希望买方承担所有进口清关的风险和费用，则应使用 DAP 术语。除非买卖合同中另行明确规定。任何增值税或其他应付的进口税款由卖方承担。

综上所述，现将《2010 通则》中的 11 种贸易术语列表如下，如表 6-2 所示。

Table 6-2 11 Types of Trade Terms

Groups	Trade Terms	Place of Delivery	Risk Transfer Limits	Mode of Transport	Transport handling and shipping costs	Insurance Handling and costs	Responsibility for export clearance	Import clearance responsibility
E	EXW	Factory of Exporter	Deliver to buyer	different kinds	Buyer	Buyer	Buyer	Buyer
F	FCA	Place designated for delivery by export countries	Deliver to carrier	different kinds	Buyer	Buyer	Seller	Buyer
	FAS	FAS port of the exporting country	FAS port	Waterway	Buyer	Buyer	Seller	Buyer
	FOB	FOB port of the exporting country	FOB port	Waterway	Buyer	Buyer	Seller	Buyer
C	CFR	CFR port of the exporting country	CFR port	Waterway	Seller	Buyer	Seller	Buyer
	CPT	Place designated for delivery by export countries	Deliver to carrier	different kinds	Seller	Buyer	Seller	Buyer
	CIF	CIF port of the exporting county	CIF port carrier	Waterway	Seller	Seller	Seller	Buyer
	CIP	Deliver to carrier of export countries	Deliver to carrier	different kinds	Seller	Seller	Seller	Buyer
D	DAT	Destination of Import countries	Disposal after deliver to carrier	different kinds	Seller	Seller	Seller	Buyer
	DAP	Agreed Destination of Import countries	Disposal after deliver to carrier	Waterway	Seller	Seller	Seller	Buyer
	DDP	Mailand of Import countries	Disposal after deliver to carrier	different kinds	Seller	Seller	Seller	Seller

表 6-2 《2010 年国际贸易术语解释通则》11 种贸易术语对照表

组别	贸易术语	交货地点	风险转移界限	适用运输方式	运输办理及运费承担	保险办理及保费承担	出口清关责任	进口清关责任
E	EXW	出口国工厂	货交买方	各种	买方	买方	买方	买方
F	FCA	出口国指定交货地点	货交承运人	各种	买方	买方	卖方	买方
	FAS	出口国装运港船边	装运港船边	水上	买方	买方	卖方	买方
	FOB	出口国装运港船上	装运港船上	水上	买方	买方	卖方	买方

续表

组别	贸易术语	交货地点	风险转移界限	适用运输方式	运输办理及运费承担	保险办理及保费承担	出口清关责任	进口清关责任
C	CFR	出口国装运港船上	装运港船上	水上	卖方	买方	卖方	买方
	CPT	出口国指定交货地点	货交承运人	各种	卖方	买方	卖方	买方
	CIF	出口国装运港船上	装运港船上	水上	卖方	卖方	卖方	买方
	CIP	出口国货交承运人	货交承运人	各种	卖方	卖方	卖方	买方
D	DAT	进口国目的地运输终端	货交买方处置后	各种	卖方	卖方	卖方	买方
	DAP	进口国目的地约定点	货交买方处置后	水上	卖方	卖方	卖方	买方
	DDP	进口国内地	货交买方处置后	各种	卖方	卖方	卖方	卖方

Section Four Component & Quotation of Goods Price
第四节 商品价格的构成与报价

1. Four Components of Unit Price 单价的四个组成部分

International commodity price are consisted of not only unit price and amount but also related liabilities, costs and risks between the seller and buyer.

国际贸易商品价格构成中，除了要表明每一计量单位的价格、金额外，还要表明买卖双方在货物交接过程中有关责任、费用、风险的划分问题。

The price of a commodity usually refers to the unit price in the international trade. The unit price consists of type of currency, price per unit, measurement unit and trade terms. For example, a price term, "Eur€ 500 per metric ton FOB Shanghai", may be understood. See Fig. 6-3.

Eur€	500	per metric ton	FOB Shanghai
type of currency	price per unit	measurement unit	trade terms

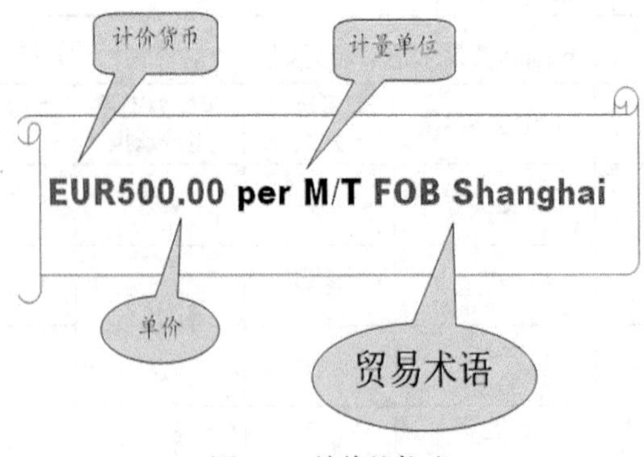

图 6-3　单价的构成

在国际贸易中，商品的价格通常指商品的单价。单价是由计价货币、单位价格金额、计价数量单位和贸易术语构成的如图 6-3 所示。例如，一项价格条款“每打 100 美元 FOB 伦敦价”可以解释如下：

每公吨	500	欧元	FOB 上海
计价数量单位	单位价格金额	计价货币	贸易术语

（1）Types of Currency 计价货币

In international trade, since the change of the value of the selected currency may directly affect their financial interests, the parties concerned should choose the currency favorable to them during pricing .In general, hard currency (e.g. US dollars, sterling)should be chosen for exports and soft currency for imports. The price for exports may be quoted in the both parties′ currency or in a third currency. See Table 6-3 and Fig. 6-4.

在国际贸易中，由于计价货币的币值变化会直接影响到进出口双方的经济利益，因此买卖双方在确定价格时应该注意选择对自己有利的计价货币，一般来说，出口应选硬通货（如美元、英镑等），而进口应选择软通货。买卖双方可选用自己国家的货币报价，也可选用第三国的货币报价，如表 6-3 和图 6-4 所示。

Table 6-3　　Common Use Type of Currency for Export 出口交易中常用的计价货币

货币名称	货币符号	简写
英镑	£	GBP
美元	US$	USD
港元	HK$	HKD
欧元	€	EURO
瑞士法郎	SF	CHF
澳大利亚元	$A	AUD
日元	¥	JPY

图 6-4　计价货币

（2）Price Per Unit 单位价格金额

While quoting an export price, first of all, the exporters should take into account the various costs and charges involved in getting the goods from the factory or warehouse in his own country to the buyer’s premises. Generally speaking, they consist of the purchasing cost of the goods, inland freight, packing expenses, warehousing, commodity inspection fees, export tariffs and entry fees, agent’s commissions, etc. In some cases, ocean freight and insurance premiums should be covered in the quotation. And the profit margin, of course, should also be considered when a price quoted.

在出口报价时，出口商首先要考虑的是把这些商品从自己国家的工厂或仓库运到买方所在地所要涉及的各种成本和费用。一般来说，主要包括购买商品的费用、内陆运输费、包装费、仓储费、商检费、出口关税、报关手续费、佣金以及其他各种费用。在有些情况下，海洋运输费和保险费也包括在出口商品报价里。当然，在计算报价时，还应考虑利润。

（3）Measurement Unit 计价数量单位

The specified measurement unit should also be mentioned, because many countries use different systems of measures and weights. For example, if "ton" is used as the measurement unit, it should be clearly indicated whether it is "metric ton", "long ton" (British) or "short ton"(America).

1 Metric Ton = 1000 kilograms
1 Short Ton = 907 kilograms
1 Long ton = 1016 kilograms

作为计价数量单位，应明确指出它是"公吨"或"长吨"（英制）或"短吨"（美制）。

（4）Trade Terms 贸易术语

In foreign trade, although the cost of certain commodities is the same ex-factory, the prices quoted by the seller will vary with the place of delivery. For example, in the case of a contract based on CIF terms as "CIF London" stated above, that means the seller bears all the cost, freight and insurance up to the named port of destination, here is "London". Trade terms ensure both exporter and importer know their own responsibilities.

在对外贸易中，某种商品在出厂价格都一样的情况下，卖方将随着交货地点的不同而报出不同的价格来。例如，以 CIF（上面提到的 CIF 伦敦）签订的合同就意味着卖方承担所有的成本、运费和保险费直至指定的目的港，在这里是"伦敦"。贸易术语使进出口双方明确各自的责任。

2 .Pricing Principles 定价原则

It is very complicated to make a good price for a product in the import and export business. In order to do it well, we should carry out correctly our pricing principles and be sure to master the changing trend of the international market. All the factor that may influence pricing should be taken into account. The calculation of cost, profit and loss must be reinforced.

在进出口业务中，确定一个合理的价格是一项十分复杂的工作。为了做好这项工作，必须正确贯彻我国进出口商品的作价原则，切实掌握国际市场价格的变动趋势，充分考虑影响价格的各种因素，加强成本和盈亏的结算。

In order to pricing properly, the following three principles should be adhered to.

在确定进出口商品价格时，必须遵循下列三项原则。

（1）According to the international market.

The international market price is made on the basis of international merits and formed in the international market competition, which can be accepted both by the buyer and the seller.

（2）Based on the situations of different policies of various countries and regions.

In order to let the foreign trade work in with the diplomatic policies, we should consider the policies of different countries and regions in the reference with the international market.

（3）Based on the purpose of purchasing.

The price of goods to be imported and exported can be made according to the international market, and be made based on the purpose of purchasing. That's to say, the price can be a little higher or lower than international market.

（1）按照国际市场价格水平定价。国际市场价格是以商品的国际价值为基础并在国际市场竞争中形成的，它是交易双方都能接受的价格。

（2）要结合国别、地区政策定价。为了使外贸配合外交，在参照国际市场价格水平的同时，也可适当考虑国别、地区政策。

（3）要结合购销意图定价。进出口商品价格在国际市场价格水平的基础上，可根据购销意图来确定，即可略高于或略低于国际市场价格。

3. Pricing Methods 定价方法

In the course of business negotiation and contract conclusion, appropriate trade terms, reasonable price and favorable money of account should be chosen. Detailed method of pricing should be included in the clause of price, and price adjustment clause should also beaded in the price term if necessary. In addition, commissions and discounts could be used as a flexible way of motivating the initiatives of the supplier and expanding the sales.

在对外磋商交易和签订合同时，应采用适当的贸易术语，合理确定商品的价格，选择有利的计价货币，价格条款中应列明具体的作价办法，必要时订立价格调整条款，还应灵活运用佣金和折扣，以调动采购商的积极性和扩大销路。

In the international sales of goods, the following methods of pricing can be used.

在国际贸易买卖中，可采取下列几种作价方法。

（1）Fixed Pricing 固定价格

The seller delivers and the buyer accepts the commodities at a fixed price agreed by both parties, neither party shall have the right to change the agreed price.

For example, USD 300 per metric ton CIF NEW YORK.

买卖双方按约定价格交接货物和收付货款，任何一方无权要求对约定价格进行变更。例如每公吨 300 美元 CIF 纽约

（2） Flexible Pricing 暂不固定价格

① The pricing time and method are specified in the price terms, for instance, "the price will be negotiated and decided by both parties 60 days before the shipment according to the international price level."

在价格条款中明确规定定价的时间和定价方法，如"在装船前 60 天，参照国际市场价格水平，协商议定正式价格。"

② Only the pricing time is fixed, for instance, "To be priced on July 1, 2012 by both parties."

只规定作价时间，如"由双方在 2012 年 7 月 1 日商定价格"。

（3）Partial Fixed Price and Partial Unfixed Price 价格部分固定，部分不固定

The parties concerned only fix the price for the commodities to be delivered recently, and leave the price of the commodities to be delivered in the long term open.

交易双方只约定近期交货部分的价格，远期交货部分的价格，则待以后商定。

（4）Floating Pricing 滑动价格

At the time of pricing, the price adjustment is also stipulated, for instance, "if the concluded price for other buyers is 5% higher or lower than the contract price, both parties will negotiate to adjust the contract price for the quantity of the contract."

在规定价格的同时，还规定价格调整条款。如"如果卖方对其他客户的成交价高于或低于合同价 5%，对本合同的数量，双方协商调整价格"。

4. Calculations of Commodity Price 有关商品价格的核算

4.1 Calculation of Commission and Discount 佣金和折扣的计算

4.1.1 Commission 佣金

（1）Definition 定义

Commission refers to the service fees charged by the agents or brokers for the transactions made in the sale or purchase of commodity. As a rule, such as the commission paid by the exporter to its sales agent, and paid by the importer to its purchasing agent. Commission is usually given on a percentage basis. The price in the contract is always expressed as CIF 5%, 5% means five percent commission is given to the middlemen.

国际贸易中因中间商介绍生意或代买代卖而向其支付一定的酬金，此项酬金叫佣金。如，出口商支付佣金给销售代理人，或进口商支付佣金给采购代理人。即，佣金又称"手续费"，是买方或卖方付给中间商的酬金。佣金通常按其一定百分比的支付。在合同中常常这样表示——成本、货运、加佣金 5%——这里 5%的佣金，就表示支付 5%的佣金给中间人。

The ratio of commission in price is defined, we call them Price with Commission. Otherwise, if the commission or discount is not included in price, we call them Net Price.

凡价格中含有佣金的称之为含佣价。凡在价格中不含佣金或折扣的称为净价。

（2）Kinds of Commission 佣金的种类

Commission can be divided into two kinds which are open commission and sleep commission.

The former marks the word "commission" in international contract and stipulates a certain percentage of the selling price of the property while the later does not mark percentage and "commission" of the letter. In any case, the commodity price is high definitely if only the commission exist.

佣金分"明佣"和"暗佣"两种。前者在合同中标明"佣金"字样，并规定某一百分比。而后者不标明百分比，甚至也不出现"佣金"字样。但不管何种方式，只要含有佣金，商品的价格就肯定要高。

（3）Three Stipulations of Commission 佣金三种规定办法

① Labeled by Words 一般用文字表示

For example, USD200 per M/T CIF London including 3% commission.

如，"每公吨 220 美元 CIF 伦敦包括 3%佣金"。

② Followed Trade Terms 在贸易术语后面加上"commission"的缩写字母"C"和所付的佣金率。

For example, USD 220 per M/T CIFC 3% London.

如，"每公吨 220 美元 CIFC 3%伦敦"。

③ Defined by Number 用数量值定义

For example, including USD 25 commission per M/T.

如，"每公吨付佣金 25 美元"。

（4）Calculation of Commission 佣金的计算

1）Relevant Formula of Calculation of Commission 有关佣金的计算公式

$$\text{Commission} = \text{C (Commission)–Inclusive Price} \times \text{Commission Rate}$$

$$\text{佣金额} = \text{含佣价} \times \text{佣金率}$$

The Formula of Calculation of Commission 佣金计算公式：

$$\text{净价}=\text{含佣价}\times(1-\text{佣金率})$$

$$\text{含佣价}=\frac{\text{净价}}{1-\text{佣金率}}$$

$$\text{Net Price} = \text{C-Inclusive Price} \times (1-\text{Commission Rate})$$

$$\text{C}-\text{inclusive Price}=\frac{\text{Net Price}}{1-\text{Commission Rate}}$$

2）Calculation　计算

Calculation of commission is based on the invoice value, whatever the trade term is used. 无论采用什么术语，佣金的基数通常按发票金额计算。

① For example, price with commission, CFRC 5%, USD100 per M/T. Calculate commission.

如，报含佣价 CFRC 5%每吨 100 美元，那么每公吨付佣金多少？

$$\text{Commission} = \text{USD}100 \times 5\% = \text{USD } 5$$

$$\text{佣金}=100 \times 5\% = 5\text{（美元）}$$

② For example, price with commission, CFRC 5%, USD100 per M/T. What is the calculate net price?

如，原报含佣价 CFRC 5%每公吨 100 美元，那么 CFR 净价多少？

$$\text{Net Price} = \text{USD}100-\text{USD}5 =\text{USD}95$$

$$\text{净价}= 100-5 = 95\text{（美元）}$$

③ For example, Net Price, USD100 per M/T, under the conditions of income unaffected. Calculate CFRC 5%.

如，报净价 CFR 每公吨 100 美元，不影响收入的条件下，CFRC 5% 含佣价多少？

CFRC 5%–105（美元）

Or 或

$$\text{CFRC5\%}=\frac{100}{1-5\%}=105.26$$

④ For example, Price with commission, CFRC 2%, USD100 per M/T, under the conditions of income unaffected. Calculate CFRC 5%.

如原报价 CFRC 2%每公吨 100 美元，不影响收入的条件下，CFRC 5%含佣价多少？

CFRC 5%=103（美元）

Or 或

$$\text{CFRC5\%}=\frac{100\times(1-2\%)}{1-5\%}=103.16$$

3）Payment Methods of Commission 佣金的支付方法

① Remove from exporting or importing price.

中间代理商直接从货价中扣除。

② Remittance from principals in a defined date and rate.

委托人收清货款后，再按事先约定的期限和佣金比率，另行付给中间代理商。

4.1.2 Discount 折扣

（1）Definition 定义

The discount is customarily the price deduction allowed by the seller to the buyer as a reward when the buyer pays for the goods

折扣（Discount; Allowance），指卖方按原价给予买方一定百分比的减让，即在价格上给予适当的优惠。

（2）Kinds of Discount 折扣的种类

In international trade, discount is aimed to motivate the initiatives of the buyer for a reward paying cash (cash discount), buying in quantity (quantity discount, volume discount), making early payment (trade discount), granting some other advantages to the seller.

在国际贸易中，除为鼓励买方积极购买而给与的一般交易折扣外，还有现金折扣、数量折扣、季节折扣、特别折扣等。此外与佣金相同，折扣也有“明扣”与“暗扣”之分。

（3）Three Stipulations of Discount 折扣三种规定办法

① Labeled by Words 一般用文字表示

For example, U.S. 500per M/T CIF London including 2% Discount.如，每吨 500 美元 CIF 伦敦含2%折扣。

② Followed Trade Terms 在贸易术语后面加上“D（discount）”或“R（rebate）”

For example, “CIFD 2% London”, “CIFR 2% London”.

如，“CIF 伦敦含 2%折扣”。

③ Defined by Number 也可以用绝对数字表示

For example, Including USD 5 discount per M/T.

如，“每吨折扣 5 美元”。

（4）Calculation of Discount 折扣的计算

① Relevant Formula of Calculation of Discount 有关折扣的计算公式

The Formula of Calculation of Discount 折扣换算公式：

单位货物折扣额=原价（或含折扣价）×折扣率

卖方实际净收入=原价−单位货物折扣价

折实售价=原价（1−折扣率）

$$\text{Discount} = \text{Original Price} \times \text{Discount Rate}$$

$$\text{Net Seller's Income} = \text{Original Price} - \text{Discount}$$

$$\text{Net Seller's Income} = \text{Original Price} \times (1 - \text{Discount Rate})$$

② Calculation 计算

For example, original price, USD100 per M/T CFR HK, Discount rate 2%. Calculate Discount.

如，报原价 CFR HK 每公吨 100 美元，折扣为 2%，那么卖方给买方的折扣是多少？

Discount = USD100×2% = USD 2

折扣额 = 100×2% = 2（美元）

（5）Payment Methods of Discount 折扣的支付方法

买方在开证时直接扣除金额或卖方在发票中扣除折扣额。

4.2 Quotations of FOB, CFR & CIF FOB、CFR & CIF 对外报价核算

4.2.1 Components of Goods Price 货物价格的构成

Now the question is how the unit price is worked out. For example, in the contract, price is usually quoted in this way, US$100 per ton FOB Shanghai. That means the complete price term consisting of currency, measuring unit, unit price, price terms, delivery port or destination. One of the exporter's tasks is to make the decision on what price to set for a product. The price setting relates to product costs, market demand, and competitive price. But first the exporter or manufacturer has to take into account the different costs, fixed cost and variable cost. Fixed cost is an element, such as rent, executive salaries, or property tax that remains constant regardless of how many items are produced. Variable cost is an element, of the cost of inputs such as cost of materials, direct labor, fuel and power, and that is directly related to production. It is equally important for the exporter to make it clear how much the foreign buyer is asked for the product and how many different kinds of costs are involved in your quoted price. The best solution is to use a costing sheet. Its purpose is to check that every expense has been covered in arriving at the selling price. The following is the detailed illustration of the costing sheet.

单价是怎样制定出来的？如合同中常以这种形式报价，上海港船上交货价格每吨一百美元。这就意味着，完整的价格条款应包括货币名称、计价单位、单价、价格术语以及装运港或目的港。出口商的工作之一，就是要决定产品定多高的价格。首先要考虑到产品成本、市场需求和竞争价格。出口商或制造商首先要考虑的是各种成本，如租金、管理人员工资、财产税。除了固定成本之外，还有可变成本，如原料消耗、直接劳动、燃料和动力等，确定了生产或销售一定数量产品的总成本之后，同样重要的是出口商须明确要国外买主付多少钱购买此产品，以及所报的价格中包含多少不同种类的费用。需要事先作精心的成本计算。目的在于查对售价中是否包含了所有的开支。以下是关于成本核算表的详细说明。

In international trade, the price of goods should take various costs, expenses /charges and expected profit factors into account.

在国际贸易中，货物的价格包括各种成本、费用和预期利润三大要素。即，

（1）Cost 成本

It simply refers to the unit of the product. This price is also purchase cost of product.

这是指产品的国内单价。这个价格就是指采购成本。

（2）Expenses/Charges 费用

The expenses /charges of goods exported mainly refer to commodity circulation fee. In practice, there are several kinds as follows:

出口货物价格中的费用主要是指商品流通费。业务中经常出现的费用有如下几种：

- Packing Costs 包装费

Here the export package refers to the transport package. Export packing calls for a great deal of money. A small cost is involved in stenciling an identification mark on each package for export.

这里所说的出口包装指的是运输包装。在出口的每一包货上刷唛头也要涉及一笔费用。

- Charges of Inland Transport 国内运输费用

The cost includes taking goods from factory to local railway station or container depot, next comes the cost of transporting the goods to the seaport for shipment abroad.

国内运输费用包括：货物从工厂运到火车站或集装箱货运站的费用，以及再运到装运港的费用。

- Charges of Port 港区港杂费用

This includes handling, wharfage and harbor dues that must be paid by the exporter to the port authorities.

港区港杂费用包括出口商必须向港务局缴纳的管理费、码头费和停泊费。

- Charges of Documents 单证费用

It mainly refers to consular documents which can be quite expensive particularly in the case of export to the Latin American countries. Initially, the exporter may wish to quote to the foreign customer a price，plus the cost of consular documents. Other documents are also very costly, such as license or inspection certificate, etc.

单证费用主要指领事发票。这笔费用也会很高，尤其在对拉丁美洲国家的出口中。报价时，出口商有时可以向外国客户要求外加“领事票据费”。其他票据如许可证或商检证书费用也很高。

- Operating Charges 业务费用

Here, space is left for the inclusion of unexpected additional expenses such as the cost of overseas telegrams or phone calls, fax charges, extra storage charges, and even “gifts” to the foreign customers.

如国际电报或电话、传真费用、附加的仓储费，甚至还要算上给外商的“礼物”。

- Ocean Freight 海运费用

When quoting in CIF and CFR, we will encounter the problem of freight. The freights are different according to different ports of shipment, different ship companies and different containers.在采用 CIF 或 CFR 价格术语对外报价时，就会涉及出口运费问题。不同的指运港、不同的船舶公司、不同的货柜对应不同的海运费。

- Freight Forward’s Fee 发运代理费

If the exporter uses the services of a freight forwarder to handle all the export documentation and book the shipping space required，allowance must be made for the fee involved.

如果出口商请发运代理人帮助办理出口手续、租船订舱，则该成本核算表中应该包括这笔费用。

- Marine Insurance 海运保险

The exporter must choose the coverage most suitable for the shipment as stipulated in the contract while they are being shipped abroad. Usually ocean shipment are insured for 10 percent of their total costs.

出口商必须按合同规定，为正在运输途中的货物选择适当的险别进行投保。通常，海运货物按其价值的 10%投保。

- Interest 垫款利息

Until receives payment, the exporter will have part of his working capital tied up in the export merchandise. Even if no credit is given, he will give credit to the foreign customer, he may have to wait for several months for payment. Consequently, the export price should include an amount to cover the cost of this working capital as well as the interest.

在收到货款之前，出口商总有部分流动资金被压在出口的货物上。即使没有出口信贷，出口商也要向国外客户提供信用，有时甚是要等好几个月才能收取货款。因此，出口价格中还应包括补偿这部分流动资本的费用和这部分利息。

- Commission 佣金

Commission refers to the reward given to middleman for his promoting business.

因中间商介绍生意或代买代卖而向其支付一定的酬金。

- Exchange Rate 汇率

When quoting in foreign currency, we should make a conversion between RMB and foreign currency. So we must take the exchange rate into consideration. Usually, the exchange rate adopted in quotation is similar to the official rate.

当采用除人民币以外的其他货币报价时，应将人民币折成外币。这就存在着汇率问题。一般情况下，报价采用的汇率在国家的外汇收购价左右，偏差不大。

- Rate of Export Rebates 出口退税率

In order to reduce、strengthen their capacity of competition, and encourage export, the domestic tax authority returns the collected domestic tax to companies.

所谓的出口退税是国家为帮助出口企业降低成本，增强出口产品在国际市场上的竞争能力，鼓励出口创汇，而实行的由国内税务机关退还出口商品国内税的措施。

（3）Expected Profit 预期利润

Expected profit is income of exporter and the mark of management.

预期利润是出口商的收入，是经营好坏的主要标志。

The above separate costs are now available for consolidation into a properly printed price list.

These are ones being used by most of the Chinese trading companies.

报价单就是在以上各种费用基础上合计而成的。绝大部分中国的贸易公司都使用这些项目。

4.2.2 Calculation Formula of Goods Price for Export 出口货物的价格核算公式

Calculate the quotation: the effective figure is kept to 2 decimal places.

计算报价：有效数字保留到小数点后第 2 位。

（1）Formula for Total Export Quotation 出口报价总公式

Export Quotation = Actual Cost of Exports + Various Expenses of Exports + Expected Profit

出口报价 = 出口货物的实际成本 + 出口过程中的各种费用 + 预期利润

（2）Formula for Cost 成本核算公式

Purchase Cost = Actual Cost + Value − added Tax

= Actual Cost + Actual Cost × Value − added Tax Rate

= Actual Cost × (1+ Value − added Tax Rate)

Actual Cost = Purchase Cost – Refund Income

Refund Income = Actual Cost × Refund Rate

Then, Refund Income = Purchase Cost ÷ (1+ Value − added Tax Rate) × Refund Rate

Actual Cost = Purchase Cost × (1+ Value − added Tax Rate − Refund Rate)

÷ (1+ Value − added Tax Rate)

购货成本 = 实际成本 + 增值税

= 实际成本 + 实际成本 × 增值税率

= 实际成本 ×(1+ 增值税率)

实际成本 = 购货成本 − 退税收入

退税收入 = 实际成本 × 出口退税率

那么，退税收入 = 购货成本 ÷（1+增值税率）× 退税率

实际成本 = 购货成本 ×（1+增值税率 − 退税率）÷（1+增值税率）

The purchase price here refers to the after-tax price, which is also called purchase cost. Foreign trade companies purchase commodities from the factory and pay as per the enterprise's value-added tax invoice, like this, we call purchase price as tax-included price. As a matter of fact, in international practice, it is necessary to remove the tax rebate (after the commodities have been exported, the Department of National Revenue offers tax rebates according to the different commodities' refund rate) from purchase price (tax price), this is our actual payment, therefore, which is also called actual cost. It is the foundation of an offer. Usually actual cost is in the form of unit price.

商品进价是指税后的购货价，也叫购货成本，是外贸公司在向工厂收购出口产品时，根据企业的增值税发票进行付款，这样，我们的采购货款就成了含税的价格。事实上，在国际贸易实际业务中，我们在计算出口产品的价格时，要从购货成本（含税价）中减去国家的退税额（在货物出口后，由国家税务部门按各商品的退税率给予退税），这样得到的价格，才是我们付款的实际成本。实际成本是计算报价的基础。通常商品进价以单价形式体现。

（3）Formula for Expenses 费用核算

Calculating the expenses, every expense are converted to into U.S. dollar, being share to the minimum quotation unit, the effective figure is kept to 4 decimal places.

计算费用：各项费用都折合成美元，并分摊到最小报价单位上，有效数字保留到小数点后第4位。

① Domestic Expenses 国内费用

Domestic Expenses = All the Cost in Domestic ÷ Total Quantity of Packages ÷ Exchange Rate

国内费用 = 所有的国内费用总和 ÷ 总件数 ÷ 汇率

For example, fixed cost of company and Lump sum charge

如，业务定额费和包干费。

Fixed Cost of Company = Purchase Cost × Fixed Cost Rate

定额费=采购成本 × 定额费率

- Fixed cost of company is a percentage of operating costs in business operation, including postage, telegram, and other communications costs, travel expenses, entertainment expenses and so on, which is specified by the exporter according to actual expenditures in previous years for the estimation of export business costs. It normally takes procurement costs as the base figure for calculations.

业务定额费是出口商人对业务操作中诸如邮电、通信、交通差旅，招待客户等业务费用，按照历年实际支出状况规定一个百分比，以方便估算出口业务费用，它的计算基数通常是出口商的

采购成本。

● Lump sum charge is the cost incurred for export clearance services by freight forwarders or other service providers, usually including transportation, loading and unloading, commodity inspection, customs declaration, documentation, and port fees.

包干费是货运代理或其他服务营运商提供出口清关服务所发生的费用，通常包括运输、装卸、商品检验、报关、单证、港口码头费用。

② Ocean Freight 海运费

Ocean freight is divided into break-bulk cargo freight and container freight.

海洋运费的计算，分为件杂货运费和集装箱货运费两类。

Break-bulk /LCL cargo freight is calculated in terms of charges per freight ton, while container freight is calculated in terms of box rates, namely, charges for the carriage of a container.

件杂货/散装货物/拼箱货物是按照每运费吨多少钱来计算的，而集装箱整箱货物的运费则是用包箱费率，即每个集装箱多少美元来计算。

First, calculate the volume of unit pack. Most export commodities have one's own packaging except nude cargo or the bulk cargo, calculate the individual packaging object.

首先，要计算单位包装体积。除了裸装货或散装货。大部分的出口商品都有自己的包装，据此算出单个包装物体积。

Second, the common quantity such as 20' container or 40' container is divided by unit of packing, then has the amount of packing. (The volume of 20- feet container is 25 cubic meters, the volume of 40-feet container is 55 cubic meters; and the weight is 17.5 kg and 24.5kg respectively.)

其次，按常规数量如一个 20 尺或 40 尺货柜的经验体积除以单位包装物体积计算出能够装下的总包装件数。（20 尺货柜最大有效容积为 25 立方米，40 尺货柜最大有效容积为 55 立方米；其最大载货重量分别为 17500 千克和 24500 千克）

There are three commonly used methods for the calculation of ocean freight which are Weight Calculation, Volume Calculation and Selection Method.

Weight measurement is the calculation of freight by the gross weight of cargo, called the "weight ton" (calculated to 3 decimal places). It is represented with "W" on the cargo scale or the freight tariff.

Volume calculation calculates freight in terms of the volume of goods, taking cubic meter as the calculation unit, called the "measurement ton" (calculated to 3 decimal places), and represented with "M" on the cargo scale or the freight tariff.

The selection method refers to the collection of freights by using either one of the above two methods whose freight is calculated to be higher. It is represented with "W/M" on the cargo scale or the freight tariff.

海洋运费的计算标准：其中最常见的为重量法、体积法和选择法。

重量法是按照货物的毛重来计算运费，称为重量吨（weight ton），吨以下取三位小数，货物等级表或运价表上用“W”来表示。

体积法是按照货物的体积来计算，以每立方米为运费计算单位，称尺码吨（measurement ton），立方米下取三位小数，货物等级表或运价表上用“M”来表示。

选择法是在重量法和体积法之间择高收取运费，该方法在运价表或货物等级表上用“W/M”来表示。

Suppose a commodity is packed in carton, the size of each carton being 47 × 36.5 × 84.5cm, and the weight of each being 18 kg. The freight of the commodity shall be calculated as follows if "W/M" is to be adopted:

The volume of each carton is 0.47×0.365×0.845=0.145m^3

The gross weight of each carton is 18/1000=0.018 tonnes.

∵ The volume is greater than the weight,

∵ therefore, volume measurement is to be used to calculated the freight.

设某商品的包装为纸箱，每个纸箱的尺寸为 47cm×36.5cm×84.5cm，每个纸箱的重量为 18 千克，如该商品的运费计算标准为 W/M，则比较方法如下：

每箱的体积为 0.47m×0.365m×0.845m=0.145 立方米

每箱的毛重换算为公吨则为 18/1000=0.018 公吨，

∵ 尺码大于重量，

∴ 按照尺码计算运费。

Based on the clear measuring criterion, the freight of the commodity could then be calculated according to the freight rates published by the shipping company.

在明确计费标准的基础上，根据船舶公司公布的运费率就可以计算出单位商品的运费。

- Freight=Quantity of Container × the Fee for Single 20’ Container or 40’ Container ÷ Total Quantity

海运费=集装箱数量×从启运地到指定地单个 20 尺或 40 尺货柜所需海运费 ÷ 总件数

③ Insurance Premium 保险费

- Insurance Premium = Insurance Amount × Premium Rate（Summary of all Risk Kinds）

保险费 = 保险金额 × 保险费率（投保险别保险费率之和）

- Insurance Amount = CIF(CIP）× (1 + Addition Rate)

保险金额 = CIF(CIP）×(1+投保加成率)

Generally, plus insurance rate is 10%. Insurance amount is on the basis of CIF(CIP）or invoice amount. Then, premium also applys formula to calculations as follows:

因为投保加成率一般是 10%，保险金额以 CIF 或 CIP 货价或发票金额为基础计算。所以，保险费又可以用下面公式计算：

- Premium = CIF × 110% × Premium Rate（Summary of all Risk Kinds）

保险费 = CIF 价 × 110% × 保险费率（投保险别保险费率之和）

④ Discount Interest 垫款利息

Discount Interest = Purchase Price × Annual Interest Rate × (Exact Discount Time ÷ Days of one year)

垫款利息 = 采购价格 × 贷款年利息率 ×（具体垫款时间一年的天数）

⑤ Bank’ Charges 银行费用

Bank Charges = Quotation × Percentage

银行费用 = 报价 × 一定比率

⑥ Profit 利润

Profit = Quotation × Profit Rate 利润=报价× 利润率(一般为 8% – 10%)

4.2.3 Calculation Process of FOB, CFR and CIF 三种贸易术语报价的核算过程

Case:

Question: Calculate the FOB price, CFR price and CIF price.

求：FOB 价，CFR 价和 CIF 价。

Commodity name: Toy Bear

Methods of packages:60pcs/ctn

Measurement: 100×41 × 40

G.W./ N.W.: G.W. 8KG，N.W. 7KG

Quotation quantity: 9120 pcs

Purchase cost: 6 RMB/pcs

Unit Lump sum charge for export: ￥0.10

Break-bulk freight:（charge standard “M/W”）USD60（freight ton）

Fixed cost:（calculation as per purchase cost）3.50%

Interest discount time：30 days

Annual interest:（calculation as per 360）6.00%

Insurance premium: all risks:0.8% and war risks 0.08%

Addition rate: 10.00%

Value-added Tax Rate:17%

Refund Rate: 15%

Ocean freight: USD1350 for per 20 feet container from Qingdao to Hamburger.

Insurance: 110 of invoice amount on the basis of CIF, covering all risks(0.8%)and war risks(0.08%)

Bank charges: quotation × 0.35%

Expected profit: quotation × 10%

Exchange rate: US$1= ￥6.35

商品名称: 毛绒玩具熊

包装方式：每箱装 60 只 pcs/ctn

纸箱尺码：100×41 × 40

毛重/净重：G.W. 8kg，N.W. 7kg

报价数量：9 120 只

采购成本：6 元/只（含增值税）

出口费用：单位商品出口的包干费约为：￥0.10

件杂货/拼箱海运费为:（计费标准“M/W”）60 美元（每运费吨）

出口定额费率为:（按采购成本计）3.50%

垫款周期为：30 天

银行贷款年利率为:（1 年按 360 天计）6.00%

海运货物保险费率为：一切险（0.8%费率）和战争险（0.08%费率）

投保加成率为：10.00%

增值税率为：17.00%

出口退税率为：15.00%

银行手续费为:（按报价计）0.35%

预期利润为:（按报价计）10%

汇率为:（1 美元兑换人民币）￥6.35

Answer:（1）Components of FOB, CFR and CIF 三种价格术语的基本构成

FOB price = cost + expenses + profit

= actual cost + (domestic expenses +bank charges) + expected profit

= actual cost + (domestic expenses +bank charges) + quotation×profit rate

= actual cost + (domestic expenses + quotation×0.5%) + quotation×profit rate

= (actual cost + domestic expenses)/(1 − 0.5% − profit rate)

FOB=成本+费用+利润

=实际成本+（国内费用+银行费用）+预期利润

=实际成本+（国内费用+银行费用）+ 报价×利润率

=实际成本+（国内费用+报价×0.5%）+报价×利润率

=（实际成本+国内费用）/（1−0.5%−利润率）

CFR price = cost + expenses + profit

= actual cost + (domestic expenses + bank charges + freight)+ expected profit

= actual cost + (domestic expenses + quotation × 0.5% + freight)+ quotation × profit rate

=（actual cost + domestic expenses + freight）/(1−0.5%−profit rate)

CFR=成本+费用+利润

=实际成本+（国内费用+银行费用+ 海运费用）+预期利润

=实际成本+（国内费用+报价×0.5%+海运费用）+报价×利润率

=（实际成本+国内费用+海洋费用）/（1−0.5%−利润率）

CIF price = cost + expenses + profit

= actual cost + (domestic expenses + bank charges + freight + premium)+ expected profit

= actual cost +[domestic expenses + quotation×0.5% + freight + quotation×(1+addition rate）×premium rate] + quotation×profit rate

= (actual cost + domestic expenses + freight)/[1−0.5%−profit rate−(1+ addition rate）×premium rate]CIF=成本+费用+利润

=实际成本+（国内费用+银行费用+海运费用+保险费）+报价×利润率

=实际成本+[国内费用+报价×0.5%+海运费用+报价×（1+投保加成）×保费率之和] +报价×利润率

=（实际成本+国内费用+海洋费用）/[1−0.5%−利润率−（1+投保加成）×保费率之和]

（2）Conversion of FOB, CFR and CIF　三种贸易术语之间的换算

CIF=FOB+F+I　　　I = CIF ×（1+10%）×premium rate

CIF=CFR+I

CIF=(FOB+F）÷ [1−(1+10%）× Insurance rate]

CFR 价=FOB 价+运费

CIF 价=FOB 价+运费+保险费

FOB价的换算：

① CFR 价=FOB 价+运费

② CIF 价=（FOB 价+运费）÷[1−(1+投保加成)×保险费率]

CFR价的换算：

① FOB 价=CFR−运费

② CIF 价=CFR 价 ÷ [1−(1+投保加成）×保险费率]

CIF价的换算：

① FOB 价= CIF 价× [1−(1+投保加成）× 保险费率]−运费

② CFR 价= CIF 价×[1−(1+投保加成）×保险费率]

③ Calculation Procedures of FOB, CFR and CIF 三种贸易术语的核算过程

The calculation process as follows: 核算过程如下：

Total measurement: since the measurement of one carton:

$$1\times0.41\times0.4 = 0.164m^3$$

And the quantity 9 120pcs，so the number of cartons needed：

$$9\ 120 \div 60 = 152\ ctn$$

so，

$$0.164\times 152 = 25m^3$$

Total weight：152× 8 = 1 216 kg

Actual Cost = Purchase cost ×(1+ Value-added Tax Rate-refund rate) ÷ (1+ Value-added Tax Rate）

= 6 ×(1+17%-15%) ÷ (1+17%)

= 5.23RMB

Refund Income = Purchase Cost ÷ (1+ Value-added Tax Rate）× Refund Rate

= 6 ÷（1+17%）×15%

= 0.769RMB

Discount interest =purchase cost× annual interest rate × discount days

=6×6% /360×30=0.03RMB

Ocean freight: since the measurement of one carton proceeds the weight of one carton, then：

25× 60 ÷ 9 120 = US$0.164/PCS

Insurance premium:= CIF Price × 110% × premium rate = CIF Price× 110% ×（0.8%+0.08%）

= 0.0096CIF Price

Fixed cost：= purchase cost × fixed cost rate = 6 × 3.5%=0.21 RMB /PCS

Lump sum charge：0.10RMB /PCS

Bank charges: quotation × 0.35%

Expected profit: quotation × 10%

Exchange rate: US$1= ￥6.35

since：

Domestic expenses = fixed cost + Lump sum charge + discount interest

=0.21+0.10+0.03 = 0.34RMB

So, FOB price：

FOB price = cost + expenses + profit

= actual cost + (domestic expenses + bank charges) + expected profit

= actual cost + (domestic expenses + FOB × 0.35%) + FOB × profit rate

= (actual cost + domestic expenses) + FOB × (0.35% + 10%)

FOB price =5.23+ 0.34+ FOB ×（0.35% + 10%）=5.57+ 0.1035 × FOB

FOB price =6.2130RMB

Finally,

Exchange foreign US currency:

FOB price = 6.2130 ÷ 6.35=US$ 0.98 /pcs

CFR price = FOB price + ocean freight = 0.98 + 0.164 = US$1.144/pcs

CIF price = CFR price + insurance premium= 1.144 +0.0 096CIF

therefore：

CIF price =US$1.155 /pcs

按如下内容核算，过程如下

货物总体积：每个纸箱体积：1×0.41×0.4 = 0.164 立方米

因为报价数量为 9 120 只，所以需要的纸箱数为：

9 120 只 ÷ 60 只/箱= 152 箱

那么，**货物的总体积**为：

0.164 立方米/箱× 152 箱 = 25 立方米

货物总毛重：152× 8=1 216 公斤

实际成本：= 购货成本 ×（1+增值税率－退税率）÷（1+增值税率）

=6 ×(1+17%-15%) ÷ (1+17%)

=5.23 人民币

退税收入：= 购货成本 ÷（1+增值税率）× 退税率

=6 ÷ (1+17%)×15%

=0.769 人民币

贷款利息：= 采购价格 × 贷款年利息率 ×（具体垫款时间一年的天数）

=6×6% /360×30=0.03 元人民币

海洋运费：因为每个纸箱体积（=0.164 立方米）每个纸箱货物总毛重（= 0.008 公吨）（船运公司根据重量吨或尺码吨从高计收），所以货物的海洋运费为：

25 立方米× US$60 /立方米 ÷ 9 120 只 = 0.164 美元/只

海运保险费：= CIF 价 × 110% × 保险费率 =CIF 价× 110% ×（0.8%+0.08%）

= 0.0 096CIF 价

出口业务定额费：定额费=采购成本 × 定额费率 = 6 × 3.5%=0.21 人民币/只

包干费：0.10 人民币元/只

银行手续费为：（按报价计）0.35%

预期利润为：（按报价计）10%

汇率为：（1 美元兑换人民币）￥6.35

因为：

国内费用 = 出口业务定额费 + 包干费 + 贷款利息=0.21+0.10+0.03 = 0.34 元人民币

所以，FOB 报价为：

FOB=成本+费用+利润

=实际成本+（国内费用+银行费用）+预期利润

=实际成本+（国内费用+FOB 报价×0.35%）+报价×利润率

=（实际成本+国内费用）+FOB 报价（0.35% +利润率）

FOB 报价=5.23+ 0.34+报价（0.35% + 10%）=5.57+ 0.1035 × FOB 报价

FOB 报价=6.2130 元人民币

折成美元：6.2130 元人民币 ÷ 6.35=0.98 美元/只

CFR 报价=FOB 价 ＋ 运费= 0.98 美元+ 0.164 美元/只=1.144 美元/只

CIF 报价=CFR 价 ＋ 保险费= 1.144 美元+0.0 096CIF 价

所以，CIF 报价=1.155 美元/只

Section Five Price Clause in a Sales Contract 第五节　合同中的价格条款

1. Contents of Price Clause 价格条款的内容

The price terms of a sale contract include unit price and total value in international trade.

进出口商品合同中的价格条款一般包括单价和总值两项基本内容。

（1）Unit Price 单价

The price of a commodity usually refers to the unit price. The unit price consists of type of the currency, price per unit, measurement unit and trade terms.

进出口合同中的单价由计量单位、单位价格金额、计价货币和贸易术语四个部分组成。

（2）Total Amount 总值

Total value is the unit price and quantity and the total amount of a deal.总值是单价与数量的乘积。

For example, Total Amount: USD5 000. 例如，总值：5 000 美元。

For example, Total Amount: USD5 000 FOB Liverpool. 例如，总值：5 000 美元 FOB 利物浦。

When writing the total amount in capital, we always add “SAY” at the beginning of the sentence, and “ONLY” at the end.

For example,

当写总值时，合同中总是在金额的开头加“SAY”，在金额的末尾加“ONLY”。

SAY UNITED STATE DOLLARS EIGHT HUNDRED AND NINETY-NINE AND TEN CENTS ONLY.

例如，总计：899.10 美元的总值合计大写如上。

2. Samples of Price in Contract 合同中价格样例

In international practice, the commonly price clause are:

国际贸易中，常见的价格条款：

（1）US$ 5 000 per metric ton net CIF Hong Kong.

每公吨 5,000 美元 CIF 中国香港净价。

（2）US$ 200 per dozen CFRC3% New York.

每打 200 美元 CFRC3%纽约。

（3）FFr600 per set FOB Shanghai less 3% discount.

每台 600 法国法郎 FOB 上海减 3%折扣。

（4）HK$1 000 per bale CIF Hong Kong.

（Remarks：The above is a provisional price，which shall be determinedseller 15 days before the month of Shipment. ）

每包 1000 港元 CIF 中国香港. (备注：上列价格为暂定价，于装运月份 15 天前由买卖双方另行协商确定价格。)

（5）500 M/T，gross for net，6% more or less.

500 公吨，以毛作净，6%上下。

Unit Price：US$1 000 per metric ton CIF Singapore.

单价：每公吨 1 000 美元 CIF 新加坡。

Total Price：US$500 000.

总值：500 000 美元。

3. 制定价格条款应注意的问题

（1）Be reasonable to make the commodity price according to the market.

（2）Select the proper type of currency.

（3）Choose the suitable trade terms.

（4）Apply various methods of price to avoid the risks of price version.

（5）Refer to the conventions of international trade, attention to the use of commission and discount.

（6）If the quality and the quantity have more or less clause, the price clause should follow it.

（1）根据国际市场行情，合理确定商品的单价。

（2）选择好计价货币。

（3）选择适当的贸易术语。

（4）灵活运用各种不同的作价办法，以避免价格变动的风险。

（5）参照国际贸易的习惯做法，注意佣金和折扣的合理运用。

（6）如交货品质和数量约定有一定的机动幅度，则对机动部分的作价也应一并规定。

【Review Questions】复习思考题

【Typical Case Link 1—典例链接 1】

Question: Is the buyer's requirement reasonable?

问题：买方的要求合理吗?

A Chinese company sold 500 metric tons of grade A rice to a foreign company on basis of FOB Qingdao. When loading, the goods received inspection and all were in good condition. After the goods were delivered, the seller informed the buyer of the shipping advice. Unfortunately, on the voyage to the destination, the goods met with huge waves and half of the goods were soaked by seawater. As a result, the quality of the rice was spoiled. When the goods arrived at the destination, they had to be sold at grade C. The buyer lodged a claim against the seller and asked for compensation for the differentials.

中国某公司向外商出售 A 级大米 500 公吨，成交条件 FOB 青岛。装船时货物经检验符合合同要求，货物出运后，卖方及时向买方发出装船通知，但是航运途中，因海浪过大，大半被海水浸泡，大米的品质受到影响。货物到达目的港后，只能按三级大米的价格出售，于是买方要求卖方赔偿差价损失。

【Typical Case Link 2—典例链接 2】

Question: Who do you think should hold the responsibilities for the loss? Why?

问题：你认为货损责任应由谁承担？为什么？

A company export, a batch of goods on the basis of CFR. Because of negligence, it failed to notify the loading and shipment. As a result, the importer did not insure the goods timely. Not long after the vessel left for the destination, it ran aground and sank, causing total loss of goods. The importer lodged a claim against the exporter and asked for compensation for the lost goods. However, the exporter refused to compensate for the lost goods because the lost happened after the goods were over the rail of the ship. So the risks should be borne by the importer. Disputes then arose.

某公司以 CFR 价出口一批货物，装运后由于工作疏忽，未能及时向买方发出装货通知，致使买方未及时投保，结果船开后，不久触礁沉没，货物全部损失，进口方向出口方提出赔偿，可是出口方认为货物损坏，发生在越过船舷之后，风险应由买方承担，故拒绝赔偿，因此发生争执。

【Typical Case Link 3—典例链接 3】

Question: In such circumstances, does the seller hold the right to buyer to pay the bill? Why ?

问题：在上述情况下，卖方有无权利凭规定的单据要求买方付款？为什么？

A Chinese importer entered into a CIF contract with an American exporter, in which the Chinese importer imported some machine components from the American exporter. The goods have been loaded on time at the shipping port stipulated in the contract. Four hours after the vessel left for the destination, it ran aground on a reef and sank. The next day, when the seller held the bill of lading, insurance policy, invoice and other shipping documents to require the buyer for payment, the buyer refused to accept document and payment, saying that all the goods had been ruined.

中国出口商与美国出口商签订一份 CIF 合同，从美国进口机械零部件一批。货物已在合同规定的时间和装运港装船，受载船只离港四小时后触礁沉没。第二天，当卖方凭手中持有的提单、保险单、发票等装运单据要求买方付款时，买方以货物全部损失为理由，拒绝接受单据和付款。

【Typical Questions Analysis 典型问题分析】

Question: Calculate the FOB price, CFR price and CIF price.

求：FOB 价，CFR 价和 CIF 价。

Commodity name: toy rabbit

Commodityinformation:60pcs/ctn,measurement:0.164m^3, 20’container(measurement:25m^3).

Purchase cost: 6 RMB/pcs.

Rate: Value-added Tax Rate17%, Refund Rate 15%.

Domestic expenses: inland freight 100RMB; inspection fee 120 RMB, declaration fee 150 RMB, Port charge 100 RMB, other expenses 3000 RMB.

Bank charges: quotation × 1%.

Ocean freight: USD1350 for per 20 feet container from Qingdao to Hamburger.

Insurance: 110 of invoice amount on the basis of CIF, covering all risks(0.8%)and war risks(0.08%).

Expected profit: quotation × 10%

Exchange rate: US$1= 6.35RMB

商品名称：毛绒玩具兔子。

商品资料：每箱装 60 只，每箱体积为 0.164 立方米，一个 20 尺的小柜（常识 25 立方米）

供货价格：每只 6 元。

税率：供货单价中均包括 17%的增值税，退税率为 15%。

国内费用：内陆运费（每立方米）100 元；报检费 120 元；报关费 150 元；港杂费 100 元；公司综合费用 3000 元。

银行费用：报价的 1%。

海运费：从青岛到汉堡港的一个 20 尺的小柜运费为 1350 美元。

货运保险：CIF 成交金额的基础上加 10%投保中国人民保险公司海运货物保险条款中的一切险（0.8%费率）和战争险（0.08%费率）。

报价预期利润：报价的 10%。

报价汇率：6.35 元人民币兑换 1 美元。

Chapter Seven International Cargo Transportation

第七章 国际货物运输

【Learning Objectives】教学目的与要求

After learning this chapter, you will be able to:

1. Understand the main means of international transport of goods;
2. Understand the various international transportation characteristics;
3. Master a variety of international transport of goods freight calculation;
4. Master contract in terms of shipment and shipment documents produced.

【Lead-in Case】引导案例

Questions: Does this action breach the contract?
问题：这是否违约?

A Chinese company A exported 1 000 tons of corn. The letter of credit stipulated “partial shipment is not allowed”. Later, the company A loaded 500 tons each on the same ship on the same voyage number in Rizhao and Qingdao.And the bill of lading also indicated different port of loading and date of shipment.

我国 A 公司向美国出口 1 000 公吨玉米，国外来证规定，“不允许分批装运”，结果 A 公司在规定的期限内分别在日照、青岛各装 500 公吨于同一航次的同一船上，提单上也注明了不同的装货港和不同的装货日期。

Section One Means of Transportation
第一节 国际货物的运输方式

The delivery of goods, in international trade, is a way to achieve both the transfer of goods, which is related to the import and export contract whether implement smoothly, due to the international transport of cargo have some features such as high risk, multi-links, involved many aspects, strong timeliness etc., it is required to select proper modes of transport and consistent terms of shipment.

国际货物运输是实现买卖双方交接货物的手段，关系到进出口合同能否顺利完成，由于国际货物运输具有风险大，环节多，涉及面广，时间性强等特点，要求买卖双方在订立合同时，应该合理地选择运输方式和相应的装运条款。

At present, international cargo transport mainly include: ocean transport, rail transport, road transport, air transport, and other means. Each mode has its own characteristics.

目前来看，国际货物运输有海洋运输、铁路运输、公路运输、航空运输等多种方式。每种运输方式都有各自的特点。

1. Ocean Transport 海洋运输

1.1 Definition and Characteristics 定义和特点

Ocean transport is the most widely used mode of transportation in international trade, it is based on the vessel for transport tool , fixed routes and sailing region, between both the ports of domestic and abroad to complete the task of transportation. At present, the total volume of international goods more than 80% of the carriage of goods by ocean transport is completed, so the ocean transportation has become the most important mode of transportation in the international trade .

海洋运输是国际贸易运输中采用最广泛的一种形式，它是以船舶为运输工具，在国内外港口之间通过一定的航线和航区来完成运输任务的一种运输方式。目前，国际货物总运量的 80%以上是利用海上运输完成的，从而使海洋运输成为国际贸易中最为重要的运输方式。

Comparing with other modes of transport, it has the following characteristics:

与其他运输方式相比较，它有以下几个特点：

（1）Large transportation quantity. The ship carrying capacity is far beyond the train, car and plane, is the strongest in transport capacity. A ship load weight of 10 000 ton is generally equal to 250 ~ 300 train paper weight.

运输量大。船舶承载能力远远大于火车、汽车和飞机，是运输能力最强的运输工具。一艘万吨船舶的载重量一般相当于 250 ~ 300 个火车皮的载重量。

（2）Strong passing capability. Oceans area of the earth surface is about 70%, it can lead in all direction of ports of natural waterway around the world together, not like the car, train which are often limited by road and rail.

通过能力强。海洋占地球表面积约 70%，可以利用四通八达的天然水路将世界各地的港口连在一起，不像汽车、火车要受公路和铁路的限制。

（3）Low freight rates. Ocean transportation by waterway is a naturally formed, the port facilities are built by the general government, and the load weight is large quantity, long distance, economies of scale, assigning to per ton of freight costs are relatively low.

运费率低。海洋运输所利用的航道是天然形成的，港口设施一般为政府所建，而且海运量大、航程远，分摊于每吨货物的运费成本相对较低，具有规模效益。

（4）Good adaptability . Because of the above characteristics make ocean transport adapted to convey a variety of goods, especially some special cargo which is unable to transport by train or automobile, such as oil derrick, the locomotive.

对货物的适应性强。由于以上特点使海洋运输适合运输各种货物，尤其是一些火车、汽车无法运输的特种货物，如石油井架、机车等。

(5) Slow speed. The measurements of the ship is rather large, the flow resistance is large, so the ship speed is slow.

速度慢。船舶体积大，水流阻力大，因此速度慢。

(6) High risk. Ocean transport cycle is relatively longer because of being subject to climate and natural condition.

风险大。海洋运输的周期相对较长，受气候和自然条件影响较大。

1.2 Operation Mode of Ocean Transport 海洋运输的经营方式

According to the different operating mode, ocean transportation can be divided into the liners and chartering.

根据营运方式不同，海洋运输可以分为班轮运输和租船运输两大类。

1.2.1 Liner/Regular Shipping Liner 班轮运输/定期船运输

The liner is also known as regular shipping liner refers to the ship in accordance with the fixed route and a predetermined schedule sailing, with stops at several fixed ports, and according to the prior published rates charged on freight transport mode. The liner is one of the main ways of ocean transport, the majority of China's import and export goods is transportd through the liner, approximately 70% of the total of China's marine transport, the liner especially suitable for shipment the goods in stability, varieties, bulk small of groceries.

班轮运输又称定期船运输，是指船舶按照固定的航线和预先规定的时间表航行，沿途停靠若干固定的港口，并按事先公布的费率收取运费的运输方式。班轮运输是海上货物运输的主要方式之一，我国绝大部分进出口物资都是通过班轮运输，约占我国海运总量的 70%以上，班轮运输尤其适合于货流稳定、货种多、批量小的杂货运输。

Characteristics of Liner 班轮运输的特点

① Four fixed. The liner has a regular sailing and arrival on a stated schedule between a group of specific port by the fixed rates.This is the main features of liners.

② The carrier is responsible for the cargo loading and unloading.

③ The B/L drawn by the shipping company is the shipping contract between the carrier and the consignor. The rights and obligations of the carrier and the consignor are base on the B/L drawn by the shipping company, as well as subject to unified international convention constraints.

④ The ship-owner usually leases part of shipping space instead of the whole ship.

Thus, use of liner shipping goods is very flexible and convenient, especially more suitable for the goods in small transaction quantity, much batch, delivery scattered port.

① 四固定。即有固定航线、固定港口、固定的船期表和相对固定的费率。这是班轮运输的基本特点。

② 船方负责货物的装卸，即通常所说的“管装管卸”。

③ 船、货双方的权利、义务与责任豁免，以船方签发的提单条款为依据并受统一的国际公约制约。

④ 船东通常出租部分舱位，而不是全部舱位。

由此可见，利用班轮运输货物是十分灵活方便的，尤其是对成交数量少、批次多、交货港口分散的货物更合适。

1.2.2 Chartering 租船运输

Shipping by chartering is also called tramp, refers to the charterer rents the whole boat for transport of goods, and pays the agreed freight. Difference with liner, it has no fixed schedule of sailing, route, a docking port is not fixed. Ship operation by the charterer and the lessor according to the charter contract. The shipping by chartering is often used in mineral or other bulk, cheap goods transport, and accounts for about 80% of the total international shipping.

租船运输又称不定期船运输，是指租船人向船主租赁整条船进行货物运输，并按商定运价交纳运费的一种运输方式。它和班轮运输不同，没有预先制定的船期表、航线、停靠港口也不固定。船舶之间的运营由租船人和出租人之间按照双方签订的租船合同确定。租船运输常用于矿产或其他大宗、低价货物的运输，约占国际海运总量的 80%左右。

（1）The Characteristics of Charter Transport 租船运输的特点

① Suitable for the transport of bulk goods. Shipping by chartering to transport low value goods such as food, feed, fertilizer, coal, is usually the whole ship.

适合运输大宗货物。租船运输主要以运输价值较低的大宗货物为主，如粮食、饲料、煤炭、化肥等，通常是整船装运。

② The price is not fixed. From the market supply and demand constraint, charter freight rate level along with the market change. In general, the charter freight rate is lower than the liner.

运价不固定。受市场供求的约束，租船运价的高低随市场行情的变化而变化。一般来说，租船运价比班轮运价低廉。

③ According to the charter contract arrangement of navigation. Charter contract is signed with the owner charterer, the ship without a predetermined schedule, routes and ports, sailing time is not fixed. Therefore, take what route, carry what goods and sailing time according to the charterer's request, confirmed by the ship-owner.

按租船合同安排航行。租船合同是租船人同船东签订的，船舶没有预定的船期表、固定的航线和港口，航行时间也不固定。因此，走什么航线、运什么货物以及航行时间等都按租船人的要求，由船东确认而定。

（2）Methods of the Chartering 租船运输的方式

① Time Charter. The charterer charters the ship for a period of time during which the ship is deployed and managed by the charterer. What concerns the charterer most is the period, not the voyage. The chartering may be for a period of one year or of several years.

During the period of chartering, the ship is managed, deployed and used by the charterer. Fuel expenses, port expenses, loading and unloading expenses which are caused by loading and unloading, stowing and trimming, should be borne by the charterer. The ship-owner should bear the wages and the vessel insurance premium, and be responsible for seaworthiness during the period of chartering.

定期租船。又称期租船，是以期限为基础的租船方式。即由船舶所有人将船舶出租给租船人使用一定期限，在此期限内由租船人自行调度和经营管理。租用时间可以是一年或数年。

在租船期间，货船的经营、管理和使用权都归承租人。同时，由于装卸货物、平仓、理仓等引起的燃油费、港口费、装卸费等也都由承租人负担。船东要负责支付船员的工资及相关费用和货船的保险费，并保证在租用期间货船适合海洋运输。

② Voyage Charter. The voyage charter is one of the carriage of goods from one specified port to another or for a round trip. It includes single voyage charter, return voyage charter and successive voyage charter. According to the route stipulated in the charter party, the ship-owner is responsible for delivering the goods to the port of destination and for managing the ship as well as bearing all expenses.

定程租船。又称“程租船”或“航次租船”，指租船人按照航程租赁全部舱位，由船舶所有人负责将货物运到指定的目的港。定程租船就其租赁方式的不同可分为：单程租船（又称单航次租船）、来回航次租船、连续航次租船。

Voyage charter's "lease" depends on the voyage transportation task is completed, the voyage charter does not require completion of a voyage or voyages the time required, so the ship owner complete a voyage time is required for most concerned, in particular he wanted to shorten the time of mooring in port. While the charterer and the ship owner to ship loading and unloading speed also is opposite, so after signing the charter, the parties also agreed to ship loading and unloading speed and handling time calculation method, and the corresponding provisions of demurrage and dispatch rate standard and calculation method.

程租船的“租期”取决于航次运输任务是否完成，由于航次租船并不规定完成一个航次或几个航次所需的时间，因此船舶所有人对完成一个航次所需的时间是最为关心的，他特别希望缩短船舶在港停泊时间。而承租人与船舶所有人对船舶的装卸速度又是对立的，所以在签订租船合同时，承租双方还需约定船舶的装卸速度以及装卸时间的计算办法，并相应地规定滞期费和速遣费率的标准和计算方法。

③ Demise Charter. Demise charter is the only charter, with the crew, in the charter period, the charterer is equipped with a full set of personnel, ship management and navigation control. This chartering way actually belongs to simple lease of property, the owner, generally will not be assured of ship to the charterer disposal. Therefore, the demise charter in chartering market uses less.

光船租船，是指只租船，不带船员，在租船期内，由租船人配备全套人员，支配船舶进行经营管理和航行。这种租船方式实际上属于单纯的财产租赁，对于船东来说，一般不放心将船交给租船人支配使用。因此，光船租船在租船市场上较少采用。

2. Air Transport 航空运输

Air transport refers to applying the mode of air transport to delivery the import and export goods. It is a modern mode of transport. The characteristics of air transport are quick, short time, high safety, low breakage rate of goods, save the packing expenses, insurance premium and storage charges; sailing facilities, not limited by ground conditions and forward the goods to the destination around the airport of world. The basic way of air transport can be grouped into Scheduled Airliner, Charter Transport and Air Express. See Fig. 7-1.

航空货物运输是指利用飞机运送进出口货物。它是一种现代化的运输方式。其特点是交货速度快，时间短，安全性能高，货物破损率小，节省包装费，保险费和储藏费，航行便利，不受地面条件限制，可以通往世界各地。航空货物运输的基本方式可以分成班机运输、包机运输、急件传递，如图 7-1 所示。

图 7-1　航空运输

The Scope of Air Transport 航空货物运输的适用范围

The main scope of air transport includes:

(1) Easy decay, spoilage of fresh goods;

(2) Timeliness goods and seasonal strong goods;

(3) Rescue, emergency goods;

(4) Valuables, precision instruments.

航空货物运输主要适合范围包括：

(1) 易腐烂、变质的鲜活商品；

(2) 时效性、季节性强的商品、节令性商品；

(3) 抢险、救急品；

(4) 贵重物品、精密仪器。

3. Railway Transport 铁路运输

International railway transportation is a major mode of transport in international trade following the ocean transport. Its major advantage is larger load weight, quick speed, transportation risk is significantly smaller than the ocean transportation, can be maintained at the sharp time to consign the goods all the year round. See Fig. 7-2.

国际铁路运输是在国际贸易中仅次于海洋运输的一种主要运输方式。其最大的优势是运量较大，速度较快，运输风险明显小于海洋运输，能常年保持准点运营等，如图 7-2 所示。

图 7-2　铁路运输

China International Rail Transport is roughly divided into two kinds, one is the international rail transport, the other is the Hong Kong and Macao railway transportation.

我国的国际铁路运输大致上分为两种，第一种是国际铁路联运，第二种是对港澳地区的铁路运输。

3.1 Railway Combined Transport 国际铁路联运

International railway through transport, consignor consign the goods from the originating station, use a railway consignment note, the railway will carry the goods to the destination according to the consignment to the consignee. In one country by rail to another country railroad the handing over of the goods, without charge, consignor to countries in Asia and Europe, according to the international treaty obligations under international railway through transport.

国际铁路联运，发货人由始发站托运，使用一份铁路运单,铁路方面根据运单将货物运往终点站交给收货人。在由一国铁路向另一国铁路移交货物时，不需收、发货人参加，亚欧各国按国际条约承担国际铁路联运的义务。

China Europe international rail transport lines have two lines: one is the use of the Siberia mainland bridge of Russia through the Middle East, Europe; the other one is from Jiangsu via Xinjiang and Kazakhstan railway connected Lianyungang, through Russia, Poland, Germany to Holland Rotterdam. The latter is called the bridge of new Asia-Europe mainland, fortune than marine 9 000km shorter than ocean transport, via the Siberia mainland bridge shortened 3 000km, and further promotes China's economic and trade exchanges with European and Asian countries, but also promote the Chinese along the region's economic development.

我国通往欧洲的国际铁路联运线有两条：一条是利用俄罗斯的西伯利亚大陆桥贯通中东、欧洲各国；另一条是由江苏连云港经新疆与哈萨克斯坦铁路连接，贯通俄罗斯、波兰、德国至荷兰的鹿特丹。后者称为新亚欧大陆桥，运程比海运缩短 9 000 公里，比经由西伯利亚大陆桥缩短 3 000 公里，进一步推动了我国与欧亚各国的经贸往来，也促进了我国沿线地区的经济发展。

3.2 Hong Kong and Macao Railway Transportation 对港澳地区的铁路运输

For district of Hong Kong-Macao railway transport according to the domestic transport handling, but it is also not the same as the general domestic transport. Goods from the mainland ships at Shenzhen to Hong kong unloading delivery as two tickets combined transport, A "cargo receipt" will be issued by company Sinotrans. The Beijing-Kowloon Railway and Shanghai harbor to after the opening of the mainland to Hong Kong, the transportation is more efficient. Because of the Hong Kong Special Administrative Region of free port, goods in the mainland and Hong Kong must apply for import. The railway transport in Macao, is the first arrival of the goods at the Guangzhou south station to ship to Macao.

对港澳地区的铁路运输按国内运输办理，但又不同于一般的国内运输。货物由内地装车至深圳到转到香港卸车交货，为两票联运，由外运公司签发“货物承运收据”。京九铁路和沪港直达通车后，内地至香港的运输更为快捷。由于香港特别行政区系自由港，货物在内地和香港间进出，需办理进出口报关手续。对澳门地区的铁路运输，是先将货物运抵广州南站再转船运至澳门。

4. Road Transport 公路运输

With the development of international trade, the highway transportation is also developing rapidly. Many European countries and the United States, Japan and other countries have built more developed road network, the automobile industry provides a solid material foundation, which prompted the highway transportation in transportation industry is jumped to the dominant position. At present developed country road transport passenger and freight turnover accounted for completion of various modes of transport in total volume of about 90%. The characteristics of highway transportation are flexible, adaptable which can realized of the"door-to-door"direct transportation, less investment, fast capital turnover, small volume, higher cost. See Fig. 7-3.

随着国际贸易的发展，公路运输发展迅速。欧洲许多国家和美国、日本等国已建成比较发达的公路网，汽车工业又提供了雄厚的物质基础，这些都促使公路运输在运输业中跃至主导地位。目前发达国家公路运输完成的客货周转量占各种运输方式总周转量的90%左右。公路运输的特点：机动灵活，适应性强；可实现“门到门”直达运输；原始投资少，资金周转快；运量较小，运输成本较高，如图 7-3 所示。

图 7-3　汽车运输

5. Pipelines Transport 管道运输

Pipelines transport are used a pipeline as a transportation tool to forward liquid and gaseous materials in long distance transportation, pipelines transport of petroleum products is higher cost than the shipping, but still cheaper than rail transport. Pipelines transport capacity, less land occupation, short construction period, low cost, safe and reliable, strong continuity, low energy consumption, low cost, good benefit. But pipelines transport also has its disadvantages, mainly in poor flexibility, high cost. See Fig. 7-4.

管道运输是用管道作为运输工具的一种长距离输送液体和气体物资的运输方式，管道运输石油产品比海洋运输费用高，但仍然比铁路运输便宜。管道运输的运量大，占地少，建设周期短，费用低，安全可靠、连续性强，耗能少，成本低，效益好。但是管道运输如有缺点，主要表现在管道运输的灵活性差，成本高，如图 7-4 所示。

图 7-4　管道运输

6. Postal Transport 邮政运输

The postal transport refers to a mode of transport which send the goods of import and export through the post office. The postal transport is relatively simple, as long as the seller handles the procedures of sending to post office according to the sale contract agreed conditions and the stipulations, for example pay the postage, obtain a receipt, which means to accomplish the delivery task. See Fig. 7-5.

邮政运输，是指通过邮局寄交进出口货物的一种运输方式。邮政运输比较简便，只要卖方根据买卖合同中双方约定的条件和邮局的有关规定，向邮局办理寄送手续，付清邮费，取得收据，就完成交货任务，如图 7-5 所示。

图 7-5　邮政运输

7. Container Transport 集装箱运输

Container transport is the most advanced modern carriage means to use container as a transport unit, which is a senior transport way in group transport form. It has"safe, rapid, simple, cheap"characteristics, which can reduce transport links. Container transport can utilize the comprehensively railway, highway, waterway and aviation and other transport modes to multimodal transport to realize the "door-to-door" transport. See Fig. 7-6.

集装箱运输是以集装箱作为运输单位进行货物运输的一种最先进的现代化运输方式，是成组运输的一种高级运输形式。它具有“安全、迅速、简便、价廉”的特点，有利于减少运输环节，可以通过综合利用铁路、公路、水路和航空等各种运输方式，进行多式联运，实现“门到门”运输，如图 7-6 所示。

图 7-6　集装箱运输

7.1 Characteristics of Container Transport 集装箱运输的特点

（1）High efficiency mode of transport, 高效益的运输方式；

（2）Highly efficient mode of transport, 高效率的运输方式；

（3）Collaborative modes of transport, 高协作的运输方式；

（4）For the organization of multimodal transport. 适于组织多式联运。

7.2 Container Types 集装箱的种类

（1）According to the cargo types: grocery container, bulk container, liquid container, refrigerated container. See Fig. 7-7.

（2）By the material: woods container, steel container, aluminum alloy container, glass steel container, stainless steel containers.

（3）By the structure: foldable container, fixed container (including sealed container, open top container, plate rack container).

（4）By weight: 30 tons, 20 tons, 10 tons, 5 tons, 2.5 tons of container.

（1）按所装货物种类可分为：杂货集装箱、散货集装箱、液体集装箱、冷藏集装箱等，如图 7-7 所示。

（2）按制造材料可分为：木集装箱、钢集装箱、铝合金集装箱、玻璃钢集装箱、不锈钢集装箱等。

（3）按结构可分为：折叠式集装箱、固定式集装箱（包括密闭集装箱、开顶集装箱、板架集装箱）等。

（4）按承重量可分为：30 吨集装箱、20 吨集装箱、10 吨集装箱、5 吨集装箱、2.5 吨集装箱等。

图 7-7 集装箱

7.3 Container Specifications 集装箱的规格

In order to unity container classes, the international organization for standardization recommends of three catena of thirteen classes of the container, in the international transport commonly used in container specifications for type IA, type IAA and type IC, our country generally use the IC type container.

Type IA is 8 feet by 8 feet by 40 feet.

Type IAA is 8.6 feet by 8 feet by 40 feet.

Type IC is 8 feet by 8 feet by 20 feet.

为了统一集装箱的规格，国际标准化组织推荐了三个系列十三种规格的集装箱，在国际运输中常用的集装箱规格为 IA 型、IAA 型和 IC 型，我国一般采用 IC 型集装箱。

IA 型，即 8 英尺 × 8 英尺 × 40 英尺。

IAA 型，即 8.6 英尺 × 8 英尺 × 40 英尺。

IC 型，即 8 英尺 × 8 英尺 × 20 英尺。

7.4　Container Packing Method 集装箱的装箱方式

（1）Full Container Load(FCL)整箱货

This is defined that the shipper is responsible for packing, count, fill in the list, and the customs seal. FCL is usually only a consignor and a consignee. The owner uses it when he has sufficient goods put in one or more FCL, in addition to some large shippers maintained a container, others from the carrier or container leasing company hire a certain container. After empty containers transport to the factory or warehouse, under the supervision of customs officers, owner put the goods into the box, lock, aluminum seal, then give it to carrier and obtain station receipt, the receipt for a bill of lading.

整箱货是指由发货人负责装箱、计数、填写装箱单，并由海关加铅封的货。整箱货通常只有一个发货人和一个收货人。这种情况通常在货主有足够货源装载一个或数个整箱时采用，除有些大的货主自己置备有集装箱外，一般都是向承运人或集装箱租赁公司租用一定的集装箱。空箱运到工厂或仓库后，在海关人员的监管下，货主把货装入箱内、加锁、铝封后交承运人并取得站场收据，最后凭收据换取提单或运单。

（2）Less than Container Load(LCL)拼箱货

Refers to the carrier (or agents) accept consignor consignment number less than FCL cargo after the vote, according to goods kind nature and destination classification. They collect a certain number of less than container to be packed a whole container for delivering to the same destination of the goods. As a result of a box with different consignor goods together, so called LCL's. In the case of the insufficient number of full FCL consignments owner uses. LCL's sorting, concentration, packing (Unboxed), delivery and other work does on the carrier dock container freight station and inland container transport station.

拼箱货是指承运人（或代理人）接受货主托运的数量不足整箱的小票货运后，根据货类性质和目的地进行分类整理。把去同一目的地的货，集中到一定数量拼装入箱。由于一个箱内有不同货主的货，它们拼装在一起，所以叫拼箱。这种情况在货主托运数量不足装满整箱时采用。拼箱货的分类、整理、集中、装箱（拆箱）、交货等工作均在承运人码头、集装箱货运站或内陆集装箱转运站进行。

7.5　Container Transfer Mode 集装箱货物交接方式

（1）FCL / FCL 整箱交，整箱接

（2）LCL / LCL 拼箱交，拆箱接

（3）FCL / LCL 整箱交，拆箱接

（4）LCL / FCL 拼箱交，整箱接

7.6　Goods Handing over Locations 集装箱运输货物交接地点

（1）Door to Door；门到门

（2）Door to CY；门到场

（3）Door to CFS；门到站

（4）CY to Door；场到门

（5）CY to CY；场到场

（6）CY to CFS；场到站

（7）CFS to Door；站到门

（8）CFS to CY；站到场

（9）CFS to CFS；站到站

8. International Multimodal Transport 国际多式联运

8.1 Concept of International Multimodal Transport 国际多式联运的概念

International multimodal transport means the conveyance of cargo includes at least two modes of transport by which the goods are carried from the place of dispatch to destination on the basis of combined transport or a multimodal contract. Under this method, the container is used an intermedium and make up of an international multimodal and join transport mode by sea, air and land.

国际多式联运是在集装箱运输的基础上产生和发展起来的一种综合性的连续运输方式。它一般以集装箱为媒介，把海、陆、空多种传统的单一运输方式有机地结合起来，组成一种国家间的连贯运输。

8.2 International Multimodal Transport Conditions 国际多式联运应具备的条件

（1）The multimodal transport operator and the shipper must sign a multimodal transport contract, in order to clear the right, obligation and immunity relationship of each other. Multimodal transport contract is determined according to the nature of multimodal transport, and the based on difference between multimodal transport and general transport.

多式联运经营人与托运人之间必须签订多式联运合同，以明确承、托双方的权利、义务和豁免关系。多式联运合同是确定多式联运性质的依据，也是区别多式联运与一般联运的主要依据。

（2）Must use M.T.D, the document is a document of title, and securities.

必须使用全程多式联运单据(M. T. D)，该单据既是物权凭证，也是有价证券。

（3）Must be full implementation of single tariff. The freight rate time charge, including the cost of transport (the sum of each transport fees), management fees and reasonable profit.

必须全程实行单一运价。这个运价一次收取，包括运输成本（各段运杂费的总和）、经营管理费和合理利润。

（4）Must be made by a multimodal transport operator with respect to the entire transportation responsibility. He signs the multimodal transport contract with the shipper, but also issues multimodal transport document or a multimodal transport bill of lading, he assumed the responsibility of the entire transport from the acceptance of the goods to the delivery of the goods.

必须由一个多式联运经营人对全程运输负总责。他是与托运人签订多式联运合同的当事人，也是签发多式联运单据或多式联运提单者，他承担自接受货物起至交付货物止的全程运输责任。

（5）Must be two different modes of coherent transport at least. This is an important distinction the general transport to multimodal transport.

必须至少是两种不同运输方式连贯运输。这是一般联运与多式联运的一个重要区别。

（6）Must be the international transport of goods. This is the difference between domestic and international transport conditions.

必须是国际间的货物运输。这是区别国内运输和国际运输的限制条件。

9. Continental Bridge Transport 陆桥运输

9.1 Land Bridge Transport 大陆桥运输

Land bridge transport refers to the use of the transcontinental railway (highway) transport system as a bridge between the mainland, both ends of the marine connecting container coherent mode of transport.

In the words, both sides is marine, middle is the land, the sea continent connected, forming a sea land transport, while the mainland play a "bridge" role, so called the continental bridge transport.

大陆桥运输是指利用横贯大陆的铁路（公路）运输系统作为中间桥梁，把大陆两端的海洋连接起来的集装箱连贯运输方式。简言之，就是两边是海运，中间是陆运，大陆把海洋连接起来，形成海—陆联运，而大陆起了“桥”的作用，因此称之为大陆桥运输。

Land bridge transport was first started in the United States, it links up the sea routes of Japan, Europe, the United States and the railway of across the United States, carried out the land and sea container transport between Japan and Europe.

大陆桥运输最早是从美国开始的，是把日本、美国、欧洲间的海上集装箱航线与横贯美国东西的铁路连接起来，开展日本—欧洲间的海陆集装箱联运。

The world's major continental bridges are the American land bridge, Canada land bridge, they are parallel, collectively referred to as the North American land Bridge; another one is Siberian land bridge connected the Pacific Ocean and the Atlantic ocean. The Baltic and Black Sea is also known as Eurasia bridge due to cross two continents-Asia and Europe. In addition, in 1992 December the official opening of the second Asia-Europe continental bridge, East China Lianyungang, via Longhai, Lanxin, North Xinjiang Railway into the CIS in direct Holland Rotterdam.

目前，世界上最主要的大陆桥有美洲大陆桥、加拿大大陆桥，它们之间是平行的，统称为北美大陆桥；另一条是连接太平洋和大西洋、波罗的海以及黑海的西伯利亚大陆桥，因地跨欧亚两洲又称欧亚大陆桥。此外，1992 年 12 月正式开通的第二条亚欧大陆桥，东起我国连云港，途经陇海、兰新、北疆铁路进入前独联体境内直达荷兰鹿特丹。

9.2 Mini Bridge Transport 小陆桥运输

Lane bridge transport means than continental bridge transportation by sea, land, sea transport to shorten the period of maritime transport, forming a sea, land, sea or land transport. For example, Japan to the United States east coast port of the Atlantic or the United States Southern Mexico bay port freight, from the original full shipping, by the Japan shipping to the United States western pacific ports, turn with special railway train to the eastern port of the Atlantic or southern Mexico port, with onshore railway bridge, the west coast of the United States with the east coast and the Gulf of Mexico to connect.

小路桥运输是指比大陆桥运输的海、陆、海运输缩短一段的海上运输，形成了海、陆或陆、海运输的方式。例如，日本至美国东海岸大西洋港口或美国南部墨西哥湾口岸的货运，由原来的全程海运，改为由日本装船运至美国西部太平洋口岸，转装铁路专用列车至东部大西洋口岸或南部墨西哥口岸，以陆上铁路为桥梁，把美国西海岸同东海岸和墨西哥湾连接起来。

Section Two　Freight of International Transportion
第二节　国际货物运输的运费

1.　Ocean Freight 海运费

1.1　Definition of Freight 运费的定义

The carrier, in the process of transportation, is to bear certain labor, consumption expenditure, and while they are selling services in labour, they need to reimburse a certain reward to compensate the consumption and expenditure for this part, and earn a certain profit, this compensation is called the freight.

承运人在运输过程中，要承担一定劳务，消耗支出，而在出售劳务的时候，需要向运输劳务的购买者，收取一定的报酬，以补偿这部分的消耗和支出，并取得一定的盈利，这部分补偿就是运费。

1.2 Payment of Freight 运费支付

（1）Freight Prepaid 预付运费

In the present international trade, most companies generally use CIF or CFR price terms, the seller has paid the freight in the port of loading before the bill of lading issued, so that the two sides are early settlement. Freight prepaid is guaranteed for the carrier to avoid the risks not received freight because of loss of or damage to goods.

在当前的国际贸易中，一般都采用 CIF 或 CFR 价格条件，在签发提单之前由卖方在装货港支付运费，以便双方尽早结汇。预付运费对承运人是有保证的，避免了因货物灭失或损坏而收不到运费的风险。

（2）Freight Collect 到付运费

Freight collect refers to pay the freight for goods shipped to the port of destination. To pay the freight, the carrier is to beat the risk.

到付运费需等待货物运到目的港，交付货物前付清运费。到付运费，对承运人来说是要承担一定的风险的。

1.3 Freight of Liners 班轮运费

Freight of liners is that the consignor pays the freight price to liner companies, include shipping costs and profits. When the liners company developed freight, in addition to consider the shipping costs, but also must pay attention to the following several main factors:

① The value of the goods and commodity characteristics;

② Volume size and efficiency of port handling;

③ Voyage distance.

班轮运量是班轮公司向货主收取的运费价格，包括航运成本和利润。班轮公司制定运价时，除了考虑航运成本费用外，还要关注以下几个主要因素：

① 货物价值和商品特性；

② 运量大小和港口装卸效率的高低；

③ 航程的远近。

1.4 Liner Freight Standard of Calculating 班轮运费的计收标准

According to the weight, volume and value is mainly divided into three kinds of calculation methods, shipping company in the freight charge often choose the most advantageous, the highest collection. Liner freight is composed of the basic freight and charges. Basic freight to be collected as follows.

根据货物的重量、体积和价值主要分为三种计算方法，船公司在收取运费时往往选择对其最有利、可收运费最高的一种计收。班轮运费由基本运费和附加费构成。基本运费的计收标准有如下几种。

（1）According to weight ton. Which is indicated by "W" in the tariff. According to the gross weight (weight ton) calculation, tons of the following and three decimal place. Applied value is not high, small size, large weight cargo.

按重量吨（weight ton）计收。运价表上用"W"表示。按货物毛重（公吨）计算，吨以下取小数三位。适用于价值不高、体积小、重量大的货物。

（2）According to the measurement ton, tariff with "W". According to the cargo volume (cubic meters) calculation, cubic meters the following three decimal places. Applied value is not high, light weight, large volume of goods. Weight ton and ton collectively is known as freight ton, abbreviation FT.

按尺码吨（measurement ton）计收。运价表上用"M"表示。按货物体积（立方米）计算，立方米以下取三位小数。适用于价值不高、重量轻、体积大的货物。重量吨和尺码吨统称为运费吨或计费吨（freight ton，缩写 FT）。

（3）According to the price charged. Commonly it is known as freight. Tariff with "Ad.Val" or "A.V.". The value of the goods as freight calculated according to FOB standard, general price to calculate the percentage. It is applicable to gold, silver, precision instruments, crafts and other precious commodities.

按价格计收。俗称从价运费。运价表上用"Ad. Val"或"A. V."表示。以货物价值作为运费计收标准，一般按 FOB 价格的百分比计算。适用于黄金、白银、精密仪器、手工艺品等贵重商品。

（4）According to the weight or measurement ton. Freight list with W / M. This is a common charge standard, the shipping company chooses the higher collection. 163

按重量吨或尺码吨计收。运价表上用 W/M 表示。这是常见的一种计收标准，由船舶公司选择其中数值较高的一种计收。

（5）According to the weight or measurement ton or freight calculated from the price. Freight list with W/M or A.V. The shipping company choose the highest collection from the three standard.

按重量吨或尺码吨或从价运费计收。运价表上用 W/M or A.V.表示。由船舶公司从三种计收标准中选择收费最高的一种计收。

（6）Choose the higher price as the standard from the weight and measurement, then add the certain freight calculated from the price. Freight list with W / M plus A.V.

按重量吨或尺码吨中收费较高的作为标准再另行加收一定百分比从价运费。运价表上用 W/M plus A.V.表示。

（7）According to the number of items (per unit / per head). As the truck by car, live animals in the collection.

按货物的件数（per unit /per head）计收。如卡车按辆，活牲畜按头计收。

（8）Instead of by open rate. Temporary agreed freight rate, such as grain, ore, coal and other bulk goods.

按议价（open rate）计收。临时商定运价，如粮食、矿石、煤炭等大宗货物。

（9）According to the minimum freight (Mini rate). Less than 1 ton (1 tons or 1 metric ton weight) of goods are according to the level of goods freight charge, called minimum freight.

按起码运费（mini rate）计收。不足 1 运费吨（1 重量吨或 1 尺码吨）的货物均按一级货收取运费，称为起码运费。

1.5　Surcharges 附加费

In addition to receive basic freight by shipping company, also a surcharge, to compensate for the lack of basic freight. There are several common surcharge:

船公司除收取基本运费外，还征收附加费，以弥补基本运费的不足。常见的附加费有以下几种：

（1）Heavy lift additional. Cargo gross weight over tariffs prescribed weight, i.e. for heavy-weight, require surcharge.

超重附加费（heavy lift additional）。一件货物毛重超过运价表规定的重量，即为超重货，需要加收附加费。

（2）Long length additional. The length of goods is longer than tariff regulation length, i.e. for super-long cargo, require surcharge.

超长附加费（long length additional）。一件货物的长度超过运价表规定的长度，即为超长货，需要加收附加费。

（3）Transshipment surcharge. Cargo transshipment port handling, shipping company in dress and transshipment procedures, and the increased cost, called transshipment surcharge.

转船附加费（transshipment surcharge）。货物转船时，船公司在转船港口办理换装和转船手续而增加的费用，称为转船附加费。

（4）Bunker adjustment factor, abbreviation BAF. Rising fuel prices, shipping companies get the extra fuel oil fee according to the basic rate of a certain percentage.

燃油附加费（bunker adjustment factor，缩写 BAF）。燃油价格上涨时，船公司按基本运价的一定百分比加收的燃油涨价费。

（5）Direct additional. To the non-base port cargo to a certain number, shipping companies can arranged to direct and they get the fees. Direct additional lower than transshipment surcharge.

直航附加费（direct additional）。运往非基本港的货物达到一定数量时，船公司可安排直航而收取的费用。直航附加费一般比转船附加费低。

（6）Port surcharge. For the Ports of the poor equipment condition or the low efficiency in loading and unloading, shipping companies get the fees caused by loss of charge for the long time stay of the ship. According to the basic rate of a certain percentage of the collection.

港口附加费（port surcharge）。对有些设备条件差或装卸效率低的港口，船公司为了弥补船舶靠港时间长造成的损失而收取的费用。一般按基本运价的一定百分比计收。

（7）Port Congestion Surcharge. For some port due to press harbor boat, longer moored ship, and therefore the owner gets the charges.

港口拥挤费（port congestion surcharge）。对有些港口由于压港压船，导致停泊时间较长，船方因此而收取的费用。

（8）Optional surcharge (additional on optional discharging port). For selecting unloading goods (optional cargo) is required in the stowage give a special arrangement, it should increase certain procedures and costs, and sometimes need to capsize (point for cargo cabin), according to the cause and the additional charges, known as optional surcharge.

选卸附加费（additional on optional discharging port）。对于选卸货物（optional cargo）需要在

积载方面给以特殊的安排，这要增加一定的手续和费用，甚至有时需要翻船（指倒舱翻找货物），根据这样的原因而追加的费用，称为选卸附加费。

（9）Deviation surcharge. Normal channel can not pass, you had to make a detour to arrival at the destination port, convenient to charge the fee of ship.

绕航附加费（deviation surcharge）。正常航道不能通行，需绕道才能到达目的港时，船方便要加收此费。

（10）Devaluation surcharge or currency adjustment factor, CAF. When the tariff provisions devaluation, the shipping company will charge a certain percentage according to the basic fare surcharge.

货币贬值附加费（devaluation surcharge 或 currency adjustment factor, CAF）。当运价表中规定的货币贬值时，船公司便按基本运价加收一定百分比的附加费。

2. Container Freight 集装箱运费

International container freight calculation approach also has basic freight and additional freight branch, LCL and FCL freight calculation method is different.

国际集装箱海运运费的计算办法也有基本运费和附加运费之分，拼箱货和整箱货的运费计算方法是不同的。

2.1 LCL Freight Calculation 拼箱货海运运费的计算

LCL freight charges, is a basis of groceries shipping calculation standards, according to the consignment of actual freight ton billing, i.e. larger size by size tons of billing, large weight by weight tons charging; in addition, the LCL freight in there and container related expenses, such as LCL service charge and so on. As a result of LCL difference relates to the consignee, the LCL cannot accept consignor puts forward relevant port or change the port of destination, so the LCL freight had not selected port surcharge and alteration of destination port surcharge.

拼箱货运费的计算，基本上是依据件杂货运费的计算标准，按所托运货物的实际运费吨计费，即尺码大的按尺码吨计费，重量大的按重量吨计费，另外，在拼箱货海运运费中还要加收与集装箱有关的费用，如拼箱服务费等。由于拼箱货涉及不同的收货人，因而拼箱货不能接受货主提出的有关选港或变更目的港的要求，所以，在拼箱货海运运费中没有选港附加费和变更目的港附加费。

2.2 FCL Freight Calculation 整箱货海运运费的计算

（1）FAK box rates: regardless of type of goods, regardless of the volume of each container, only provides uniform charge rate.

FAK 包厢费率：不分货物种类，不计货量，只规定统一的每个集装箱收取的费率。

（2）FCS box rates: according to the different class of goods freight.

FCS 包厢费率：按不同货物等级计算运费。

（3）FCB box rates: according to the different class of goods or goods as well as the calculation of standard rates.

FCB 包厢费率：按不同货物等级或货类以及计算标准制定的费率。

2.3 Additional Charges 附加费的计算

As ordinary liner, the international container freight except collect basic freight, also want to add a variety of additional charges of standard and project of surcharge, according to the routes and goods are different and have different regulations.

与普通班轮一样，国际集装箱海运运费除计收基本运费外，也要加收各种附加费。附加费的标准与项目，根据航线和货种的不同而有不同的规定。

3. Rail Freight of International Carriage of Goods 国际铁路货物运输运费

3.1 Freight Calculation Principle 运费计算的原则

（1）The railway freight sending countries and reached nation, according to the national regulations.

发送国家和到达国家铁路的运费，均按铁路所在国家的国内规章办理。

（2）Transit railway freight carriage, according to the unified price of goods shall be calculated by the consignor or consignee. the goods are delivered between in the state in international railway cargo agreement and did not in the international railway cargo agreement, the international railway freight that was not in the international railway cargo agreement, calculate the freight according to its participation in another transport agreement.

过境国铁路的运费，均按承运当日统一货价格规定计算，由发货人或收货人支付。如在参加国际铁路货物协定的国家与未参加国际铁路货物协定的国家之间运送货物，则有关未参加国际铁路货物协定的国家的铁路运费，可按其所参加的另一种联运协定计算。

（3）China's transport of exported goods, delivery conditions are generally provided in the vehicle of the sellers, so I shall be responsible to the exit border station costs. But the transport of imported goods, should burden transit transportation costs and China railway section of the cost.

我国出口的联运货物，交货共同条件一般均规定在卖方车辆上交货，因此我方仅负责至出口国境站一段的运送费用。但联运进口货物，则要负担过境运送费和我国铁路铁路段的费用。

3.2 Basic Formula of Freight 运费的基本计算公式

Basic freight amount = goods freight rate × charging weight

Total freight = basic freight amount × (1 + bonus rate)

Add rate refers to the freight amount should be checked classes in basic freight volume based on the increase in the percentage. Express freight transport by slow freight 100%, less-than-truckload cargo plus 50% plus 100%. With passenger train hanging transport vehicle fees plus 200%.

基本运费额=货物运费率 × 计费重量

运费总额=基本运费额 ×（1+加成率）

加成率是指运费总额应按托运类别在基本运费额基础上所增加的百分比。快运货物运费按慢运运费加 100%，零担货物加 50%后再加 100%。随旅客列车挂运整车费，另加 200%。

3.3 Calculation of freight Classification 运费计算分类

（1）Vehicle cargo freight = ton freight × weight billing (by weight billing)

In which: per ton of freight = to value × freight mileage

整车货物运费 = 每吨运价 × 计费重量(按重量计费)

其中，每吨运价 = 发到基价 × 运价里程

（2）LTL freight =10 kilogram of freight × charging weight/ 10

In which: 10 kg rate = to price + operating base price × freight mileage

零担货物运费 = 10 公斤运价 × 计费重量/10

其中，10 公斤运价=发到基价+运行基价 × 运价里程

（3）The container freight = every box freight × box number

In which: each box price = to the base price + operating base price x box number

Calculated for each batch of goods freight mantissa insufficient 1 angle, press four to five homes in processing.

集装箱运费 = 每箱运价 × 箱数

其中，每箱运价=发到基价+运行基价 × 箱数

计算出的每批货物的运费尾数不足 1 角时，按四舍五入处理。

Transportation of out-of-gauge goods, the station should be the out-of-gauge goods grades in the bill of lading indicate, according to the following provisions billing:

（1）A class of goods: as per out-of-gauge freight rate plus 50%;

（2）Two levels of out-of-gauge goods: as per rate plus 100%;

（3）Super out-of-gauge goods: according to rate plus 150%.

On the installation of out-of-gauge goods inspection rack to the vehicle, not the other freight.

运输超限货物，发运站应将超限货物的等级在货物运单内注明，按下列规定计费：

（1）一级超限货物：按运价率加 50%；

（2）二级超限货物：按运价率加 100%；

（3）超级超限货物：按运价率加 150%。

对安装超限货物检查架的车辆不另收运费。

Section Three　Shipment Clauses and Shipping Documents in a Sales Contract
第三节　合同中的装运条款及装运单据

1. Shipping Clauses 装运条款

Terms of transportation is the main clauses in the contract, reasonably, clearly stipulates shipment terms, is the important condition to ensure that the import and export fulfill. This section describes the contract terms of shipment, including the time of shipment, loading port, port of destination, transshipment and partial shipment, shipment and demurrage dispatch clause.

装运条款是买卖合同中的主要条款，合理、明确地规定装运条款，是保证进出口履行的重要条件。因此本节主要介绍合同的装运条款，包括装运时间、装运港、目的港、分批装运和转运、装运通知以及滞期速遣条款等。

1.1　Shipment Time 装运时间

Time of shipment, refers to the seller by the sale of the contract to deliver the goods to the buyer or carrier period, this is the main provisions of the contract, if the seller breach this condition, the buyer has the right to cancel the contract, and to require the seller to compensate the loss.

装运时间又称装运期，是指卖方按买卖合同规定将货物交付给买方或承运人的期限，这是合

同的主要条款，如果卖方违反该条件，买方则有权撤销合同，并要求卖方赔偿其损失。

1.1.1 Stipulation Methods of Shipment Time 装运时间的规定方法

（1）Defined the Specific time of Shipment 明确规定具体装运时间

① Time of shipment is stipulated in a month or cross month shipment, that is, limited to a period of time. For example, shipment during March 2011, the seller may be in March 1st, 2011 to March 31st this period at any time during the shipment of exports, shipment during July / August 2011, the seller may be in the July 1st, 2011 to August 31st this period at any time during the shipment of exports.

规定在某月或跨月装运，即装运时间限于某一段确定时间。例如：在 2011 年 3 月装运，即卖方可在 2011 年 3 月 1 日至 3 月 31 日这一段期间的任何时间装运出口；在 2011 年 7 月至 8 月装运，即卖方可以在 2011 年 7 月 1 日至 8 月 31 日这一段期间的任何时间装运出口。

② The provisions in the end of June or one day before the shipment is stipulated in the contract, a latest date of shipment, in the prior to the date of shipment. For example, shipment at or before the end of March 2011, whereby the seller no later than March 31st shipment. Shipment not later than July 15th, namely the contract date, seller no later than July 15th shipment. 【Typical Case Link 1】

规定在某月月底或某日前装运，即在合同中规定一个最迟装运日期，在该日期前装运有效。例如，在 2011 年 3 月底前装运，即卖方最迟不能超过 3 月 31 日装运；在 7 月 15 日前装运，即合同订立之日起，卖方最迟不能超过 7 月 15 日装运。【典例链接 1】

（2）Provided credit is received within a specified period of time after shipment 规定在收到信用证后一定期限内装运

In the buyer's credit to understand enough or prevent the buyer may be due to some reasons not to perform the contract, but using this method a shipment date, at the same time can make a restrictive provisions, regulations of credit or served to protect the benefit of duration, in generally, ocean transport shall not less than one month, near ocean transport not less than 20 days. For example, the shipment within 30 days after receipt of L / C, i.e., within 30 days after receipt of the shipment.

在对买方资信了解不够或防止买方可能因某些原因不按照合同履行的情况下，可采用此种方法规定装运时间，同时可订立一个限制性条款，规定信用证的送达期限，以保障卖方利益。一般来说，远洋运输规定不少于一个月，近洋运输不少于 20 天。例如，Shipment within 30 days after receipt of L/C，即收到信用证后 30 天内装运。

（3）General Provisions Near Shipment 笼统规定近期装运

Immediate shipment is arranged, shipped as soon as possible (shipment immediately), it is used when the seller has the goods, the buyer has the cash to goods. This method does not require a specific term, said only "shipment immediately", "prompt shipment", "shipped as soon as possible", on these words had no uniform explanation, easy to cause the dispute, so should try to avoid used in addition to the seller has a consistent understanding.

立即装运或称为即装、尽快装运（shipment immediately），往往是在卖方备有现货、买方要货情况下使用。此种方法不规定具体期限，只是表示"立即装运"、"即刻装运"、"尽快装运"等，国际上对这些词语并无统一的解释，易引起纠纷，因此除买卖双方有一致理解外，应尽量避免使用。

1.1.2 Attention of shipment time matters 规定装运时间的注意事项

(1) Consider the actual situation of the sources of goods and ships to determine the time of shipment, avoid the ship and goods line.

考虑货源和船源的实际情况来确定装运期，避免船、货脱节。

(2) Explicitly stipulated time of shipment, using little or no general method stipulate time of shipment.

明确规定装运期，少用或不用笼统规定装运期的方法。

(3) Consider the issuing date of the rule is reasonable or not, pay attention to avoid the "double due", namely, the letter of credit settlement period and shipment date are expiring. Generally the seller should strive for the settlement period longer than the shipment 7 ~ 15 days after shipment, in order to have enough time to handle the formalities for foreign exchange settlement.

考虑开证日期的规定是否明确合理，注意避免“双到期”，即信用证结汇有效期与装运期同时到期。一般卖方应争取结汇有效期长于装运期 7 ~ 15 天，以便于货物装船后有足够的时间办理结汇手续。

(4) Consider loading conditions of the port of loading or port of destination and special cases. For example, shipping period may be short to have direct access to the ship and voyage of more ports, shipping period is longer for no direct vessel or remote port, it should try to avoid the shipment in frozen period or the rainy season in some countries or regions.

考虑装运港或目的港的装运条件和特殊情况。例如，对有直达船和航次较多的港口，装运期可短一些，对无直达船或偏僻的港口，装运期要长一些；对某些国家或地区，应尽量避免装运期在冰冻期或雨季。

1.2 Port of Loading and Port of Destination 装运港和目的港

1.2.1 Port of Shipment 装运港

The loading port is the port where goods are shipped firstly. In generally, the port of shipment is choosed by the seller, the buyer agrees to determine. In principle, convenient transportation options close to the origin, low cost, good infrastructure.

装运港是指货物起始装运的港口。一般情况下，装运港由卖方提出，经买方同意后确定。原则上选择靠近产地、交通便利、费用较低、基础设施较完善的地方。

Should pay attention to the following questions to port of shipment choice. 装运港的选择，应注意以下几个问题。

(1) Should not accept our country policy does not permit the dealings of the port for loading / unloading port.

不能接受我国政策不允许往来的港口为装卸港口。

(2) The foreign port regulations should be specific and clear, not too general.

对国外装卸港的规定应力求具体明确，不宜过于笼统。

(3) Should not accept inland city for the loading and unloading conditions, because once you accept this condition, we should take from the port to the inland city of this stretch of road freight and risk.

不能接受内陆城市为装卸的条件，因为一旦接受这一条件，我方要承担从港口到内陆城市这段路程的运费和风险。

(4) Must be considered in port specific circumstances and loading and unloading conditions,

including having no direct liner shipping, port loading and unloading conditions as well as the freight and additional levels.

必须考虑港口具体情况和装卸条件，主要包括有无直达班轮航线、港口装卸条件以及运费和附加水平等。

（5）Pay attention to the same name of port of shipment.

注意装卸港有无重名问题。

1.2.2 Destination Port 目的港

Port of destination refers to final port of discharge. General filed by the buyers, the consent of the seller to determine.

目的港是指最终卸货的港口。一般由买方提出，经卖方同意后确定。

In the export business, the port of destination choice should pay attention to the following questions:

出口业务中，目的港的选择应注意以下问题：

（1）Should not to our government is not allowed to trade between countries or regions as the port of destination. 不能以我国政府不允许进行贸易往来的国家或地区作为目的港。

（2）The port of destination must be a ship can safe berth port. 目的港必须是船舶可以安全停泊的港口。

（3）The port of destination should be clear and specific provisions, avoid using such as “major Asian ports” generalities.目的港的规定应明确具体，避免采用如“亚洲主要港口”等笼统说法。

（4）Unless in multimodal transport, or generally do not accept the inland city conditions for the destinations. 除非以多式联运方式运输，否则一般不接受内陆城市为目的地的条件。

（5）Reasonable use the “select port”. 合理使用“选择港”。

（6）Pay attention to the same name of port of destination. Many ports around the world have the same name, such as Victoria Harbour, 12 of the world, so you should indicate in the contract the destination country and position. 注意目的港有无重名问题。世界各国港口重名的很多，如维多利亚港世界上有 12 个，因此应在合同中标明目的港所在国家和所处方位。

1.3 Partial Shipment and Transshipment 分批装运和转运

1.3.1 Partial Shipment 分批装运

Partial shipment refers to a transaction of goods in several batches of shipment. In commodity trading, buyers and sellers according to the number of delivery, transport conditions and market needs and other factors, may stipulate in the contract that partial shipment clause.

分批装运指一笔成交的货物分若干批次装运。在大宗货物交易中，买卖双方根据交货数量、运输条件和市场销售需要等因素，可在合同中规定分批装运条款。

According to the Uniform Customs and Practice for Documentary Credits concerned regulation, partial shipment should pay attention to the following points.

根据《跟单信用证统一惯例》的有关规定，分批装运应注意以下几点。

（1）If the credit without partial shipment prohibited, it can be regarded as a partial shipment. But in the actual business, expressly stated in the contract as to partial shipment allowed.

如果信用证中没有规定禁止分批装运，可视为允许分批装运。但实际业务中，还是在合同中明确规定允许分批装运为宜。

（2）For the same vessel, with a voyage and the same destination port of shipment shipping documents for many times, even on the surface indicating different date of shipment or different port of shipment, also should not be regarded as partial shipment. 【Typical Case Link 2】

对于同一船只、同一航次及同一目的港的多次装运，即使运输单据表面上注明不同的装运日期或不同的装运港口，也不应视为分批装运。【典例链接 2】

（3）For the partial shipment of the goods, the seller should be in strict accordance with the provisions of the contract, set number of quantitative, regular delivery, any such a batch of goods not in accordance with the provisions of the shipment, the goods and after the goods shall be void.

对于分批装运的货物，卖方应严格按合同规定定批、定量、定期分运，如果其中任何一批货物未按规定装运，则该批货物及以后各批货物均告失效。

1.3.2 Transshipment 转运

Transshipment refers to the goods from the port of shipment to the port of destination in the transport process, from a conveyance to another kind of transportation, or by a mode of transportation to another kind of means of transportation behavior. In generally, when the goods are shipped without the direct ship docked, or although have direct vessel sailing voyage and indefinite or interval too long port, can be specified in the contract “allowing transshipment clause”.

转运，是指货物从装运港至目的港的运输过程中，从一种运输工具转移到另一种运输工具上，或是由一种运输方式转为另一种运输方式的行为。一般来说，当货物运往无直达船停靠，或虽有直达船而船期不定或航次间隔时间太长的港口，可在合同中规定“允许转运条款”。

According to the Uniform Customs and Practice for Documentary Credits Provisions, such as credit card does not require transshipment is prohibited, as transshipment is allowed, but in the actual business, in order to clear the responsibility and easy to arrange shipment, both parties agree transport or not and related transport method and transport freight burden problem, should be spctified in the import and export contracts.

根据《跟单信用证统一惯例》规定，如信用证中没有规定禁止转运，可视为允许转运，但实际业务中，为了明确责任和便于安排装运，交易双方是否同意转运以及有关转运的办法和转运费的负担等问题，都应在进出口合同中具体注明。

1.4 Shipment Advice 装运通知

Advice of shipment refers to that under the situation of transporting bulk cargo by charter, it agreed the terms in the contract. Its purpose is to clear both sides duty, make both parties cooperate each other, joins the good job. No matter what kind of trade contract terms, both parties shall bear the obligation to inform each other.

装运通知是在采用租船运输大宗进出口货物的情况下，在合同中加以约定的条款。其目的在于明确买卖双方的责任，促使买卖双方互相配合，共同做好船货衔接工作。不论按哪种贸易术语成交，交易双方都要承担相互通知的义务。

According to general practice in international trade, in FOB turnover conditions, the seller should send to the buyer the goods ready notes before the start of the shipment generally is 30 or 45 days, , in order that the buger sent a ship cargo at time. The buyer received the notice of readiness, should according to the agreed time, the name of the carrying ship, ship to port loading date notice to the seller, so the seller arrange for shipment of goods and ready for shipment.

按照国际贸易的一般做法，在按 FOB 条件成交时，卖方应在约定的装运期开始以前，一般是

30 天或者 45 天，向买方发出货物备妥通知，以便买方及时派船接货。买方接到卖方发出的备货通知后，应按约定的时间，将船名、船舶到港受载日期等通知卖方，以便卖方及时安排货物出运和准备装船。

In addition, after shipment, the seller shall notify the buyer at the appointed time, usually in 48 hours, the contract number, description of goods, quantity, weight, invoice value, name of vessel and shipment date and other contents,so the buyer handles insurance and do a good job of handling cargo ready, timely handle the import customs formalities.

此外，在货物装船后，卖方应在约定时间通常是 48 小时之内，将合同号、货物的品名、件数、重量、发票金额、船名及装船日期等项内容电告买方，以便买方办理保险并做好接卸货物的准备，及时办理进口报关等手续。

1.5 Time for Loading in and Unloading, Demurrage, Dispatch 装卸时间、滞期费、速遣费

In the international transport, bulk cargo commonly used charter, transport, in order to bind each other, make it complete the charterer loading and unloading tasks in the agreed tme, the charterer usually in the import and export contract handle the time, demurrage, dispatch, as part of the terms of shipment. The terms are in accordance with the corresponding provisions in the charter party.

国际货物运输中，大宗货物一般采用程租船方式运输，租船人为了约束对方，促使其按照约定时间定额完成装卸任务，一般都会在进出口合同中规定装卸时间、滞期费、速遣费，作为装运条款的组成部分。该项条款应与租船合同中的相应条款保持一致。

1.5.1 Lay Time 装卸时间

Loading and unloading time is defined as stipulated in the contract to complete cargo handling by time. To stay or expressed in days or hours.

装卸时间是指合同中规定的完成货物装卸所用的时间。一般以天数或小时数来表示。

On handling time of starting and stopping, more general rules are: if the captain to submit “loaded / unloaded notice of readiness.” In the morning 8～12 are served, from 2 p.m. starting; as in the afternoon 2 ~ 6 points from the next day delivery, 8 a.m. starting. End time with one final goods or discharged from the ship.

关于装卸时间的起算和止算，较为普遍的规定是：如船长递交“装/卸准备就绪通知书”在上午 8 ~ 12 点送达，则从下午 2 点起算；如在下午 2～6 点送达，则从次日上午 8 点起算。终止时间则以最后一件货物装上船或卸下船为准。

1.5.2 Demurrage and Dispatch 滞期费和速遣费

Responsible for loading and unloading the goods, if at the appointed time failed to allow the loading and unloading of cargo handling, the ships in the harbor time extended to the ship, the economic losses caused by delay, loss during the day, should be agreed by the certain amount compensation level of the ship, the compensation is called demurrage. Conversely, such as in the agreed loading and unloading time, ahead of the completion of loading and unloading task, so that the ship to save the ship in port fees and expenses, can from the ship received the award, known as the dispatch. By convention, dispatch usually bends half demurrage.

负责装卸货物的一方，如果在约定的允许装卸时间内未能将货物装卸完，致使船舶在港内停泊时间延长，给船方造成经济损失，则延迟期间的损失，应按约定每天若干金额补偿船方，这项补偿金称为滞期费。反之，如在约定的装卸时间内，提前完成装卸任务，使船方节省了船

舶在港口的费用开支，则可从船方获得奖励，称为速遣费。按惯例，速遣费一般为滞期费的一半。

2. Shipping Documents in Contract of Sales 合同中的装运单据

After receipt of the goods by the carrier transport document is issued to the shipper certifying documents, it is the transfer of cargo, handling and settling claims and bank settlement or instrument for important documents. In the international transport of goods, transport documents of many types, including bill of lading, railway bill, cargo receipt, bill of lading and parcel post receipt.

运输单据是承运人收到货物后签发给托运人的证明文件，它是交接货物、处理索赔和理赔以及向银行结算货款或进行议付的重要单据。在国际货物运输中，运输单据的种类很多，其中，包括海运提单、铁路运单、承运货物收据、航空运单和邮包收据等。

2.1 Bill of Lading 海运提单

Bill of lading, is the carrier of the cargo on demand of the shipper, on receipt of the goods after the rules issued to the shipper for a document. The 1978 UN Convention on carriage of goods by sea in China and maritime law article seventy-first of the bill of lading bill of lading under the definition: "refers to a contract of carriage of goods by sea and to prove that the goods have been taken in charge or shipped on board by the carrier, and the carrier according to the development and ensure the delivery of documents."

海运提单，简称提单，是货物承运人应托运人的要求，在收到货物归其掌管后签发给托运人的一种单据。《1978 年联合国海上货物运输公约》以及我国《海商法》第 71 条都对提单下了定义："提单是指一种用以证明海上货物运输合同和货物已由承运人接管或装船，以及承运人据发保证交付货物的单证。"

2.1.1 Ocean Bill of Lading and Function 海运提单的性质和作用

In international marine cargo transportation, shipper and carrier between the generally need a contract of carriage and the issuance of bills of lading to define the rights and obligations of both parties and exemption from liability. Therefore, the bill of lading is a very important document in international shipping, only to its property and function have a clear understanding, to correctly handle according to the bill of lading for transport operations.

在国际海洋货物运输中，托运人与承运人之间一般需要通过订立运输合同和签发提单来确定双方的权利和义务以及责任豁免。因此，提单是国际海运中十分重要的单据，只有对其性质和作用有一个清楚的认识，才能正确处理按提单进行运输的各项业务。

（1）The bill of lading is a receipt for goods 提单是货物收据

Bill of lading is the goods receipt that the carrier or its agent issued to the shipper, proven carrier has been received the consignment of goods according to the bill of lading. Laws generally, bill of lading is by the captain, the carrier or his agents issued that it has received, or take the goods.

提单是承运人或其代理人签发给托运人的货物收据，证明承运人已经按提单所列内容收到托运货物。各国法律一般认为，提单是由船长、承运人或其代理人签发的，证明其已收到或接管货物。

（2）The bill of lading is a document of title 提单是物权凭证

The carrier or his agents at the port of delivery, delivery to the holder of the bill of lading. Because the bill of lading is represented by a certificate of ownership of the goods, the lawful holder of bills of lading can be at the port of destination to the shipping company to take delivery of the goods, it can also transfer.

承运人或其代理人在目的港交货时，必须向提单持有人交货。因为提单是代表货物所有权的凭证，提单的合法持有人可以凭提单在目的港向轮船公司提取货物，也可以有偿转让。

（3）The bill of lading is the shipper and carrier transport between contract certificates 提单是托运人与承运人之间的运输契约证明

Contract of carriage of goods by sea including bill of lading as evidence by the contract of carriage. In the liner in the carriage of goods, bills of lading only transport contracts in the presence of a proof, rather than the contract of carriage. In addition, the bill of lading is establishment of the contract, it is to fulfill a contract of carriage appeared during the process of one kind of evidence, and the contract is actually the shipper to the carrier or its agent booking, check has been established. Specifically, the carrier or his agent in the shipper on consignment note on the seal, bearing, consignment contract between was set up.

海上货物运输合同包括提单所证明的运输合同。在班轮货物运输中，提单只是运输合同中存在的一种证明，而不是运输合同。另外，提单的签发是在合同成立之后，它只是在履行运输合同的过程中出现的一种证据，而合同实际上在托运人向承运人或其代理人订舱、办理托运手续时就已成立。确切地说，承运人或其代理人在托运人填制的托运单上盖章后，承、托运之间的合同才成立。

2.1.2 Classification of Bill of Lading 海运提单的种类

A bill of lading can be from a variety of different angle classification.

海运提单可以从各种不同的角度分类。

（1）According to whether the goods shipped on board can be divided into 根据货物是否已装船可分

① On Board B/L 已装船提单

This bill of lading is also known as the bill of loading, refers to the shipping company to ship the goods on the specified ship after the bill of lading, its characteristic is the bill of lading must to text indicates that the goods have been loaded on a ship, and indicate the shipment of cargo ships and the date of completion of loading. In international trade by convention provisions, export to the bank for negotiation of payment must be submitted on board bill of lading.

这种提单又称为装运提单，是指轮船公司将货物装上指定轮船后所签发的提单，其特点是提单必须以文字表明货物已装上某条船，并注明装运货物的船舶名称和货物实际装船完毕的日期。在国际贸易中按惯例规定，出口人向银行议付货款时必须提交已装船提单。

② Received for Shipment B/L 备运提单

This bill of lading is also called the received for shipment bill of lading, refers to the shipping company in the consignment of goods to await shipment is yet shipped bill of lading issued during the period. As a result of this bill of lading the goods without loading, name of vessel, date of shipment is not specified, the arrival time is not guaranteed, it is adverse to the buyer, so the buyer is generally not willing to accept a bill of lading.

这种提单又称收讫待运提单，是指轮船公司在托运货物等待装运即尚未装船期间所签发的提单。由于这种提单上的货物没有装船，没有载明船名、装船日期，到货时间没有保证，对买方很不利，因此买方一般不愿意接受备运提单。

（2）According to the consignee a column filled with different contents, namely, look up can be divided into different 根据提单收货人一栏填写内容的不同，即抬头不同分

① Straight B/L 记名提单

Straight bill of lading refers to the consignee fill in specific consignee name, the carrier at the port of discharge to the handing over of the goods to the named consignee bill of lading. This bill of lading in principle cannot be transferred to third party, so it is generally only in the transport of precious cargo or exhibits used.

记名提单是指在提单收货人一栏填写特定的收货人姓名，承运人在卸货港只能将货物交给提单上所指定的收货人。这种提单原则上不能转让给第三者，因此一般只有在运输贵重货物或展览品时才采用。

② Blank B/L 不记名提单

A blank B/L consigned column without specifying any name, but only the holder of the bill of lading marked words, who hold a bill of lading, who can pick up the goods, the carrier delivery voucher only, not with the people. Bill of lading without endorsement can transfer liquidity strong. But once it is lost or stolen, the great risk. So in the international trade is rarely used.

不记名提单是指提单收货人一栏内没有指明任何收货人名称，而只注明提单持有人字样，谁持有提单，谁就可以提货，承运人交货只凭单，不凭人。不记名提单无需背书即可转让，流通性极强。但一旦丢失或被窃，风险极大。所以在国际贸易中很少使用。

③ Order B/L 指示提单

An order B/L refers to in the bill of lading consigned column fill in “to order” or “to order of some people” of a bill of lading. This bill of lading can endorsement, so widely used in international trade.

指示提单是指在提单上收货人一栏内填写“凭指示”或“凭某人”字样的一种提单。这种提单可以经背书转让，因此在国际贸易中广泛使用。

Bill of lading endorsed a “blank” and “endorsement” two. At present, in the actual business, is the most frequently used “by order and blank endorsed bill of lading marked”, traditionally called “made out to order, blank endorsed”.

提单背书有“空白背书”和“记名背书”两种。目前在实际业务中，使用最多的是“凭指示”并注明空白背书的提单，习惯上称其为“空白抬头、空白背书提单”。

“Made out to order, blank endorsed” refers to the consignee in the column to fill in “with the indication” in the back of the bill of lading, only to write endorsed name.

Order bill of lading in the shipper (seller) is not specified, the consignee, the seller retains the ownership of the goods, such as the endorsed in blank, then becomes the bearer bill, but as bills of lading receipt voucher; if the endorsement is made up of straight bill of lading.

“空白抬头、空白背书提单”指在提单收货人一栏内填写“凭指示”字样，在提单的背面只写上背书人的名称。

指示提单在托运人（卖方）未指定收货人之前，卖方仍保有货物所有权，如经空白背书，则成为不记名提单，而作为凭提单收货的凭证；如经记名背书后即成为记名提单。

175

（3）According to the bill of lading on cargo semblance condition has no adverse comment can be divided into 根据提单上对货物外表状况有无不良批注分

① Clean Bill of Lading 清洁提单

Clean bill of lading bill of lading indicates that the goods without additional surface condition of defective qualified bill of lading. If the carrier issued a clean bill of lading, that accepted the surface of goods or packaging intact, the carrier shall post to faulty packing of cargo for delivery to shirk their responsibility. Bank settlement generally only accept a clean bill of lading.

清洁提单指提单上未附加表明货物表面状况有缺陷的批注的提单。承运人如签发了清洁提单，就表明所接受的货物表面或包装完好，承运人不得事后以货物包装不良等为由推卸其运送责任。银行在结汇时一般只接受清洁提单。

② Unclean Bill of Lading 不清洁提单

Unclean bill of lading has demonstrated in a defective condition of the bill of lading the goods surface. Unless otherwise stipulated in the credit of banks can accept the bill of lading case, the general will refuse to accept the un clean bill of lading for settlement.

不清洁提单指在提单上批注有表明货物表面状况有缺陷的提单。银行除非在信用证规定可以接受该类提单的情况下，一般会拒绝接受不清洁提单办理结汇。

（4）According to the Mode of Transport can be Divided into 根据运输方式分

① Direct B/L 直达提单

A direct B/L is halfway without transshipment directly to the goods to the destination bill of lading. The port of discharge column write only final port of destination. Where a credit requires transshipment is prohibited, must use the straight bill of lading.

直达提单是指中途不经转船直接将货物运往目的地的提单。提单的卸货港一栏只写最终目的港。凡信用证中规定不准转船者，必须使用这种直达提单。

② Transshipment B / L 转船提单

Transshipment bill refers to the consignments in transit undirectly to the port of destination, but in the middle of the need to convert another ship to the port of destination, including bill of lading issued throughout the ship. In the bill of lading marked “transshipment” or “in the port of transshipment × ×”. Transshipment bill often consists of the first issued by the carrier.

转船提单是指当货物的运输不是由一条船直接运到目的港，而是在中途需转换另一船舶运往目的港时，船方签发的包括全程的提单。在提单上注明“转船”或“在××港转船”字样。转船提单往往由第一承运人签发。

③ Through B/L 联运提单

Bill of lading is the shipping and other different transportation modes of transport, from the first carrier including issuance of bill of lading and for the entire transport under a cargo transshipment and transfer procedures.

联运提单是海运与其他不同运输方式组成的联合运输，由第一程承运人签发包括全程运输的提单并办理下一程货物的转船和交接手续。

（5）According to whether was paid or not can be freight be divided into 依是否已付运费分

① Freight Prepaid B/L 运费预付提单

Freight prepaid bill of lading refers to specify the shipper has been paid to the carrier at the port of loading freight bill of lading.

运费预付提单是指载明托运人在装货港已向承运人支付运费的提单。

② Freight to be Collected B/L 运费到付提单

Freight collect bill of lading refers to indicate the consignee in the port of destination delivery to pay the freight to the carrier's bill of lading.

运费到付提单是指载明收货人在目的港提货时向承运人支付运费的提单。

2.1.3 Contents of Bill of Lading and Preparation 提单的内容及编制

（1）Positive Items of B/L 提单正面的记载事项

Bill of lading positive contained items, each shipping company have the same approximately to bill of lading, generally include the following:

关于提单正面的记载事项，各航运公司拟制的提单大致相同，一般包括下列各项：

① The name and principal place of business 承运人的名称和主营业所；

② The name of the shipper 托运人的名称；

③ The name of the consignee 收货人的名称；

④ The notify party 通知方；

⑤ The name of the ship 船舶名称；

⑥ The port of loading and discharge 装货港和卸货港；

⑦ The description of the goods, mark, number of packages or the number, weight or volume 货物的品名、标志、包数或者件数、重量或者体积；

⑧ Order bill of lading date, location and number of copy 提单的签发日期、地点和份数；

⑨ Payment of freight 运费的支付；

⑩ The carrier or his representative's signature 承运人或者其代表的签字。

（2）Back Clause of B/L 提单背面条款

Bill of lading is usually contained on the back of the parties rights and obligations under the terms . Bill of lading format terms are not the same, but the content is basically the same:

海运提单的背面通常载有关于双方当事人权利和义务的条款。各种提单格式的条款虽不尽相同，但主要内容基本上是一致的：

① The jurisdiction and choice of law clause 管辖权和法律适用条款；

② The carrier's liability clause 承运人责任条款；

③ The carrier's exemption 承运人的免责；

④ The period of carrier's responsibility clause 承运人责任期间条款；

⑤ The limit of liability clause 赔偿责任限额条款；

⑥ The special clause 特殊货物条款；

⑦ The lien clause 留置权条款；

⑧ General average and new Jason clause 共同海损和新杰森条款；

⑨ Both to blame collision clause. In addition, the bill of lading is about war, quarantine, frozen, strike, crowded, transit and other content terms.

双方有责碰撞条款。此外，提单中还有关于战争、检疫、冰冻、罢工、拥挤、转运等内容的条款。

BILL OF LADING

海运提单

<table>
<tr><td colspan="2">1）SHIPPER（托运人）</td><td rowspan="6">10）B/L NO.SSAB02
COSCO
中国远洋运输（集团）总公司
CHINA OCEAN
SHIPPING(GROUP)CO.

ORIGINAL
COMBINED TRANPORT BILL OF LADING</td></tr>
<tr><td colspan="2">2）CONSIGNEE（收货人）</td></tr>
<tr><td colspan="2">3）NOTIFY PARTY（被通知人）</td></tr>
<tr><td>4）PLACE OF RECEIPT（收货地点）</td><td>5）OCEAN VESSEL（船名）</td></tr>
<tr><td>6）VOYAGE NO.（航次）</td><td>7）PORT OF LOADING（装货港）</td></tr>
<tr><td>8）PORT OF DISCHARGE（卸货港）</td><td>9）PLACE OF DELIVERY（交货地点）</td></tr>
</table>

<table>
<tr><td>11）MARKS
唛头</td><td>12）NOS.&KINDS OF PKGS
13）DESCRIPTION OF GOODS
（包装件数、商品描述）</td><td>14）G.W.(M/T)
（毛重）</td><td>15）MEAS(m^3)
（尺码）</td></tr>
<tr><td colspan="4">16）TOTAL NUMBER OF CONTAINERS OR PACKAGES(IN WORDS)
集装箱数或件数合计（大写）</td></tr>
</table>

<table>
<tr><td>FREIGHT & CHARGES
（运费与附加费）</td><td>REVENUE TONS</td><td>RATE
（运费率）</td><td>PER
（每）</td><td>PREPAID
（运费预付）</td><td>COLLECT
（运费到付）</td></tr>
<tr><td>PREPAID AT
（预付地点）</td><td colspan="2">PAYABLE AT
（到付地点）</td><td colspan="3">17）PLACE AND DATE OF ISSUE
（签发地点及日期）</td></tr>
<tr><td>TOTAL PREPAID
（预付总额）</td><td colspan="2">18）NUMBER OF ORIGINAL B(S)L（正本提单份数）</td><td colspan="3"></td></tr>
<tr><td colspan="3">LOADING ON BOARD THE VESSEL
19）DATE（日期）</td><td colspan="3">20）SIGNED ON BEHALF OF THE CARRIER
COSCO
AS CARRIER（签字）</td></tr>
</table>

（3）Making of B/L 提单的缮制

① The Shipper 托运人

The shipper or consignor, is commissioned by the transport of the parties. If a credit without special requirements, should be the beneficiary as shipper. If the beneficiary is a middleman, the goods are shipped directly from producing area, then can also be practical for the consignor.

托运人也称发货人(Consignor)，是指委托运输的当事人。如信用证无特殊规定，应以受益人为托运人。如果受益人是中间商，货物是从产地直接装运的，这时也可以实际卖方为发货人。

② The Consignee 收货人

This is bill of lading payable, bank audit projects. With the consignment note “consignee” fill in exactly the same, and in accordance with the stipulations of the credit. The column must fill out the credit requires consistent with. Any be negligent and the easy way out filling law may be discrepant documents.

这是提单的抬头，是银行审核的重点项目。应与托运单中“收货人”的填写完全一致，并符合信用证的规定。收货人栏的填写必须与信用证要求完全一致。任何粗心大意和贪图省事的填法都可能是不符合单证。

③ The Notify Party 被通知人

The buyer’s agent, the goods at the port of destination by the carrier to inform their customs clearance delivery procedures.

即买方的代理人，货到目的港时由承运人通知其办理报关提货等手续。

Ⅰ. If a credit contains provisions, should be strictly in accordance with the stipulations of the credit to fill in, as the detailed address, telephone, telex, fax numbers, so that the circular smooth.

如果信用证中有规定，应严格按信用证规定填写，如详细地址、电话、电传、传真号码等，以使通知顺利。

Ⅱ. If the card does not specific about the notify party, then it should put the name of the applicant, the address in the bill of lading on this column, this column while the originals remain empty or filled the buyer can also be. Bill of lading must fill in the notify party, is convenient for the port of destination agents contact the consignee delivery.

如果来证中没有具体说明被通知人，那么就应将开证申请人名称、地址填入提单副本的这一栏中，而正本的这一栏保持空白或填写买方亦可。副本提单必须填写被通知人，是为了方便目的港代理通知收货人提货。

Ⅲ. If l / C stipulated in Notify ... Only, means only notify × ×, Only is a word not be missed.

如果来证中规定 Notify...only，意指仅通知某某，则 Only 一词不能漏掉。

Ⅳ.If a credit does not state notify address, and the shipper on bill of lading notify back filling detailed address, banks can accept, but without the audit.

如果信用证没有规定被通知人地址，而托运人在提单被通知人后面加注详细地址，银行可以接受，但无需审核。

④ The Pre-carriage by / Port of Transshipment 前段运输/转船港

If the goods need transport, then in two columns respectively fill the first ship’s name and port of transit.(Port of transshipment)

如果货物需转运，则在此两栏分别填写第一程船的船名和中转港口名称。

⑤ Name of Vessel 船名

If the goods are required to transfer, in this column fill in the second name of the ship; if the goods do not need to transfer, in this column filled first name of vessel. Fill in the second carrier, based mainly on the requirements of the letter of credit, if the credit is no requirements, even though transshipments, also do not need to fill in the second name of ship.

如果货物需转运，则在这栏填写第二程的船名；如果货物无需转运，则在这栏填写第一程船的船名。是否填写第二程船名，主要是根据信用证的要求，如果信用证并无要求，即使需转船，也不必填写第二程船名。

⑥ Port of Lading 装运港

Port of Lading should be strictly in accordance with the stipulations of the credit to fill out, if the credit also specifies several port of shipment (ground), bill of lading only fill out the actual shipped that a name of the port.

装运港应严格按信用证规定填写，如信用证同时列明多个装运港（地），提单只填写实际装运的那一个港口名称。

⑦ Place of Destination 最终目的地

If the destination is the port of destination, blank this column. Fill in the port of destination or ground should pay attention to the following questions.

如果货物的目的地就是目的港，这一栏保持空白。填写目的港或目的地应注意下列问题。

Ⅰ. Except FOB price terms, the port of destination is not general name, must list the port name. A duplicate name exists on the international port, also should be added.

除 FOB 价格条件外，目的港不能是笼统的名称，必须列出具体的港口名称。如果是国际上的重名港口，还应加国名。

Ⅱ. If the port of destination Intransitto ... In CIF or CFR condition, price, can according to adding, only in the other blank or marks in the text to indicate to fill the inland transportation costs borne by the buyers.

如果来证目的港后有 Intransitto…在 CIF 或 CFR 价格条件，则不能照加，只能在其他空白处或唛头内加注此段文字以表示转入内陆运输的费用由买方自理。

Ⅲ. If a credit port of destination stipulated for the Kobe / Negoga / Yokohama, which is expressed as the port, only playing one of bill of lading. If a credit states that OptionKobe / Negoga / Yokohama, such that the selected port, bill of lading should order all photo shoot.

如信用证规定目的港为 Kobe/Negoga/yokohama，此种表示为卖方选港，提单只打一个即可。如来证规定 OptionKobe/Negoga/yokohama，此种表示为买方选港，提单应按次序全部照打。

⑧ Marks 唛头

Marks for loading and unloading, transportation and storage process to facilitate the identification and brush on the outer packing, shipping marks, is one of the important contents of bill of lading, bill of lading and goods is the main contact elements, but also the important basis for the delivery of the consignee. Bill of lading marked with invoices and other documents as well as the actual cargo to keep consistent, otherwise it will give delivery and settlement difficult.

唛头即为了装卸、运输及存储过程中便于识别而刷在外包装上的装运标记，是提单的一项重要内容，是提单与货物的主要联系要素，也是收货人提货的重要依据。提单上的唛头应与发票等其他单据以及实际货物保持一致，否则会给提货和结算带来困难。

⑨ Numbers and Kinds of Packages 件数和包装种类

This column fill in the number of packages and packaging unit. If the bulk cargo without number, can be expressed as “In bulk”. Types of packaging must be in accordance with L / C.

本栏填写包装数量和包装单位。如果散装货物无件数时，可表示为散装。包装种类一定要与信用证一致。

⑩ Description of Goods 商品名称

Description of goods shall be stipulated in the credit and other documents such as invoices name to fill, should be attention to avoid unnecessary described, but not superfluous to add content. If a credit on commercial shoes, it must not be arbitrarily detailed description of Men’s canvas shoes, or Ladies’casual shoes.

商品名称应按信用证规定的品名以及其他单据如发票品名来填写，应注意避免不必要的描述，更不能画蛇添足地增加内容。如信用证上商品是Shoes(鞋子),绝不能擅自详细描述成Men's canvas shoes（男式帆布鞋），或 Ladies'casual shoes（女式轻便鞋）等。

⑪ Freight Clause 运费条款

Freight clause should be accordance with the stipulations of the credit. If a credit is not clear, according to the price terms are included freight decided how to annotate. For the cargo shipping charges and handling fee burden problem, often the requirements shown on the bill of lading related articles.

运费条款应按信用证规定注明。如信用证未明确，可根据价格条件是否包含运费决定如何批注。对于货物的装船费和装卸费等负担问题，船方经常要求在提单上注明有关条款。

⑫ Place and Date of Issue 提单签发地点和日期

List address is usually the carrier receiving the goods or shipping address, but also sometimes inconsistent, for example, receive or shipment of goods in Xingang and signing in Tianjin. Some do not even in the same country or region. The bill of lading date not later than the time of shipment stipulated in the credit, the exporter can safely is important. Front of this bill of lading clause has loaded terms (Shipped on board the vessel named above ...), in this case the signing date will be deemed to be the date of shipment.

签单地址通常是承运人收受货物或装船的地址，但有时也不一致，例如，收受或装运货物在新港而签单在天津。也有的甚至不在同一国家或地区。提单签发的日期不得晚于信用证规定的装运期，这对出口商能否安全收汇很重要。本提单正面条款中已有装上船条款(Shipped on board the vessel named above…)，在这种情况下签单日期即被视为装船日期。

⑬ Signed for the Carrier Signature 提单签发人签字

According to UCP600 regulations, have the right to issue the bill of lading is the carrier or a named agent for or on behalf as the carrier, or the master or a named agent for or on behalf of as captain. If it is the agent, agent name and identity and being the agent's name and identity should be specified.

按照 UCP600 规定，有权签发提单的是承运人或作为承运人的具名代理或代表，或船长或作为船长的具名代理或代表。如果是代理人签字，代理人的名称和身份与被代理人的名称和身份都应该列明。

2.2 Air Transport Document 航空运输单据

An air transport document known as the air waybill, is between consignor and carrier transport contract, cargo receipt, can handle the negotiated settlement, but it is not a document of title, not by virtue of delivery, not endorsed. Consignee only with a "Notice of delivery" delivery procedures. Air waybill three originals, first note the "Original for the shipper" the inscription, the delivery man; second note the "Original for the issuing carrier", carrier for accounting; third note the "Original for the consignee" the inscription, the consignment, as consignee nuclear cargo basis.

航空运输单据称为航空运单，是发货人与承运人之间的运输合同，是货物收据，可凭此办理议付结汇，但它不是物权凭证，不能凭此提货，不能背书转让。收货人只能凭“提货通知单”办理提货手续。航空运单正本三份，第一份注有“Original for the shipper”字样，交发货人；第二份注有“Original for the issuing carrier”字样，交承运人留作记帐；第三份注有“Original for the consignee”字样，随货走，作为收货人核收货物依据。

2.3 Multimodal Transport Document 多式联运单据

Multimodal transport document, is the proof of international multimodal transport contract and proof of the multimodal transport operator takes over the goods and is responsible for the delivery of goods pursuant to the terms of the contract documents. It is adapt to the international container transportation needs, using in the process of international multimodal transport operations.

多式联运单据，是指证明国际多式联运合同以及证明多式联运经营人接管货物并负责按照合同条款交付货物的单据，是为适应国际集装箱运输需要而产生的，在办理国际多式联运业务时使用。

2.4 Post Parcel Receipt 邮包收据

Post parcel receipt is the main document of parcel post transport, it is not only the post office received the sender post issued certificates, but also with the recipient to extract the cargo certificate, when the package is damaged or destroyed, it can also be used as the basis for claims and settlement of claims. But the parcel post receipt is not the property certificate.

邮包收据，是邮包运输的主要单据，它既是邮局收到寄件人的邮包后所签发的凭证，也是收件人凭以提取货物的凭证，当邮包发生损坏或灭失时，它还可以作为索赔和理赔的依据，但邮包收据不是物权凭证。

【Review Questions】复习思考题

【Typical Case Link 1—典例链接1】

Question：Are we right to do this? Why?

问题：我们这样做是否可以？为什么？

A Chinese foreign trade company export 60 000 boxes of goods to American, contracting to ship the goods in each lot during. March to August, 10 000 boxes each month, payment by confirmed irrevocable letter of credit.The customer duly sent letter of credit on which the total amount are in conformity with the contract, but the shipping clauses indicated “the latest date of shipment is 31st, August, by partial shipment.” Our exporter dispatched 10 000 boxes in March,12 000 boxes in April, 20 000 boxes in May and 18 000 boxes in June.The customer raise an objection to this

我国某外贸公司向美国出口商品 60 000 箱，合同规定 3 月至 8 月按月等量装运，每月装运 10 000 箱，凭不可撤销信用证付款，客户按时开来信用证，信用证上总金额与总数量均与合同相符，但装运条款规定为：“最迟装运期 8 月 31 日，分数批装运。”我方 3 月装出 10 000 箱，4 月装出 12 000 箱，5 月装出 20 000 箱，6 月装出 18 000 箱，客户发现后向我方提出异议。

【Typical Case Link 2—典例链接2】

Question:Is the bank’s dishonor reasonable? Why?

问题：银行的拒付是否合理？为什么？

A Jiangsu company export a group of Soyabean overseas, the foreign customer open an irrevocable letter of credit, with shipment terms: “Shipment from Chinese port to Singapore in August. Partial shipment prohibited”. Because of shortage of supply, prior to August 15th,loaded 200 metric tons of peanuts at the port of Lianyungang by S.S. “HuangShi”, and obtained a bill of lading; then they got a number of sources in Yantai, under the premise that the exporter should bear the related costs the ship sailed to Yantai port and 300 metric tons of peanuts were installed on the same ship. On August 20th obtained the bill of lading. After that the exporter submitted two sets of bills within the credit period to the bank for negotiation, the dishonored on the grounds of partial shipment which is not consistent to the L/C.

江苏省某公司向国外出口一批黄豆，国外客户开来不可撤销信用证，证中的装运条款规定："8 月从中国港口装船运往新加坡，不允许分批装运。"出口公司因货源不足，先于 8 月 15 日在连云港将 200 公吨花生仁装上"黄石"轮，取得一套提单；后又在烟台联系到一批货源，在中国公司承担相关费用的前提下，该轮船又驶往烟台港装了 300 公吨花生仁于同一轮船，8 月 20 日取得有关提单。然后在信用证有效期内将两套单据交银行议付，银行以分批装运、单证不符为由拒付货款。

Chapter Eight International Cargo Insurance

第八章 国际货物保险

【Learning Objectives】教学目的与要求

After learning this chapter,you will be able to:

1. Understand the insurance categories;
2. Master marine cargo insurance coverage and insurance principles;
3. Master the China's international cargo transportation insurance coverage and insurance clause.

【Lead-in Case】引导案例

Question: Please try to analyze the two kinds of situations, whether are the losses both partial losses? Why?

问题：试分析这两种情况的损失是否都属于部分损失？为什么？

A consignment on the voyage caught a cabin fire, endangering the cargo, for the sake of the common security the captain ordered irrigation to rescue. The goods originally in the captain were 500 bales of cotton, in addition to the part being burned, the remaining part suffered severe water stain and could only be sold as pulp to paper mills, at a rate of 30% of the original price of goods, namely the value of the loss was 70% of the price; there were also 500 package of rice originally in the cabin, upon inspection it suffered only water-soaked loss, without burning or hot smoked losses. After dried treatment, they were sold as inferior-rice, at a total price 40% of the original price. In accordance with the above, the value of the loss of cotton accounted for 70% of the original price, value of the loss of rice accounted for 60% of the original price.

某一艘货轮在航行中有一船舱发生火灾，危及船货的共同安全，经船长下令灌水施救后被扑灭。事后检查该船舱的货物，原装在该船舱内的 500 包棉花，除被烧毁部分外，剩下部分有严重水渍，只能作为纸浆出售给造纸厂，价值占原货价值的 30%，即损失货价 70%；原装在该舱内尚有 500 包大米，经检查这 500 包大米只有水渍损失，而无烧毁或热熏的损失，经晒干处理后，作为次等米出售，得价占原价的 40%。按照上述情况，棉花损失价值占原价的 70%，大米损失价值占原价的 60%。

Section One Risk and Loss of International Cargo Transport 第一节 国际货物运输风险与损失

The consignments in transit often encounter a variety of risk which resulted in damage or loss of goods.

进出口货物在运输过程中常常会遇到各种风险而导致损失或灭失。

1. Risk 风险

Risk is the reason why the loss of the goods or expenses caused.The risks of marine cargo transportation insurance can be attributed to the perils of the sea and extraneous risk. See Table 8-1.

风险是造成货物损失或发生费用的原因。海上货物运输保险中的风险可归结为海上风险和外来风险两大类，如表 8-1 所示。

Table 8-1

Types of risk	Risk elements
Perils of the Sea	Natural Disaster: bad weather, lightning, tsunami, earthquake, flood, volcano, washing overboard.etc.
	Fortuitous Accidents: grounding, stranding, sunk, collision, fire, explosion,etc.
Extraneous Risks	General extraneous risks: theft,breakage, leakage, contamination, leakage, broken, odor, moisture, heat, rust and hook damage.etc.
	Special extraneous risks: War, strike, failure to delivery, rejection,etc.

表 8-1

风险类型	风险内容
海上风险	自然灾害：恶劣气候、雷电、海啸、地震、洪水、火山爆发、浪击落海等。
	意外事故：船舶搁浅、触礁、沉没、互撞、失火、爆炸等。
外来风险	一般外来风险：偷窃、雨淋、短量、沾污、渗漏、破碎、串味、受潮、受热、锈损和钩损等。
	特殊外来风险：战争、罢工、交货不到、拒收等。

1.1 Marine Risks 海上风险

The so-called marine risk, also known as the shipwreck, refers to the ship, cargo at sea, sea and land, inland waters or barge connected transport processes occurring in the risk. From the nature of risk, marine risk covers by insurer are major grouped into natural disasters and accidents.

所谓海上风险，也称海难，是指船舶、货物在海上、海上与陆地及内河或驳船相连的水域运输过程中发生的风险。从风险的性质上分，保险人所承保的海上风险主要有自然灾害和意外事故两种。

（1）Natural Disasters is caused by natural forces, including bad weather, lightning, tsunami, earthquake, volcano erupts, washing overboard.

自然灾害是指不以人们意志为转移的自然力量所引起的灾害，主要包括恶劣气候、雷电、海啸、地震、火山爆发、浪击落海等。

（2）Fortuitous Accidents refers to the accidents caused by unexpected haphazard, mainly including stranding, sinking, capsizing, collision, fire, explosion, land transportation, goods, overturning or derailment of sling damage, the master or crew of illegal behavior and etc.

意外事故是指偶然的非意料之中的事故，主要包括搁浅、触礁、沉没、倾覆、碰撞、火灾、爆炸、陆上运输工具倾覆或出轨、抛货、吊索损害，船长或船员不法行为等。

1.2 Extraneous Risk 外来风险

Extraneous risks generally refers to the unexpected risks resulting in losses other than Perils of the Sea, including General Extraneous Risks and Special Extraneous Risks.

外来风险一般是指海上风险以外的其他外来原因所造成的风险，包括一般外来风险和特殊外来风险两种。

（1）General extraneous risks includes theft, leakage, short quantity, damaged, broken, hook damage, rust, stains, odor, fresh and rain water, heat and moisture, etc.

（2）Special extraneous risk includes war, strike, rejection and failure to delivery.

（1）一般外来风险。主要包括偷窃、渗漏、短量、碰损、破碎、钩损、生锈、沾污、串味、淡水雨淋、受热受潮等。

（2）特殊外来风险主要包括战争、罢工、拒收以及交货不到等。

2. Loss 损失

Marine losses refer to any loss or damage due to natural calamities and fortuitous accidents and the related cost incurred in the process of transit. According to the degree of loss, it can be divided into total loss and partial loss.

海上损失是指被保险货物在海洋运输途中，因遭遇海上风险所引起的损坏或灭失。按损失的程度划分，海上货物运输损失可以分为全部损失和部分损失两类。

2.1 Total Loss 全部损失

Total loss, can be divided into an actual total loss or a constructive total loss.

全部损失简称全损，可分为实际全损和推定全损。

2.1.1 Actual total loss is also called absolute total loss, refers to the insured goods in transit from total destruction, the main reason is as follows:

实际全损又称绝对全损，指的是投保的货物在运输途中全部灭失，造成全损的主要原因有：

（1）The insured goods arc completely destroyed;

被保险的货物已经完全灭失；

（2）The insured goods suffered serious damage to the loss of the original use, already did not have any use value;

被保险货物遭受严重损害丧失原有用途，已不具有任何使用价值；

（3）The insured cargo loss is irreversible;

被保险货物丧失已无可挽回；

（4）Missing ship.

船舶失踪。

2.1.2　Constructive Total Loss 推定全损

Constructive total loss means the cargo is not totally lost, but the actual total loss shall be unavoidable,when a ship or a cargo is so badly damaged, the cost of repair or the effect of rescue would be greater than the market value of the ship or cargo.The following is the constructive total loss:

推定全损是指被保险货物虽未完全灭失，但实际损失不可避免，若进行施救、整理需要的费用要超过货物完好状态的价值。凡有下列情况下之一者即为推定全损：

（1）The insured goods suffered serious damage, loss is unavoidable already completely;

被保险货物遭受严重损害，完全灭失已不可避免；

（2）The insured goods are damaged, repair cost is estimated to be over after repair of the value of goods;

被保险货物受损后，修理费用估计要超过货物修复后的价值；

（3）The goods insured suffered serious damage, to reach their destination freight has exceeded the residual value of the goods;

被保险货物遭受严重损害之后，继续运抵目的地的运费已超过残存货物的价值；

（4）The goods insured from within responsibility of insurance accident, the insured loss of the insured goods ownership, and the withdrawal of the ownership, the cost will exceed the insured value of the goods back.

被保险货物遭受保险责任范围内的事故，使被保险人失去被保险货物所有权，而收回这一所有权所需费用将超过收回被保险货物的价值。

2.2　Partial Loss 部分损失

Partial loss of the insured goods loss is not reached all the degree of loss, according to the partial loss of different reasons, can be divided into general average and particular average.

部分损失是被保险货物的损失没有达到全部损失的程度，根据部分损失产生原因的不同，部分损失可分为共同海损和单独海损两种。

2.2.1　General Average 共同海损

General average means a partial and deliberate sacrifice of the ship, freight, cargo, or the additional expense incurred to rescue a ship and its cargo from impending danger or for the common safety of the adventure under a peril of the sea or some other hazards. Four conditions forming GA is as follows:

共同海损指的是货物在运输途中遇到海难的时候，为了船舶和货方的共同利益，船方有意识的采取合理的救助措施而直接造成的费用和支出，该费用和支出由有关各方共同分摊。其构成条件如下：

（1）The ship in transit will be or have suffered a natural disaster or extraneous accident, the ship and cargo are both damaged, the captain has to take measures to protect the safety of the ship and cargo;

船舶在运输途中将要或已经遭遇自然灾害或意外事故，船舶和货物受到损害，船长为维护船货安全而必须采取措施；

（2）Distress and risk must be real rather than speculating, loss caused by captain judgment errors is not belong to general average;

海难与危险必须是真实的而不是推测的，因船长判断错误所造成的损失不属于共同海损；

（3）A general average act must be artificial, deliberate, rational behavior;

共同海损行为一定是人为的、故意的、合理的行为；

（4）Losses and expenses must be extra, special.

损失和开支必须是额外的、特殊的。

2.2.2 Particular Average 单独海损

Particular Average is defined in the general average partial loss outside. This loss only by subject matter owner individual burden. Compared with general average particular average is not a person intentionally, partial loss of the insured goods itself, but the loss of the insured alone, not by the ship, goods each common share. For example, 500 boxes of food fell into the sea in unloading, this loss is not the ship for the common good conscious measures, it is a particular average.

单独海损是指除共同海损以外的部分损失。这种损失只能由标的物所有人单独负担。与共同海损相比较，单独海损不是人为有意造成的部分损失，而是被保险货物本身的损失，该损失由被保险人单独承担，不能由船、货各方共同分摊。例如，500 箱食品在货物装卸时不慎掉落到海里，这种损失不是船方为了共同利益有意识的采取的措施，因此属于单独海损。

Section Two Insurance of Ocean Cargo Transport
第二节 海洋运输货物保险险别

According to the people's Insurance Company of China "ocean marine cargo clauses" provisions, marine insurance can be divided into basic risks and additional risks. Basic insurance mainly includes FPA, WPA and all risks.

根据中国人民保险公司制定的《海洋运输货物保险条款》规定，海洋运输保险可以分为基本险和附加险。基本险主要包括平安险、水渍险和一切险。

1. The Basic Insurance 基本险

1.1 The F.P.A. 平安险

F.P.A. English meaning "free from particular average". And fundamentally speaking, it is a kind of limited liability insurance, The responsibility range of F.P.A. includes：

平安险的英文意思为“单独海损不赔”。因而从根本上讲，它是一种有限制的保险责任，平安险的责任范围主要包括以下内容。

（1）Total or Constructive Total Loss of the whole consignment hereby insured caused un the cause of transit by natural calamities heavy weather, lightning, tsunami, earthquake, floods and other natural disasters. In case a constructive total loss is claimed for, the insured shall abandon to the company the damage goods and all his rights and title pertaining thereto. The goods on each lighter to or from the seagoing vessel shall be deemed a separate risk.

被保险货物在运输途中由于恶劣气候、雷电、海啸、地震、洪水等自然灾害造成的整批货物的全部损失或推定全损。被保险人要求推定全损的时候，需要将受损货物及其权利委付给保险公司。如果被保险货物用驳船运往或远离海轮时候，每一驳船所装的货物视为一个整批。

（2）Total or Partial Loss caused by accidents-the carrying conveyance being stranded, sunk, rocks, collisions, and ice or other object collision and fire, explosion and other accidents.

由于运输工具遭受搁浅、触礁、沉没、互撞、与流冰或其他物体碰撞以及失火、爆炸等意外事故造成货物的全部或部分损失。

（3）Partial loss of the insured goods attributable to heavy weather, lightning and tsunamis, where the conveyance has been grounded, stranding, sunk or burnt, irrespective of whether the event or events took place before or after such accident.【Typical Case Link1】

在运输工具已经发生搁浅、触礁、沉没、焚毁等意外事故的情况下，货物在此前后又在海上遭受恶劣气候、雷电、海啸等自然灾害所造成的部分损失。【典例链接 1】

（4）Partial or total loss consequent on falling of entire package or packages into sea during loading, transshipment or discharge.

在装卸或转运时由于一件或数件货物落海造成的全部或部分损失。

（5）Reasonable cost incurred by the insured in salvaging the goods or averting or minimizing a loss recoverable under the policy, provided that cost shall not exceed the sum insured of the consignment.

被保险人对遭受承保责任内危险的货物采取抢救、防止或减少货损的措施而支付的合理费用，但以不超过该批被救货物的保险金额为限。

（6）Losses attributable to discharge of the insured goods at a port of distress following a sea peril as well as special charges arising from loading, warehousing and forwarding of the goods at an intermediate port of call or refuge.

运输工具遭遇海难后，在避难港由于卸货所引起的损失以及在中途港，避难港由于卸货、存仓以及运送货物所产生的特别费用。

（7）Sacrifice and contribution to general average and salvage charges.

共同海损的牺牲、分摊和救助费用。

（8）Such proportion of losses sustained by the ship owners as is to be reimbursed by the cargo owner under the contract of Affreightment “Both to Blame Collision” clause.

运输合同中订有“船舶互撞责任”条款，根据该条款规定应由货方偿还船方的损失。

1.2 W.P.A. 水渍险

W.P.A .covers wider than F.P.A. English meaning is “responsible for the particular average”. Aside from the risks covers under F.P.A. conditions as above, this insurance also covers partial losses of the insured goods caused by heavy weather, lightning, tsunami, earthquake, floods and other natural disasters. One thing to note is, F.P.A. and W.P.A .for sea water caused by various responsible for the loss of the insured goods compensation, because fresh water, rain, snow and ice melting loss caused by the additional risk to bear.

水渍险的赔偿范围比平安险要广，水渍险的英文含义是“负责赔偿单独海损”。除平安险的各项责任外，水渍险还负责被保险货物由于恶劣气候、雷电、海啸、地震、洪水等自然灾害所造成的部分损失。需要注意的一点是，平安险和水渍险只对海水所致的各种损失负责赔偿，被保险货物由于淡水、雨水、冰雪融化所造成的损失，由附加险来承担。

1.3 All Risks 一切险

All risks are the three basic risks insured range is the widest, the risks in addition to the F.P.A. and W.P.A .'s area of responsibility, also responsible for the compensation of the insured goods in transit due to external causes the loss of all or part. External causes generally refers to external causes, such as theft, TPND, rain and freshwater, short quantity, confounding, leakage, contamination, smell, sweat and heating, breakage of packing, fishing loss, clash and breakage, rust and other reasons, not because of the war, strikes, riots and other special extraneous reasons caused the loss. And all risks only responsible for general extraneous causes physical loss of or damage to the goods, the inherent defects of natural loss, not at all risks of responsibility.【Typical Case Link2】

一切险是三种基本险别中投保范围最广的，该险除包括平安险和水渍险的各项责任范围外，还负责赔偿被保险货物在运输途中由于外来原因所致的全部或部分损失。外来原因指一般外来原因，例如偷窃、提货不着、淡水雨淋、短量、混杂、沾污、渗漏、串味异味、受潮受热、包装破裂、钩损、碰损破碎、锈损等原因，不包括由于战争、罢工、动乱等特殊外来原因所造成的损失。并且，一切险只负责赔偿一般外来原因造成的物理性灭失或损坏，货物的内在缺陷、自然损耗不在一切险的责任范围之内。【典例链接 2】

1.4 Exclusions 除外责任

Maritime transportation insurance three kinds of risks stipulated exclusion, the following is not liable for any loss:

（1）The insured caused by the intentional act or fault of the loss;

（2）Belong to the liability of the consignor loss;

（3）Prior to commencement of insurance liability, the insured goods already exist in the inferior quality or shortage caused by the loss;

（4）The insured goods natural loss, intrinsic defect, characteristics as well as a falling market, transport delay caused by the losses and expenses;

（5）Marine cargo transportation, cargo war risk clauses and strike clause provisions of the scope of liability and exemption of liability.

海上运输保险的三种险别规定了除外责任，对下列损失不负赔偿责任：

（1）被保险人的故意行为或过失所造成的损失；

（2）属于发货人责任所引起的损失；

（3）在保险责任开始前，被保险货物已经存在的品质不良或数量短差所造成的损失；

（4）被保险货物的自然损耗、本质缺陷、特性以及市价跌落、运输延迟所引起的损失和费用；

（5）海洋货物运输、货物战争险条款和货物运输罢工险条款规定的责任范围和除外责任。

1.5 Insurance Duration 保险期限（保险责任的起讫）

We take the practice stipulated by the International Insurance Market called Warehouse to Warehouse Clause to decide the insurance duration.

我国采用国际保险市场上有关保险责任起讫规定的惯例：仓至仓条款。

W/W indicates that the insurance company undertakes an insurance liability over the insured cargo from the warehouse or the place of storage of the shipper named in the policy until the cargo has arrived at the warehouse or the place of storage of the receiver named in the policy.The insurance liability terminates once the cargo arrives at the warehouse of the receiver.

仓至仓条款是保险责任起讫的条款。它是指自被保险货物远离保险单所载明的启运地发货人的仓库时生效，包括正常的运输过程，直至该货物运交保险单所载明的目的地收货人的仓库时为止。当货物一进入收货人的仓库，保险责任即行终止。

2. Additional Risks 附加险

Additional risk is the basic insurance liability to extend and complement, additional risks can be divided into two types: general additional risks and special additional risks. Additional risks must be insured against all risks, and since have included general additional insurance against all risks, so it is no longer required insurance general additional risks.

附加险是基本险责任的扩大和补充，附加险可以分为两种：一般附加险和特殊附加险。附加险不能单独投保，而且由于一切险已经包括了一般附加险，所以投保一切险就无需再投保一般附加险。

2.1 General Additional Risks 一般附加险

General additional insurance coverage due to general extraneous risks caused by the loss, the people's Insurance Company of China insurance general additional risks are mainly 11 kinds.

（1）Theft, pilferage and non-delivery clause(TPND).

（2）Fresh water and rain damage clause.【Typical Case Link3】

（3）Shortage clause.

（4）Intermixture and contamination clause.

（5）Leakage clause.

（6）Clash and breakage clause.

（7）Trint of odor clause

（8）Sweating and Heating clause.

（9）Hooks damage clause.

（10）Breakage of packing clause.

（11）Rust clause.

一般附加险承保由于一般外来风险所造成的损失，中国人民保险公司承保的一般附加险主要有 11 种。

（1）偷窃、提货不着险。

（2）淡水雨淋险【典例链接 3】。

（3）短量险。

（4）混杂、沾污险。

（5）渗漏险。

（6）碰损、破碎险。

（7）串味异味险。

（8）受潮受热险。

（9）钩损险。

（10）包装破裂险。

（11）锈损险。

2.2 Special Additional Risks 特殊附加险

Special additional risks means must be attached to the main risks, due to the special risk of causing losses to the subject matter insured liability insurance. Special additional risks to insure the responsibility has exceeded all risks coverage. It is selected according to the transport of goods need. Special additional risks include:

（1）War risk;

（2）Strike risk;

（3）Failure to delivery clause;

（4）Import duty risk clause;

（5）On deck risk;

（6）Rejection risk;

（7）Aflatoxin risk;

（8）Fire risk extension clause for storage of cargo at destination Hong Kong, including Kowloon or Macao.

特殊附加险是指必须附属于主要险别项下，对因特殊风险造成的保险标的的损失负赔偿责任的附加险。特殊附加险所承保的责任已超出了一切险的范围。要根据货物运输的需要选择加投。特殊附加险包括：

（1）战争险；

（2）罢工险；

（3）交货不到险；

（4）进口关税险；

（5）舱面险；

（6）拒收险；

（7）黄曲霉素险；

（8）出口货物到香港或澳门存仓火险。

Section Three Insurance of Other Cargo Transport
第三节 其他运输货物保险

1. Overland Transportation Insurance 陆上运输货物保险

Overland transportation insurance main underwriting to train, automobile and other land transport vehicles cargo transport insurance. According to the January 1st, 1981 revision of the Chinese people's Insurance Company "overland transportation cargo insurance clauses", overland transportation cargo insurance basic risks have the overland transportation risks and overland transportation all risks.

陆上运输货物保险主要承保以火车、汽车等陆上运输工具进行货物运输的保险。根据 1981 年 1 月 1 日修订的中国人民保险公司《陆上运输货物保险条款》，陆运货物保险的基本险有陆运险和陆运一切险两种。

Coverage of overland transportation insurance is similar with the ocean marine cargo clauses "W.P.A.".

陆运险的承保责任范围与海洋运输货物保险条款中的“水渍险”相似。

The range of all risks in overland transportation is similar with "all risks" in marine cargo transportation insurance clauses.

陆运一切险的承保责任范围与海上运输货物保险条款中的“一切险”相似。

Duration of overland transportation insurance adopts a "warehouse to warehouse clause".

陆上运输货物险的责任起讫也采用“仓至仓”责任条款。

Overland transportation insurance claims of effectiveness for a given period of time: from the insured goods at the final destination station all is unloaded from the vehicle, not more than two years.

陆上运输货物险的索赔时效为：从被保险货物在最后目的地车站全部卸离车辆后，最多不超过两年。

2. Air Transportation Insurance 航空运输货物保险

Air transportation insurance is the cargo insurance taking the aircraft as a way of transportation. In order to meet the development of foreign trade of our country needs, the people's insurance company of china is also acceptable to cover for air transportation risks, and to develop air transportation risk and all risks of air transportation.

航空运输货物保险是以飞机为运输工具的货物运输保险。为了适应我国对外贸易发展的需要，中国人民保险公司也接受办理航空运输货物的保险业务，并制定有航空运输险和航空运输一切险两种基本险条款。

3. Parcel Post Insurance 邮递货物保险

Parcel Post Insurance mainly through the post office to parcel delivery goods, because the parcel in transit by natural disasters, accidents or external causes the loss of goods. The people's insurance company of China with reference to international practices, combined with China's postal parcel business actual situation, revised in January 1, 1981 and released a set of complete mail cargo insurance clauses, including mail and parcel post all risks insurance.

邮递货物保险亦称邮包保险，主要承保通过邮局以邮包递运的货物，因邮包在运输途中遭到自然灾害、意外事故或外来原因造成的货物损失。中国人民保险公司参照国际上的通行做法，结合我国邮政包裹业务的实际情况，于 1981 年 1 月 1 日修订并公布了一套完备的邮递货物保险条款，包括邮包险和邮包一切险。

Section Four　Insurance Premium
第四节　保险费用

1. Insurance Premium 保险费用

Insurance Premium refers to the fee of insurer (insurance company) undertake the insurance responsibility.

保险费用主要是指保险人（保险公司）承保保险责任的费用。

1.1　Rescue Expenses 施救费用

The rescue expenses refer to the insured goods from inside insurance extent of liability accident, the insured person and agent is to avoid or reduce the losses and take the rescue, protection, cleaning and other measures to pay reasonable costs. In general, the rescue fees do not include general average and by the insurer and the insured to the third party other than the salvage charges.

施救费用是指被保险货物在遭受保险责任范围内的灾害事故时，被保险人及其代理人为了避免或减少损失而采取的抢救、保护、清理等措施所需支付的合理费用。一般而言，施救费用不包括共同海损及由保险人和被保险人以外的第三者救助而产生的费用。

1.2　Salvage Charges 救助费用

Salvage charges mean the insured goods in transit from the scope of coverage of natural disasters, the insurer and the insured outside the third take the rescue action saved by being saved, paid the savor.

救助费用是指被保险货物在运输途中遭受的承保范围内的自然灾害事故时，由保险人和被保险人以外的第三者采取救助行为而获救，由被救方付给救助方的报酬。

2. Calculation Formula Premium 国际货物运输保险费的计算公式

The insures or the insurant shall pay the premium to insure the goods based on the insurance total amount, and according to certain insurance ratio be calculated.

投保人或被保险人应缴纳的保险费是以投保货物的保险金额为基础，按一定的保险费率计算出来的。

保险费的计算公式为：保险费=保险金额×保险费率

其中保险金额的计算公式为：保险金额＝CIF 货价×（1＋加成率）

【Review Questions】复习思考题

【Typical Case Link 1—典例链接1】

Question: Should the insurance company compensate for the loss?

问题：试分析保险公司是否负责赔偿？应赔多少？

A batch of goods was insured FPA for 110% of the invoice value, a seagoing vessel carrying the goods on August 3rd encountered storms at sea, making the goods partially damaged, the loss value was 2 000 yuan; the ship continued sailing again on August 8th ran aground, also making some of the goods damaged, with the loss value of 4 000 yuan.

Please analyze whether the insurance company is responsible for compensation? How much should be compensable?

有一批货物按发票总值 110%投保了平安险（FPA），运载该批货物的海轮于 8 月 3 日在海面遇到暴风雨的袭击，使得该批货物受到部分损失，损失货值为 2 000 元；该海轮在继续航行中，又于 8 月 8 日发生触礁事故，再次使该批货物发生部分损失，损失货值为 4 000 元。

【Typical Case Link 2—典例链接2】

Question: Is it right?

问答：是否正确?

An exporter exported a batch of China, in case of collision and breakage, covering all risk additional with risk of clash and breakage.

某公司出口瓷器一批，为防碰撞、破碎，投保了一切险另加碰撞险。

【Typical Case Link 3—典例链接3】

Question：Should the insurance company make compensation?

问答：保险公司是否赔偿?

Shandong exporter exported 2 000 bales of gray cloth to American, covering WAP 150 bales were wetted as a result of leakage of the pipe during transit.

山东省某外贸公司向美国出口坯布 2 000 包，投保水渍险，货在海运途中因船舱使用水管漏水，致使该批货物中 150 包浸水渍。

Chapter Nine Payment of Goods

第九章 货物的支付

【Learning Objectives】教学目的与要求

After learning this chapter, you will be able to:

1. Acquire the most commonly used instruments of settlement and the modes of payment in international trade;

2. Grasp skillfully the relationships and differences between the various modes of international settlement and procedures of business;

3. Master the payment convention in international contract, and apply relevant knowledge to analyze the case.

【Lead-in Case】引导案例

Question: Is it reasonable for the US exporter to do so?

问题：美方此举是否合理？

A Chinese company imported 200 metric tons of steel on FOB Vessel New York basis at the price of USD 242 per metric ton. The importer established the L/C on time for USD 48 400, but the U.S. exporter required the importer to increase the amount of the L/C to USD50 000, otherwise, any export tariff and certificate fee should be paid by the importer separately by T/T.

中国某公司按每公吨242美元F.O.B. Vessel New York 进口200公吨钢材。中方如期开出48 400美元信用证，但美方来电要求增加信用证金额至50 000美元，不然有关出口捐税及签证费用应由中方另行电汇。

Section One Instruments of Payment in International Trade
第一节 国际货款结算工具

1. Bill of Exchange/Draft 汇票

1.1 Definition 汇票的含义

Bill of exchange, also called draft or draught, is defined as "an unconditional order in writing, addressed by one person to another, signed by the person giving it, requiring the person to whom it is addressed to pay on demand, or at a fixed or determinable future time, a sum certain in money, to the order of a specified person, or to bearer".

汇票是由一人向另一人签发的无条件的书面命令，要求接受命令人在见票时或在指定的或可以确定的将来某一日期，支付一定的金额给特定的人或其指定的人或持票人。

1.2 The Parties to a Bill of Exchange 汇票的基本当事人

（1）Drawer: The person who writes the order and gives directions to the person to make a specific payment of money. He is usually the exporter or the appointed bank in international trade.

出票人：即签发汇票的人，在国际贸易中，出票人一般是出口商或其指定的银行。

（2）Drawee: also called Payer. The person to whom the order is addressed and who is to pay the money. He is usually the importer or the appointed bank under a letter of credit in international trade.

受票人：又称付款人，即接受支付命令而付款的人，在国际贸易中，通常是进口商或其指定的银行。

（3）Payee: The person (individual, firm, or bank) to whom the payment is ordered to be made. The payee is usually the exporter or his appointed bank in international trade.

受款人：又称收款人（个人、公司或银行），即受领汇票所规定金额的人，在国际贸易中，通常是出口商或其指定的银行。

1.3 Elements of Bill of Exchange 汇票的基本内容

（1）Bill of Exchange，Draft “汇票”字样；

（2）Unconditional Order to Pay 无条件的支付命令；

（3）the Sum Certain in Money 确定的金额；

（4）Payer，Drawee 付款人名称；

（5）Payee 收款人名称；

（6）Date and Place of Issue 出票日期及地点；

（7）Tenor 付款期限；

（8）Drawer 出票人签章。

See Fig.9-1 Contents of Bill of Exchange. 如图 9-1 所示票的内容。

1.4 Classification of Bill of Exchange 汇票的种类

1.4.1 According to different drawer, the Bills of Exchange can be classified into Banker's Draft and Commercial Draft 按出票人的不同，分为银行汇票和商业汇票

（1）Banker's Draft: If the drawer is a bank, the bill is called a banker's bill. It is mainly used in funds transfers, such as remittance. See Fig.9-2.

汇票

BILL OF EXCHANGE

No. 汇票编号　　　　Date: 出票日期

For: 汇票金额

At 付款期限 sight of this second of exchange (first of the same tenor and date unpaid) pay to the order of 受款人 the sum of

Drawn under 出票条款

L/C No. ________ Dated

To. 付款人

出票人签章

图 9-1　汇票的内容

银行汇票:是指由银行签发的汇票，其付款人也是银行，通常用于资金转移（如汇款）业务，如图 9-2 所示。

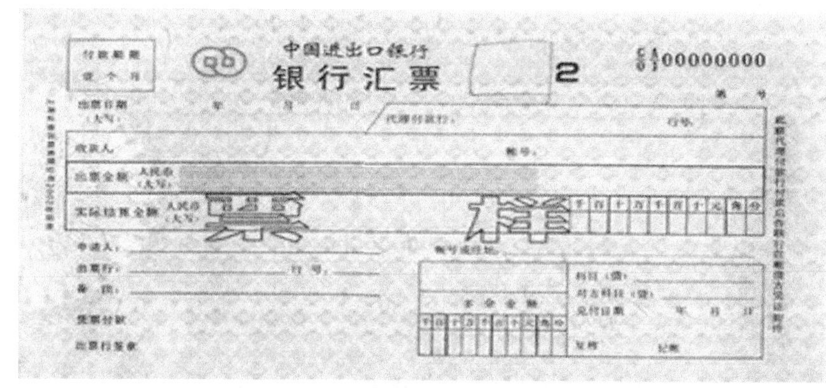
中国进出口银行
银行汇票　2
付款期限 壹个月
出票日期（大写）　年　月　日
代理付款行：　行号：
收款人：　帐号：
出票金额 人民币（大写）
实际结算金额 人民币（大写）
千 百 十 万 千 百 十 元 角 分
票样
申请人：
出票行：　行号：
备注：
帐号或住址：
多余金额
科目（借）
对方科目（贷）
兑付日期　年　月　日
凭票付款
出票行签章
复核　记帐

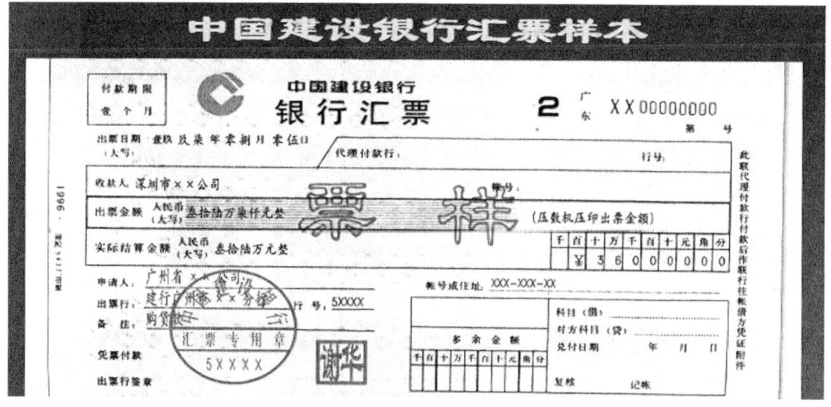
中国建设银行汇票样本
中国建设银行
银行汇票　2　广东 XX00000000
付款期限 壹个月
出票日期（大写）
代理付款行：　行号：
收款人：深圳市××公司
出票金额 人民币（大写）叁拾陆万柒仟元整 （压数机压印出票金额）
实际结算金额 人民币（大写）叁拾陆万元整
¥ 3 6 0 0 0 0 0 0
票样
申请人：广州省××公司
出票行：建行广州市××分行　行号：5XXXX
备注：购货款
帐号或住址：XXX-XXX-XX
汇票专用章 5XXXX
多余金额
科目（借）
对方科目（贷）
兑付日期　年　月　日
凭票付款
出票行签章
复核　记帐
此联代理付款行付款后作联行往帐借方凭证附件

图 9-2　银行汇票样本

（2）Commercial Draft：If the drawer is a commercial concern or individual, the bill is called a commercial bill. The payer can be firms, individuals, or a bank.

商业汇票：是指由工商企业或个人签发的汇票。付款人可以是企业、个人，也可以是银行。

1.4.2　According to the time when the bill falls due, Bills of Exchange may be divided into Sight (or demand)Bill or Time (or usance)Bill

按付款时间的不同，分为即期汇票和远期汇票

（1）Sight Draft: Demand immediate payment by the drawee at the sight of the bill. It doesn't require acceptance. There are the words “at sight” at the date of payment. See Fig.9-3.

即期汇票:在提示或见票时立即付款的汇票。即期汇票无须承兑，在付款日期中用“at sight”字样，如图 9-3 所示。

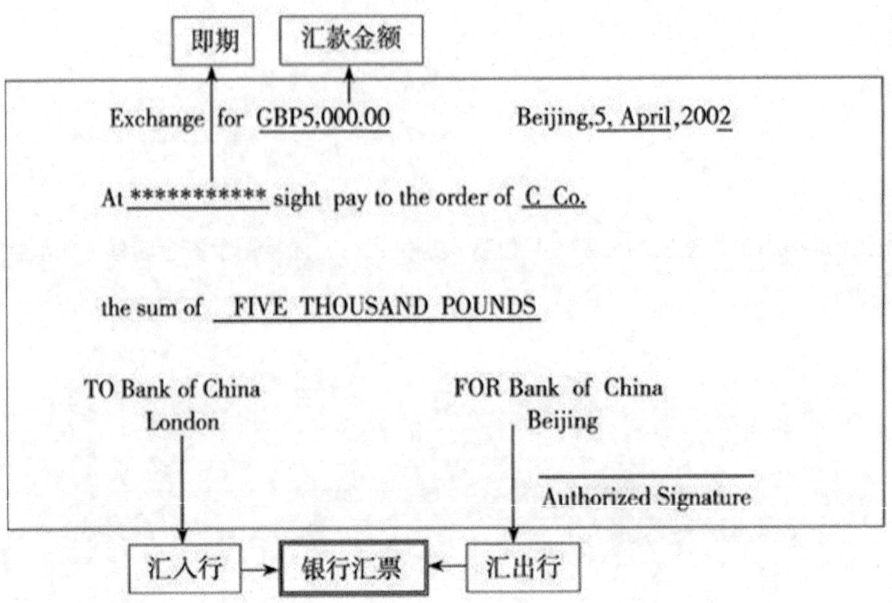

Exchange for HKD21 500.00 Tianjin,15 April 2004

D/P At***sight of this first Exchange(Second of the same tenor and date unpaid)pay to the order of

The Industrial and Commercial Bank of China

Hong Kong dollars twenty one thousand five hundred only

Drawn against shipment of 22 bales of pongee from Tianjin to Hong Kong for collection

To Sunlight garments Company

314 Locky Road,

Hong Kong

图 9-3 即期汇票样本

（2）Time Draft/ Usance Draft: The drawee is required to accept it firstly and pay it at a fixed or determinable future time. It requires acceptance before payment, see fig.9-4.

远期汇票:在一个指定的日期或一定期限内付款的汇票，远期汇票需先承兑，如图 9-4 所示。

The ways of payment time of time draft as follows.【 Typical Case Link 1 】

远期汇票的付款时间，有以下规定方法。【典例链接 1 】

① At…days after sight,such as 30 days sight ,60 days sight or 90 days sight 见票后若干天付款，如见票后 30 天、60 天、90 天等;

② At…days after date of draft 出票日后若干天付款;

③ At…days after date of B/L 提单签发日后若干天付款;

④ Fixed date 指定日期付款;

⑤ At…days after date of arrival of goods 货物到达后若干天付款。

> Exchange for HKD18 600.00　　Tianjin, 20 April 2004
> D/A　At 30 days after sight of this first Exchange(Second of the same tenor and date unpaid)pay to the order of Nanyang Commercial Bank Ltd.
> Hong Kong dollars eighteen thousand six hundred only
> Drawn against shipment of Cashmere Coats from Tianjin to Hong Kong for collection
> To Sunlight garments Company
> 314 Locky Road,
> Hong Kong

图 9-4　远期汇票样本

1.4.3　According to different acceptor, the bills of exchange can be classified into commercial acceptance draft and banker's acceptance draft 按承兑人的不同，分为商业承兑汇票和银行承兑汇票

（1）Commercial Acceptance Draft: In time or usance commercial bill, the bill is accepted by the commercial firm or individual is called a commercial acceptance bill. It is based on the commercial credit. See Fig. 9-5.

商业承兑汇票:企业或个人为汇票承兑人的远期汇票，以商业信用为基础，如图 9-5 所示。

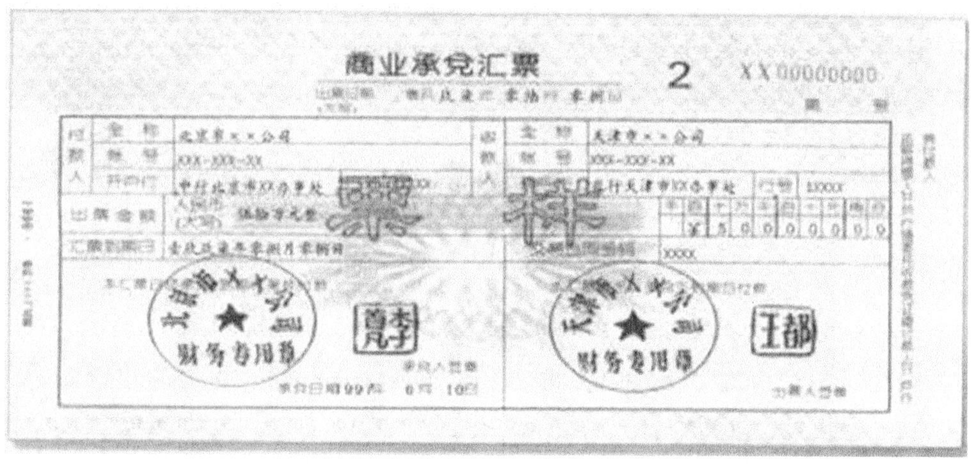

图 9-5　商业承兑汇票样本

（2）Banker's Acceptance Draft: In time or usance commercial bill,when the drawee is a bank, the bill is accepted by the bank is called a banker's acceptance bill. It is based on the bank credit.

See Fig.9-6

银行承兑汇票:以银行为汇票承兑人的远期汇票，以银行信用为基础，如图 9-6 所示。

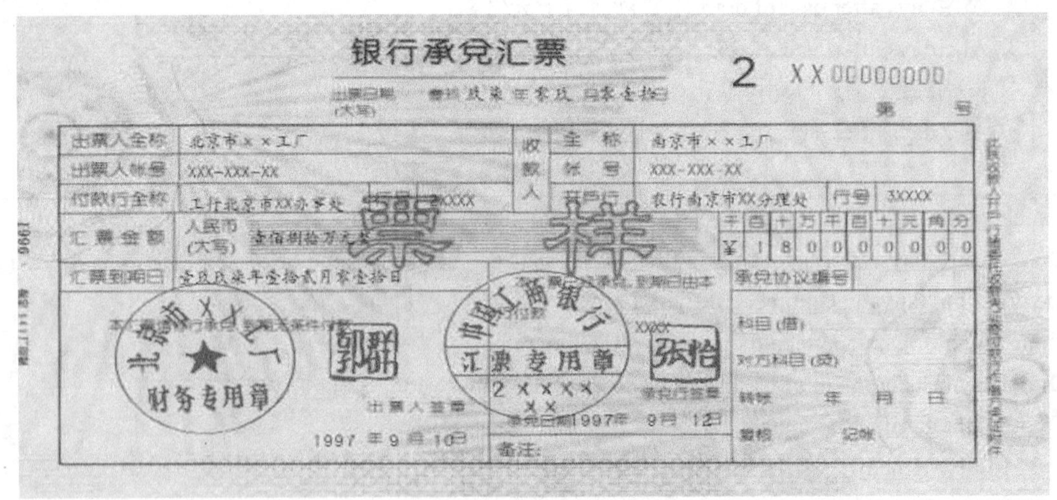
银行承兑汇票

2 XX 00000000

出票日期（大写）

第 号

出票人全称	北京市××工厂	收款人	全称	南京市××工厂
出票人帐号	XXX-XXX-XX		帐号	XXX-XXX-XX
付款行全称	工行北京市XX办事处		开户行	农行南京市XX分理处　行号 3XXXX
汇票金额	人民币（大写）			¥ 1 8 0 0 0 0 0 0 0
汇票到期日				承兑协议编号

票样

北京市××工厂 财务专用章

中国工商银行 汇票专用章 2××××××

出票人签章

1997 年 9 月 10 日

承兑日期 1997 年 9 月 12 日

承兑行签章

备注:

科目（借）

对方科目（贷）

转帐 年 月 日

复核 记帐

图 9-6　银行承兑汇票样本

1.4.4　According to the bill of exchange is accompanied by shipping documents or not, the bills of exchange can be classified into clean draft and documentary draft 按是否随附货运单据，分为光票和跟单汇票

（1）Clean Draft: It refers to the bill of exchange isn't accompanied by shipping documents. Banker's draft usually is clean draft. In international trade, clean draft mostly is used in remaining fund or non-trade settlement.

光票:指不附带任何货运单据的汇票。银行汇票一般为光票，在国际贸易中，光票多用于尾款或非贸易结算。

（2）Documentary Draft: It refers to the bill of exchange is accompanied by shipping documents. Commercial draft usually is documentary draft. In international trade, most draft is the documentary draft.

跟单汇票：指附带有货运单据的汇票。商业汇票一般为跟单汇票，在国际贸易中，大多使用的是跟单汇票。

1.5　Bills of Exchange Act 汇票的行为

（1）To Draw 出票

To Draw: the drawer fills the date of drawing,the name of the drawee, the time,the place and amount of the payment, etc in a bill of exchange. The draft is signed by the drawer and then sent to the payee.

出票是指出票人在汇票上填写付款人、付款金额、付款日期和地点、收款人等项目，经签字后，将汇票交给收款人的行为。

After the issuance of bills of exchange, the drawer takes responsibility for the bill of acceptance or payment. When a bill of exchange is not acceptance or payment, the payee can claim to drawer.

出票人签发汇票后，即承担该汇票被承兑或付款的责任。当汇票得不到承兑或付款时，收款人可以向出票人追索。

There are three kinds of ways to fill up the payee.

① Restrictive payee, such as pay to × ×not transferable pay to × ×only.

② To order, such as pay to × × or order or pay to the order of...This type requires endorsement when transferable.

③ To bearer, such as pay to bearer. This type requires no endorsement.

出票时，汇票抬头（收款人）有三种写法。

① 限制性抬头，如：付给 × ×，不得转让（Pay to × × not transferable）或仅付给（Pay to × × only），这种汇票不可转让，只能由抬头人收取货款。

② 指示性抬头，如：付给 × × 或其指定人（Pay to × × or order 或 Pay to the order of × ×），这种汇票经背书后可进行转让。

③ 持票人或来人抬头，如：付给来人（Pay to bearer），这种汇票无需背书，仅凭交付即可转让。

（2）Presentation 提示

Presentation: The holder takes the bill to the drawee and demands the payment or accept the bill is known as presentation.

提示：是持票人将汇票提交付款人要求承兑或付款的行为。

（3）Acceptance 承兑

Acceptance: The formal act whereby the drawee adopts the bill as his own obligation is known as acceptance. Acceptance is the written signification by the drawee of his assent to the order of the drawer. This is accomplished in the regular manner by writing the word "Acceptance", with the date and the signature of the drawee, across the face of the bill. When the bill is accepted by the drawee, he is then known as an acceptor.

承兑:是付款人对远期汇票表示承担到期付款的责任的行为。在汇票被提示时，付款人在汇票正面写上"承兑"（Accepted）字样，注明承兑日期，并签章后交还持票人。付款人对汇票做出承兑，即成为承兑人。

（4）Payment 付款

Payment: It is the payment behavior that the drawee is required to make the payment when the bill is presented to him by the holder within a specified time and place.

付款:是持票人在规定时间内、在规定地点，向付款人做出付款提示时，付款人付款的行为。

Under a sight bill, the drawee is required to make the payment when the bill is presented to him while for a time bill; the drawee is required to accept the bill when the bill is presented to him and make the payment at the maturity of the bill. When paid, the bill is retained by the payer while the receipt is made and signed by the holder of the bill.

即期汇票，在持票人（Holder）提示汇票时，付款人即应付款；远期汇票，付款人经过承兑后，在汇票到期日付款。付款后，汇票上的一切债务责任即告结束。

（5）Endorsement 背书

Endorsement: Endorsement is done when the payee has signed his name or the edorsee's name on the back of the bill and give the acceptor. After endorsement，the right of Bill billing transfers to the endorsee.

背书:是由汇票持票人在汇票的背面签上自己的名字或再加上受让人（即被背书人 Endorsee）的名字，并把汇票交与受让人的行为。经背书后，汇票的收款权利就转让给了受让人。

Modes of Endorsement 背书的方式

① Demonstrative Endorsement: A demonstrative endorsement is one which specifies the person to whom, or to whose order, the bill is to be payable, such as "Pay ...or to order of".

指示性背书，背书人在汇票背面其签字上方写明被背书人，但允许其继续转让。例如"付给 × ×

或其指定人”。

② Blank Endorsement or Endorsement in blank: A blank endorsement, or endorsement in blank is one which specifies no payee.

空白背书,又称不记名背书，是背书人仅在汇票背面签名，而不记载被背书人的背书形式。

③ Restrictive Endorsement: The endorser may write clearly on the upper part of the signature on the back of the bill the endorsee with restrictive conditions. A restrictive endorsement is one which limits the bill for further negotiation, such as “Pay to × ×Co. only”; “ Pay to × ×Co.，not transferable”.

限制性背书,即不可转让背书，是指背书人对支付给被背书人的指示带有限制性的词语。例如，仅付给××公司; 付给××公司，不可转让。

（6）Dishonor 拒付

Dishonor: It is called dishonor by non-acceptance or by non-payment in case that the bill is not accepted or not paid when the bill is presented by the bill holder for the acceptance. Dishonor also happens when the payer returns the bill, keeps away from the bill, dies, or is bankrupted.

持票人提示汇票要求承兑时，遭到拒绝承兑，或遭到拒绝付款，均称为拒付。付款人避不见票、死亡、破产，也称退票。

（7）Recourse 追索

Recourse: Upon the dishonor, the bill holder has the right to claim for the settlement of the payment and the relevant charges against the prior endorser (or the drawer).

追索:是汇票如果遭到拒付，汇票持票人可以对其前手（背书人、出票人）请求偿还汇票金额及费用。

（8）Discount 贴现

Discount: It means that the usance bill after the acceptance but undue is sold to a bank or a discounting house for the immediate payment with the discounting interest deducted from the payment sum based on a certain discounting rate.

贴现:是指远期汇票承兑后尚未到期，由银行或贴现公司从票面金额中扣除按一定贴现率计算的贴现息后，将余款付给持票人的行为。

Discounting Interest= Face Amount × Discounting Days /360 × Discount Rate

贴现息=票面金额×贴现天数/360×贴现率

Net Amount= Face Amount − Discounting Interest

Or Net Amount= Face Amount ×(1 − Discounting Days/360 × Discount Rate)

净款 = 票面金额 − 贴现息

或净款=票面金额×（1 − 贴现天数/360 × 贴现率）

2. Promissory Note 本票

2.1 Definition 本票的含义

Promissory Note: It is an unconditional promise in writing made by the drawer to the payee or the holder signed by the drawer engaging to pay on demand or at a fixed or determinable future time a certain sum of money to or to the order of a specified person or to the bearer.

本票：是出票人签发的，承诺自己在见票时或可以确定的时间，无条件支付确定的金额给收款人或者持票人的票据。

2.2 Essential Elements of Promissory Note 本票的基本内容

Specimen of Promissory Note.本票必要项目式样。

PROMISSORY NOTE

Promissory Note for USD5000.00 New York, 10th May 2011

At 90 days after date we promise to pay to the order of Bank of China, Qingdao Branch the sum of FIVE THOUSAND U.S. DOLLARS ONLY.

For New York Export and Import Company

(1) Promissory Note. "本票"字样。

(2) Unconditional Payment Promise. 无条件支付的承诺。

(3) the Sum Certain in Money. 确定的金额。

(4) Payee. 收款人名称。

(5) Date of Issue. 出票日期。

(6) Tenor. 付款期限。

(7) Drawer. 出票人签章。

2.3 Classification of Promissory Note 本票的种类

According to different drawer, promissory note can be classified into Commercial Promissory Note and Bank Promissory Note.

根据出票人不同，本票分为商业本票和银行本票

(1) Commercial Promissory Note: Promissory notes can be made by commercial firms or individual called commercial promissory notes.Commercial promissory notes can be sight promissory notes or times promissory notes.

商业本票：由企业或个人签发的本票称为商业本票或一般本票。商业本票有即期和远期之分。

(2) Bank Promissory Note: Promissory notes can be made by bankers, called bank promissory notes, while bank promissory notes can only be sight. See Fig.9-7.

银行本票：由银行签发的本票称为银行本票。银行本票只有即期，没有远期，如图 9-7 所示。

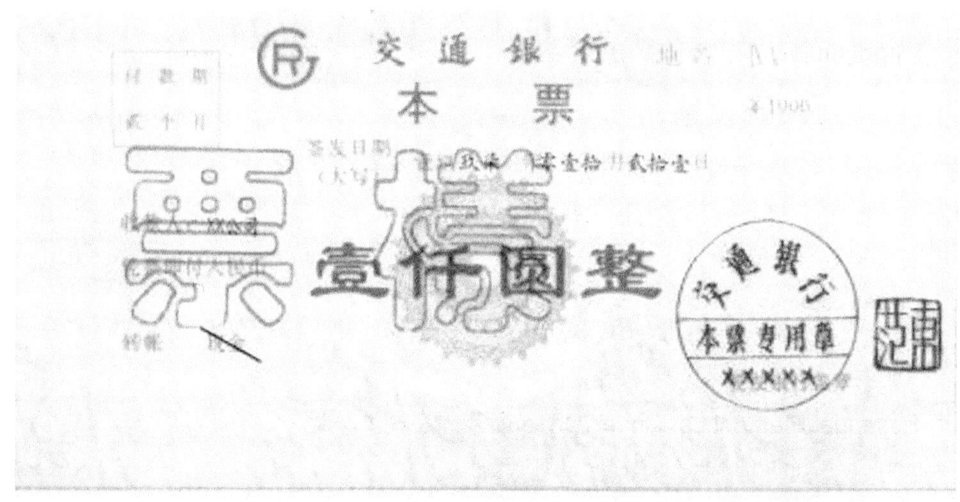

本票样本

中国工商银行 上海市分行

付款期 壹个月	本票 1	本票号码 XI 第 号

签发日期（大写） 壹玖 年 月 日

收款人	
凭票即付 人民币（大写）	
转帐 | 现金	科目（付） 对方科目（付） 兑付日期 年 月 日 出纳 复核 经办

此联签发行结清本票时作付出传票

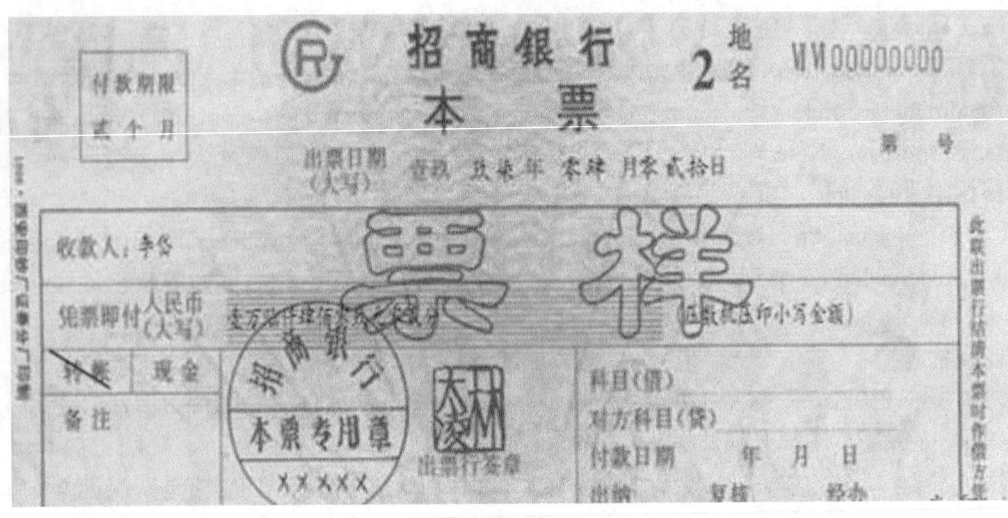

招商银行 本票 2

地名 WW00000000

付款期限 贰个月

第 号

出票日期（大写）

收款人：

凭票即付 人民币（大写）

转帐 现金

备注

本票专用章

出票行签章

科目（借）

对方科目（贷）

付款日期 年 月 日

出纳 复核 经办

图 9-7 银行本票样本

3. Check/Cheque 支票

3.1 Definition 支票的含义

Cheque, Check: A check is an unconditional order in writing drawn on banker signed by the drawer, requiring the banker to pay on demand a sum certain in money to or to the order of a specified person or to bearer. Cheque can only be sight.

支票：支票是银行存款户对银行签发的授权银行对特定的人或其指定人或持票人在见票时无条件支付一定金额的书面命令。支票都是即期的。

3.2 Essential Elements of Check/Cheque 支票的基本内容

Specimen of Cheque/Check. 支票必要项目式样。

CHEQUE	
Cheque for GBP10000.00	London,6th April, 2011
Pay to Tianjin Economic and Development Corp.Or order the sum of ten thousand pounds only.	
To: National Westminster Bank	For British Trading Co.
London, England	Signed

（1）the Words of Cheque/Check. “支票”字样。

（2）Unconditional Payment Promise. 无条件支付承诺。

（3）a Certain Amount of Money. 一定金额的货币。

（4）the Issuance Date and Place. 出票日期和出票地点。

（5）Name and Location of Paying Bank. 付款行名称和地点。

（6）Tenor. 付款期限。

（7）Payee. 收款人。

（8）Drawer. 出票人签章。

3.3　Classification of Check/Cheque 支票的种类

3.3.1　According to whether there are two parallel lines drawn on the face of the cheque or not, Check/Cheque can be classified into Crossed Cheque and Open Cheque 按支票票面上有无划线，分为划线支票和非划线支票

（1）Crossed Cheque 划线支票

Crossed Cheque：A crossed cheque refers to two parallel lines drawn on the face of the cheque, and usually this is done on the top left corner of the cheque. It implies that the cheque amount should be paid into a bank account and can not be exchanged for cash over the counter. The purpose of crossing a cheque is to ensure the right holder to obtain the payment.

划线支票：是在支票的正面有两道平行线的支票。这种支票，持票人只能委托银行代收票款入账，不能提取现金。使用划线支票的目的是为了在支票遗失被人冒领时，可以通过银行方面的线索追回货款。

（2）Uncrossed Check/Open Cheque/非划线支票

Uncrossed Check/Open Cheque：It refers to the one which is written on “plain” blank form, implying that the cheque can be exchanged for cash over the counter when the payee/holder presents the cheque for payment to the drawee bank.

非划线支票：是在支票的正面无两道平行线的支票。这种支票，持票人既可以委托银行代收票款入账，又可以提取现金。

3.3.2　Traveler’s Cheque 旅行支票

Traveler’s Cheque：A traveler’s check is a specially printed form of check issued by a financial institution, leading hotels, and other agencies in preprinted denominations for a fixed amount to a customer for use when he is going to travel abroad. See Fig.9-8.

旅行支票：是银行或旅行社为了方便游客在旅行期间安全携带和支付旅行费用而发行的一种固定面额票据，如图 9-8 所示。

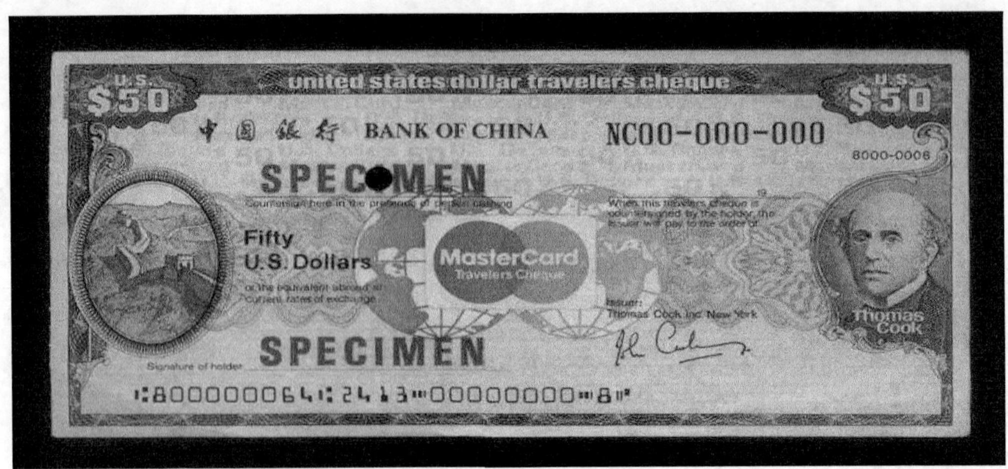

图 9-8　旅行支票样本

3.3.3　Cash Cheque or Money Transfer Cheque 现金支票和转账支票

Cash Cheque or Money Transfer Cheque：Cash cheque can only be used to withdraw cash. Money Transfer Cheque can only be used by banks or other financial institution transfers. See Fig.9-9 Sample of Cash cheque, Fig.9-10 Sample of Money Transfer Cheque.

现金支票和转账支票：现金支票只能用于支取现金；转账支票只能用于通过银行或其他金融机构转账，如图 9-9 现金支票样、图 9-10 转账支票样本所示。

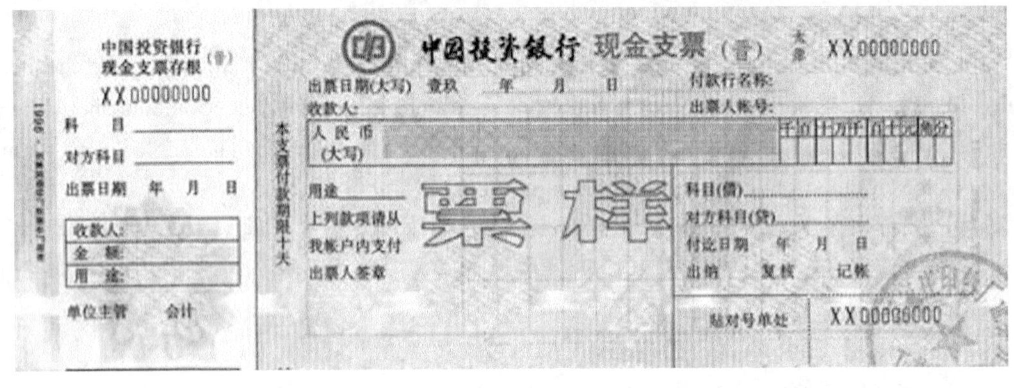

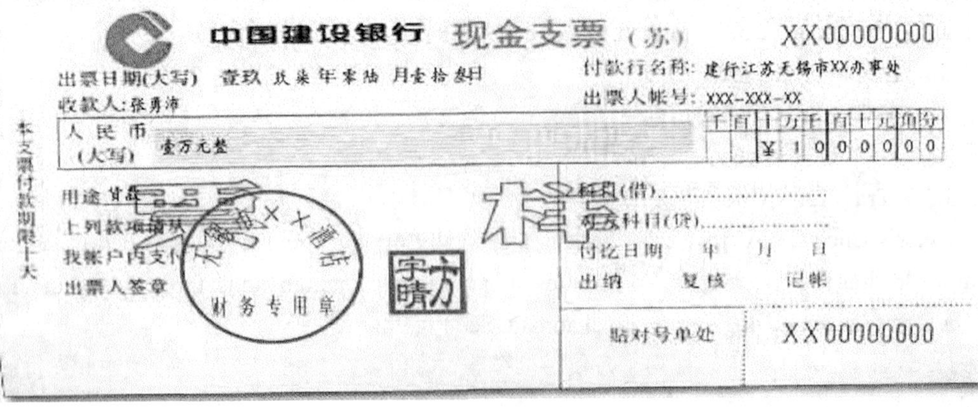

图 9-9　现金支票样本

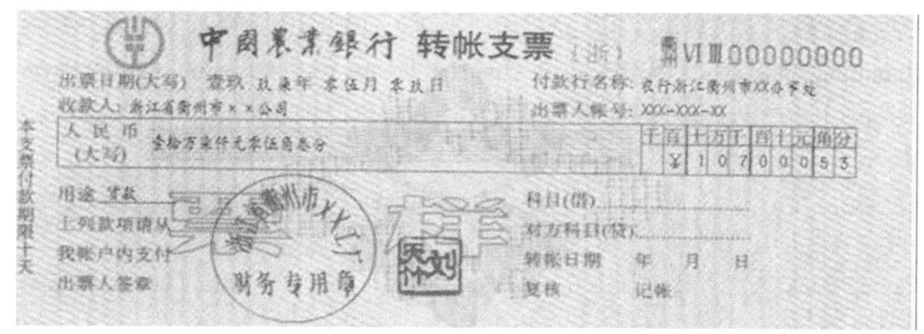
中国农业银行 转帐支票（浙）
出票日期（大写） 贰玖 玖柒年 零伍月 零玖日　付款行名称：农行浙江衢州市双办事处
收款人：浙江省衢州市××公司　出票人帐号：XXX-XXX-XX
人民币（大写） 壹拾万柒仟元零伍角叁分　千 百 十 万 千 百 十 元 角 分　¥ 1 0 7 0 0 0 5 3
本支票付款期限十天
用途 货款
上列款项请从
我帐户内支付
出票人签章　财务专用章
科目（借）
对方科目（贷）
转帐日期　年　月　日
复核　记帐

图 9-10　转账支票样本

4. The Differences between Bill of Exchange, Promissory Note and Cheque 汇票、本票与支票的区别

Instrument 工具	The Parties 当事人	Payer Identity 付款人身份	Tenor 付款期限	The Main Debtor 主债务人	Note Behavior 票据行为
Cheque 支票	Drawer，Payer，Payee 出票人、付款人、收款人	Bank of deposit 吸收存款的银行	can only be sight 只有即期	Drawer 出票人	no acceptance requirement 不需要承兑
Bill of Exchange 汇票	Drawer，Payer，Payee 出票人、付款人、收款人	No restriction 不受限定	can be sight or times 有即期，也有远期	before acceptance is the drawer，after accceptanceisthe acceptor 承兑前是出票人，承兑后是承兑人	Thereis acceptance requirement for times 远期需要承兑
Promissory note 本票	Drawer，Payee 出票人、收款人	Drawer 出票人	can be sight or times 有即期，也有远期	Drawer 出票人	no acceptance requirement 不需要承兑

Section Two Modes of International Payment 第二节 国际结算方式

1. Remittance 汇款

1.1 Definition of Remittance 汇款的含义

Remittance: Remittance refers to a bank (the remitting bank), at the request of its customer (the remitter), transfers a certain sum of money to its overseas branch or correspondent bank (the paying bank) instructing it to pay to a named person (the payee/beneficiary) domiciled in that country.

汇款：又称汇付，是指汇款人委托银行，以一定的方式将款项汇交收款人的结算方式。

1.2 Parties in Remittance 汇款的当事人

（1）Remitter: The party who will make the payment. Person requires his bank to remit funds to the beneficiary in a foreign country. In international trade, the remitters are usually the importer.

汇款人：是向银行交付款项，并委托银行将该款项交给收款人的人。在国际贸易中，汇款人通常是进口商。

（2）Payee: It refers to the party who accepts the payment. In international trade, the payee is usually the exporter.

收款人：是接受汇款的人。在国际贸易中，收款人通常是出口商。

（3）Remitting Bank: The bank remits the funds at the request of a remitter to the paying bank and instructs the latter to pay a certain mount of money to a beneficiary. In international trade, remitting bank is usually the importer's bank.

汇出行：是接受汇款人的委托，办理汇出款项的银行。在国际贸易中，汇出行通常是汇款人所在地的银行，即进口方银行。

（4）Paying Bank: A paying bank is the bank entrusted to by the remitting bank to pay a certain sum of money to a beneficiary. The paying bank usually locates in the same city as that of the exporter and is often the exporter's bank in international trade.

汇入行：又称解付行。是接受汇出行委托，将款项解付给收款人的银行。在国际贸易中，汇入行通常是收款人所在地的银行，即出口方银行。

1.3 Classification of Remittance 汇款的种类

（1）Telegraphic Transfer, T/T 电汇

Telegraphic Transfer, T/T: The remitting bank, at the request of the remitter, transfers funds by means of cable/telex/SWIFT message to the paying bank, asking the latter to pay a certain sum of money to the beneficiary.

电汇：是汇出行应汇款人的要求，以电报、电传或 SWIFT 等电信方式向汇入行发出付款委托的一种汇款方式。

The characteristics of T/T are speedy, safe and reliable, but the cost is higher. In international trade, T/T is one of the most commonly used ways in the method of remittance.

电汇的特点是付款速度快，安全可靠，但费用较高。在国际贸易中，电汇是各种汇款方式中使用最多的一种方式。

（2）Mail Transfer, M/T 信汇

Mail Transfer, M/T: The remitting bank, at the request of the remitter, transfers the funds by means of mailing a payment instruction to the paying bank, asking the latter to pay a certain sum of money to the payee.

信汇：汇出行应汇款人的要求，以航空邮件方式向汇入行发出付款委托的一种汇款方式。

Mail transfer is characterized by relatively low cost, but long time for receiving the payment. Therefore, it is rarely used. See Fig.9-11.

信汇的特点是费用较低，但耗时长，因此，目前使用得很少，如图 9-11 所示。

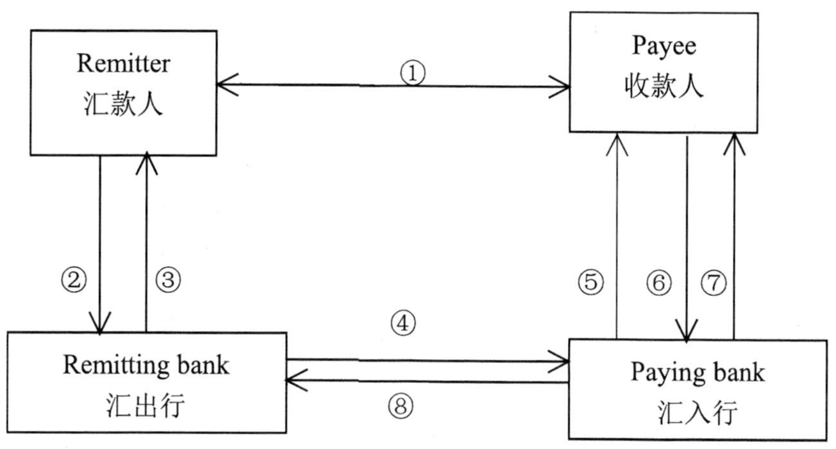

图 9-11 电/信汇业务程序图

Description 说明。

① Buyers and sellers conclude a contract, confirm to use T/T or M/T to pay.买卖双方订立合同，确认采用电汇或信汇方式付款。

② The remitter gives his signed written application to his bank,instructing to transfer the funds through T/T.汇款人填写电汇或信汇申请书，交款付费。

③ The remitting bank will stamp on the application form and return the customer's copy to the remitter for record.汇出行向汇款人签发回执。

④ The remitting bank will debit the remitter's a/c with the amount to be remitted together with its commission and cable charges (if any) and then issue and send the payment instruction by cable/telex/ SWIFT to the paying bank.汇出行向汇入行发出汇款委托书。

⑤ Upon receipt the cable message, the paying bank verifies it against the test key or SEIFT authenticate key (SAK) before it notifies the beneficiary with a copy of the cable message.汇入行向收款人发出电、信汇通知书，通知收款人提款。

⑥ The beneficiary presents the copy to the paying bank for payment.收款人凭取款通知书到汇入行取款。

⑦ The paying bank checks the identity of the beneficiary before releasing the funds to him.汇入行付款给收款人。

⑧ The paying bank will claim reimbursement according to the reimbursement clause stated in the cable message. 汇入行向汇出行发出付讫通知书。

（3）Remittance by Banker's Demand Draft, D/D 票汇。

Remittance by Banker's Demand Draft, D/D: The remitting bank,at the request of the remitter,draws a bill of exchange on the paying bank ordering the latter to pay on demand a certain sum of money to the beneficiary who will also be the payee of the draft. See Fig.9-12 The Business Process Diagram of D/D.

票汇：是汇出行应汇款人的要求，开立以其分行或代理行为付款行的银行即期汇票，并将该汇票交给汇款人，由其自行交给收款人，由收款人凭票向付款行收款的一种汇款方式，如图 9-12 所示。

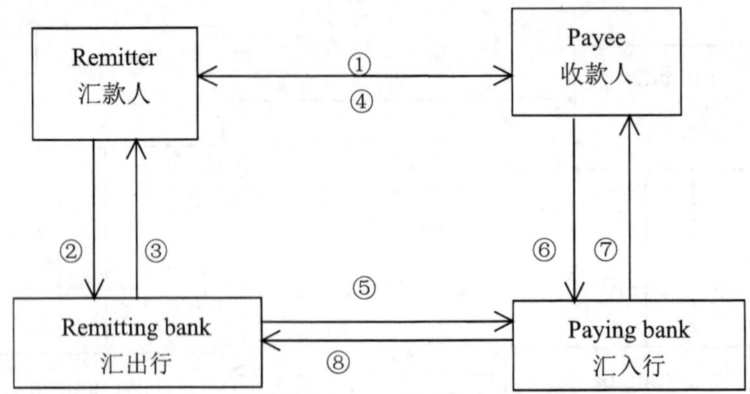

图 9-12　票汇业务流程图

说明：

① Buyers and sellers conclude a contract, confirm to use D/D to pay.买卖双方订立合同，确认采用票汇方式付款。

② The remitter gives his signed written application to his bank instructing the bank to transfer the funds by D/D.汇款人向汇出行提交票汇申请并交款付费。

③ The remitting bank will check the remitter's account with him. If it is positive, the remitting bank will debit the account and draw a draft on the paying bank payable to the beneficiary.汇出行签发银行即期汇票给汇款人。

④ The remitter will send the draft to the beneficiary.汇款人将汇票寄给收款人。

⑤ The remitting bank will keep the paying bank aware of the remittance via inter-bank system.汇出行将汇票通知书寄汇入行。

⑥ Upon receipt of the draft, the beneficiary will present the draft for payment to the paying bank.收款人凭银行即期汇票到汇入行取款。

⑦ After authentication of the draft against authorized signature,the paying bank will release the funds to the beneficiary.汇入行核对汇票，向收款人付款。

⑧ The paying bank will claim reimbursement against the remitting bank.汇入行将付讫通知书寄送汇出行。

1.4　Characteristics of Remittances 汇款的特点

In the remittance business, banks only offer services ，assume no payment responsibilities, so remittance is established on the basis of commercial credit payment.

在汇款业务中，银行参与其间只提供服务，不承担付款责任，故汇款是建立在商业信用基础上的结算方式。

2. Collection 托收

2.1　Definition 托收的含义

Collection is an arrangement whereby the goods are shipped and the relevant instrument is drawn by the seller on the buyer, and/or document(s) is sent to the seller's bank with clear instructions for collection through one of its correspondent banks located in the domicile of the buyer.

托收体现商业信用。出口商（或债权人）开立金融票据或商业单据或两者兼有，委托托收行通过其联行或代理行向进口商（或债务人）收取货款或劳务费用的结算方式。

2.2 Parties 托收的当事人

（1）Principal: It refers to the customer entrusts the bank to handle collections, usually is the exporter.

委托人是指委托银行办理托收业务的客户，通常是出口商。

（2）Remitting Bank: refers to the bank which accepts the seller's request and on behalf of the payee, usually is the bank of export place.

托收行是指接受委托人的委托，代为收款的银行，一般为出口地银行。

（3）Collecting Bank: refers to the bank of import place which accepts the remitting bank's request and collecting cheques from the payer. The collecting bank is usually the remitting bank's foreign branch or agency.

代收行是指接受托收行的委托,向付款人收取票款的进口地银行。代收银行通常是托收行的国外分行或代理行。

（4）Payer: refers to the person responsible for payment, also called Drawee. They are usually the exporters.

付款人是支付款项的人，即为汇票的受票人，通常为进口商。

2.3 Classifications 托收的种类

Classifications of Collection is shown in Fig.9-13. 托收的种类，如图 9-13 所示。

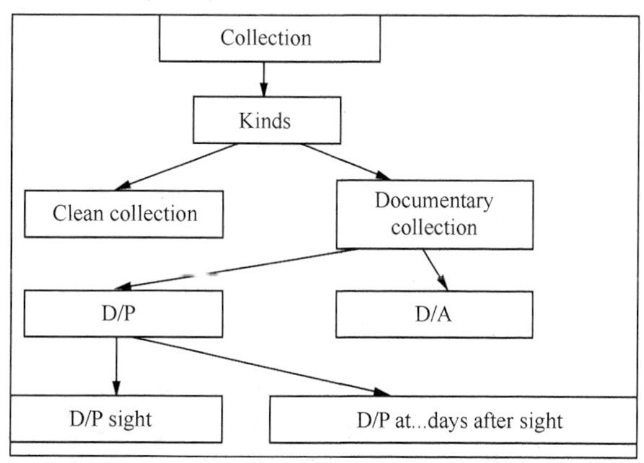

图 9-13　托收的种类

（1）Clean Collection 光票托收

Clean Collections are collections on financial instruments without being accompanied by commercial documents, such as invoice, bill of lading, insurance policy, etc.

光票托收是指出口商仅开立汇票而不附任何商业单据，委托银行收取货款的一种托收方式，如发票、提单、保险等。

（2）Documentary Collection 跟单托收

Documentary Collections may be described as collections on financial instruments and commercial documents or collections on commercial documents without being accompanied by financial instruments.

跟单托收是指附有金融票据和商业单据的托收或者仅随附商业单据而没有金融票据的托收。

The documentary collection is widely used in international trade. In terms of release of documents, documentary collection falls into two kinds: documents against payment (D/P)and documents against acceptance (D/A).

国际贸易中货款的收取大多采用跟单托收。在跟单托收的情况下，按照向进口商交单条件的不同，又可分为付款交单和承兑交单两种。

① Documents against Payment D/P 付款交单

Under D/P, the exporter is to ship the goods ordered and deliver the relevant shipping documents to the buyer abroad through the remitting bank and the collection bank with instructions not to release the documents to the buyer until the full payment is effected. According to the different time of payment, document against can be further divided into D/P at sight and D/P after sight.

在付款交单支付方式下，出口人交出单据后指示托收行和代收行在国外的买方付清贷款后才交出单据。根据付款时间不同，付款交单可分为即期付款交单和远期付款交单。

- Documents against Payment at Sight D/P at Sight 即期付款交单

Under D/P at sight,seller draws a sight draft, and sends it with the shipping document to the collecting bank.Then the collecting bank presents the sight of draft and shipping document to the buyer. When the buyer sees them he must pay the money at once, then he can obtain the shipping documents.This method is also called “Cash against Documents”.

在即期付款交单方式下，卖方开具即期汇票并通过银行向买方提示，买方见票后马上付款，只有付款清货后才能领取单据。这种方式也称“凭单据付款”。

- Documents against Payment after Sight, D/P after Sight 远期付款交单

Under D/P after Sight, the seller draws a time (or usance) draft. The collecting bank presents the time draft and shipping documents to the buyer.When the buyer sees them he just accepts the time bill and then effects payment at maturity of the draft.When receiving the money from the buyer, the collecting bank hands over the shipping documents to him. See Fig.9-14.

在远期付款交单方式下，卖方开立远期汇票。代收银行将此汇票向买方提示汇票和货运单据。买方见票后仅须承兑汇票，等汇票到期支付贷款。代收行收到货款后，即向他交付单据，如图 9-14 所示。

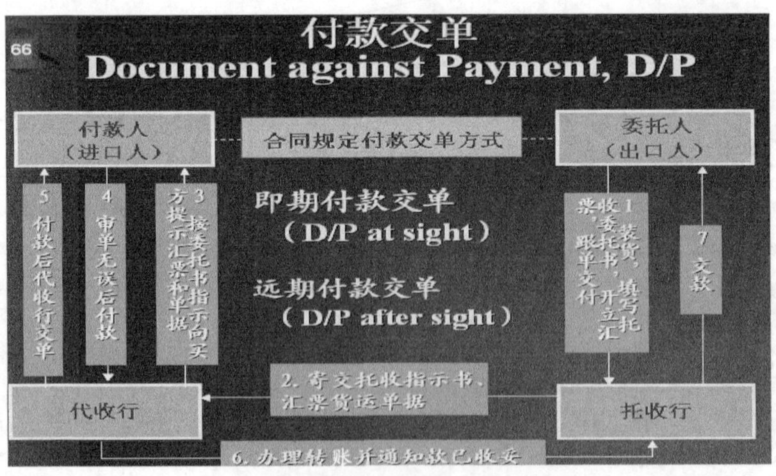

图 9-14　付款交单业务流程图

② Documents against Acceptance, D/A 承兑交单

D/A is applicable only to a time bill that is used in documentary collection, in which the collecting bank will release the shipping documents to the buyer without any payment but merely against the acceptance of the bill by the buyer to honor the draft at a certain future date agreed upon between the seller and the buyer D/A is always after sight. See Fig.9-15.

承兑交单是指出口人的交单以进口人在汇票上承兑为条件。即出口人在装运货物后开具远期汇票连同货运单据，通过银行向进口人提示，进口人承兑汇票后，代收行即将货运单据交给进口人，进口人在汇票到期时才履行付款义务，如图 9-15 所示。

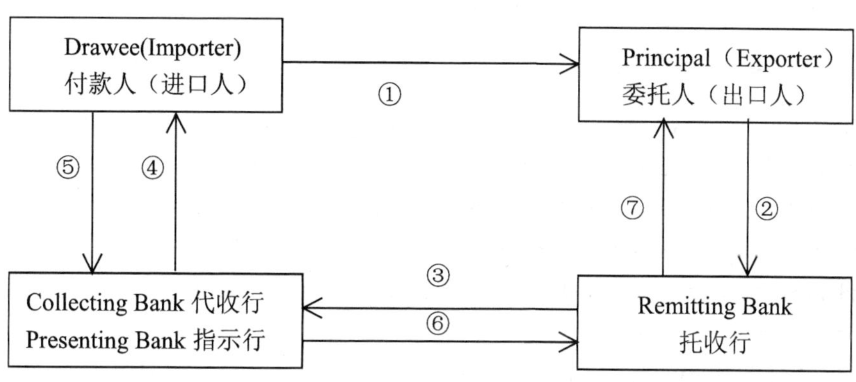

图 9-15 跟单托收业务流程图

Description 说明：

① The buyer and the seller conclude the sales contract, confirming to use Documentary Collection to pay.买卖双方订立合同，并规定以跟单托收方式结算。

② The exporter authorizes the local bank to effect the collection, submitting the full set of shipping documents with draft to the remitting bank.出口人委托当地银行代收货款，将全套单据和汇票交托收行。

③ The remitting bank sends the draft and the shipping documents to the collecting bank of the importer's country together with the instructions received from the exporter.托收行将汇票和货运单据寄交进口地银行（代收行），并说明托收委托书上的各项指示。

④ The presenting bank makes presentation of the payment advice to the buyer. 提示行向买方作付款提示。

⑤ The importer makes the payment and gets the documents. 进口人付清货款，赎取全套单据。

⑥ The collecting bank informs the remitting bank and makes transfer of the payment to the remitting bank.代收行电告托收行，款已收妥转账。

⑦ The remitting bank credits the payment to the account of the exporter. 托收行将货款交出口人。

2.4 Characteristics of Collection 托收的特点

（1）Risky 风险大

In Collection practice, banks only provide services, without obligations to provide any credit and guarantees.

托收业务中，银行仅提供服务，不提供任何信用和担保。

（2）Low Expenses 费用低

Under collection, the importer can spare expenses of formalities for the opening of L/C applied. Collection is usually used as a force means in the keen market to expand the sales.

进口商可以免去申请开立信用证的手续费用。在激烈的市场竞争情况下，托收常被出口商用来作为一种争夺客户，扩大销售的竞争手段。

（3）Facilitates Funds Circulation 有利于资金融通

Under D/P after sight, it can avoid to tie up a number of funds circulated for the importer.

如能争取到远期付款，还可不占用或少占用资金。

3. Letter of Credit 信用证

Letter of Credit (L/C) is a payment term mainly used in international trade. Under the circumstance that the seller and the buyer don't know much of each other, lacking mutual trust, the payment term of (L/C)is a good solution to solve this difficult problem, which replaces commercial credit with bank credit, getting a bank involved in the payment obligations. The availability of the payment promise to the seller from a bank before the delivery of goods helps the transactions go well, further boosting the development of international trade.

信用证是目前我国外贸进出口结算的一种主要方式，它以银行信用取代商业信用，以银行的付款责任取代买方的付款责任，在买卖双方缺乏信任、互不熟悉的情况下，信用证的付款方式很好地解决了支付中的难题，使卖方在交货以前就能得到银行付款的承诺，使交易得以顺利进行，有利于国际贸易的快速发展。

L/C payment is in favor of buyers, too. In a sales transaction by L/C, the buyer can restrict the seller with the clauses of L/C to the fulfillment of the contract, ensuring the quality, quantity and delivery time of the goods. The seller cannot be paid if it breaches the contract.

在信用证交易中，买方也有得天独厚的好处，它可以利用信用证条款约束卖方履行合同，保证所购买货物的品质、数量、交货期符合合同的规定， 卖方如果违约将得不到偿付。

3.1 Definition 信用证的含义

According to the Uniform Customs and Practice for documentary credits, documentary credit, letter of credit is a kind of conditional document in written form, opened by a bank, with a promise to make payment. In details, it is a kind of warrant issued by a bank at the request of the buyer, addressed to the exporter, in a certain amount, under a certain condition, promising to make payment. The said "a certain amount, a certain condition" means that the payment made by the opening bank is under the condition that the seller presents the documents complying with the L/C clauses.

As defined in *the UCP 600,* a letter of credit means "any arrangement, however named or described, whereby a bank acting at the request and on the instructions of a customer or on its own behalf, is to make a payment to or to the order of a third party, or is to accept and pay bill of exchange drawn by the third party".

根据国际商会《跟单信用证统一惯例》的解释，信用证是一种银行开立的、有条件的、承诺付款的书面文件。具体地说，就是银行（开证行）应进口人的请求和指示，向出口人开立的、一定金额的、在一定条件下保证付款的凭证。所谓“一定金额、一定条件”，是指开证行的付款是以卖方提交符合信用证的单据为条件。

UCP 600 给信用证下的定义是："指一项不可撤销的安排，无论其名称或描述如何，该项安排构成开证行对相符交单予以承付的确定承诺"。

3.2 Characteristics of L/C 信用证的特点

（1）L/C is a guarantee from the bank，opening bank undertaking the responsibility of the first payer. 信用证是一种银行信用，开证行承担第一付款人的责任。

The issuing bank gives guarantee to the beneficiary, if the beneficiary carries out contract according to the L/C, the issuing bank shall pay. 【Typical Case Link 2】

信用证是一种银行开立的有条件承诺付款的书面文件，只要出口商在信用证规定的期限内提交符合信用证规定的单据，开证行就必须付款。【典例链接 2】

（2）L/C is an independent instrument【Typical Case Link 3】

信用证是独立于合同之外的一种自足的文件。【典例链接 3】

（3）L/C is a kind of transaction of document.

信用证业务是一种单据买卖。

3.3 Parties Involved 信用证的当事人

Parties involved in a L/C business include: the applicant, the opening bank, the beneficiary (exporter or actual supplier), the advising bank, the negotiating bank and the paying bank.

信用证的当事人包括开证申请人、开证银行、受益人（出口人或实际供货人）、通知银行、议付银行和付款行。

（1）Applicant, Opener 开证申请人

The Applicant (Opener) refers to the party which applies to the bank for the opening of a letter of credit, namely, the importer.

开证申请人是指向银行申请开立信用证的人，即进口人。

（2）Opening /Issuing Bank 开证银行

The Opening Bank (the Issuing/Opening/Establishing Bank), which is the bank receiving the application from the applicant to issue the letter of credit and will be responsible for the payment. It is usually the bank at the place where the importer is located.

开证银行是指接受开证申请人的申请，开立信用证的银行，承担第一付款的责任。开证银行一般是进口商所在地银行。

（3）Beneficiary 受益人

The party entitled to be reimbursed under a credit and specified in the credit, usually the exporter.

受益人是指信用证上所指定的有权使用该证的人，一般是出口人。

（4）Advising /Notifying Bank 通知银行

The Advising Bank hands the letter of credit to the exporter under instructions from the issuing bank. It only proves the authenticity of the letter of credit and is not responsible for other things. The advising bank usually is the bank at the place where the exporter is located.

通知银行是指受开证行的委托，将信用证转交出口人的银行。通知银行只鉴别信用证的表面真实性，不承担其他义务。一般是出口商所在地的银行。

（5）Negotiating Bank 议付银行

The Negotiating Bank is the bank ready to pay or discount the documentary bill by the beneficiary under the letter of credit. The negotiating bank has the right of recourse on the beneficiary if it was dishonored.

议付银行是指根据开证行的授权，买入或贴现受益人开立和提交的符合信用证规定的汇票及/或单据的银行。议付行如果遭到拒付，它有权向受益人追索垫款。

（6）Paying Bank 付款银行

The Paying Bank is the bank responsible for payment mentioned in the letter of credit. It is usually the issuing bank or it may be another bank appointed by the issuing bank. When the paying bank makes the payment, it has no recourse on the beneficiary.

付款银行是信用证指定的付款银行。一般是开证行，也可以是它指定的另一家银行。付款行一旦付款后可以向开证行索偿，无权向受益人追索。

3.4 Essential Elements of L/C 信用证的基本内容

（1）General Information of L/C 关于信用证本身的说明

Including credit number, the issuing date, expiry date and place, whether there is an expiry date outside territory and so on.

包括信用证的编号、开证日期、到期日和到期地点、是否有境外有效期等。

（2）Types of L/C 信用证种类

（3）Parties to a L/C 信用证当事人

（4）Clause in Bill of Exchange 汇票条款

Under a letter of credit with draft,the information about the types of bill of exchange, drawer, drawee,sum，and other main terms must be specified in the draft.

如使用汇票，要明确汇票的种类、出票人、受票人、汇票金额、主要条款等内容。

（5）Clause in Goods 货物条款

Including name, number, quantity, packing，price and so on, must be stated in a credit.

包括货物的名称、货号、数量和包装、价格等。

（6）Currency of Payment and L/C Amount 支付货币和信用证金额

Including currency and total amount.The type of currency usually includes abbreviations and capitalization of the currency. Amount in total usually should write down the capital words and Arabic numerals.

包括币种和总额，币别通常包括货币的缩写和大写，总额一般分别用大写汉字与阿拉伯数字书写。

（7）Clause in Shipping and Insurance 装运与保险条款

Including the provisions of the shipment time, port of loading or the place of shipment, the port of discharge or destination, time of shipment, can be partial shipment or not, can transship or not and how to be partial shipment and transship.

包括装运时间、装运港或启运地、卸货港或目的地、装运期限、 可否分批装运、可否转运以及如何分批装运、转运的规定。

（8）Clause in Documents 单据条款

It may usually require submitting commercial invoice, bill of lading, insurance policy, packing list, certificate of origin and so on.

通常要求提交商业发票、提单、保险单、装箱单、原产地证等及其他单据。

（9）Special Clause 特殊条款

It means some special instruction or special requirement for the negotiation, or payment route, or confirmation or not.

银行对议付或付款路线或是否保兑，做出特别指示，或有特别要求。

3.5 Procedure of L/C 信用证的业务流程

Procedures of L/C are shown in Fig.9-16.

信用证的业务流程如图 9-16 所示。

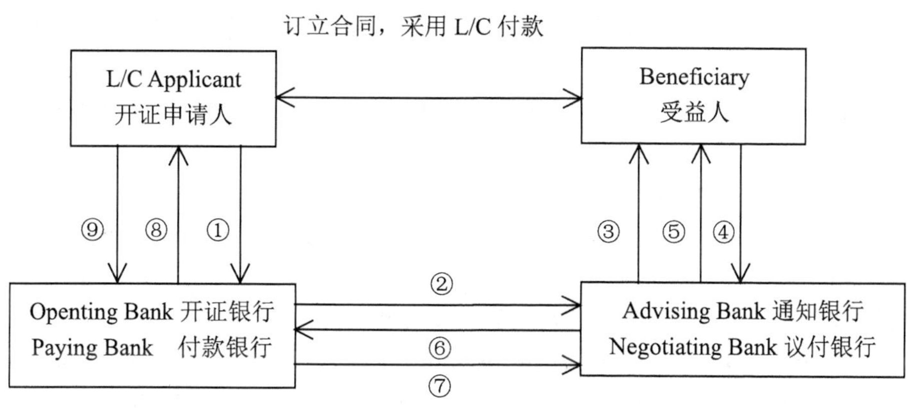

图 9-16 信用证的业务流程

① The buyer makes application for a L/C with his bank and pays a number of deposit and issuing fees.

开证申请人根据合同规定向当地银行提出开证申请，并交纳若干押金和开证手续费。

② The opening bank accepts the application for a L/C and forwards the letter of credit to the advising bank.

开证银行接受开证申请，开出信用证并寄交通知行。

③ The advising bank identifies the signature and delivers the letter of credit to the beneficiary.

通知行接到信用证，核对印鉴无误后，将信用证交给受益人。

④ Having examined the L/C, the beneficiary ships the goods to the buyer. After that, the beneficiary prepares documents, draws a draft and presents them to his bank.

受益人审查信用证无误后，按信用证规定装船、制作单据送交议付行议付。

⑤ The beneficiary’s bank negotiates the documents and pays funds to the beneficiary in accordance with the letter of credit.

议付行审单后，按汇票金额扣除利息，垫付货款给受益人。

⑥ The negotiating bank forwards the documents to the opening bank and demands the payment.

议付行将单据寄交开证行或付款行要求付款。

⑦ The opening bank receives the documents to check them. If the documents are in order and comply with the letter of credit, the opening bank credits the negotiating bank’s account.

开证行或付款行审单后，向议付行付款。

⑧ The opening bank notifies the buyer to make payment for documents.

开证行通知开证申请人付款赎单。

⑨ Having examined the documents , the buyer makes the payment.

开证申请人审单无误后，付款赎单。

3.6 Types of Letter of Credit 信用证的种类

3.6.1 According to whether the L/C is accompanied by a shipping document, letter of credit can be classified into documentary L/C and clean L/C 依据信用证项下是否附有货运单据划分，分为跟单信用证和光票信用证

（1）Documentary L/C 跟单信用证

Documentary L/C: The opening bank makes payment against the documentary draft or only the documents under a documentary L/C.The documentary letter of credit is widely used in international trade.

跟单信用证是指开证行凭跟单汇票或仅凭单据付款的信用证。国际贸易中使用的信用证，绝大部分是跟单信用证。

（2）Clean L/C 光票信用证

Clean L/C: It refers to the letter credit that requires the opening bank can make payment by the presentation of the draft without documents.

光票信用证是指开证行仅凭不附单据的汇票付款的信用证。

3.6.2 According to the nature of the issuing bank's payment guarantee, letter of credit can be classified into irrevocable L/C and revocable L/C 依据开证行付款保证的性质划分，分为不可撤销信用证和可撤销信用证

（1）Irrevocable L/C 不可撤销信用证

The Irrevocable of Credit means that once the credit is issued it cannot be cancelled or amended before the expiry date without the agreement of the beneficiary.Under such a credit, the exporter can rely on payment being made as soon as he has shipped the goods and produced the shipping documents called for in accordance with the terms of the letter of credit.

不可撤销信用证是指信用证一经开出，在有效期内，未经受益人及有关当事人的同意，开证行不得片面修改和撤销，只要受益人提供的单据符合信用证规定，开证行必须履行付款义务。

（2）Revocable L/C 可撤销信用证

The Revocable Letter of Credit can be cancelled or amended during the term of validity without notice to the beneficiary. It does not constitute a legally binding undertaking by the banks concerned.

可撤销信用证是指开证行对所开信用证不必征得受益人或有关当事人的同意，有权随时撤销的信用证。

3.6.3 According to whether the bank confirms, letter of credit can be classified into Confirmed L/C and Unconfirmed L/C 依据是否加以保兑划分，分为保兑信用证和不保兑信用证

（1）Confirmed L/C 保兑信用证

A confirmed L/C is a credit issued by the issuing bank, and guaranteed by another bank to fulfill the payment for the consistent presentation of documents. The bank who adds its confirmation to the credit is called as Confirming Bank.

保兑信用证是指开证行开出的信用证，由另一银行保证对符合信用证规定的单据履行付款义

务的信用证。对信用证加保兑的银行，叫做保兑行。

（2）Unconfirmed L/C 不保兑信用证

An unconfirmed L/C means that the credit issued by the issuing bank is not confirmed by another bank. An unconfirmed credit is usually issued when the issuing bank is with a good reputation.

不保兑信用证是指开证银行开出的信用证没有经过另一家银行保兑的信用证。当开证银行资信好时，一般都使用这种不保兑的信用证。

3.6.4 According to the payment time, letter of credit can be classified into Sight L/C and Usance L/C 依据付款时间划分，分为即期信用证和远期信用证

（1）Sight L/C 即期信用证

Sight L/C refers to the negotiating bank makes payment immediately upon the presentation of the sight draft and shipping documents as stipulated in the letter of credit by the seller.

即期信用证是指受益人凭即期汇票或凭装运单据即可向指定银行提示，请求立即付款的信用证。

（2）Usance L/C 远期信用证

A usance L/C is a letter of credit under which the payment is made by the issuing bank or paying bank within the stipulated time upon receipt of documents.

远期信用证是指开证行或付款行收到信用证的单据时，在规定期限内履行信用证规定凭远期汇票收取货款的信用证。

Usance L/C can be divided into two types as follows:

远期信用证可分为常见的有下列两种：

① Acceptance L/C 承兑信用证

Acceptance L/C: The paying bank accepts the time draft and documents after receiving L/C when the beneficiary presents the time draft to the bank, and pays the amount on the due date. It is usually used in usance transaction.

承兑信用证是开证行对于受益人开立以开证行为付款人或以其他银行为付款人的远期汇票，在审单无误后，应承担承兑汇票并于到期日付款的信用证。承兑信用证用于远期付款的交易。

② Deferred Payment L/C 延期付款信用证

Deferred Payment L/C: In which the buyer deliver the goods by accepting the documents and agree to pay the bank after a fixed period of time.

延期付款信用证是指开证行在信用证中规定货物装船后若干天付款，或开证行收取单据后若干天付款的信用证。

3.6.5 According to whether the beneficiary can transfer the L/C or not, letter of credit can be classified into Transferable L/C and Non-transferable L/C 依据受益人对信用证的权利是否可转让划分，分为可转让信用证和不可转让信用证

（1）Transferable L/C 可转让信用证

Transferable L/C: The beneficiary may allow transferring all or part of the proceeds (payment) of the L/C to second beneficiary, usually the ultimate supplier of the goods.

可转让信用证是指信用证受益人（第一受益人）要求时，可将信用证全部或部分转让给一个

或数个受益人（第二受益人）使用的信用证。

（2）Non-Transferable L/C 不可转让信用证

Non-Transferable L/C: Beneficiary has no right to transfer the L/C to the others, and L/C without the "TRANSFERABLE" is not transferable one.

不可转让信用证是指受益人不能将信用证的权利转让给他人的信用证。只有信用证中明确注明“可转让”时才可转让，否则视为不可转让信用证。

3.6.6 Reciprocal L/C 对开信用证

A Reciprocal L/C is that two parties open letters of credit in favor of each other.

对开信用证是指两张信用证的开证申请人互以对方为受益人而开立的信用证。

The features of reciprocal L/C: the drawer and beneficiary of one L/C are usually the drawee and payer of another one; the opening bank of one L/C is the advising bank of another one. The amount of the two credits is same or almost same. The two credits can be opened to each other at the same time or one by one.

对开信用证的特点是第一张信用证的受益人（出口人）和开证申请人（进口人）就是第二张信用证的开证申请人和受益人，第一张信用证的通知行通常就是第二张信用证的开证行。两张信用证的金额相等或大体相等，两证可同时互开，也可先后开立。

Reciprocal L/C is often used in barter trade, processing trade.

对开信用证多用于易货交易或来料加工业务。

3.6.7 Back to Back L/C 背对背信用证

Back to Back L/C means that beneficiary requires the advising bank of the original credit or other bank to issue a new credit with similar contents on the basis of the original L/C.

背对背信用证又称转开信用证，是指受益人要求原证的通知行或其他银行以原证为基础，另开一张内容相似的新信用证。

A back to back letter of credit must be irrevocable.

背对背信用证的开证银行只能根据不可撤销信用证来开立。

3.6.8 Soft Clause L/C 软条款信用证

It is a credit with some special clauses added by the L/C applicant, appearing to be an irrevocable credit, but an invalid actually, and cannot be utilized by the beneficiary smoothly.

In legal sense, a credit with soft clauses is against the nature and principle of L/C with fraud. It is also called as trap L/C.

由于信用证的开证申请人在信用证中加列了某些特殊条款使受益人无法利用信用证，表面上的不可撤销信用证实际上是无效的信用证。

从法律上说，软条款信用证从根本上违反了信用证的性质和原则，带有某些欺诈性质，有人把它称为陷阱信用证。

3.7 L/C Check and Modification 审核与修改信用证

The beneficiary shall verify the L/C firstly after receiving it, confirming that the L/C contents are in compliance with the sales contract. In case of any discrepancies, unacceptable L/C clauses or soft clauses, the beneficiary shall notify the buyer to amend the L/C. See Fig 9-17.

受益人接到信用证后应首先审核信用证，检查买方开证时是否与买卖合同相符。如发现不符、某些条款不能接受或有软条款，应立即通知买方修改信用证，如图 9-17 所示。

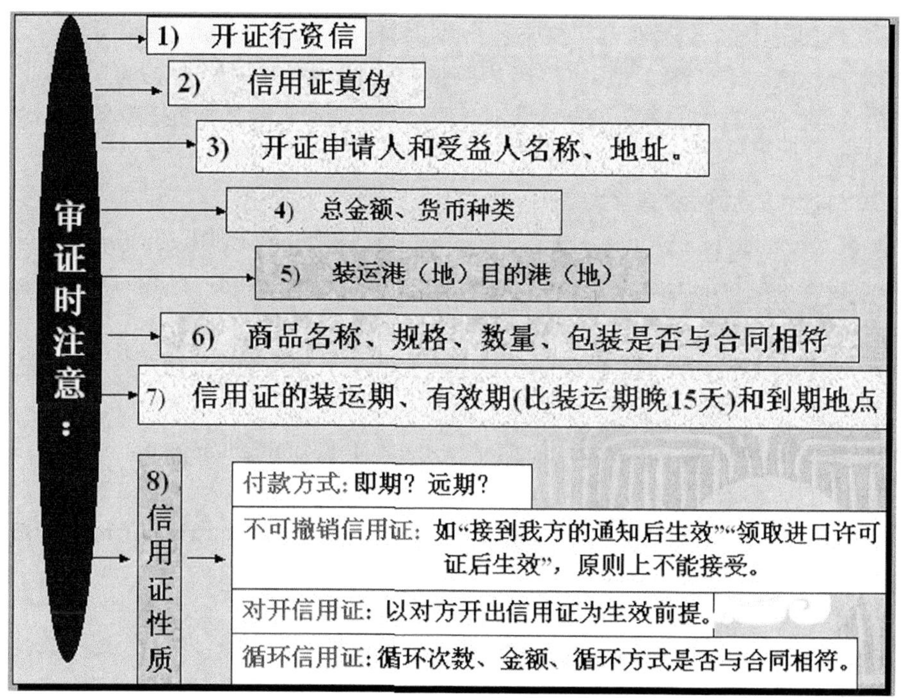

图 9-17　审证注意事项

It is stipulated in *UCP600* as follows: "an issuing bank is irrevocably bound by an amendment as of the time it issues the amendment"; "a credit can neither be amended nor cancelled without the agreement of the issuing bank, the confirming bank, if any, and the beneficiary"; "the terms and conditions of the original credit (or a credit incorporating previously accepted amendments) will remain in force for the beneficiary until the beneficiary communicates its acceptance of the amendment to the bank that advised such amendment. The beneficiary should give notification of acceptance or rejection of an amendment. If the beneficiary fails to give such notification, the shipping documents presented are consistent with the L/C and any not yet accepted amendment, the beneficiary will be deemed to have given such notification of acceptance of such amendment. As of that moment the credit will be amended".

UCP600 中规定："开证行自发出修改之时起，即不可撤销地受其约束"；"未经开证行、保兑行（如果有的话）及受益人同意，信用证既不得修改，也不得撤销"；"在受益人告知修改的银行接受其该修改之前，原信用证（或含有先前被接受的修改的信用证）的条款对受益人仍然有效。受益人应提供接受或拒绝修改的通知。如果受益人未能给予通知，当交单与信用证以及尚未表示接受的修改的要求一致时，即视为受益人已做出接受修改的通知，并且从此时起，该信用证被修改"。

4. Banker's Letter of Guarantee, L/G 银行保函

In international trade, due to the lack of mutual understanding and trust between both parties in a transaction, it is hindered to conclude deals and fulfill contracts smoothly. In order to solve these problems, the banks and other financial institutions with excellent credit offer the service of letter of guarantee, through which, the warrantor promises the L/G applicant will fulfill the liability or obligation under the concerning business contract or other economic contracts, further in favor of the transaction's fulfillment.

在国际经济贸易中，交易双方往往缺乏了解和信任，因而给达成交易和履行合同造成一定障碍。为了解决这些问题，就出现了由信誉卓著的银行以及其他金融机构办理的保函业务，担保人保证申请人履行双方签订的有关商务合同或其他经济合同项下的某种责任或义务，从而有利于交易的顺利进行。

4.1 Definition 银行保函的含义

A letter of guarantee is a written promise by a bank at the request of its customer, undertaking to make payment to the beneficiary within the limits of a stated sum of money in the event of non-performance of the contractual obligations by the principal.

银行保函是银行因客户要求，保证对受益人由于委托人未能履行合约义务而在一定的范围内支付规定金额货币的书面保证。

Guarantees are used as secure mechanism for payment of the contract amount.

银行保函是付款的安全机制。

A contractor uses a guarantee as default instrument that covers the risk of non-performance or defective performance by the contractor.

银行保函作为违约工具涵盖了不履约以及履约有缺陷的风险。

4.2 Parties of Letter of Guarantee 银行保函的当事人

4.2.1 Basic Parties 基本当事人

（1）Principal 委托人

The principal or applicant is the person who requests a bank issues a guarantee for him. If the principal fails to fulfill his contractual obligations, he will be claimed after the payment being effected by the guarantor.

委托人或投保人是指向银行提出申请并委托银行开立保函的当事人。如果委托人不履行其合同义务，担保人付款后会向其索赔。

（2）Beneficiary 受益人

Beneficiary is the party in whose favor the guarantee is issued. He is secured against the risk of the principal's not fulfilling his obligations towards the beneficiary.

受益人即基础合同的债权人，接受保函并有权按保函规定向担保银行提出索赔的当事人。受益人是基础合同中与委托人相对的当事人。

（3）Guarantor 担保人

The guarantor is a surety, a bank or financial institution that issues a letter of guarantee undertaking to make payment to the beneficiary in the event of default of the principal against the presentation of a written demand and other specified documents.

担保人，即开立保函的银行，是指接受委托人的申请开立保函的银行，并由此向保函的受益人承担了有条件或无条件付款保证责任的银行。担保人开立保函后，在同受益人构成一种或有负债的同时，也从委托人那里获得了一种或有债权。

4.2.2 Possible Parties 可能涉及的相关当事人

（1）Advising Bank 通知行

Advising Bank: also called transmitting bank, it's the bank that notifies to the beneficiary according to guarantor bank's requirement and entrustment.

通知行又称转递行。即根据担保行的要求和委托，将保函通知给受益人的银行。

（2）Confirming Bank 保兑行

Confirming Bank: it refers to the bank which adds its confirmation to the credit is called as Confirming Bank.

对信用证加保兑的银行叫保兑行。

4.3　Essential Elements of Letter of Guarantee 银行保函的基本内容

（1）Party Involved 有关当事人

（2）Basis for Opening for a Letter of Guarantee 开立保函的依据

（3）Amount of Guarantee 担保金额

（4）the Terms for Payment 要求付款的条件

（5）Expiry Date or Events of Letter of Guarantee 保函失效日期或失效事件

（6）Applicable Laws of Letter of Guarantee 保函所适用的法律

4.4　Types of L/G 银行保函的种类

（1）Performance Guarantee 履约保函

Performance Guarantee is a promise made by a guarantor, that a guarantor will make payment to beneficiary with the agreed sum in case that guarantee applicant (contractor)fails to fulfill the contract concluded by beneficiary (owner)and contractor. 【Typical Case Link 4】

履约保函是指保证人的承诺，如果担保申请人（承包人）不履行他与受益人（业主）之间订立的合同，应由保证人在约定的金额限度内向受益人付款。【典例链接 4】

（2）Repayment Guarantee 还款保函

Repayment guarantee is a guarantee issued by bank, insurance company or other involving party upon request the application of one party of a contract to the other party of a contract. It is stipulated in the repayment guarantee, that the bank is committed to making reimbursement in case that the applicant fails to fulfill the obligation agreed in the contract, not returning or repaying the deposit or paid amount to the beneficiary.

还款保函是指银行、保险公司或其他当事人应合同一方当事人的申请，向合同另一方当事人开立的保证书。保证书规定，如申请人不履行他与受益人订立的合同的义务，不将受益人预付、支付的款项退还或还款给受益人，银行则向受益人退还或支付款项。

Appendix: A Letter of Credit in Chinese and English

实例：中英文对照的信用证

<table>
<tr><td colspan="2">CITIBANK N.A.
P.O.BOX 2685 NEWYORK
花旗银行纽约分行
邮政信箱 2685 纽约 ORIGINAL

ORIGINAL
正本</td></tr>
<tr><td>CABLE ADDRESS: “CITIBANK”
电报挂号：“CITIBANK”</td><td>PLACE&DATE OF ISSUE: NEWYORK USA 23 July, 2007
开证地点&时间：美国纽约 2007 年 7 月 23 日</td></tr>
<tr><td>DOCUMENTARY CREDIT 跟单信用证
IRREVOCABLE 不可撤销</td><td>CREDIT NUMBER OF ISSUING BANK
开证行信用证
277-54672</td></tr>
</table>

ADVISING BANK 通知行 CITI BANK OF SHANGHAI BRANCH, CHINA 中国花旗银行上海分行	APPLICANT 开证申请人 JAMES BROTHER INTERNATIONAL CO., 詹姆斯兄弟国际有限公司 Room 1005-1011 Convention Plaza, 108 Harbor NEWYORK USA
BENEFICIARY 受益人 FUJIAN TITIAN IMPORT&EXPORT COMPANY 13th Floor, JiaFa Mansion, 210 Siping Road. Fuzhou, China 中国福建体天进出口公司 福州清泉路 210 号佳发大厦 13 层 Tel:0086-0591-55151779 Fax:0086-0591-55151770	AMOUNT 金额 *USD 230 000.00* (SAY US DOLLARS TWO HUNDRED AND THIRTY THOUSAND ONLY) EXPIRY 有效期 DATE: Sept.10, 2007 日期：Sept.10, 2007 THE COUNTER OF CITIBANK NEWYORK 到期地点在纽约花旗银行

Dear sir(s)阁下：

We hereby issue in your favor this documentary credit which is available by your 30 days'sight draft(s) drawn on CITI BANK N.A. NEWYORK USA for 100% invoice value accompanied by the following documents:

我们兹开出以你方为受益人的跟单信用证，本证凭你方按发票金额的全额开出的以花旗银行纽约分行为付款人的 30 天远期汇票付款。并随附下列单据：

1)2/3 original clean on board ocean bill of lading dated no later than August 31,2007 made out to order, blanked endorsed , notify APPLICANT marked freight prepaid.

三份正本其中两份（提交银行）清洁已装船海运提单签发日期不迟于 2007 年 8 月 31 日，做成凭我行指示，通知开证申请人注明运费到付

2) Commercial invoice in triplicate and duly signed

已签署的商业发票一式三份

3) Packing list in quadruplicate stating gross weight of package and certifying that the goods are packed in export cartons

装箱单一式四份，注明每箱毛重，并证明货物用出口纸箱包装

4) Beneficiary's certificate stated that 1/3 set of original bill of lading has been airmailed directly to the applicant without 48 hours after shipment.

受益人的一份证明声明三份正本提单中的一份已经在装船后的 48 小时内以航空邮件直寄开证申请人。

5) Insurance policy or certificate in duplicate in the currency of the credit and in assignable form for the full invoice value plus 110 pct, covering Institute Cargo Clauses Clause A

保险单或保险凭证一式两份按照信用证的货币做成可转让的形式，按发票金额全额另加 10%投保协会货物条款 ICC(A)

Covering: 40 000 pairs of sport shoes as per sales Contract No. FD-AN2007 FM079dated July 16,2007CIF NEWYORK

对货物的描述：40000 双运动鞋，详见销售合同号 FD-AN2007 FM079，日期为 2007 年 7 月 16 日 CIF 纽约 Man's

Art no.13996: White 5000pa USD 5.50/pa Black 5000pa USD 5.50/pa Gray5000pa USD 5.50pa

Art no.13998: White 5000pa USD 6.00/pa Black 5000pa USD 6.00/pa Gray5000pa USD 6.00pa

Lady's

Art no.13265: White 2000pa USD 5.50/pa RED 2000pa USD 5.50/pa Blue1000pa USD 5.50pa

Art no.13266: White 2000pa USD 6.00/pa Black 2000pa USD 6.00/pa Blue1000pa USD 6.00pa

男鞋：

货号 13996：白 5000 双 5.50 美元/双 黑 5000 双 5.50 美元/双 灰 5000 双 5.50 美元/双

货号 13998：白 5000 双 6.00 美元/双 黑 5000 双 6.00 美元/双 灰 5000 双 6.00 美元/双

女鞋：

货号 13265：白 2000 双 5.50 美元/双 红 2000 双 5.50 美元/双 蓝 1000 双 5.50 美元/双

货号 13266：白 2000 双 6.00 美元/双 黑 2000 双 6.00 美元/双 蓝 1000 双 6.00 美元/双

总额：230 000.00 美元(SAY US DOLLARS TWO HUNDRED AND THIRTY THOUSANG ONLY)

Shipment from Chinese ports to New York USA no later than August 31, 2007, partial shipment allowed and transshipment prohibited.

装运：从中国港口到纽约港，不迟于 2007 年 8 月 31 日，允许分批，不允许转船。

Documents must be presented within 10 days after the date of shipment but within the validity of the credit.

<table>
<tr><td>
单据必须在提单签发的 10 天之内向银行交单，但还必须在信用证的有效期内。
SPECIAL CONDITIONS:
特别提示：
1. The documents beneficiary presents should include an inspection certificate signed by the applicant or its agent.
受益人提交的单据中必须包含一份由开证申请人或其代理所签发的检验证书。
2. Each draft accompanying documents must indicate the credit number , name of issuing bank and name of advising bank (if indicated).
3. This credit is non-operative unless of carrying vessel has been approved by applicant and to be advised by L/C issuing bank in form of an L/C amendment to beneficiary.
本证未生效，除非开证申请人同意载货船舶（装船）并通过开证行以信用证修改书的形式通知受益人。
4. All charges outside America for account of the beneficiary
所有美国以外的银行费用由受益人承担
</td></tr>
</table>

<table>
<tr><td>
We hereby agree with the drawers, endorsers and bona fide holders of drafts drawn under and in compliance with the terms of this credit that such drafts will be duly honored on due presentation to the drawee if negotiated on or before expiry date and paid on maturity.
我们兹向根据本证开出并符合本证条款的汇票的出票人、背书人和正当持票人承诺，只要你们在汇票的有效期内向付款行提示或议付（远期汇票在汇票的到期日向付款行提示），将立即得到付款。
The advising bank is requested to notify the beneficiary without adding their confirmation.
请通知行通知受益人本证未加保兑。
In reimbursement, the drawee bank will debit our account No.184542 with our New York Office, making reference to our letter of credit No. Documents are to be airmailed directly to us.
关于偿付，付款行将借记我花旗行纽约分行的账户 184542， 将参照本信用证号，单据请直邮我行。
Your faithfully, 此致
AUTHORIZED SIGANATURE
CARMEN　WILLAL GBOS　(签名)
</td><td>
Advising Bank Notification
通知行注意
</td></tr>
</table>

In the case, after examination of L/C, the clauses underlined are soft clauses or the clauses to be amended, as follows.

实例中信用证经过审证，其中加粗划线为软条款或需要修改的条款，一一列明如下。

Mistakes: 错误之处：

（1）The sum in words and figures are not complying with each other.

金额大小写不符。

（2）The expiry time abroad is not acceptable usually. It shall be revised to be expiry date in the export country. The expiry place is such as “at beneficiary’s country”, “at your country”or “in China”.

境外效期一般不可接受。应改为在出口国到期。到期地点如：“受益人国家”，“在到达国”，“在中国”。

（3）It is unacceptable for the clause like “2/3 original clean on board ocean bill of lading”, and it shall be recasted into 3/3 or full set original clean on board ocean bill of lading.

不能 3 份提单只提交给银行 2 份。应改为 3/3 或 full set original clean on board ocean bill of lading。

（4）The clauses like “Beneficiary’s certificate stated that 1/3 set of original bill of lading has been airmailed directly to applicant within 48 hours after shipment” shall be deleted. It brings a great risk to the beneficiary.

应删除条款 “Beneficiary’s certificate stated that 1/3 set of original bill of lading has been airmailed directly to applicant within 48 hours after shipment”。其中，一份正本提单直寄开证申请人，这一条款对受益人风险非常大。

（5）“Transshipment allowed”shall be remarked in the credit if the goods need to be transshipped.

如果在出运时必须转船，则在信用证的转运条款应允许转船。

（6）The requirement in the credit like “Documents must be presented within 10 days” is not reasonable for the presentation time is too short. According to UCP600, the presentation time of the seller is usually within 15 days or 21 days.

信用证中要求“单据必须在提单签发的 10 天之内向银行交单”，交单时间短。按《惯例 600》卖方的交单期限一般有 15 天或 21 天。

Soft Clauses: 含有软条款为：

（1）In SPECIAL CONDITIONS, the 1st clause is soft clause, the inspection certificate presented to the negotiating bank by the seller shall not be signed by the credit applicant, and the soft clause will put the document offered by the seller in the buyer’s control, leading to the seller’s passive standing. So, it shall be amended to the inspection certificated issued by a 3rd party or deleted.

在 SPECIAL CONDITIONS 中，第 1 条为软条款，卖方提交给银行的商检证书不应由开证申请人来签署，该软条款的规定使卖方提交给银行的单据掌握在买方手中，使卖方处于被动地位，应修改为第三方出具或删除该条款。

（2）In SPECIAL CONDITIONS, the 3rd clause is soft clause, the credit is effective once it is issued. If its effectiveness is controlled by the buyer, the clause shall be deleted as it is a trap clause.

在 SPECIAL CONDITIONS 中，第 3 条为软条款，信用证一旦开出即已生效。如果信用证的生效受买方控制。这属于陷阱条款，应删除该条款。

Section Three Payment Clause in a Sales Contract 第三节 合同中的支付条款

1. Remittance Clause 汇款条款

In international trade, using remittance as the method of payment should make clear the time, the mode, and the amount of remittances.

国际贸易中，使用汇款方式时应明确汇款时间、方法和金额。

For example 例如:

The buyers shall pay 100% of the sales proceeds in advance by T/T (M/T or D/D) to the Sellers before × × ×.

买方应于×年×月×日前将全部货款以电汇（信汇/票汇）方式预付给卖方。

The buyers shall pay 20% of the total value to the sellers in advance by T/T (M/T or D/D) not later than × × ×, the rest will be paid against receiving the fax of the original B/L, the shipping documents are to be delivered against payment only.

买方应于×年×月×日前将 20%货款以电汇（信汇/票汇）方式预付给卖方，余款在收到卖方正本提单（传真）后支付，付款后交单。

2. Collection Clause 托收条款

In international trade, using Collection as the method of payment, the contract should provide for the collection type, condition and time of payment and so on.

国际贸易中，采用托收方式结算时，合同中应规定托收种类、交单条件和付款时间等。

For example: 例如：

（1）D/P at Sight 即期付款交单

Upon first presentation the buyers shall pay against documentary draft drawn by the sellers at sight. The shipping documents are to be delivered against payment only.

买方凭卖方开具的即期跟单汇票，于第一次见票时立即付款，付款后交单。

（2）D/P after Sight 远期付款交单

The buyers shall duly accept the documentary draft drawn by the sellers at ×× days after sight upon first presentation and make payment on its maturity. The shipping documents are to be delivered against payment only.

买方对卖方开具的见票后××天付款的跟单汇票，于第一次提示时承兑，并应于汇票到期日付款，付款后交单。

（3）D/A 承兑交单

The buyers shall duly accept the documentary draft drawn by the sellers at ×× days after sight upon first presentation and make payment on its maturity. The shipping documents are to be delivered against acceptance.

买方对卖方开具的见票后××天付款的跟单汇票，于第一次提示时承兑，并应于汇票到期日付款，承兑后交单。

3. Letter of Credit/ Clause 信用证条款

In international trade, using L/C as the method of payment, the contract should make clear the beneficiary, the opening date, the opening bank, L/C type, the amount of money, the validity period and so on.

国际贸易中，采用信用证方式结算时，合同中应明确受益人、开证时间、开证银行、信用证种类、金额、有效期等。

For example: 例如：

（1）L/C at Sight Clause 即期信用证条款

The buyers shall open through ×× bank an irrevocable letter of credit at sight in the favor of the sellers for the full amount of the invoice to reach the sellers ×× days before the month of shipment and it shall be valid for negotiation in Qingdao until 15th day after the month of shipment.

合同中规定："买方应通过××银行于装运月份前××天开立并送达装运口岸以卖方为受益人全部发票金额的不可撤销即期信用证，有效期至装运月份15天在青岛议付"。

（2）Usance L/C Clause 远期信用证条款

The buyers shall open through ×× bank an irrevocable letter of credit at 30 day's sight to reach the sellers ×× days before the month of shipment , valid for negotiation in Qingdao until 15 day after the month of shipment.

合同中规定："买方应通过××接受的银行于装运月份前××天开立并送达卖方不可撤销见票后30天付款的信用证，有效期至装运月份15天在青岛议付。

4. Clause of Partial L/C and Partial Collection 部分信用证、部分托收条款

Using partial L/C and partial collection as the method of payment should be aware of the relevant shipping documents must all come under a bill of collection, after full payment received, the bank can give the documents to the buyer. Generally speaking, the contract can include the following or a similar provision.

采用部分信用证和部分托收方式时，应注意有关装运单据必须全部随附托收项下的汇票，待全部货款收妥后，银行才能将单据交给买方。一般在合同中可以作如下或类似的规定。

The buyers shall open through a bank acceptable to the seller all irrevocable L/C to reach the sellers ×× days before the month of shipment, stipulating that 80% of the invoice value available against clean draft at sight while the remaining 20% on D/P at sight. The full set of the shipping documents of 100% invoice value shall accompany the collection item and shall only be released after full payment of the invoice value. If the buyers fail to pay full invoice value, the shipping documents shall be held by the issuing bank at sellers disposal.

"买方应通过卖方所接受的银行于装运月份前××天开立以卖方为受益人的不可撤销即期信用证，规定80%发票金额凭即期光票支付，余下20%即期付款交单。100%发票金额的全套装运单据随附托收项下，于买方付清发票的全部金额后交单。如买方不付清全部发票金额，则装运单据须由开证行掌握凭卖方指示处理。"

【Review Questions】复习思考题

【Typical Case Link 1—典例链接1】

Question: Please analyze the possibilities of getting back the money when the draft is on due, and provide your suggestions of how to solve the problem.

问题：试分析A公司于汇票到期时收回货款的可能性，并提出处理该案的建议。

Company A from China exported to Company B of South Korea. Payment was to be made by D/P at 90 days after sight. After the shipment of goods, draft and shipping documents were sent to the foreign collection bank through remitting bank in the exporter's country. Company B had accepted the draft. After the arrival of the goods at the port of destination, Company B presented the trust receipt and took delivery of the goods for resale in advance against the borrowed shipping documents from the local collecting bank, because B was in urgent need of the goods. When the draft was falling due, B became insolvent because of poor management. The collecting bank informed the remitting bank that the drawee rejected the payment and suggested Company A to collect the money back directly from Company B. There was another 30 days left before the draft was due.

中国A公司向韩国B公司出口一批货物，付款方式为付款交单90天后付款。货物出运后。汇票及货运单据通过出口地的托收银行寄抵国外代收行，B公司进行了汇票承兑。货抵目的港后，由于用货心切，B商于是出具了信托收据向本地代收行借得货运单据，先行提货转售。当汇票到期时，B商因经营不善，失去偿付能力。代收行以汇票付款人拒付为由通知托收行，并建议由A公司直接向B商索取货款。此时距离汇票到期日还有30天。

【Typical Case Link 2—典例链接2】

Question: Is it right for Bank of China to do so? Why?

问题：试问，中国银行这样做是否有理？为什么？

An import and export company A from Changsha, Hunan Province imported a batch of small household electrical appliance. The goods were to be shipped in two lots, and payment was to be made by negotiable irrevocable letter of credit. A branch of Bank of China was to open a letter of credit for each lot. After the first shipment, the seller presented the documents to the bank for negotiation. The negotiating bank, after checking, found no discrepancy and thus negotiated the draft. The branch office of Bank of China later reimbursed the negotiating bank. The company A received the first shipment and found the quality of the goods did not match the stipulations of the contract, and then asked the Bank of China to refuse the payment for the second lot of the goods under the second L/C. The Bank of China refused the importer's requirement.

湖南长沙市某进出口公司 A 向外国某公司进口一批小家电产品。货物分两批装运，支付方式为不可撤销议付信用证。每批分别由中国银行某分行开立一份信用证。第一批货物装运后，卖方在有效期内向银行交单议付，议付行审单后，未发现不符点，即向该商议付货款，随后中国银行某分行对议付行作了偿付。A 公司在收到第一批货物后，发现货物品质不符合合同规定，进而要求中国银行对第二份信用证项下的单据拒绝付款，但遭到中国银行的拒绝。

【Typical Case Link 3—典例链接3】

Questions:

(1) Does the bank have the right to refuse the payment? Why ?

(2) How should the seller deal with the problem?

问题：

(1) 银行是否有权拒付货款？为什么？

(2) 作为卖方，应当如何处理此事？

A foreign importer signed a contract with an import and export company in China for 500 metric tons of wheat. The contract stipulated that the L/C should be established before January 20th, 2009 and the shipment should be effected before February 5th. On January 28th, the importer opened the L/C which was valid for negotiation until February 10th. It became difficult for the seller to effect shipment on time, so the seller asked the buyer to extend the time of shipment to February 17th and the validity of L/C to February 20th respectively. The buyer agreed but didn't inform the opening bank. The goods were shipped on board on February 17th and the seller presented the shipping documents to the bank for negotiation, the bank refused.

国外一家贸易公司与中国某进出口公司订立合同，购买小麦 500 公吨。合同规定，2009 年 1 月 20 日前开出信用证，2 月 5 日前装船。1 月 28 日买方开来信用证，有效期至 2 月 10 日。由于卖方按期装船发生困难，故电请买方将装船期延至 2 月 17 日并将信用证有效期延长至 2 月 20 日，买方回电表示同意，但未通知开证银行。2 月 17 日货物装船后，卖方到银行议付时，遭到拒绝。

【Typical Case Link 4—典例链接4】

Questions: What should the Chinese exporter do according to your opinion? Explain the reasons briefly.

问题：对此，你认为中方应如何处理好？简述理由。

A Chinese exporter received an irrevocable L/C from a foreign country, this L/C was advised and confirmed by a foreign bank located in China. The Chinese company effected the shipment and was to present the documents for negotiation, suddenly it was informed by the foreign bank in China that the opening bank had declared bankruptcy and thus that foreign bank in China claimed it had no obligation to negotiate the L/C or to make payment for the L/C. However, it could help the exporter to collect the payment back directly from the buyer under the instruction and authorization of the exporter.

中国出口企业收到国外开来的不可撤销信用证一份，由设在中国境内的某外资银行通知并加保兑。中国出口企业在货物装运后，正打算将有关单据交银行议付时，忽然该外资银行通知，由于开证银行已宣布破产，该行不承担对该信用证的议付或付款责任，但可接受中国出口公司委托向买方直接收取货款的业务。

Chapter Ten Commodities Inspection and Customs Declaration

第十章 商品的检验与报关

【Learning Objectives】教学目的与要求

After learning this chapter, you will be able to:

1. Understand what is a commodity inspection and customs declaration;
2. Know how to stipulate inspection clauses in sales contract;
3. Master the procedures of inspection application and customs clearance.

【Lead-in Case】引导案例

Question: What should my company do?

问题：我公司该怎么办？

My company imported a Singapore production testing equipment on CIF basic. The contract availed of the simplified standard format, and insurance policy simply provided that "Insurance will be for seller's account". After arrival, my company found that some deformation of the equipment affected normal use. So they reflected the requirements of compensation to the foreign side, the foreign side answer that there rigorous testing when the equipment out of the factory with the quality certificate, non-responsibility for them. After inspection by the inspection bureau,the problem was caused by vibration and compression.

我公司以 CIF 价格条件引进一套新加坡产检测仪器，合同采用简式标准格式，保险条款一项只简单规定"保险由卖方负责"。到货后，我公司发现一部件变形影响其正常使用。我公司向外商反映要求索赔，外商答复仪器出厂经严格检验，有质量合格证书，非他们责任。后经我商检局检验认为是运输途中部件受到振动、挤压造成的。

Section one Commodities Inspection
第一节 商品的检验

1. Definition 定义

The inspection of commodities refers to the inspection conducted by an authorized party to testify whether the quality, specification, quantity weight, package, would be exactly in conformity with terms stipulated in the contract, to determine who should be responsible for the losses or damages to the goods in transit, if any. The results of inspection should conform to the standards of relative safety and sanitation conditions, environmental and labor protection conditions regarding the goods, or quarantine of plants and animals as per the laws and regulations of relevant countries. And issues the relevant certificate as the evidence for the delivery of goods, and the settlement of payment and claims. Commodity inspection has become the indispensable part in international trade, which is the extension of the quality clause of contract and the warranty of it as well.

商品检验是指在国际货物买卖中，对卖方交付的货物或拟交付的合同规定的货物进行质量、规格、数量、重量、包装等方面的检验，同时分清各方当事人的责任。检验结果应该与一国法律或政府法令的规定进行的卫生、安全、环境保护和劳动保护等条件的检验以及动植物病虫害检疫的要求一致。出具的证书，作为交接货物，结算货款，处理索赔，理赔的依据。商检已成为国际贸易中不可缺少的环节。商检是合同中品质条款的延续，是品质条款的保证。

2. Inspection Time and Place 检验的时间和地点

The inspection time and the inspection place refer to when and where the inspection is implemented to the goods. The so-called inspection right means that the buyer or the seller has the right to exercise inspection on the traded goods, with the inspection result as the evidence for the delivery and the acceptance of the goods. The confirmation of the inspection time and place means to confirm which party exerts the inspection right, that is to say, to confirm which party's inspection certificate is taken as the final inspection result.

检验的时间和地点是指何时、何地行使对货物的检验权。所谓检验权，是指买方或卖方有权对所交易的货物进行检验，其检验结果即作为交付与接受货物的依据。确定检验的时间和地点，实际上就是确定买卖双方中哪一方行使对货物的检验权，也就是确定检验结果以哪一方提供的检验证书为准。

Buyer's inspection Right. 买方对货物的检验权。

According to *united Nations Convention on contracts for the international Sale of Goods,* the buyer shall implement the inspection or have others to do it in the shortest practical time. The inspection can be put off to the time when the goods arrive at the destination in case of the involvement of the transportation.

根据《联合国国际货物销售合同公约》的规定，买方必须在按实际情况可行的最短时间内检验货物或由他人检验货物。如果合同涉及运输，检验可推迟到货物到达目的地后进行。

The re-inspection right of buyer is not compulsory，nor the basic condition for the acceptance of goods，depending on the buyer's selection.The buyer must finish the re-inspection within a reasonable time if the re-inspection is needed.The reasonable time is regulated in the contract and shall be specified in the contract to the specific property of the cargo. 【Typical Case Link 1】

买方对到货的复验权不是强制性的，也不是接受货物前提条件，由买方自决，如进行复验，买方必须在合理的时间内完成。合理时间的期限由买卖双方在合同中规定，并根据货物性质的不同来规定具体的时间。【典例链接 1】

There are the following 4 ways to regulate the inspection time and place.

关于检验时间和地点的规定有以下 4 种方法。

（1）Inspection in Export Country 在出口国检验

There are two ways including the inspection at manufacturing place (factory) and the inspection at the loading port.

这种方法又分为在产地（工厂）检验和在装运港检验两种。

For the inspection at the loading port, it is also called as "Shipping Quality, Shipping Weight", means the inspection authority specified in the sales contracts makes the inspection and appraisal on the cargo's quality, weight (quantity) and the like, and the inspection certificate issued by the authority is taken as the final evidence. The seller is not responsible for the changes of the cargo after the delivery. Therefore, the clause is a great disadvantage to the buyer as it denies the re- inspection right of the buyer.

在装运港检验，也称为"离岸品质，离岸重量"(Shipping Quality, Shipping Weight)，是指货物在装运港或装运地交货前，由买卖合同中规定的检验机构对货物的品质、重量（数量）等项内容进行检验鉴定，并以该机构出具的检验证书作为最后证据。卖方对交货后货物所发生的变化不承担责任。因此，这种规定办法从根本上否定了买家的复验权，对买方极为不利。

（2）Inspection in Import Country 在进口国检验

It is also divided into the inspection at the destination port and the inspection in the buyer's business location or the final user's location.

这种方法又分为在目的港检验和在买方营业处所或最终用户所在地检验。

The inspection at the destination port or discharging port is also called as "Landed Quality, Landed weight", means that the cargo is inspected by the inspection authority specified in the contract within the specified time on the spot after the cargo arrives in the destination port or place, and the inspection certificate issued by the organization is taken as the final evidence of the cargo delivered by the seller. In the way, the buyer has right to claim for the compensation with the inspection result made at the destination port or place in case that the quality, weight (quantity)is not in conformity with the involving requirement.

在目的港/ 地卸货后检验， 也称为"到岸品质，到岸重量"（Landed Quality, Landed Weight），是指货物运达目的港或目的地时，由合同规定的检验机构在规定的时间内，就地对商品进行检验，并以该机构出具的检验证书作为卖方所交货物品质、重量（数量）的最后依据。采用这种方法时，买方有权根据货物运抵目的港或目的地时的检验结果，对属于卖方责任的品质、重量（数量）不符合，向卖家索赔。

The clause is disadvantageous to the seller. Under the trade term of CIF (CIP,CFR,CRT), the seller is responsible for carry the goods to the destination, but according to *International Rules for the Interpretation of Trade Terms of* 2000, the obligation of the seller has been completed after the goods are loaded on the ship (delivered to the carrier) in the export country, the risk has been transferred to the buyer when the goods are over the shipboard. The regulation of the inspection time and place means that the conditions of the goods are subject to the final inspection result in the destination, actually transferring the risks of the cargo losses occurred during the transportation to the seller. During the transportation, the goods have been out of supervision of the seller, but under the control of the carrier, so it is quite unfair to the seller with the inspection clause against the regulation of the seller's obligation in the above-mentioned trade terms.

这种规定方法对卖方不利。因为在使用 CIF(CIP、CFR、CPT)术语的情况下，虽然卖方要负责把货运到目的地，但按照《2000 年国际贸易术语解释通则》的解释，卖方的交货义务实际上是在出口国装运港装上船（或交承运人）时即完成，风险在装运港越过船舷时转移至买方。这种检验时间、地点的规定方法以最后到目的地的港的检验为准，实际上要把运输途中产生的货损、货差的风险由卖方承担。在运输途中，货物已经脱离了卖方的监管，是在承运人的监控之下，这对卖方极不公平，违反了上述贸易术语有关卖方义务的规定。

（3）Inspection in Export Country and Re-inspection in Import Country 出口国检验，进口国检验

The inspection certificate issued by the export county's inspection authority is taken as one of the bank negotiating documents for payment, but not as the final inspection proof. After the arrival of the cargo, the inspection certificate issued by the import country's inspection authority is taken as the final inspection result to confirm if the quantity and the quality of the goods are right and the proof for the buyer's claims. 【Typical Case Link 2】

以出口国检验机构出具的检验证书，作为卖方向银行议付货款的单据之一，不作为最后的依据。货到目的港后，以进口国检验机构出具的检验证书，作为卖方交货品质数量合格与否的最后依据，也是买方索赔的依据。【典例链接 2】

It is fair and reasonable for the buyer and the seller to regulate the inspection time and inspection place in this way, so it is the way used mostly in international trade, complying with the international usual practice.

这种检验时间、地点的规定方法对买卖双方公平合理，因而它是国际贸易中目前最常用的一种规定方法，符合国际惯例。

（4）Weight Inspection in Export Country and Quality Inspection in Import Country 出口国检验重量，进口国检验品质

It is also called as "Shipping Weight, Landed Quality", means that for the inspection of goods in large amount, in order to conciliate the conflict of the buyer and the seller on the inspection, the inspection on the weight and the quality are respectively carried out. That is to say, the inspection certificate issued by the inspection authority at the loading port or place is taken as the final proof of the commodity weight, and the inspection certificate issued by the inspection authority at the destination port is taken as the final proof of the commodity quality.

出口国检验重量，进口国检验品质也称为“离岸重量，到岸品质”（Shipping Weight, Landed Quality），是指在大宗商品交易的检验中，为了调和买卖双方在商品检验问题上存在的矛盾，常将商品的重量和品质检验分别进行，即以装运地验货后检验机构出具的重量检验证书，作为卖方所交货物重量的最后依据，以目的港或目的地检验机构的品质检验证书，作为商品品质的最后依据。

3. The Inspection Range in China 我国商检机构实施法定检验的范围

Law of the People's Republic of China on Import and Export Commodity Inspection has stipulated the work of the inspection authorities of China and the range of the legal inspection. The commodity inspection is the inspection and supervision on the production, sales of the exported commodities and the imported commodities, which is performed by the government according to the related regulations and rules.

《中华人民共和国进出口商品检验法》规定了我国商检机构的任务和法定检验的实施范围。商品检验体现为国家对进出口商品的生产，销售按规定实施检验和监管。

The governmental inspection authorities implement the compulsory inspection on the important imported and exported commodities related to the national economy and the people's livelihood in accordance with the concerning laws and regulations. The commodities, which are not inspected or failed to pass the inspection, the goods are not permitted to be released by the customs.

根据有关的法律、法规，国家检验机构对关系到国计民生的重要进出口商品实施强制性检验。未经检验或检验不合格的商品，海关不予放行。

It is not all commodities that are compulsory to be inspected. The specific regulations on the commodities which are compulsory to the inspection are as follows:

并不是所有的商品都必须进行法定检验，国家对必须进行法定检验的商品做了明确的规定，主要有以下几种：

（1）The commodities which are listed in the Catalogue of Enter-Exit Goods that shall be Inspected and Quarantined by Enter-exit Inspection and Quarantine Authorities (hereinafter referred to as "the Catalogue");

列入《出入境检验检疫机构实施检验检疫的进出口商品目录》(简称《目录》) 的商品；

（2）The exported food stuff shall be inspected for their sanitary purpose;

对出口食品的卫生检验；

（3）The appraisal for the function and operation of the packing container for the exported dangerous goods;

对出口危险货物包装容器的性能鉴定和使用鉴定；

（4）The inspection of the container and cabin's adaptability for the transportation of the perishable food stuff and the frozen food stuff;

对装运出口易腐烂变质食品、冷冻品的船舱，集装箱等运输工具的适载检验；

（5）The inspection on the imported and exported commodities which are required to be inspected by the inspection authorities according to the involving international treaties;

对有关国际条约规定须经商检机构检验的进出口商品的检验；

（6）The inspection of the imported and exported commodities which are required to be inspected according to other laws or administrative regulation and rules.

对其他法律、行政法规规定必须经商检机构检验的进出口商品的检验。

4. Inspection Authority and Inspection Certificate 检验机构和证书

（1）Inspection Authority 检验机构

The inspection organizations can be divided into the following two types, which one is governmental inspection authority, the others are non-governmental ones.

检验机构的类型大体可归纳为官方检验机构和非官方检验机构两种。

① The governmental inspection authority is owned and supervised by governments and specializes in inspection of particular commodities or commodities subject to mandatory inspection by government.

For example, the Food and Drugs Administration (FDA) in the United States which specializes in inspection of particular merchandise like grain and drug. In China, the State Administration for Commodity Inspection (SACI) and its designated provincial divisions are in charge of the inspection of import and export commodities (According to the regulation of "Law of the People's Republic of China on Import and Export Commodity inspection" ("Law of inspection" for short), AQSIQ (General Administration of Quality Supervision, inspection and Quarantine of the People's Republic of China) is in charge of the inspection of the imported and exported commodities throughout the whole country ,the local Entry-exit inspection and Quarantine Bureaus are in charge of the local inspection of the imported and exported commodities.

官方的检验机构是指由国家或地方政府投资，按照国家有关法律法令对出入境商品实施强制性检验检疫和监督管理的机构，只对特定商品（粮食、药物等）进行检验，如美国食品药物管理局（FDA）和中国国家质检总局负责进出口商品的检验。根据我国《商检法》的规定，国家质检总局主管全国进口商品检验工作，国家质检总局设在各地的出入境检验检疫局管理其所辖地区内的进口商品检查工作。进出口商品的检验工作由地方出入境检验检疫机构和经国家质检总局认可的检验机构负责。

② In international trade, the inspections of commodities are mainly undertaken by non-governmental bodies which have the same legal status as notary organizations and associations. The famous ones include Societe Generale De Surveillance S.A.(SGS) in Geneva, Swiss, Underwriters Laboratory (UL) in the USA, Lloyd Surveyor, B.V.in Britain and Japan Marine Surveyor & Sworn Measurer`s Association (NKKK), etc.

国际贸易中的商品检验主要由民间机构承担，民间商检机构具有公证机构的法律地位。比较著名的有：瑞士日内瓦通用鉴定公司（SGS）、美国保险人实验室（UL）、英国劳合氏公证行（Lloyd's Surveyor）、日本海外货物检验株式会社（OMIC）等。

（2）Inspection Certificate 检验证书及作用

An inspection certificate is a kind of testifying document in written form issued and signed by the inspection authority after the inspection and appraisal of the imported and exported commodities.

检验证书是检验机构对进出口商品进行检验、鉴定后签发的书面证明文件。

The common inspection certificate used in international commercial transaction are as follows:国际贸易中常见的检验证书有以下几种类型。

① 品质检验证书 (Inspection Certificate of Quality)；

② 数量检验证书 (Inspection Certificate of Quantity)；

③ 重量检验证书 (Inspection Certificate of Weight)；

④ 价值检验证书 (Inspection Certificate of Value)；

⑤ 产地检验证书 (Inspection Certificate of Origin)；

⑥ 卫生检验证书 (Sanitary Inspection Certificate)；

⑦ 兽医检验证书 (Veterinary Inspection Certificate)；

⑧ 消毒检验证书 (Disinfection Inspection Certificate)；

⑨ 验残检验证书 (Inspection Certificate on Damaged Cargo)。

All kinds of inspection certificate are used to certify the condition of the nature, quantity, weight and sanitary situation of the goods respectively. In China, inspection certificate is usually issued by the Entry-Exit Inspection and Quarantine of the People's Republic of China. The certificate also may be issued by the exporter or manufacturer depending on the specific situation if there is no specific stipulation in the concerning contract or credit. It shall be paid attention that the certificate in the contract and the listed items or inspection result must be in conformity with the stipulated in the contract and credit. The issuing date of inspection certificate must be no later than the issuing date of B/L.

各种检验证书分别用以证明货物的品质、数量、重量和卫生条件等方面的状况。在我国，这类证书一般由国家出入境检验检疫局出具，如合同或信用证无特别规定，也可以根据不同情况，由出口公司或生产企业出具。但应注意证书的名称及所列项目或检验结果，应与合同及信用证规定相同，出证日期迟于提单日期的商检证书无效。

Functions:

（1）to certify if the quality, quantity, packing and the clean situation of the goods delivered by the seller are complying with the requirements stipulated in the contract;

（2）for customs to release the goods;

（3）for the sellers to settle the payment;

（4）as the evidence of making claims and the settlement.

其作用：

（1）证明卖方所交货物的品质、数量、包装以及卫生条件等方面是否符合合同规定的依据；

（2）海关验关放行的依据；

（3）卖方办理贷款结算的依据；

（4）办理索赔和理赔的依据。

5. Inspection Bases and Inspection Methods

检验依据和检验方法。

（1）Inspection Bases 检验依据

The commodities are usually inspected in accordance with the confirmed samples, contract with samples, letter of credit, and standards, etc.

商品的检验依据主要有成交样品、标样合同、信用证、标准等。

The inspection standard is the measures and rules adopted for the inspected commodity and inspection process，which are the criteria to appraise and identify if the inspected.

检验标准是指检验机构从事检验工作在实体和程序方面所遵循的尺度准则，是评价检验对象是否符合规定要求的准则。

According to Law of Inspection，all the imported and exported commodities listed in the catalogue must be inspected according to the government technical regulations；for the commodities which are not required by the governmental technical regulations, the inspection can be made in reference to the related standards of foreign countries，stipulated by national commodity inspection body.

根据《商检法》的规定，凡列入目录进出口商品，按照国家技术规范的强制性要求进行检验；没有国家技术规范的强制性要求的，可以参照国家商检部门制定的国外有关标准进行检验。

（2）Inspection Methods 检验方法

The inspection results are different for the same commodity inspected in different ways. Therefore, it is better to specify in which way to inspect the goods in order to avoid any dispute.

同一商品用不同的方法进行检验可以得出完全不同的结果。所以，最好在合同中明确规定用哪种方法进行检验，以免事后发生纠纷。

In the business of import and export, the inspection is made according to the following standards:

① according to the requirement in the import contact about the quality, specification, packing, and sampling inspection;

② according to the standard of the manufacturing country, the import country, or the usual standard adopted internationally in case that the standard is not specified in the contract;

③ the law and rule of state and the international usual practice are prior to the contract clauses;

④ for some international standards such as ISO 9000 or the standard of international wool secretariat, it is decided by both seller and buyer to adopt them or not.

在进出口业务中，一般按以下检验标准进行。

① 按进口合同中对品质、规格、包装、抽样检验的规定办理。

② 合同未规定标准的一般按生产国标准、进口国标准，或按国际上已用标准，无国际标准的按进口国标准。

③ 有国际法规、国际惯例的，按法规、惯例优先于合同进行。

④ 是否采用某些国际标准，由买卖双方自愿决定，如 ISO 9000、国际羊毛局标准等。

6. Procedures of Inspection Application 报检程序

（1）Procedures for Export 出口报检程序

The exporter makes application to the commodity inspection bureau for the export inspection. For all the commodities which are required by government or stipulated in contract to go through the inspection of China Entry-Exit Inspection and Quarantine Bureau of the local branches, the exporter shall apply for inspection after the goods get ready. The customs will not release the goods before the goods are inspected and approved by the local Entry-Exit Inspection and Quarantine Bureau. The goods are not permitted to be exported if they fail the pass of inspection.

报检是指出口方向商品检验机构申报检验。凡属国家规定法检的商品，或合同规定必须经中国进出口商品检验检疫局验证出证的商品，在货物备齐后，应向商品检验局申请检验。只有取得商检局发给的合格的检验证书，海关才准放行。经检验不合格的货物，一般不得出口。

The general inspection procedures are as follows.

报检的程序一般如下。

① Application 申报

Fill in the application form of CIQ, and submit the application to the local Entry-Exit Inspection and Quarantine Bureau. After the application, in case that the contents in the application form are found to be wrong , or the goods are changed due to the credit amendment, the exporter shall ask for the modification of the application form and make explanation for the modification reasons.

凡需要法定检验出口的货物，应填制《出口商检验申请书》，向商检局办理申请报验手续。

申请检验后，如出口公司发现“申请单”内容填写有误，或因国外进口人修改信用证以致货物规格有变动时，应提出更改申请。并改为“申请单”，说明更改事项和更改原因。

② Inspection 查验

The local inspection bureau inspects the commodities by sampling according to the relevant law or the inspection standard stipulated in contract. The inspection contents include the quality, quantity, weight, packing and the grade of safe, health and so on.

商检机构对出口商品抽样，应当按照法律或合同规定的检验标准进行检验。检验的内容包括商品的质量、规格、数量、重量、包装及是否符合安全、卫生要求等。

③ Issuance of Inspection Certificate 出证

The inspection bureau will issue the inspection certificate after the commodity passed the inspection. The exporter shall make shipment within the validity of the inspection certificate. In case that the shipment has exceeded the validity, the exporter shall apply for the extension of inspection and re-inspection. The goods must be exported after passing the re-inspection. The validity of the inspection certificate keeps in effect for two months from the issuance of the inspection certificate, two or three weeks for fruits and eggs, three weeks for plants. The re-inspection shall be effected when the validity is over before the shipment.

商品检验合格后，即由商检局发给检验证书，进出口公司应在检验证书规定的有效期内将货物运出。如超过有效期装运出口，应向商检局申请展期，并由商检局进行复验，经复验合格货物才能出口。检验证书的有效期，一般货物是从发证起两个月内有效，鲜果、鲜蛋类为 2 ~ 3 个星期内有效，植物检验为 3 个星期。如果超过有效期，装运前应向商检局申请复验。

（2）Check and Accept of Goods 进口验收货物

After getting the bill of lading (B/L)from the exporter, the importer give it to the shipping company and get the delivery order (D/O)in return. For the commodities under legal inspection or required to be inspected in contract, the importer shall make application for inspection before getting through customs clearance, then get into inspection or guaranty. The importer fills in an entry inspection form, attached with import contract, commercial invoice, packing list and other concerning documents to obtain an entry inspection approval certificate.

买方取得“提单”后，向船公司换取“提货单”，俗称“小提单”。如是法定检验商品或合同规定必须检验的商品，应“先报检后通关再检验检疫”。入境报检时，应填写“入境货物报检单”，随附进口合同、商业发票、装箱单等有关单证，获得“入境货物通关单”。

After the arrival of the imported goods, in case that the goods are found in short, the harbor bureau shall fill the short landed report timely and send it to the shipping company for confirmation with the written statement claiming for the recourse right. In case that the goods are found broken or damaged, the goods shall be stored in the nominated site waiting for the verification and inspection of the insurance company and the inspection institute and the proper settlement.

进口货物运达港口卸货时，如果港务局在卸货核对时发现货物短缺，应及时填制“短卸报告”交由船方签认，并向船方提出保留索赔权的书面声明。卸货时如发现残损，货物应存放于海关指定的地方，待保险公司会同商检机构检验后作出处理。

It is stipulated in the law, that the imported commodities under the legal inspection list are not permitted to be sold and used without the inspection of the relative inspection institute. Meanwhile, the buyer is regarded to quit the right claiming for compensation in case that the inspection cannot be effected within in specified inspection time in the contract. Therefore, the goods under the legal inspection list or required in contract to carry out inspection at the discharging port, to make payment after inspection, with a short claim time, or found to be damaged, broken or non-delivery, shall be inspected at the discharging port; other imported goods may be inspected at the site of client by the local inspection bureau.

我国法律规定，凡属法定检验的进口商品，不经商检机构的检验就不得销售和使用，同时如果商检不能在合同规定检验期内进行，买方即被视为放弃索赔权。因此，凡是属于法定检验或合同规定在卸货港检验后付款，合同规定的索赔期较短，或卸离海轮时已发现残损或有异状或提货不着的商品，均应在卸货港进行检验；其他进口商品则可以在用货企业所在地，由当地商检机构进行检验。

For the imported goods under the legal inspection list, the importer shall make application for the inspection to the inspection bureau at the discharging port or the arrival place. The goods uninspected are not allowed to be put into production, sold or used. If the inspector goods are found broken or damaged, the importer shall claim for compensation with the inspection certificate issued by the inspector. For the goods required in contract to be inspected at the discharging port, the goods found to be damaged or broken, or the goods with the time of claiming for compensation close to the expiry time, all of them need to be inspected at the discharging port.

对于法定检验的进口货物，必须向卸货地或到达地的商检机构报验，未经检验的货物不准投产、销售和使用。如进口货物经商检机构检验，发现有残损短缺，应凭商检机构出具的证书对外索赔。对于合同规定的卸货港检验的货物，或已发现残损短缺有异状的货物，或合同规定的索赔期即将届满的货物等，都需要在港口进行检验。

For the possible claim, the concerning documents such as invoice, packing list, weight list, quality certificate, usage manual, technical drawing and the like information, damaged cargo list, over short landed report, business memo and so on may be taken as important evidence and reference to make claim.

一旦发生索赔，有关的单证，如国外发票，装箱单，重量明细单，品质证书，使用说明书，产品图纸等技术资料，理货残损单，溢短单，商务记录等都可以作为重要的参考依据。

7. Inspection Clause in Sales Contract 合同中的检验条款

（1）Inspection Clauses 检验条款的主要内容

The inspection clauses cover these as follows:

① inspection time and place; 检验时间、地点；

② inspection authority; 检验机构；

③ inspection certificate; 检验证书；

④ inspection methods, contents and standards; 检验方法、内容、依据；

⑤ re-inspection. 商品复验。

（2）The inspection clauses in a sales contract are usually as follows:

在买卖合同中，检验条款通常如下规定的：

"It is mutually agreed that the inspection Certificate of quality and quantity (weight) issued by the China Import and Export Commodity Inspection Bureau at the port of shipment shall be part of the documents to be presented for negotiation under the relevant L/C. The buyers shall have the right to re-inspect the quality and quantity (weight)of the cargo. The re-inspection fee shall be borne by the buyers. Should the quality and /or quantity (weight)be found not in conformity with that of the contract, buyers are entitled to lodge with the sellers a claim, which should be supported by survey reports, issued by a recognized surveyor approved by the sellers. The claim, if any, shall be lodged within × × days after arrival of the cargo at the port of destination."

"双方同意中国进出口商品检验局签发的品质和数（重）量检验证书作为信用证项下议付单据的一部分。买方有权对货物的品质、数（重）量进行复验。复验费由买方负担。如发现品质和/或数（重）量与合同不符，买方有权向卖方索赔。索赔期限为货到目的港× ×天内。"

In addition, for an import transaction, the import contract is important especially for the buyer. The buyer must be familiar with the involving international usual practice and operate the business in flexible ways with implementing the principle of equality and mutual benefit, avoiding the economic losses. The inspection clauses in an import contract are usually as follows.

另外，在进口贸易中，作为买方，进口合同要特别慎重，既要贯彻平等互利的原则，又要熟悉和了解有关的国际惯例，采取灵活做法，在经济上避免遭到损失。在进口合同中的检验条款通常做如下规定。

Inspection : It is mutually agreed that the certificate of quality and quantity or weight issued by the manufacturer（or × × × surveyor）shall be a part of the documents for payment under the relevant L/C. However, the inspection of quality and quantity or weight shall be made in accordance with the following.

商品检验：双方同意以制造厂出具的品质及数量或重量证明书作为有关信用证项下付款的单据之一。但是，货物的品质及数量或重量检验应按下规定办理。

In case the quality, quantity or weight of the goods be found not in conformity with those stipulated in this contract after re-inspection by the China Import and Export Commodity Inspection Bureau within × × days after arrival of the goods at the port of destination, the buyers shall return the goods to or lodge claims against the sellers for compensation of losses upon the verification of Inspection Certificate issued by the said Bureau, except for the claims for which the insurers or the carriers are liable. All expenses (including insurer's fees) and losses arising from the refusal of the goods or claims should be borne by the sellers. In such case the buyers may, if so requested, send a sample of the goods is question to the sellers provided that the sampling is feasible.

货到目的港××天内，经中国进出口商品检验局复检，如发现品质或数量或重量与本合同规定不符时，除属保险公司或船公司负责之外，买方凭中国进出口商品检验局出具的检验说明书，向卖家提出退货或索赔。所有因退货或索赔引起的一切费用（包括检验费）及损失，均由卖家负担。在此情况下，凡货物适于抽样者，买方可应卖方要求，将货物的样品寄交卖方。

Section Two Customs Declaration 第二节 商品的报关

1. Customs Declaration 报关

Customs Declaration covers the whole procedures that the exporter has to go through with the customs including customs declaration, customs clearance before the goods are shipped.

报关是指进出口商品装船出运之前向海关申报的手续。

Customs Clearance refers to the consignee of the imported and exported goods or his agent presents the concerning shipment shipping documents to customs for customs declaration. Customs declaration must be operated by the enterprises which are registered in customs. The operator of customs declaration must be trained, assesses and approved by customs.

进出口报关是指进出口货物的收货人或它的代理人向海关交验有关单证，办理进出口货物申报手续的法律行为。进出口报关必须有在海关办理登记注册手续的有关企业才能报关。报关员须经海关培训和考核认可。

2. Kinds of Enterprise of Customs Declaration 报关企业的类型

Exporters may make customs declaration in the following three ways: through the professional customs clearance service, through the customs clearance agent, the exporter who goes through customs clearance by itself.

报关企业的类型有三种：专业报关企业、代理报关企业和自理报关企业。

3. Time Limit of Customs Declaration 报关期限

（1）Time Limit of Export Customs Declaration 出口报关期限

Except being permitted by the customs, the consigner or its agent of the export commodities should declare customs 24 hours before lading. This regulation make the custom have enough time to check the commodities before lading. If the consigner or its agent fails to do that in time, the custom may reject the declaration. So we should declare customs as soon as possible.

出口货物的发货人或其代理人除海关特许外，应当在装货的 24 小时以前向海关申报。

（2）Time Limit of Import Customs Declaration 进口报关期限

The consignee or its agent should declare customs 14 days after the means of shipment applying to enter a country. This regulation is for the sake of accelerating port transport, diminishing mistakes and avoiding malpractice. If the consignee fails to declare customs in 14 days, the custom will impose the late fee. It begins at the 15th day after the means of shipment applying for entering; the 15th day after commodities arrive the destination for transshipment; the 15th day after commodities arrive post office for mailing. The collecting rate of late fee is 0.5% of the commodities prices per day, and the bottom line is 10 Yuan.

The formula is: total amount of late fee = the arriving price × days × 0.5%

if the delay exceeds 3 months, the cargo will be sold off by the customs.

进口货物的发货人或其代理人应当自载运该货物的运输工具申报进境之日起 14 天内向海关办理进口货物的通关申报手续。如果在法定的 14 天内没有向海关办理申报手续，海关将征收滞报金。

滞报金总额=货物的到岸价 × 滞报天数 × 0.5%

超过 3 个月未向海关申报的，由海关提交变卖。

4. Procedures of Customs Declaration 报关的程序

（1）Procedures or Export 出口报关程序

Procedures of customs clearance: before the shipment, the exporter must fill in the export customs declaration form, then makes declaration to customs together with the commercial invoice, packing list, inspection certificate, exporter approval certificate etc. And the involving contract if necessary, credit copy. After the customs check and verify the goods and documents with stamping "PLEASE" on the shipping order, the goods may be shipped on board with it. The exporter may go through customs clearance by itself or through professional customs clearance service or international forwarder.

报关的程序：出口公司在装船前，必须填写"出口货物报关单"，向海关申报，并应随附商业发票、装货单、商检证书、出口许可证等，必要时提供合同、信用证副本。海关对货、证核查无误后，在装货单上加盖"放行"章，即可凭以装船。出口公司可以自行办理报关手续，也可以委托专业的报关行和国际货运代理公司办理。

（2）Procedures for Import 进口报关程序

After arrival of the imported cargo, the importer, his forwarder or his customs declaration agent shall in "Import Customs Declaration Form" based on the shipment shipping documents, then to ask customs declaration with the form attached with the invoice, bill of lading, packing list, insurance policy, import license & other approval documents, import contract, certificate of origin and other documents required by customs, the inspection approval certificate shall for the imported commodities subject to the legal inspection.And to make customs declaration and get through the documents examination of customs, custom tariff collection, cargo checking and release.

进口货物运到后，由进出口公司或委托货运代理公司或报关行根据进口单据填具"进口货物报关单"向海关申报，并随附发票、提单、装箱单、保险单、许可证及审批文件、进口合同、产地证和所需的其他证件。如属法定检验的进口商品，还需随附商品检验证书。以便海关审单、计征、查验放行。

After getting through customs clearance, the delivery order is notated with "RELEASE" stamp by customs. The buyer arranges for transportation and warehouse with the domestic client making payment and taking goods.

通关后，海关在提货单上加盖"放行章"，买方安排运输入库，国内客户付款提货。

In detail，there are four steps as follows: 具体地讲，包含如下 4 步：

① Declaration 申报

When the consignee and consigner or their agents deal with import or export, they should report to the custom about the commodities situation by writing or EDI; submit relative shipment and business documents. And they bear legal responsibilities for the authenticity and accuracy.

申报是指出口货物的发货人、进口货物的收货人或者他们的代理人在进出口货物时，在海关规定的期限内，以书面或者电子数据交换方式（EDI）向海关报告其进出口货物的情况，并随附有关货运和商业单据，申请海关审查放行，并对所报告内容的真实准确性承担法律责任的行为。申报也即是人们常说的"报关"。

（一般的进出口货物应填制报关单一式三联，俗称基本联，其中第一联为海关留存联，第二联为海关统计联，第三联为企业留存联。在已实行报关自动化系统，利用计算机报关进行数据录入的口岸报关，报关员只需填写一份报关单，交指定的预录入中心将数据输入计算机）

② Customs Examination 查验

In order to confirm that the commodities' characteristics, original place, status, quantity and value are the same with the detailed content of declaration, the customs carry through actual check of the commodities according to the regulation of law after accepting declaration.

查验是指海关在接受报关单位的申报后，依法为确定进口货物的性质、原产地、货物状况、数量和价值是否与货物申报单上已填报的详细内容相符，对货物进行实际检查的行政执法行为。

③ Customs Collection 纳税

It means the customs collect the taxation of import link of cargoes imported and exported according to the relevant policies. According to the relevant provisions of "customs law " and "tariff regulations of the imports and exports ", the imported and exported goods are except that the state has other regulations, should tariff . The tariff is collected according to "customs' imports and exports "tariff" by the customs.

税费计征是指海关根据国家的有关政策、法规对进出口货物征收关税及进口环节税费。根据《海关法》和《进出口关税条例》的有关规定，进出口的货物除国家另有规定外，均应征收关税。关税由海关依照《海关进出口税则》征收。

The calculation method of the import duty is as follows: first step, to confirm the value based on which the duty amount is calculated, namely the duty-paying value; then the duty amount is worked out by the applicable duty rate .The import duty of China is calculated based on the price of CIF China port.

进口关税的计算方法是：首先，确定计算税额的价格，即完税价格；然后按进口货物适应的进口税税率计算出税额。我国计算进口关税是以货物到达我国口岸的 CIF 价格作为完税价格。

④ Release 放行

It means customs after accepting declaration of cargoes imported and exported , through verify document of declaring at the customs , check the goods , imposing the expenses of taxation in accordance with the law to release, make the decision to finish customs' spot control to the cargoes imported and exported.

Customs need to declare at the customs document sign, namely "customs release chapter ", the consignee or consignor of the cargoes imported and exported whereby goes through formalities of drawing the imported goods or shipping the export goods.

海关放行是指海关在接受进出口货物的申报后，经过审核报关单据、查验货物、依法征收税费，对进出口货物作出结束海关现场监管决定的工作程序。

海关在决定放行进出口货物后，需在有关报关单据上签章，即"海关放行章"，进出口货物的收发货人凭此办理提取进口货物或装运出口货物手续。对于海关监管货物来说，盖有"海关放行章"的报关单也是海关核销的依据。

To the goods needing of export tax rebate, the consignor of the export goods should enclose one more pale yellow special-purpose customs declaration of export tax rebate, while entering out. After releasing , have affix "examine form " and verify stamped signature , and the antifalse label, return and declare the unit at the customs , deliver to the tax authority of the refund of tax.To declare high tax rate products that export, customs is imprison customs declaration copy it declare at the customs unit (declare at the customs unit export consignor to pass on) send refund to tax authority of tax refund.

对需出口退税的货物，出口货物的发货人应在向海关申报出口时，增附一份浅黄色的出口退税专用报关单。海关放行后，在报关单上加盖"验讫单"和已向税务机关备案的海关审核出口退税负责人的签章，并加贴防伪标签后，退还报关单位，送交退税地税务机关，对申报出口的高税率产品，海关将报关单制作关封退报关单位（或由报关单位转交出口发货人）送交退税地税务机关。

5. Filling in the Form of Customs Declaration 报关单的填制

General demand for filling the customs declaration. 填制报关单的一般要求如下。

（1）It must be true to make a report on , should accomplish two accord: First, the document agrees, namely the customs declaration conforms with contract , written instructions, invoice , packing list ,etc.; Second, the goods agree with document, namely the content and situation of real cargoes imported and exported offered must be true in the customs declaration, can't present the mistake , and make a false report.

（1）报关单的填报必须真实，要做到两个相符：一是单证相符，即报关单与合同、批文、发票、装箱单等相符；二是单货相符，即报关单中所报内容与实际进出口货物情况必须真实，不得出现差错，更不能伪报、瞒报及虚报。

（2）The goods of different contract, can't fill out on the same customs declaration; The same sets of goods have different trade goods of way, must use different customs declaration.

（2）不同合同的货物，不能填在同一份报关单上；同一批货物中有不同贸易方式的货物，也须用不同的报关单向海关申报。

（3）If it has many kinds of different goods on a customs declaration, should make a report clearly, but can't exceed five goods on a same customs declaration.

（3）一张报关单上如有多种不同商品，应分别填报清楚，但一张报关单上最多不能超过五项海关统计商品编号的货物。

（4）The materials that processing imports materials is used for domestic market, should fill in imported goods customs declaration too.

（4）进料加工、来料加工的料、件进口后经批准转内销或作为以产顶进，也应填写进口货物报关单，如批准内销以产顶进的产成品，则仍应填报相关的进口料、件。

（5）The project in the customs declaration should be accurate, complete. Every listed column of customs declaration should be filled in detail item by item, the content is errorless. Demand typing as much as possible , if write with the pen, the writing should be known , neat , good, can't use pencil (or red carbon paper); if alter, must affix the chapter of checking.

（5）报关单中填报的项目要准确、齐全。报关单所列各栏要逐项详细填写，内容无误；要求尽可能打字填报，如用笔写，字迹要清楚、整洁、端正，不可用铅笔（或红色复写纸）填报；填报项目，若有更改，必须在更改项目上加盖校对章。

（6）In order to implement the need that declares automation at the customs, besides filling in the relevant projects on the customs declaration , should also fill out the code about project .

（6）为实行报关自动化的需要，申报单位除填写报关单上的有关项目外，还应填上有关项目的代码。

（7）The customs declaration which should use the computer inputs, its content must be totally unanimous with the primitive customs declaration. The declarant should check conscientiously, prevent mistake, once find mistake, should submit to and make it input again in time.

（7）电脑预录入的报关单，其内容必须与原始报关单完全一致。报关员应认真核对，防止录错，一旦发现有异，应及时提请录入人员重新录入。

（8）The customs declaration, because of various kinds of reasons, is inconsistent with real cargoes imported and exported, need to correct to the customs immediately, fill in the correct declaration of customs declaration, what is the fault, change anything.

However, if the content altered involves the change of the piece of the goods, except the piece of the goods should be altered, the project related to piece, for instance quantity, weight , amount of money of the goods ,etc. should do the corresponding change too; If one customs declaration have two more than different goods, correction declaration should list which goods is altered.

（8）向海关申报的进出口货物报关单，事后由于各种原因，出现原来填报的内容与实际进出口货物不相一致，需立即向海关办理更正手续，填写报关单更正单，对原来填报项目的内容进行更改，更改内容必须清楚，一般情况下，错什么，改什么；但是，如果更改的内容涉及货物件数的变化，则除应对货物的件数进行更改外，与件数有关的项目，如货物的数量、重量、金额等也应作相应的更改；如一张报关单上有两种以上的不同货物，更正单上应具体列明是哪项货物作了更改。

（9）The export goods after declaring and releasing, because of the transport match, all goods or some goods can't load accord with transport declared, consignor should submit "apply to the export goods altered " to customs.

（9）对于海关接受申报并放行后的出口货物，由于运输工具配载等原因，全部货物或部分货物未能装载上原申报的运输工具的，出口货物发货人应向海关递交《出口货物报关单更改申请》。

【Review Questions】复习思考题

【Typical Case Link 1—典例链接1】

Question: Should the seller agree on the buyer's requirements? Why?

问题：中方应否同意对方的要求？为什么？

An import and export company in China reached a transaction of exporting sickle to a Mexico importer by "sale by samples". The contract stipulated that the valid period of re-inspection was within 60 days after the goods after arrival at the port of destination. The Mexico importer did not raise any objections to the goods after the re-inspection of the arrival goods at the port of destination. 100 days later, however, the Mexico importer called, saying that, all the sickles were rusted and had to be on sale. Therefore the Mexico importer claimed a 50% of the total price as a compensation for their losses .Then the seller immediately reviewed our retained sample, also found the similar problem.

中国某进口公司与墨西哥某进口商凭样品成交达成一笔出口镰刀的交易。合同中规定复验有效期为货物到达目的港后 60 天。货物到达目的港经墨西哥进口商复验后，未提出任何异议。但事隔 100 天，墨西哥进口商来电称：镰刀全部生锈，只能降价出售，要求按成交价的 50%赔偿其损失。中方接电后，立即查看我方留存的复样，也发现类似情况。

【Typical Case Link 2—典例链接2】

Question: What did we learn from the case?

问题：应吸取什么教训？

One Chinese exporting company signed a contract with a British company of exporting a set of products. The quality specifications in the contract were as follows: the quality of the delivery is subject to the final quality inspection of China Commodity Inspection Bureau. The quality of the goods was proved up-to-standard by China Commodity Inspection Bureau quality inspection certificate of quality specifications before shipment. When the goods arrived in British, the foreign company said: despite the inspection certificate, the quality of goods was inferior to that of the sample's. The Chinese company disagreed and then put forward the goods were agricultural products, in other words, it`s impossible to make them exactly like the sample. Hence, the British company asked an inspection company in British to inspect the quality of goods. The inspection company`s report showed that on average the quality was inferior to the sample. Because the sample of the Chinese company was lost and could not be presented as evidence, the Chinese company paid a sum of money of inferior quality.

中国某出口公司与英国一家公司签订出口一批农产品的合同。交货品质以中国商检局品质检验为最后依据。货物装运前由中国商检局品质检验签发品质规格合格证书。货物运抵英国后，该外国公司提出：虽然有检验证书，但货物品质比样品差。中方公司不服，提出该产品是农产品，不可能做到与样品完全相符，于是，英国公司请该国某检验公司检验，出具了所交货物平均品质比样品差的检验证明。由于中方公司留存的样品遗失，无法证明，最终只好赔付一笔品质差价。

Chapter Eleven　Disputes Claim Force Majeure and Arbitration

第十一章　争议、索赔、不可抗力和仲裁

【Learning Objectives】教学目的与要求

After learning this chapter, you will be able to:

1. Understanding of international trade dispute and the concept of cause;
2. Master the claim and settlement main business program;
3. To understand the characteristics and functions of arbitration;
4. Master in dispute dealing with the use of arbitration procedures and matters needing attention.

【Lead-in Case】引导案例

Question: In such circumstance, whether should the trader claim against the factory, claim 5% or 3%?

问题：在这种情况下，贸易商是否可以向工厂索赔，索赔 5%还是 3%?

A trader placed an order for a batch of goods with a Chinese factory on FOB basis. The sales contract stipulated that if the Chinese factory could not effect shipment before the end of July, it should pay 5% down payment as penalty due to breach of contract. After then, the factory delayed shipment for 5 days, which led to the trade claimed by its buyer for 3% down payment as compensation.

某贸易商以 FOB 价向中国某厂订购一批货物，在买卖合同中规定若工厂未能于 7 月底之前交运，则工厂应赔付货款 5%的违约金。后工厂交货延迟 5 天，以致贸易商被其买方索赔货款的 3%。

Section One　Dispute and Claim
第一节　争议与索赔

1. Dispute and Claim 争议与索赔

In international trade, disputes often arise between the two parties when one party thinks that the other fails to carry out the duties stipulated in the contract wholly or partially, which very likely leads to claim, arbitration and legal action. There are many reasons for disputes, but the main reasons are the following three.

在国际贸易中，争议是指交易的一方认为另一方未能全部分或部分履行合同规定的责任而引起的业务纠纷。争议很可能引起诉讼、仲裁或法律行为。究其原因归纳为以下三种情况。

1.1　Exporter's Breach of Contract 出口方违约

（1）The exporter does not delivery the goods, or delay the goods of delivery;

出口方不交货，或不按时交货；

（2）The exporter delivery the goods which are not according to the quality, quantity and packing clause of stipulations in the contract;

出口方未按合同规定的品质、包装条款交货；

（3）Documents presented by exporter have some discrepancies from the letter of credit.

出口方所提交的单据与信用证不符。

1.2　Importer's Breach of Contract 进口方违约

（1）The importer does not open or delay to open the letter of credit;

进口方不开或缓开信用证；

（2）The importer does not pay or not duly pay;

进口方不付款或不按时付款赎单；

（3）The importer is irrational rejection of goods;

进口方无理拒收货物；

（4）The importer under the F.O.B. terms do not despatch the ship on time.

进口方在 F.O.B.条件下不按时派船接货等。

1.3　Contract without Specific Clauses 合同规定欠明确

Stipulations of the contract are unclear such as "prompt shipment", "quantity about 10000 M/T", "main ports in Europe" etc. which may bring about different disputes.

合同规定欠明确。如采用"立即装运"、"大约 1 万公吨"、"欧洲主要港口"之类的规定方法，造成双方对合同条款的理解和解释不一致，以致产生争议。

2. Claim 索赔

Claim means that in international trade, one party breaks the contract and causes losses to the other party directly or indirectly, the party suffering the losses may ask for compensation for the losses. In some contract, the two parties often stipulate clauses on settlement of claim as well as inspection and claim clauses. There are two kinds of claim clauses in contract of import and export: one is the clause of dispute and claim for compensation, the other is penalty clause.

索赔就是指争议发生后，遭受损害的一方向违约方提出赔偿的要求。买卖双方通常都会在合同中写明索赔的办法以及有关商检和索赔条款。进出口合同中的索赔条款有两种规定方式：一种是异议和索赔条款，另一种是罚金条款。

2.1　Discrepancy and Claim Clause异议与索赔条款

Discrepancy and claim clause also include, besides stipulating that if any party breaches a contract the other party is entitled to lodge claim against the party in breach, other aspects in respect of proofs presented when lodging a claim and effective period for filling a claim etc.

异议和索赔条款的内容除规定一方如违反合同另一方有权索赔外，还包括索赔期限和赔付的金额等。

The proofs for lodging a claim are mainly covering the necessary proofs or certificates for claims, and the relevant certificate issuing authorities. Proofs for claims include legal proof and fact proof. The former refers to the trade contract and the related national laws and regulations while the latter refers to the facts and written evidence of the breach to verify the truth of the breach.

索赔依据主要规定索赔必需的证据和出证机构，包括法律依据和事实依据两个方面，前者是指贸易合同和有关的国家法律规定，后者则指违约的事实真相及其书面证明，以证实违约的真实性。

2.2 Penalty Clause 罚金条款

Clause in respect of penalty in a contract should stipulate that "any party who fails to perform the contract shall pay an agreed amount as penalty for compensating the other party for the damages". Penalty clause is fixed when the seller fails to make timely delivery; the buyer fails to open the relevant L/C or the buyer fails to take goods on time, and the penalty ceiling is also included in the contract.

合同规定，当一方未履行合同义务时，应向另一方支付合同约定的金额，以补偿对方的损失。罚金条款一般适用于卖方延期交货，或买方延迟开立信用证或延期接货的情况下。

Section Two Force Majeure 第二节 不可抗力

1. Force Majeure 不可抗力概念

Force majeure is to trade after the signing of the contract, the parties to the contract is not due to the fault or negligence, but as a result of the parties to a contract cannot foresee, to be unable to prevent, to be unable to avoid and control events, so as not to perform or fails to perform the contract, the accident of one side can be exempted from responsibility for the performance of the contract or delay the performance of the contract. Therefore, the force majeure is an exemption clause.

不可抗力(Force Majeure)是指买卖合同签订后，不是由于合同当事人的过失或疏忽，而是由于发生了合同当事人无法预见、无法预防、无法避免和无法控制的事件，以致不能履行或不能如期履行合同，发生意外事故的一方可以免除履行合同的责任或推迟履行合同。因此，不可抗力是一项免责条款。

2. Constituting Conditions of Force Majeure 构成不可抗力的意外事故应具备的条件

① The occurrence of a Force Majeure event is after the conclusion of the contract.

意外事故是在签订合同以后发生的。

② The event is beyond of the control of the parties involved, which mainly includes two kinds of situations, one is due to natural forces caused by flood, drought, typhoon, earthquake, etc.; another is social causes, such as war, blockade, the government ban.

意外事故是当事人所不能预见、不能避免和不可控制的。不可抗力的事故主要包括两种情况，一种是由于自然力量引起的，如水灾、风灾、旱灾、地震等；另一种是社会原因引起的，如战争、封锁、政府禁令等。

③ The event is not resulting from the fault or neglect of the parties involved.

意外事故的引起不是因为当事人双方自身的过失或疏忽而导致的。

3. Stipulation of Force Majeure Clause 不可抗力条款的规定

① Scope of Force Majeure Event 不可抗力事件的范围

Natural disasters such as earthquakes, floods, hurricanes, cold, volcano, snow, fire, ice disaster, storm ,etc.

由自然原因引起的，如地震、洪水、飓风、寒流、火山爆发、大雪、火灾、冰灾、暴风雨等；

Social disasters such as war, strike, government ban, blockade, etc.【Typical Case Link 1】

由社会原因引起的，如战争、罢工、政府禁令、封锁等。【典例链接 1】

② In the event of force majeure range, should be in the contract prescribed. Usually the following three laws: 关于不可抗力事件的范围，应在买卖合同中订明。通常有下列三种规定办法；

A. Brief stipulation 概括式规定

That is not specified in the contract of the event of force majeure, only for the general provisions. 在合同中不具体规定不可抗力事件的范围，只作概括的规定。

For example: 举例：

If the fulfillment of the contract is prevented due to force majeure, the seller shall not be liable. However, the seller shall notify the buyer by cable and furnish the sufficient certificate attesting such event or events.

如果由于不可抗力的原因导致卖方不能履行合同规定的义务时，卖方不负责任，但卖方应立即电报通知买方，并须向买方提交证明发生此类事件的有效证明书。

B. Concrete Stipulation 列举式规定

That is expressly specified in the contract of the event of force majeure, where the contract is not prescribed, as the event of force majeure shall not be quoted.

在合同中明确规定不可抗力事件的范围，凡在合同中没有订明的，均不能作为不可抗力事件加以援引。

For example: 举例：

IF the shipment of the contracted goods is delayed by reason of war, flood, fire, earthquake, heavy snow and storm, the seller can delay to fulfill, or revoke part or the whole contract.

如果由于战争、洪水、火灾、地震、雪灾、暴风的原因致使卖方不能按时履行义务时，卖方可以推迟这些义务的履行时间，或者撤销部分或全部合同。

③ Synthesized stipulation 综合式规定

Using generalizations and enumeration and integrated ways. In China's import and export contract, such provisions generally adopt the approach.

采用概括和列举综合并用的方式。在我国进出口合同中，一般都采取这种规定办法。

For example: 举例：

If the fulfillment of the contract is prevented by reason of war or other causes of force majeure, which exists for three months after the expiring the contract, the non-shipment of this contract is considered to be void, for which neither the seller nor the buyer shall be liable.

如果因战争或其他人力不可控制的原因，买卖双方不能在规定的时间内履行合同，如此种行为或原因，在合同有效期后继续三个月，则本合同的未交货部分即视为取消，买卖双方的任何一方，不负任何责任。

④ Settlement of force majeure event 不可抗力事件的处理

There are two kinds of legal consequences arising from a force majeure event: termination of the contract and postponement of the contract fulfillment. The adoption of the settlement ways is dependent on the effect of the force majeure event.

不可抗力引起的法律后果有两种：解除合同和延期履行合同。

至于什么情况下可以解除合同，什么情况下延期履行合同，要看不可抗力事故对履行合同的影响程度。

Section Three Arbitration 第三节 仲裁

1. Definition and Characteristics of Arbitration 仲裁的含义和特点

The Definition of Arbitration 仲裁的含义

Arbitration means that the two parties, before or after the disputes arise, reach a written agreement that they will submit the disputes which cannot be settled through amicable negotiations to the third party for arbitration.

所谓仲裁又称公断，是指买卖双方在争议发生之前或发生之后签订书面协议，自愿将争议提交双方同意的仲裁机构裁决，以解决争议的一种方式。

The Characteristics of Arbitration. 仲裁的特点。

① An arbitration who is familiar with the technical or social setting of the dispute may be chosen.

可以选择熟悉争议处理技巧、争议社会背景的仲裁员。

② The arbitration procedure is simple, low cost, rapid processing problems by arbitration;

仲裁程序简单、费用低，通过仲裁处理问题比较迅速。

③ Since procedure is more informal than in court, the parties may choose not to be represented by lawyers.

仲裁程序不如诉讼正式，当事人可以不请律师。

④ Privacy can be maintained in both the arbitration bearing and award.

仲裁的审理和裁决可以不公开。

⑤ The parties concerned may choose the arbitrator from the Arbitration Organization.

双方可以在仲裁机构中自由选择仲裁员。

⑥ The arbitration award is final and has binding force upon the parties concerned.

裁决一般是终局的，对双方当事人都有约束力。

2. Arbitration Clause 仲裁条款

① Place of arbitration 仲裁地点

In the arbitration clause arbitration, determine in which country, generally applicable to the country's arbitration law. China's import and export trade contracts in the place of arbitration, as the different trading object and different situations, commonly used in three provided methods：Strive to provisions in the arbitration in China；Sometimes the provisions of arbitration are in the country of the defendant；In the third country provisions agreed to arbitration.

在仲裁条款中，确定在哪国仲裁，一般就适用该国的仲裁法律。我国进出口贸易合同中的仲裁地点，视贸易对象和情况的不同，一般采用三种规定方法之一：力争规定在我国仲裁；有时规定在被告所在国仲裁；规定在双方同意的第三国仲裁。

② Arbitration body 仲裁机构

Disputes in international trade can be either referred to a permanent arbitration organization for arbitration as can be stipulated in the arbitration agreement by parties concerned or submitted for arbitration to a interim arbitration tribunal as formed by the arbitrators agreed by the two parties. In China, China International Economic and Trade Arbitration Commission and Maritime Arbitration Commission are permanent arbitration organizations. Most of the countries and some of the international organizations in the world have their permanent arbitration organizations specialized in the settlement of commercial disputes. Both parties choose which country (region)of the arbitration proceedings, make specific instructions in the contract.

国际贸易中的仲裁，可由双方当事人在仲裁协议中规定在常设的仲裁机构进行，也可以由当事人双方共同指定仲裁员组成临时仲裁庭进行仲裁。我国主要的常设仲裁机构是中国国际经济贸易仲裁委员会和海事仲裁委员会。国际上许多国家（地区）和一些国际组织都设有专门从事处理商事纠纷的常设仲裁机构。当事人双方选用哪个国家（地区）的仲裁机构审理争议，应在合同中做出具体说明。

③ Applicable arbitration rules 仲裁规则的适用

The country where the arbitration is going to be made and the relevant applicable arbitration rules should be made clear in the sales contract. If Chinese arbitration rules are applicable, then the Chinese International Economic and Trade Commission Rules shall apply. It should be noted that arbitration rules do not always go with the arbitration place. According to the usual international practice of arbitration, the arbitration rules in the arbitration place shall in principle apply, but it is legal for the parties concerned to agree in their contract that the arbitration rules of the arbitration organization in other country, other than the arbitration rules of the country where the arbitration is going to be made, shall apply.

在买卖合同中，应订明进行仲裁的所在国以及适用的仲裁规则。适用我国的仲裁规则，是指适用《中国国际经济贸易仲裁委员会仲裁规则》，但所采用的仲裁规则与仲裁地并非绝对一致，按国际仲裁的一般做法，原则上采用仲裁所在地的仲裁规则，但有的法律上也允许双方当事人在合同中约定，采用仲裁地点以外的其他国家仲裁机构的仲裁规则进行仲裁。

④ Arbitral award 仲裁的裁决

The arbitration award is final and shall have binding force upon the two parties. 【Typical Case Link 2】

仲裁的裁决一般是终局的，对双方有约束力。【典例链接 2】

【Review Questions】复习思考题

【Typical Case Link 1—典例链接1】

Question: Please analyze if the compensation is reasonable or not?

问题：请分析中方的索赔要求是否合理。

An importer ordered a batch of wood from a Brazil lumber exporter. The contract stipulated that "if it suffers government intervention, the contract's period of validity should be extended or the contract should be cancelled." But the Brazil tropical rain forest suffered accelerating destroys and the Brazil government set limitation on wood exportation, which led difficulty on the contract fulfillment before validity day on the seller's side. The exporter required the importer to either delay carrying out the contract or canceling it for the reason of force majeure. The importer of China didn't accept this requirement and claimed for compensation.

中国进口商向巴西木材出口商订购一批木材，合同规定"如受到政府干预，合同应当延长，以至取消"。签约后适逢巴西热带雨林破坏加速，巴西政府对木材出口进行限制，致使巴西出口商在合同规定期内难以履行合同，并以不可抗力为由要求中方延迟合同执行或解除合同，中方不同意对方要求，并提出索赔。

【Typical Case Link 2—典例链接2】

Question: What shall the Chinese buyer do?

问题：中方应如何处理？

A British exporter made an offer of raw materials in 20 000 tons in term of CIF Shanghai to a Chinese importer. The applicable law for the contract is the law of UK. Before the delivery, the Gulf War broke out, the UK seller had to ship the goods to China port via Cape of Goods Hope of South Africa due to failing to go through Suez Canal, thus the exporter asked for the Chinese buyer to raise the price or remove the contract.

某英国商人向中国出口原料 2 万吨，价格条件为 CIF 上海。合同适用的法律为英国法。交货前，海湾事件发生，英国商人如交货就要通过南非好望角航线，不能直航苏伊士运河，故要求中方或提高价格或解除合同。

Chapter Twelve Procedures of Practice and Operation for Export Business

第十二章 一票出口业务的实训操作流程

出口方案设计（出口价格核算）

请根据下列数据，算出每一台玩具车的 FOB\CFR\CIF 报价

品名：R/C Gas Toy 货号：TY9806			
计量单位：	辆	包装：	纸箱
包装方式：	2pcs/ctn		
每个纸箱尺码：	32cm（长）	20cm（宽）	30cm（高）
每个纸箱毛重/净重：	G.W.: 14.20kg	N.W.: 11.2kg	
报价数量	200 辆	Conveyance: Qty/20' FCL: 360pcs Qty/40' FCL: 744pcs	LCL

核算数据

采购成本：150 元人民币/辆（含增值税）

出口费用：单位商品出口的包干费约为：￥2.50
件杂货/拼箱海运费率为：（计费标准“M/W”）US＄60.00
出口定额费率为：（按采购成本计）3.50%
垫款周期为：30 天
银行贷款年利率为：（1 年按 360 天计）6.00%
海运货物保险费率为：0.70%
投保加成率为：10.00%
增值税率为：17.00%
出口退税率为：13.00%
国外客户的佣金为：（按报价计）3.00%
银行手续费率为：（按报价计）0.35%
汇率为：（1 美元兑换人民币）￥7.80
预期利润：销售利润率为 10.00%

出口业务成本核算表

计算项目	计算过程	计算结果	单位
货物总体积	(32 × 20 × 30)/1000 × 200/2	1.92	立方米
货物总毛重	1420/1000 × 200/2	1.42	公吨
实际成本	150 × (1+17%−13%)/(1+17%)	133.33	人民币元/辆
退税收入	150 × 13%/(1+17%)	16.67	人民币元/辆
贷款利息	150 × 6%/360 × 30	0.75	人民币元/辆
海洋运费	1.92 × 60/200 × 7.80	4.4928	人民币元/辆
海运保险费	CIF × 110% × 0.70%	0.0077CIF	人民币元/辆
出口业务定额费	150 × 3.50%	5.25	人民币元/辆
包干费		2.50	人民币元/辆
FOB 报价	(133.33+5.25+2.5+0.75)/ (1−3%−0.35%−10%)/7.8	20.9848	美元/辆
CFR 报价	(133.33+5.25+2.5+0.75+4.4298)/ (1−3%−0.35%−10%)/7.8	21.6495	美元/辆
CIF 报价	(133.33+5.25+2.5+0.75+4.4298)/ [1-3%-0.35%-10%-(1+10%) × 0.70%]/7.8	21.8437	美元/辆

出口合同缮制题目

请根据下列信息缮制销售确认书

出口商：上海东海进出口公司

SHANGHAI DONGHAI TRADE IMP. AND EXP. CORPORATION

55 ZHONGSHAN ROAD (S2), SHANGHAI 200001 CHINA

TEL：+0086-21-68952314

FAX：+0086-21-68952316

进口商：SEEDO INTERNATIONAL CO., LTD.

NADEEM QAISER C/LISZT 63 STACOLOMA DE GRAMENET(08923) BARCELONA, SPAIN

TEL：+34 93 496 1616

FAX：+34 93 216 0286

货物明细

商品名称：R/C Gas Toy

货号：TY9806

货号	数量	单价	包装方式	包装种类	毛重	净重	尺码
TY9806	200PCS	USD21.84	100	CTNS	14.20KGS	11.2KGS	32×20×30CM

合同号：SC1105　　日期：2011-5-10

价格条款：CIF BARCELONA

保险：卖方按发票金额的 110%，根据中国人民保险公司 1981 年 1 月 1 日的海运货物保险条款，投保一切险

付款：提单日后 30 天付款信用证，2011 年 7 月 15 日前开到

装运：2011 年 9 月 15 日前一次性装运，允许转运但不允许分批装运

卖方代表：程一新

买方代表：Keiko Nakamura

注：出口价格等相关项目在谈判后正式确定

SALES　CONFIRMATION

S/C No.　SC1105

Date:　2011-5-10

Seller:
SHANGHAI DONGHAI TRADE IMP. AND EXP. CORPOTATION
55 ZHONGSHAN ROAD (S2), SHANGHAI 200001
CHINA
TEL:+0086-21-68952314
FAX:+0086-2168952316

Buyer:
SEEDO INTERNATIOANL CO., LTD.
NADEEM QAISER C/ LISZT 63
STACOLOMA DE GRAMENET(08923)
BARCELONA, SPAIN
TEL:+34 93 496 1616
FAX:+34 93 216 0286

Art. No.	Name of Commodity & Specifications	Quantity	Unit Price	Amount
			CIF BARCELONA	
TY9806	R/C Gas Toy	200PCS	USD21.84	USD4368.00
Total A mount in Words:	SAY US DOLLARS FOUR THOUSAND THREE HUNDRED AND SIXTY-EIGHT ONLY.			

PACKING:　TO BE PACKED IN CARTONS OF 2PCS EACH ONLY.

SHIPMENT:　FROM: SHANGHAI, CHINA.
TO: BARCELONA, SPAIN.
TO BE EFFECTED BEFORE SEP.15, 2011
WITH PARTIAL SHIPMENT NOT ALLOWED BUT TRANSSHIPMENT ALLOWED.

INSURANCE:　THE SELLER SHOULD COVER INSURACNE FOR 110% OF THE TOTAL INVOICE VALUE AGAINST ALL RISKS AS PER OCEAN MARINE CARGO CLAUSES OF PICC DATED 1/1/1981.

PAYMENT:　THE BUYER SHOULD OPEN THROUGH A BANK ACCEPTABLE TO THE SELLER. AN IRREVOCABLE L/C PAYABLE AT SIGHT FOR 100% OF TOTAL CONTRACT VALUE TO REACH THE SELLER BEFORE JUL.15,2011 AND VALID FOR NEGOTIATION IN CHINA UNTIL THE 30TH DAY AFTER THE DATE OF SHIPMENT.

The contract is made out in two original copies, one copy to be held by each party.

Confirmed by.

Seller: SHANGHAI DONGHAI TRADE IMP. AND EXP. CORPOTATION
程一新

Buyer:

Remarks:

1. The buyer shall have the covering letter of credit reach the Seller 30 days before shipment, failing which the Seller reserves the right to rescind without further notice, or to regard as still valid whole or any part of this contract not fulfilled by the Buyer, or to lodge a claim for losses thus sustained, if any.
2. In case of any discrepancy in Quality, claims should be filed by the Buyer within 30 days after the arrival of the goods at port of destination; while for quantity discrepancy, claims should be filed by the Buyer within 15 days after the arrival of the goods at port of destination.
3. For transactions concluded on C.I.F. basis, it is understood that the insurance amount will be for 110% of the invoice value against the risks specified in the Sales Confirmation. If additional insurance amount or coverage required, the Buyer must have the consent of the Seller before Shipment, and the additional premium is to be borne by the Buyer.
4. The Seller shall not hold liable for non-delivery or delay in delivery of the entire lot or a portion of the goods hereunder by reason of natural disasters, war or other causes of Force Majeure. However, the Seller shall notify the Buyer as soon as possible and furnish the Buyer within 15 days by registered airmail with a certificate issued by the China Council for the Promotion of International Trade attesting such event(s).
5. All deputes arising out of the performance of, or relating to this contract, shall be settled through negotiation. In case no settlement can be reached through negotiation, the case shall then be submitted to the China International Economic and Trade Arbitration Commission for arbitration in accordance with its arbitral rules. The arbitration shall take place in Shanghai. The arbitral award is final and binding upon both parties.
6. The Buyer is requested to sign and return one copy of this contract immediately after receipt of the same. Objection, if any, should be raised by the Buyer within 3 working days, otherwise it is understood that the Buyer has accepted the terms and conditions of this contract.
7. Special conditions: (These shall prevail over all printed terms in case of any conflict.)

出口合同执行题目

一、请根据销售确认书审核信用证

合同中未规定的FORM A 信用证的补充有效

二、请根据银行来证及货物明细，缮制全套出口单据。

发票号码：INV1105　　发票日期：2011-9-10　　汇票日期：2011-9-20

Form A 号码：G11110300010001　　原产地标准：P

装运船名：NOBLERIVER　　航次：532W　　装船日期：2011-9-15

提单号码：TD879076

集装箱号码：COSCCQI192

投保单投保日期：2011-09-10

报检单位登记号：310091680　报检日期：2011-9-10

保单号码：ICC611426057　　保单日期：2011-9-11

报关单经营单位代码 3100916809

内装箱（CFS）地址：上海市中山北路1000号

电话：021-58789807

物资备妥日期：2011年9月12日

H.S.编码：95030082

预计收汇日期：2011-9-25

出口收汇核销单的报关有效截止：2011-9-15

出口收汇核销单的报关单编号：224820110567890876

货运订舱委托书编号：SH110456

保险代理：JAFIOUES INSURANCE CO.
18TH FL.， SUNBRIGHT PLAZA
BARCELONA, SPAIN

运输标志：SIC
INV1105
BARCELONA
C/No. 1-UP

卖方经办人：程一新
买方经办人：Keiko Nakamura
承运人：CHINA MARINE SHIPPING AGENCY
SHANGHAI CO.， LTD.
钟浩明

资料：

信用证：

SEQUENCE OF TOTAL *27 :1/1
FORM OF DOCUMENTARY CREDIT *40A :IRREVOCABLE
DOCUMENTARY CREDIT NUMBER *20 :CS2S769801
DATE OF ISSUE *31C :110910
APPLICABLE RULES *40E :UCP LATEST VERSION
DATE AND PLACE OF EXPIRY *31D :111122 CHINA
APPLICANT *50 : SEEDO INTERNATIONAL CO.,LTD.
NADEEM QAISER C/LISZT 63
STACOLOMA DE GRAMENET(08923)
BARCELONA,SPAIN

TEL: +34 93 496 1616
FAX: +34 93 216 0286
BENEFICIARY *59 : SHANGHAI YONGSHENG IMP. & EXP. CO.
21 WEST ZHONGSHAN ROAD SHANGHAI CHINA
CURRENCY CODE, AMOUNT *32B :USD4368,00
AVAILABLE WITH/BY *41D :ADVISING BANK ONLY
BY NEGOTIATION
DRAFTS AT ... *42C :SIGHT
DRAWEE *42D :STARDARD CHARTERED BANK.
BARCELONA BRANCH
PARTIAL SHIPMENTS *43P :NOT ALLOWED
TRANSSHIPMENT *43T :NOT ALLOWED
PORT OF LOADING/AIRPORT OF DEPARTURE *44E:
SHANGHAI PORT
PORT OF DISCHARGE/AIRPORT OF DESTINATION *44F:
BARCELONA PORT
LATEST DATE OF SHIP. *44C :110918
DESCRIPT. OF GOODS *45A :
R/C GAS TOY AS PER SALES CONTRACT NO. SC1105
DATED 110731
DOCUMENTS REQUIRED *46A :
+SIGNED COMMERCIAL INVOICE IN THREE FOLDS EVIDENCING THAT GOODS SHIPPIED AND
INVOICE ALL CONFORM TO THOSE DESCRIBED ON PROFORMA INVOICE NO.CHQ110811
DATED 110704
+FULL SET CLEAN BOARD BILLS OF LADING FOR GOODS ON BOARD MADE OUT TO ORDER
OF ISSUING BANK MARKED FREIGHT PREPAID NOTIFY TO APPLICANT

+PACKING LIST IN THREE FOLDS
+CERTIFICATE OF ORIGIN FORM A PLUS ONE COPY ISSUED BY COMPETENT AUTHORITY OF THE PEOPLE' S REPUBLIC OF CHINA, SPECIFYING ON IT THE CONTRACT NO.
+INSURANCE POLICY OR CERTIFICATE ISSUED FOR 110 PERCENT INVOICE VALUE COVERING C.I.C. ALL RISKS AND CLAIMS ARE PAYABLE AT BARCELONA
+COPY OF BENEFICIARY' S FAX ADDRESSED TO THE APPLICANT ADVISING ALL SHIPMENT DETAILS

ADDITIONAL CONDITIONS *47A : DELIVERY CIF BARCELONA

CHARGES *71B :ALL BANK CHARGES AND COMMISSIONS OUTSIDE SPAIN INCLUDING REIMBURSEMENT CHARGES ARE FOR BENEFICIARY ACCOUNT

PERIOD FOR PRESENTATION *48
:DOCUMENTS HAVE TO BE PRESENTED WITHIN 15 DAYS AFTER DATE OF SHIPMENT BUT WITHIN VALIDITY DATE

CONFIRMATION INSTRUCTIONS *49 :WITHOUT

INSTRUCTIONS TO THE PAYING/ACCEPTING/NEGOTIATING BANK *78 :
ON RECEIPT BY US CONFORM AND REGULAR DOCUMENTS IN UTILIZATION OF THIS DOCUMENTARY CREDIT. WE SHALL CREDIT YOU THROUGH THE AMERICAN BANK THAT YOU'LL INDICATE TO US IF ALL TERMS ARE COMPLIED WITH.

'ADVISE THROUGH' BANK *57D :STANDARD CHARTERED BANK, SHANGHAI BRANCH

SENDER TO RECEIVER INFORMATION *72 :
DOCUMENTS HAVE TO BE PRESENTED TO :
STANDARD CHARTERED BANK,
BARCELONA BRANCH
1055 WEST GEORGIA STREET
BARCELONA, SPAIN

SALES CONFIRMATION

S/C No. SC1105
Date: 2011-5-10

Seller:
SHANGHAI DONGHAI TRADE IMP. AND EXP. CORPORATION
55 ZHONGSHAN ROAD (S2), SHANGHAI 200001 CHINA
TEL: +0086-21-68952314
FAX: +0086-21-68952316

Buyer:
SEEDO INTERNATIONAL CO., LTD.
NADEEM QAISER C/LISZT 63 STACOLOMA DE GRAMENET(08923) BARCELONA, SPAIN
TEL: +34 93 496 1616
FAX: +34 93 216 0286

Art. No.	Name of Commodity&Specifications	Quantity	Unit Price	Amount
TY9806	R/C GAS TOY	200PCS	CIF BARCELONA USD21.84	USD4368.00
Total Amount in Words:	SAY US DOLLARS FOUR THOUSAND THREE AND SIXTY EIGHT ONLY			

PACKING: TO BE PACKED IN CARTONS OF 2 PCS EACH ONLY

SHIPMENT: FROM: SHANGHAI, CHINA
TO:BARCELONA, SPAIN
TO BE EFFECTED BEFORE NOV. 20, 2011
WITH PARTIAL SHIPMENT NOT ALLOWED AND TRANASHIPMENT ALLOWED

INSURANCE: THE SELLER SHOULD COVER INSURANCE FOR
110% OF THE TOTAL INVOICE VALUE AGAINST
ALL RISKS AS PER OCEAN MARINE CARGO CLAUSES
OF PICC DATED 1/1/1981.

PAYMENT: THE BUYER SHOULD OPEN THROUGH A BANK ACCEPTABLE TO THE SELLER
AN IRREVOCABLE L/C PAYABLE AT SIGHT FOR 100% OF TOTAL
CONTRACT VALUE TO REACH THE SELLER BEFORE SEP. 15, 2011 AND VALID FOR
NEGOTIATION IN CHINA UNTIL THE 15TH DAY AFTER THE DATE OF SHIPMENT

The contract is made out in two original copies. one copy to be held by each party.

Confirmed by.

Seller: Buyer:

SHANGHAI DONGHAI TRADE IMP. AND EXP.
CORPORATION

程一新

信用证修改表单

序号	代码（T ag）	修改后内容
1	31D	将“111122”改为“111015”
2	31C	将“110910” 改为“110715”
3	59	改为“SHANGHAI DONGHAI TRADE IMP. AND EXP.CORPORATION 55 ZHONGSHAN ROAD SHANGHAI 200001 CHINA”
4	42D	将“STARDARD”改为“STANDARD”
5	43T	将“NOT ALLOWED”改为“ALLOWED”
6	44C	将“110918”改为“110915”
7	45A	将“110731”改为“110510”
8	46A	将“C.I.C.”改为“PICC”和将“AT BARCELONA”改为“AT SHANGHAI”
9	71B	将“INCLUDING”改为“EXCEPT”

商业发票
Commercial Invoice

<table>
<tr><td colspan="3" rowspan="2">1. 出口商 Exporter
SHANGHAI DONGHAI TRADE IMP. AND EXP. CORPORATION
55 ZHONGSHAN ROAD (S2), SHANGHAI 200001 CHINA
TEL: +0086-21-68952314
FAX: +0086-21-68952316</td><td colspan="3">4. 发票日期和发票号 Invoice Date and No.
SEP.10,2011 INV1105</td></tr>
<tr><td colspan="2">5. 合同号 Contract No.
SC1105</td><td>6. 信用证号 L/C No.
CS2S769801</td></tr>
<tr><td colspan="3" rowspan="2">2. 进口商 Importer
SEEDO INTERNATIONAL CO.,LTD.
NADEEM QAISER C/LISZT 63 STACOLOMA
DE GRAMENET(08923) BARCELONA,SPAIN
TEL: +34 93 496 1616
FAX: +34 93 216 0286</td><td colspan="3">7. 原产地国 Country/region of origin
CHINA</td></tr>
<tr><td colspan="3">8. 贸易方式 Trade mode</td></tr>
<tr><td colspan="3">3. 运输事项 Transport details
FROM SHANGHAI,CHINA TO BARCELONA,SPAIN
WITH PARTIAL SHIPMENT NOT ALLOWED AND
TRANASHIPMENT ALLOWED</td><td colspan="3">9. 交货和付款条款 Terms of delivery and payment
Delievery: BEFORE NOV.20,2011
Payment: IRREVOCABLE L/C AT SIGHT FOR 100% OF
TOTAL CONTRACT VALUE</td></tr>
<tr><td>10. 运输标志和集装箱号
Shipment marks;Container No.</td><td colspan="2">11. 包装类型及件数；商品编码；商品描述
Number and kind of packages;Commodity No. ;Commodity description</td><td>12. 数量
Quantity</td><td>13. 单价
Unit Price</td><td>14. 金额
Amount</td></tr>
<tr><td>SIC
INV1105
BARCELONA
C/NO.1-UP

COSCCQI192</td><td colspan="2">100 CARTONS

HS NO.:95030082

R/C GAS TOY AS PER SALES
CONTRACT NO. SC1105
DATED 110510</td><td>200PCS</td><td>CIF BARCELONA
USD21.84</td><td>USD4368.00</td></tr>
<tr><td colspan="6">15. 总值（用数字和文字表示）Total amount (in figure and word)
SAY UNITED STATE DOLLARS FOUR THOUSAND THREE HUNDRED AND SIXTY EIGHT ONLY.</td></tr>
<tr><td colspan="3"></td><td colspan="3">16. 出口商签章
Exporter stamp and signature

SHANGHAI DONGHAI TRADE IMP. AND EXP. CORPORATION
程一新</td></tr>
</table>

装箱单
Packing List

1. 出口商 Exporter SHANGHAI DONGHAI TRADE IMP. AND EXP. CORPORATION 55 ZHONGSHAN ROAD (S2), SHANGHAI 200001 CHINA TEL: +0086-21-68952314 FAX: +0086-21-68952316	3. 装箱单日期 Packing List Date SEP. 12, 2011		
2. 进口商 Importer SEEDO INTERNATIONAL CO.,LTD. NADEEM QAISER C/LISZT 63 STACOLOMA DE GRAMENET(08923) BARCELONA, SPAIN TEL: +34 93 496 1616 FAX: +34 93 216 0286	4. 合同号 Contract No. SC1105	5. 信用证号 L/C No. CS2S769801	
	6. 发票日期和发票号 Invoice Date and No. SEP.10, 2011　INV1105		

7. 运输标志和集装箱号 Shipment marks;Container No.	8. 包装类型及件数；商品编码；商品描述 Number and kind of packages;Commodity No.;Commodity description	9. 毛重 kg Gross weight	10. 净重 kg Net weight	11. 体积 m^3 Cube
SIC INV1105 BARCELONA C/NO.1-UP COSCCQI192	100 CARTONS HS NO.:95030082 R/C GAS TOY AS PER SALES CONTRACT NO. SC1105 DATED 110510	1420	1120	1.92

12. 出口商签章

Exporter stamp and signature

Exporter stamp and signature
SHANGHAI DONGHAI TRADE IMP. AND EXP. CORPORATION
程一新

货运订舱委托书

<table>
<tr><td colspan="2">经营单位
（托运人）</td><td colspan="4">SHANGHAI CONGHAI TRADE IMP. AND EXP. CORPORATION</td><td colspan="2">编　号</td><td colspan="2">SH110456</td></tr>
<tr><td rowspan="3">提单项目要求</td><td>发货人：
Shipper:</td><td colspan="8">SHANGHAI CONGHAI TRADE IMP. CORPORATION</td></tr>
<tr><td>收货人：
Consignee:</td><td colspan="8">TO ORDER OF STANDARD CHARTERED BANK. BARCELONA BRANCH</td></tr>
<tr><td>通知人：
Notify Party:</td><td colspan="8">SEEDO INTERNATIONAL CO. LTD</td></tr>
<tr><td colspan="2">海运费（ ）
Sea freight</td><td colspan="2">预付（ ）或（ ）到付
Prepaid or Collect</td><td>提单
份数</td><td>FULL SET</td><td>提单寄送
地　址</td><td colspan="3">STANDARD CHARTERD BANK. BARCELONA BRANCH.</td></tr>
<tr><td>起运港</td><td>SHANGAI PORT</td><td>目的港</td><td>BARCELONA PORT</td><td colspan="2">可否转船</td><td>ALLOWED</td><td>可否分批</td><td colspan="2">NOT ALLOWED</td></tr>
<tr><td colspan="3">集装箱预配数</td><td colspan="2">20’× 40’</td><td>装运期限</td><td>NOV.20.2011</td><td>有效期限</td><td colspan="2">NOV. 22. 2011</td></tr>
<tr><td colspan="2">标记唛码</td><td>包装
件数</td><td colspan="2">中英文货号
Description of goods</td><td>毛重
（公斤）</td><td>尺寸
（立方米）</td><td colspan="3">成交条件
（总价）</td></tr>
<tr><td colspan="2">SIC INV1105
BARCELONA
C/NO.1-UP</td><td>100 CARTONS</td><td colspan="2">R/C GAS TOY AS PER SALES CONTRACT NO. SC1105 DATED 110510</td><td>1420</td><td>1.92</td><td colspan="3">CIF BARCELONA USD4368.00</td></tr>
<tr><td colspan="3" rowspan="2">内装箱（CFS）地址</td><td colspan="2" rowspan="2">上海市中山北路 1000 号
电话：021-58789807</td><td rowspan="2">特种货物
□冷藏货
□危险品</td><td colspan="4">重件：每件重量</td></tr>
<tr><td colspan="2">大件
（长 × 宽 × 高）</td><td colspan="2">32 × 20 × 30cm</td></tr>
<tr><td colspan="3" rowspan="2">门对门装箱地址</td><td colspan="2" rowspan="2">55 ZHONGSHAN ROAD (S2),SHANGHAI 200001 CHINA</td><td colspan="5">特种集装箱：（　　　）</td></tr>
<tr><td colspan="3">物资备妥日期</td><td colspan="2">SEP.12.2011</td></tr>
<tr><td colspan="3" rowspan="2">外币结算账号</td><td colspan="2" rowspan="2"></td><td colspan="5">物资进栈：自送（ ）或派送（ ）</td></tr>
<tr><td colspan="4">人民币结算单位账号</td><td></td></tr>
<tr><td colspan="5" rowspan="7">声明事项</td><td colspan="5">托运人签章</td></tr>
<tr><td>电话</td><td colspan="4">TEL:+0086-21-68952314</td></tr>
<tr><td>传真</td><td colspan="4">FAX:+0086-21-68952316</td></tr>
<tr><td>联系人</td><td colspan="4">程一新</td></tr>
<tr><td>地址</td><td colspan="4">55 ZHONGSHAN ROAD(S2), SHANGHAI 200001 CHINA</td></tr>
<tr><td colspan="5">制单日期：SEP.12, 2011</td></tr>
</table>

中保财产保险有限公司上海市分公司

The People's Insurance (Property) Company of China, Ltd. Shanghai Branch

进出口货物运输保险投保单

Application From form I/E Marine Cargo Insurance

被保险人 Assured's Name	SHANGHAI DONGHAI TRADE IMP. AND EXP. CORPORATION		
发票号码（出口用）或合同号码（进口用） Invoice No. or Contract NO.	包装数量 Quantity	保险货物项目 Description of Goods	保险金额 Amount Insured
INV1105	100 CARTONS	R/C GAS TOY AS PER SALES CONTRACT NO. SC1105 DATED 201150510	CIF BARCELONA USD4805.00

装载运输工具 S.S.NOBLERIVER 航次、航班或车号 532W 开航日期 AS PER B/L

Per Conveyance　Voy. No.　Slg. Date

自 SHANGHAI, CHINA 至 BARCELONA, SPAIN 转运地＿＿＿＿ 赔款地 SHANGHAI, CHINA

From　To　W/Tat　Clainn Payable at

承保险别：

Condition&/or

Special Coverage

AGAINST ALL RISKS AS PER OCEAN MARINE CARGO CLAUSES OF PICC DATED 1/1/1981

投保人签章及公司名称、电话、地址：

Applicant's Signature and Co.'s Name , Add. And Tel. No.

SHANGHAI DONGHAI TRADE IMP. AND EXP. CORPORATION

55 ZHONGSHAN ROAD (S2), SHANGHAI 200001 CHINA

程一新

投保日期：

Date　Sep. 10, 2011

备注：

Remarks

保险公司填写：　报单号：　费率：

货物运输保险单
CARGO TRANSPORTATION INUSRANCE POLICY

PICC 中国人保财险

北京2008年奥运会保险合作伙伴

OFFICIAL INSURANCE PARTNER OF THE BEIJING 2008 OLYMPIC GAMES

总公司设于北京　　一九四九年创立

Head Office Beijing　　Established in 1949

发票号　（INVOICE NO.）INV1105

合同号　（CONTRACT NO.）SC1105

信用证号（L/C NO.）CS2S769801

保单号次

POLICY NO. ICC611426057

被保险人：

INSURED SHANGHAI DONGHAI TRADE IMP.AND EXP.CORPORATION

中国人民财产保险有限公司（以下简称本公司）根据被保险人的要求，由被保险人向本公司缴付约定的保险费，按照本保险单承保险别和背面所载条款与下列特款承保下述货物运输保险，特立本保险单。

THIS POLICY OF INSURANCE WITNESSES THAT PICC PROPERTY AND CASUALTY COMPANY LIMITED (HEREINAFTER CALLED "THE COMPANY") AT REQUEST OF THE INSURED AND IN CONSIDERATION OF THE AGREED PREMIUM PAID TO THE COMPANY BY THE INSURED, UNDERTAKES TO INSURANCE. THE UNDERMENTIONED GOODS IN TRANSPORTATION SUBJECT TO THE CONDITIONS OF THIS POLICY AS PER THE CLAUSES PRINTED OVERL AND OTHER SPECIAL CLAUSES ATTACHED HEREON.

标记 MARKS & NOS.	包装及数量 QUANTITY	保险货物项目 DESCRITION OF GOODS	保险金额 AMOUNT INSURED
SIC INV1105 BARCELONA C/NO. I-UP	100 CARTONS	R/C GAS TOY AS PER SALES CONTRACT NO. SC1105 DATED 20110510	CIF BARCELONA USD4805.00

总保险金额：

TOTAL AMOUNT INSURED SAY US DOLLARS FOUR THOUSAND EIGHT HUNDRED AND FIVE ONLY

保费：　　启运日期：　　装载运输工具：S.S.

PREMIUM AS ARRANGED　DATE OF COMMENCEMENT AS PER B/L　PER CONVEYANCE NOBLERIVER

自　　经　　至

FROM SHANGHAI, CHINA　VIA　TO BARCELONA, SPAIN

承保险别：

CONDITIONS

COVERING PICC ALL RISKS

所保货物，如发生保险单项下可能引起索赔的损失或损坏，应立即通知本公司代理人查勘。如有索赔，应向本公司提交保单正本（本保险单共有 2 份正本）及有关文件。如一份正本已用于索赔，其余正本自动失效。

IN THE EVENT OF LOSS OR DAMAGE WHICH MAY RESULT IN A CLAIM UNDER THIS POLICY, INNEDIATE NOTICE MUST BE GIVER TO THE COMPANY' S AGENT AS MENTIONED HEREUNDER CLAIMS, IF ANY ONE OF THE ORIGINAL POLICY WHICH HAS BEEN ISSUED IN TWO ORIGINAL TOGETHER WITH THE RELEVENT DOCUMENTS SHALL BE SURRENDERED TO THE COMPANY. IF ONE OF THE ORIGINAL POLICY HAS BEEN ACCOMPLISHED. THE OTHERS TO BE VOID.

中国人民财产保险股份有限公司上海市分公司

PICC Property and Casualty Company Limited, Shanghai Branch

赔款偿付地点

CLAIM PAYABLE AT/IN SHANGHAI

出单日期

ISSUING DATE SEP. 11, 2011

GENERAL MANAGER

中华人民共和国出入境检验检疫
出境货物报检单

报检单位（加盖公章）：　　　　　　　　　　　　　　　　*编号＿＿＿＿＿＿

报检单位登记号：310091680　　联系人：程一新　电话：　　　　报检日期：2011 年 9 月10日

<table>
<tr><td rowspan="2">发货人</td><td colspan="5">（中文）上海东海进出口公司</td></tr>
<tr><td colspan="5">（外文）SHANGHAI DONGHAI TRADE IMP. AND EXP. CORPORATION</td></tr>
<tr><td rowspan="2">收货人</td><td colspan="5">（中文）</td></tr>
<tr><td colspan="5">（外文）SEEDO INTERNATIONAL CO., LTD</td></tr>
<tr><td>货物名称（中/外文）</td><td>H.S. 编码</td><td>产地</td><td>数/重量</td><td>货物总值</td><td>包装种类及数量</td></tr>
<tr><td>摇控玩具汽车
R/C GAS TOY</td><td>95030082</td><td>上海</td><td>200PCS</td><td>USD4368.00</td><td>. 100 CARTONS</td></tr>
</table>

<table>
<tr><td>运输工具名称号码</td><td>NOBLERIVER</td><td>贸易方式</td><td>一般贸易</td><td>货物存放地点</td><td>本公司仓库</td></tr>
<tr><td>合同号</td><td>SC1105</td><td>信用证号</td><td>CS2S769801</td><td>用途</td><td>其他</td></tr>
<tr><td>发货日期</td><td>2011.09.15</td><td>输往国家（地区）</td><td>西班牙</td><td>许可证/审批号</td><td>***</td></tr>
<tr><td>启运地</td><td>上海</td><td>到达口岸</td><td>巴塞罗那</td><td>生产单位注册号</td><td>***</td></tr>
<tr><td>集装箱规格、数量及号码</td><td colspan="5">COSCCQI192</td></tr>
</table>

<table>
<tr><td>合同、信用证订立的检验检疫条款或特殊要求</td><td>标记及号码</td><td colspan="2">随附单据（划“√”或补填）</td></tr>
<tr><td>无</td><td>SIC
INV1105
BARCELONA
C/NO.
1-UP</td><td>☑合同
☐信用证
☑发票
☐换证凭单
☑装箱单
☑厂检单</td><td>☑包装性能结果单
☐许可/审批文件
☐
☐
☐
☐</td></tr>
</table>

<table>
<tr><td colspan="2">需要证单名称（划“√”或补填）</td><td colspan="2">*检验检疫费</td></tr>
<tr><td rowspan="7">☐品质证书　＿正＿副
☐重量证书　＿正＿副
☐数量证书　＿正＿副
☐兽医卫生证书　＿正＿副
☐健康证书　＿正＿副
☐卫生证书　＿正＿副
☐动物卫生证书　＿正＿副</td><td rowspan="7">☐植物检疫证书　＿正＿副
☐熏蒸/消毒证书　＿正＿副
☐出境货物换证凭单　＿正＿副
☐出境货物通关单　＿正＿副
☐
☐
☐</td><td>总金额
（人民币元）</td><td></td></tr>
<tr><td>计费人</td><td></td></tr>
<tr><td>收费人</td><td></td></tr>
</table>

<table>
<tr><td rowspan="3">报检人郑重声明：
1. 本人被授权报检。
2. 上列填写内容正确属实，货物无伪造或冒用他人的厂名、标志、认证标志，并承担货物质量责任。
签名：程一新</td><td colspan="2">领取证单</td></tr>
<tr><td>日期</td><td></td></tr>
<tr><td>签名</td><td></td></tr>
</table>

注：有“*”号栏由出入境检验检疫机关填写　　　　　　◆国家出入境检验检疫局制

[1-2 (2000.1.1)]

中华人民共和国海关出口货物报关单

预录入编号:　　　　　　　　　　　　　　海关编号:　224820110567890876

出口口岸 上海海关	备案号	出口日期	申报日期
经营单位 上海东海进出口公司 3100916809	运输方式 水路运输	运输工具名称 NOBLERIVER/532W	提运单号 TD879076
发货单位 上海东海进出口公司 3100916809	贸易方式 一般贸易0110	征免性质 一般征税101	结汇方式 信用证

许可证号	运抵国(地区) 西班牙	指运港 巴塞罗那	境内货源地 上海

批准文号 312345456	成交方式 CIF	运费 502/60/2	保费 0.7/1	杂费

合同协议号 SC1105	件数 200PCS	包装种类 纸箱	毛重(公斤) 1420	净重(公斤) 1120

集装箱号 COSCCQI192/20	随附单据 B:******	生产厂家

标记及备注

SIC
INV1105
BARCELONA
C/NO. 1-UP

项号	商品编号	商品名称、规格型号	数量及单位	最终目的国(地区)	单价	总价	币制	征免
01	95030082	摇控玩具车 TY9806	200辆	西班牙	21.84	4368.00	美元	照章征税

税费征收情况

录入员　录入单位	兹声明以上申报无讹并承担法律责任	海关审单批注及放行日期(签单) 审单　审价
报关员　程一新 单位地址 邮编　电话	申报单位(签章) 上海东海进出口公司 填制日期	征税　统计 查验　放行

装运通知
Shipping Note

<table>
<tr><td rowspan="2">1. 出口商 Exporter
SHANGHAI DONGHAI TRADE IMP. AND EXP. CORPORATION
55 ZHONGSHAN ROAD (S2), SHANGHAI 200001 CHINA
TEL: +0086-21-68952314
FAX: +0086-21-68952316</td><td colspan="2">4. 发票号 Invoice No.
INV1105</td></tr>
<tr><td>5. 合同号 Contract No.
SC1105</td><td>6. 信用证号 L/C No.
CS2S769801</td></tr>
<tr><td rowspan="2">2. 进口商 Importer
SEEDO INTERNATIONAL CO.,LTD.
NADEEM QAISER C/LISZT 63 STACOLOMA
DE GRAMENET(08923) BARCELONA,SPAIN
TEL: +34 93 496 1616
FAX: +34 93 216 0286</td><td colspan="2">7. 运输单证号 Transport document No.
TD89076提单号</td></tr>
<tr><td colspan="2">8. 价值 Value
USD4368. 00</td></tr>
<tr><td>3. 运输事项 Transport details
FROM SHANGHAI PORT TO BARCELONA PORT BY VESSEL</td><td colspan="2">9. 装运口岸和日期 Port and date of shipment
SHANGHAI PORT
SEP. 15, 2011</td></tr>
<tr><td>10. 运输标志和集装箱号
Shipment marks;Container No.</td><td colspan="2">11. 包装类型及件数；商品编码；商品描述
Number and kind of packages;Commodity No.;Commodity description</td></tr>
<tr><td>SIC
INV1105
BARCELONA
C/NO. 1-UP

COSCCQI192</td><td colspan="2">PACKED IN 100 CARTONS
95030082
R/C GAS TOY</td></tr>
<tr><td></td><td colspan="2">12. 出口商签章
Exporter stamp and signature</td></tr>
</table>

出口收汇核销单
存根

（沪）编号：312345456

出口单位：上海东海进出口公司
单位代码：3100916809
出口币种总价：USD4368. 00
收汇方式：
约计收款日期：
报关日期：
备注： 上海海关
此单报关有效截止到 2011. 09. 15

（出口单位盖章）

出口收汇核销单

（沪）编号：312345456

<table>
<tr><td colspan="5">出口单位：</td></tr>
<tr><td colspan="5">单位代码：</td></tr>
<tr><td rowspan="2">银行签注栏</td><td>类别</td><td>币种金额</td><td>日期</td><td>盖章</td></tr>
<tr><td></td><td></td><td></td><td></td></tr>
<tr><td colspan="5">海关签注栏：</td></tr>
<tr><td colspan="5">外汇局签注栏：
年　月　日（盖章）</td></tr>
</table>

（出口单位盖章）

（海关盖章）

出口收汇核销单
出口退税专用

（沪）编号：312345456

<table>
<tr><td colspan="3">出口单位：</td></tr>
<tr><td colspan="3">单位代码：</td></tr>
<tr><td>货物名称</td><td>数量</td><td>币种总价</td></tr>
<tr><td colspan="3">遥控玩具车
100箱
USD4368. 00</td></tr>
<tr><td colspan="3">报关单编号：
22482011056789C</td></tr>
<tr><td colspan="3">外汇局签注栏：
年　月　日（盖章）</td></tr>
</table>

未经核销此联不得撕开

ORIGINAL

1. Goods consigned from (Exporter's business name, address, country) SHANGHAIDONGHAITRADE IMP.AND EXP. CORPORATION 55 ZHONGSHAN ROAD(S2), SHANGHAI 200001 CHINA TEL:+0086-21-68952314 FAX:+0086-21-68952316	Reference No. GENERALIZED SYSTEM OF PREFERENCES CERTIFICATE OF ORIGIN (Combined declaration and certificate) FORM A Issued in THE PEOPLE'S REPUBLIC OF CHINA (country) See Notes overleaf
2.Goods consigned to (Consignee's name, address, country) SEEDO INTERNATIONAL CO.,LTD. NADEEM QAISER C/LISZT 63 STACOLOMA DE GRAMENET(08923) BARCELONA,SPAIN TEL: +34 93 496 1616 FAX: +34 93 216 0286	
3.Means of transport and route (as far as known) FROM SHANGHAI PORT TO BARCELONA PORT BY VESSEL	4.For official use

5.Item number	6.Marks and numbers of packages	7.Number and kind of packages; description of goods	8.Origin criterion (see Notes overleaf)	9.Gross weight or other quantity	10.Number and date of invoices
1	SIC INV1105 BARCELONA C/NO.1-UP 100 CARTONS	100 CARTONS R/C GAS TOY AS PER SALES CONTRACT NO. SC1105 DATED 110510	"P"	G.W 1420KGS	INV1105 SEP.10,2011

11.Certification It is hereby certified, on the basis of control carried out, that the declaration by the exporter is correct. SHANGHAI,CHINA SEP.10, 2011 程一新 Place and date, signature and stamp of certifying authority	12.Declaration by the exporter The undersigned hereby declares that the above details and statements are correct, that all the goods were produced in CHINA (country) and that they comply with the origin requirements specified for those goods in the Generalized System of Preferences for goods exported to (importing country) Place and date, signature and stamp of authorized signatory

商业汇票

No. INV1105

For USD4368.00　　**BILL OF EXCHANG**　　SEP.20, 2011

Date

At ______******______ sight of this SECOND BILL of EXCHANGE (first of the same and date unpaid) pay to the order of STANDARD CHARTERED BANK, SHANGHAI BRANCH the SAY UNITED STATE DOLLARS FOUR THOUSAND THREE HUNDRED AND SIXTY EIGHT ONLY.

Drawn under STANDARD CHARTERED BANK, BARCELONA BRANCH

L/C No. CS2S769801 Dated SEP.10.2011

TO. STANDARD CHARTERED BANK, BARCELONA BRANCH 1055 WEST GEORGIA STREET BARCELONA, SPAIN

SHANGHAI DONGHAI TRADE IMP. AND EXP. CORP

55 ZHONGSHAN ROAD (S2), SHANGHAI 200001 CHI

参 考 文 献

1. 黎孝先，石玉川. 国际贸易实务. 北京：对外经济贸易大学出版社，2008
2. 傅龙海，丛晓明. 国际贸易实务双语教程. 北京：对外经济贸易大学出版社，2011
3. 易露霞，陈原. 国际贸易实务双语教程. 北京：清华大学出版社，2009
4. 黄霜林. 外贸合同与信用证. 武汉：武汉理工大学出版社，2008
5. 杨金玲. 进出口单证实训操作. 天津：天津大学出版社，2009
6. 程淑琴. 外贸单证实务. 合肥：中国科学技术大学出版社，2010
7. 庞红. 国际结算. 北京：中国人民大学出版社，2009
8. 程惠. 国际货物运输与保险. 大连：大连理工大学出版社，2008
9. 鲁广斌. 国际货运代理实务与集装箱运输业务. 北京：清华大学出版社，2010
10. 全国国际商务单证培训认证考试办公室. 国际商务单证理论与实务. 北京：中国商务出版社，2007
11. 海关总署教材编审委员会. 2009 年报关员资格全国统一考试教材. 北京：中国海关出版社，2009
12. （美）布朗奇（Alan, E. Branch）. 出口实务与管理（第四版）孔雁，蔡荣生译. 北京：清华大学出版社，2007
13. 黄飞雪，李志浩. 跟单信用证统一惯例（UCP600）与 ISBP681 述评及案例. 厦门：厦门大学出版社，2009
14. 吴安南，李卫. 国际贸易实务. 大连：大连理工出版社，2006
15. 商务部网站（http://www. Mofcom. gov. cn/）
16. 北京出入境检验检疫局网站（http://www. Bjciq. Gov. cn/）
17. 严平. 《对外经济贸易业务知识大全》（上下册）. 上海：上海人民出版社
18. 沙麟，强连庆. 《中国外经贸大全》（上下册）. 上海：复旦大学出版社
19. 刘文广，张晓明. 国际贸易实务. 北京：高等教育出版社，2006
20. 易露露，方玲玲， 尤彧聪. 国际贸易实务案例教程（双语）. 北京：清华大学出版社，2010
21. 《2000 年国际贸易术语解释通则》. 北京：中信出版社
22. 《跟单信用证统一惯例》（国际商会第 600 号出版物）
23. 《托收统一规则》（国际商会第 522 号出版物）
24. 《联合国国际货物销售合同公约》